ON INFORMATION TECHNOLOGY

Video education courses are available on these topics through
National Education Training Group, 1751 West Diehl Road,
Naperville, IL 60563-9099 (tel: 800-526-0452 or 708-369-3000).

Database	Telecommunications	Networks and Data Communications	Society
AN END USER'S GUIDE TO DATABASE	TELECOMMUNICATIONS AND THE COMPUTER (third edition)	PRINCIPLES OF DATA COMMUNICATION	THE COMPUTERIZED SOCIETY
PRINCIPLES OF ATABASE MANAGEMENT (second edition)	COMMUNICATIONS SATELLITE SYSTEMS	TELEPROCESSING NETWORK ORGANIZATION	TELEMATIC SOCIETY: A CHALLENGE FOR TOMORROW
OMPUTER DATABASE ORGANIZATION (third edition)	**Distributed Processing**	SYSTEMS ANALYSIS FOR DATA TRANSMISSION	TECHNOLOGY'S CRUCIBLE
MANAGING THE ATABASE ENVIRONMENT (second edition)	COMPUTER NETWORKS AND DISTRIBUTED PROCESSING	DATA COMMUNICATION TECHNOLOGY	VIEWDATA AND THE INFORMATION SOCIETY
DATABASE ANALYSIS AND DESIGN	DESIGN AND STRATEGY FOR DISTRIBUTED DATA PROCESSING	DATA COMMUNICATION DESIGN TECHNIQUES	**SAA**: Systems Application Architecture
SAM: ACCESS METHOD SERVICES AND GRAMMING TECHNIQUES	**Office Automation**	SNA: IBM's NETWORKING SOLUTION	SAA: COMMON USER ACCESS
B2: CONCEPTS, DESIGN, AND PROGRAMMING	IBM OFFICE SYSTEMS: ARCHITECTURES AND IMPLEMENTATIONS	LOCAL AREA NETWORKS: ARCHITECTURES AND IMPLEMENTATIONS (second edition)	SAA: COMMON COMMUNICATIONS SUPPORT: DISTRIBUTED APPLICATIONS
MS/R: CONCEPTS, DESIGN, AND PROGRAMMING	OFFICE AUTOMATION STANDARDS	DATA COMMUNICATION STANDARDS	SAA: COMMON COMMUNICATIONS SUPPORT: NETWORK INFRASTRUCTURE
Security		COMPUTER NETWORKS AND DISTRIBUTED PROCESSING: SOFTWARE, TECHNIQUES, AND ARCHITECTURE	SAA: COMMON PROGRAMMING INTERFACE
SECURITY, ACCURACY, AND PRIVACY IN COMPUTER SYSTEMS		TCP/IP N ARCH ADMIN AND PR	

TCP/IP NETWORKING

A *James Martin* **BOOK**

THE JAMES MARTIN BOOKS
currently available from Prentice Hall

- Application Development Without Programmers
- Building Expert Systems
- Communications Satellite Systems
- Computer Data-Base Organization, Second Edition
- Computer Networks and Distributed Processing: Software, Techniques, and Architecture
- Data Communication Technology
- DB2: Concepts, Design, and Programming
- Design and Strategy of Distributed Data Processing
- An End User's Guide to Data Base
- Fourth-Generation Languages, Volume I: Principles
- Fourth-Generation Languages, Volume II: Representative 4GLs
- Fourth-Generation Languages, Volume III: 4GLs from IBM
- Future Developments in Telecommunications, Second Edition
- Hyperdocuments and How to Create Them
- IBM Office Systems: Architectures and Implementations
- IDMS/R: Concepts, Design, and Programming
- Information Engineering, Book I: Introduction and Principles
- Information Engineering, Book II: Planning and Analysis
- Information Engineering, Book III: Design and Construction
- An Information Systems Manifesto
- Local Area Networks: Architectures and Implementations, Second Edition
- Managing the Data-Base Environment
- Object-Oriented Analysis and Design
- Principles of Data-Base Management
- Principles of Data Communication
- Principles of Object-Oriented Analysis and Design
- Recommended Diagramming Standards for Analysts and Programmers
- SNA: IBM's Networking Solution
- Strategic Information Planning Methodologies, Second Edition
- System Design from Provably Correct Constructs
- Systems Analysis for Data Transmission
- Systems Application Architecture: Common User Access
- Systems Application Architecture: Common Communications Support: Distributed Applications
- Systems Application Architecture: Common Communications Support: Network Infrastructure
- Systems Application Architecture: Common Programming Interface
- TCP/IP Networking: Architecture, Administration, and Programming
- Technology's Crucible
- Telecommunications and the Computer, Third Edition
- Telematic Society: A Challenge for Tomorrow
- VSAM: Access Method Services and Programming Techniques

with Carma McClure

- Action Diagrams: Clearly Structured Specifications, Programs, and Procedures, Second Edition
- Diagramming Techniques for Analysts and Programmers
- Software Maintenance: The Problem and Its Solutions
- Structured Techniques: The Basis for CASE, Revised Edition

TCP/IP NETWORKING
Architecture, Administration, and Programming

JAMES MARTIN
with
Joe Leben

P T R PRENTICE HALL
Englewood Cliffs, New Jersey 07632

Library of Congress Cataloging-in-Publication Data

Martin, James (date)
   TCP/IP networking : architecture, administration, and programming /
James Martin, Joe Leben.
     p. cm.
   Includes index.
   ISBN 0-13-642232-2
   1. TCP/IP(Computer network protocol) 2. Internet (Computer
network) I. Leben, Joe. II. Title.
TK5105.55.M37 1994
004.6'2—dc20
                                       93-46380
                                        CIP

Editorial/production supervision: *Kathryn Gollin Marshak*
Liaison: *John Morgan*
Jacket design: *DeFranco Design*
Jacket photo: *Stock Works, Stock Illustration,* © *Rafael Lopez*
Manufacturing buyer: *Alexis Heydt*

Published by P T R Prentice-Hall, Inc.
A Paramount Communications Company
Englewood Cliffs, New Jersey 07632

The publisher offers discounts on this book when ordered
in bulk quantities. For more information, write:
          Corporate Sales Department, P T R Prentice Hall
          113 Sylvan Avenue
          Englewood Cliffs, NJ 07632
          Phone: (201) 592-2863; Fax: (201) 592-2249

ISBN 0-13-642232-2

Printed in the United States of America

10 9 8 7 6 5 4 3 2

ISBN 0-13-642232-2

Prentice-Hall International (UK) Limited, *London*
Prentice-Hall of Australia Pty. Limited, *Sydney*
Prentice-Hall Canada Inc., *Toronto*
Prentice-Hall Hispanoamericana, S.A., *Mexico*
Prentice-Hall of India Private Limited, *New Delhi*
Prentice-Hall of Japan, Inc., *Tokyo*
Simon & Schuster Asia Pte. Ltd., *Singapore*
Editora Prentice-Hall do Brasil, Ltda., *Rio de Janeiro*

Contents

Preface *xi*

List of Acronyms *xiii*

PART I   ARCHITECTURE

1   Internetworking with TCP/IP *3*

TCP/IP Internets 4; TCP/IP Components 4; Physical Network Technologies 5; Physical Network Implementation 8; TCP/IP Networking Software 10; Administration Functions 11; TCP/IP Internetworking 12; Summary 13

2   The Worldwide Internet *15*

Internet Hierarchical Structure 16; Internet Administration 17; Connecting to the Internet 18; Internet Information Resources 18; Locating Internet Resources 18; Requests for Comments 20; Protocol States and Status Levels 21; Summary 21; Reference 22

3   TCP/IP Architecture *23*

Network Architectures 24; Communication Protocols 25; OSI Reference Model 27; TCP/IP Functional Layers 31; Application Layer 31; Transport Layer 32; Internet Layer 38; Network Interface Layer 38; Hardware Layer 39; Summary 39

4   TCP/IP Addressing *41*

Three Levels of Identifiers 41; Identifier Conversions 43; Internet Addressing 44; Internet Addressing Authority 46; Subnetting 46; Routers and Multihomed Hosts 48; Internet Routing 48; Local Host Name and Address 49; Summary 49

PART **II**   APPLICATION LAYER PROTOCOLS
              AND SERVICES

     5   Application Services   *53*

              Application Layer Service Categories 54; Ping Connectivity Testing 55;
              Telnet Interactive Login 56; Rlogin Interactive Login 59;
              Rsh Remote Execution 59; FTP File Transfer 60; NFS Remote File Access 63;
              TFTP File Transfer 63; Name Resolution 65; SMTP Electronic Mail 66;
              X Windows Presentation 68; Kerberos Security 69; Remote Procedure Calls 70;
              Time Services 71; SNMP Network Management 72; Summary 72

     6   Network File System   *75*

              NFS Client-Server Architecture 75; Network Information Service 76;
              Remote Procedure Calls 76; NFS File System Model 76; Mount Protocol 77;
              NFS Protocol 77; NFS Implementation 78; Summary 78

     7   Domain Name System   *81*

              Name Resolution Using hosts Files 82;
              Name Resolution Using the Domain Name System 82;
              Internet Naming Scheme 82; DNS Client and Server Software 86;
              Name Resolution Operations 87; Caching 88; DNS Message Format 88;
              Summary 90

PART **III** TRANSPORT LAYER PROTOCOLS

     8   User Datagram Protocol   *95*

              UDP Connectionless Service 95; UDP Applications 96;
              UDP User Datagram Format 96; UDP Protocol Mechanisms 96; Summary 98

     9   Transmission Control Protocol   *99*

              TCP Connection-Oriented Service 99; TCP Applications 100;
              TCP Segment Format 100; TCP Protocol Mechanisms 101; Summary 104

PART **IV**   INTERNET LAYER PROTOCOLS

     10   Internet Protocol   *107*

              IP Users 107; IP Connectionless Service 108; IP Datagram Format 109;
              IP Protocol Mechanisms 109; IP Routing 111; Router Routing Tables 115;
              Summary 116

11 **ARP and RARP Address Resolution** *117*

Address Resolution Protocol 117; ARP Packet Format 120; ARP Example 121;
Reverse Address Resolution Protocol 122; Summary 123

12 **Internet Control Message Protocol** *125*

Uses for ICMP 125; ICMP General Message Format 126;
ICMP Message Types 126; ICMP Error Messages 126;
ICMP Query Messages 129; Summary 132

13 **Routing Protocols** *133*

Routing Algorithms 133; Autonomous Systems 136;
TCP/IP Gateway Protocols 137; Interior Gateway Protocols 137;
Exterior Gateway Protocols 139; Summary 141

PART **V** **INTERNET ADMINISTRATION**

14 **Network Management** *145*

ISO CMIP Approach to Network Management 145;
Approaches to TCP/IP Network Management 147;
Ad Hoc Network Management Tools 147;
Simple Network Management Protocol 148; CMOT (CMIP over TCP/IP) 151;
Summary 152

15 **Installation and Administration** *155*

Configuring an Internet 155; Installing the Domain Name System 160;
Expanding the Internet 162; Connecting to the Worldwide Internet 165;
Summary 167

16 **Troubleshooting** *169*

Categories of Problems 169; Problem Resolution Tools 170;
Error Diagnosis 170; Summary 173

PART **VI** **CLIENT-SERVER PROGRAMMING**

17 **Client-Server Computing** *177*

Client-Server Models and Distribution Technologies 178;
Infrastructure Functions 179; Client-Server Computing Models 181;
Distribution Technologies 188; Remote Database Access Mechanisms 189;
Message Passing Mechanisms 192; Remote Procedure Call Mechanisms 193;
Choosing a Distribution Mechanism 194; Summary 197

18   TCP/IP Programming Fundamentals *199*

*Client-Server Relationship 199; Client Component 199;
Server Component 200; Associations 201; Support Function Calls 202;
Transport Layer Protocol Ports 205; Communication Programming APIs 206;
Summary 207; Reference 208*

19   Socket Programming *209*

*Three Types of Sockets 209; Socket System Calls 212;
Application Protocols 212; Socket System Call Descriptions 218; Summary 225*

20   Remote Procedure Call Programming *227*

*Procedure Call Mechanism 227; Remote Procedure Call Functional Model 229;
RPC Call Semantics 230; RPC Implementations 232; Sun RPC Examples 233;
Summary 237*

PART VII   APPENDICES

A   Physical Network Technologies *241*

*Local Area Network Data Link Technology 241;
IEEE/ANSI/ISO LAN Architecture Layers and Sublayers 241;
IEEE/ANSI/ISO LAN Standards 243; Local Area Networking Addressing 243;
Subnetwork Network Access Protocol 246; Repeaters and Bridges 248;
Wide Area Networking Data Links 248;
Conventional Common Carrier Links 249; High-Level Data Link Control 249;
Serial Line Interface Protocol 251; Point-to-Point Protocol 252; X.25 253;
Frame Relay 255; Asynchronous Transfer Mode 256;
Other Wide Area Networking Technologies 262*

B   OSF Distributed Computing Environment *265*

*DCE Cell Architecture 265; DCE Middleware Services 266;
DCE Remote Procedure Call Service 266; DCE Threads Service 270;
DCE Directory Service 273; DCE Distributed File Service 281;
DCE Distributed Time Service 281; DCE Security Service 285*

C   Requests for Comments *289*

Glossary *295*

Index *323*

Preface

The TCP/IP protocol suite forms the basis for one of the most widely used networking technologies in the world. The acronym TCP/IP stands for the names of the two core protocols that make up the full set of TCP/IP protocols—the *Transmission Control Protocol* (TCP) and the *Internet Protocol* (IP).

Development of these communication protocols began in 1969 with funding provided by the U. S. Department of Defense. The protocols that eventually grew into the TCP/IP protocol suite began with the protocols used to build the ARPANET, the world's first packet-switching network. The ARPANET lead to the development of today's Worldwide Internet, one of the word's largest heterogeneous computer networks.

The TCP/IP protocol suite is used in the Internet and is also used in many smaller, private computer networks, especially in networks that connect computing systems that run the UNIX operating system. It is possible, although far from certain, that the protocols that have been developed by the International Organization for Standardization (ISO) for the OSI model will eventually displace the TCP/IP protocol suite in many environments. However, the TCP/IP protocols will probably be extensively used by many organizations well into the next century. TCP/IP is today an extremely important form of networking technology. This book describes the protocols that make up the TCP/IP protocol suite.

The primary purpose of this book is to enable technical staff members to choose TCP/IP internet hardware and software products to best satisfy their specific requirements. Another objective of this book is to provide an overall framework that will enable the reader to more easily gain the knowledge necessary to install and maintain specific TCP/IP products. The book can be used as the text for an introductory course on computer networking.

WHO SHOULD READ THIS BOOK

Readers who will benefit from this book include computer users who employ the facilities of a TCP/IP internet for resource sharing, for communication with other computer users, and for accessing the facilities of host computing systems; technicians who are responsible for installing TCP/IP hardware and software products; technical staff members who are responsible for maintaining and administering a TCP/IP internet; and systems analysts, designers, and programmers who will be designing and implementing client-server applications that use TCP/IP internets for communication.

PLAN OF THE BOOK

The chapters of this book are divided into six parts. Part I introduces the environment in which TCP/IP networking is generally used and describes the overall architecture of the TCP/IP protocol suite. The chapters in Part I introduce the internetworking concept, examine the Worldwide Internet that today serves the needs of government, education, and commercial organizations, present the functional layers that make up the TCP/IP architecture, and describe the addressing mechanisms used to identify computing systems in a TCP/IP internet.

Part II describes the TCP/IP protocols and services that are employed by end users for doing useful work. The chapters in Part II provide an overview of the most commonly used application services and further describe two protocols that are widely used in most TCP/IP internets—the Network File Service (NFS) facility that provides access to remote files and the Domain Name System (DNS) that provides a global directory service for mapping between the names of network resources and their network addresses.

Part III describes the two major data transport protocols that are used in a TCP/IP internet. The two transport protocols described in the chapters in Part III are the User Datagram Protocol (UDP) that provides a best-efforts datagram data delivery service and the Transmission Control Protocol (TCP) that provides a reliable, stream-oriented data delivery service.

Part IV investigates the low-level protocols in the TCP/IP protocol suite that are used to provide basic packet delivery facilities. The chapters in Part IV describe the Internet Protocol (IP) that provides routing and relaying functions, the Address Resolution Protocol (ARP) and Reverse Address Resolution Protocol (RARP) that map between internet addresses and physical hardware addresses, the Internet Control Message Protocol (ICMP) that allows systems to report on error conditions, and routing protocols that are used by routers to maintain their routing tables.

Part V concentrates on network management, administration, and troubleshooting procedures that system and network administrators employ in keeping a TCP/IP internet running.

Part VI introduces the programming techniques that are used in writing application programs that communicate over a TCP/IP internet. The chapters in Part VI introduce the client-server approach to distributed computing, describe general programming techniques that are employed with TCP/IP networking software, and describe two commonly used approaches to TCP/IP network programming—the socket approach and the remote procedure call approach.

James Martin
Joe Leben

List of Acronyms

ANSI. American National Standards Institute.

API. Application programming interface.

ARP. Address Resolution Protocol.

ARPA. Advanced Research Projects Agency.

ASC. Accredited Standards Committee.

ASCII. American Standard Code for Information Interchange.

ASN.1. Abstract Syntax Notation One.

ATM. Asynchronous Transfer Mode.

B-ISDN. Broadband integrated services digital network.

BGP. Border Gateway Protocol.

CCITT. International Telegraph and Telephone Consultative Committee.

CDS. Cell Directory Service.

CMIP. Common Management Information Protocol.

CMOT. Common Management Information Protocol over TCP/IP.

CSMA/CD. Carrier Sense Multiple Access with Collision Detection.

DARPA. Defense Advanced Research Projects Agency

DCE. Distributed Computing Environment.

DCE CDS. Distributed Computing Environment Cell Directory Service.

DCE DFS. Distributed Computing Environment Distributed File Service.

DCE DTS. Distributed Computing Environment Distributed Time Service.

DCE GDS. Distributed Computing Environment Global Directory Service.

DCE RPC. Distributed Computing Environment Remote Procedure Call.

DFS. Distributed File Service.

DNS. Domain Name System.

DQDB. Distributed Queue Dual Bus.

DTS. Distributed Time Service.

EBCDIC. Extended Binary-coded Decimal Interchange Code.

EGP. Exterior Gateway Protocol.

FDDI. Fiber Distributed Data Interface.

FQDN. Fully-qualified domain name.

FTP. File Transfer Protocol.

GDS. Global Directory Service.

HDLC. High-level Data Link Control.

IAB. Internet Activities Board.

IANA. Internet Assigned Numbers Authority.

ICMP. Internet Control Message Protocol.

IEEE. Institute of Electrical and Electronics Engineers.

IETF. Internet Engineering Task Force.

IP. Internet Protocol.

ISDN. Integrated services digital network.

ISO. International Organization for Standardization.

LAN. Local area network.

LLC. Logical Link Control.

LLC-PDU. Logical-link-control-protocol-data-unit.

LLC-SDU. Logical-link-control-service-data-unit.

MA. Management agent.

MAC. Medium Access Control.

MAC-PDU. Medium-access-control-protocol-data-unit.

MAC-SDU. Medium-access-control-service-data-unit.

MAN. Metropolitan Area Network.

MBPS. Megabits per second.

MIB. Management Information Base.

NDR. Network Data Representation.

NE. Network element.

NFS. Network File System.

NIC. Network interface card, Network Information Center.

NIDL. Network Interface Definition Language.

NIS. Network Information Service.

NMA. Network management application.

NMS. Network management station.

NOC. Network Operations Center.

NREN. National Research and Education Network.

NSS. Nodal switching system.

NTP. Network Time Protocol.

NVT. Network virtual terminal.

OSF. Open Software Foundation.

OSF DCE. Open Software Foundation Distributed Computing Environment.

OSI. Open systems interconnection.

OSPF. Open Shortest Path First.

PCI. Protocol-control-information.

PDU. Protocol-data-unit.

PPP. Point-to-Point Protocol.

PTT. Postal, Telegraph, and Telephone Administration.

RARP. Reverse Address Resolution Protocol.

RFC. Request for Comments.

RIP. Routing Information Protocol.

RPC. Remote procedure call.

SAP. Service-access-point.

SDU. Service-data-unit.

SMDS. Switched Multimegabit Data Service.

SMFA. Specific management functional area.

SMI. Structure and identification of Management Information.

SMTP. Simple Mail Transfer Protocol.

SNAP. Subnetwork Access Protocol.

SNAP LLC-PDU. Subnetwork Access Protocol logical-link-control-protocol-data-unit.

SNAP PDU. Subnetwork Access Protocol protocol-data-unit.

SNMP. Simple Network Management Protocol.

SPF. Shortest path first.

SQL. Structured Query Language.

TCP. Transmission Control Protocol.

TCP/IP. Transmission Control Protocol/Internet Protocol.

TFTP. Trivial File Transfer Protocol.

TLI. Transport Layer Interface.

UDP. User Datagram Protocol.

WAN. Wide area network.

WWW. Worldwide Web.

XDR. External Data Representation.

TCP/IP NETWORKING

PART ▌

ARCHITECTURE

Chapter 1   Internetworking with TCP/IP   Chapter 3   TCP/IP Architecture

Chapter 2   The Worldwide Internet   Chapter 4   TCP/IP Addressing

Chapter 1

Internetworking with TCP/IP

In today's computing environment, the hierarchical, terminal-based networks of the past are becoming less important. Modern computer networking technologies allow organizations to construct flexible enterprise internetworks that permit intelligent computing devices of all types to be interconnected to solve business problems. TCP/IP, which is an acronym for *Transmission Control Protocol/Internet Protocol,* represents a particularly important form of internetworking technology that allows organizations to extend the reach of their computing systems.

The term TCP/IP refers to a set of protocols, or a *protocol suite,* that defines the rules governing how messages are exchanged in a computer network. The TCP/IP protocol suite grew out of a research project that began in 1969 and was funded by the U. S. Department of Defense. The TCP/IP protocols are based on the packet-switching ideas developed for an early research computer network called the *ARPANET,* whose acronym was based on the name of the *Advanced Research Projects Agency* (ARPA) that funded its development. ARPA is now known as the *Defense Advanced Research Projects Agency* (DARPA). The early ARPANET tied together a number of research computers using conventional leased telecommunications lines.

The original idea behind the TCP/IP protocol suite was to define a standard set of procedures to allow individual computer networks to be connected to the ARPANET. Today, the main purpose of the TCP/IP protocol suite is to allow diverse types of physical networks to be tied together so that any networked computer can talk to any other computer. The TCP/IP protocols allow the interconnected individual networks to give the appearance of a single, unified network—called an *internet*—in which all computers can freely exchange data as if they were all directly connected. The TCP/IP protocols make it appear to a system that there is a simple point-to-point connection to any other system in the internet, even though data might have to follow a quite complex path in traveling from one system to another.

TCP/IP INTERNETS

The ARPANET and the TCP/IP protocol suite were extremely successful, and the TCP/IP protocols are used throughout the world in a great number of computer networks. The world's largest TCP/IP internet grew from the original ARPANET and has evolved into what is now often called the Worldwide Internet, or simply the Internet.* Today's Worldwide Internet interconnects thousands of networks containing millions of computers in universities, national laboratories, and commercial organizations. Although the TCP/IP protocol suite is used for connecting to the Worldwide Internet, TCP/IP protocols are widely used in implementing the private internets of many organizations as well.

TCP/IP COMPONENTS

Figure 1.1 shows the major components that are used to construct a TCP/IP internet. The following are descriptions of the three major components:

- **Hosts.** With TCP/IP, the term *host* is used to refer to any computing system that is attached to an internet and communicates using the TCP/IP protocols. Hosts run the application programs that communicate with one another. A host can be a large mainframe, a minicomputer, a midrange departmental processor, a graphics workstation, or a personal computer.

- **Networks.** TCP/IP hosts are attached to individual *networks*. A *network* is a collection of two or more hosts that are interconnected using a particular form of data link technology. The TCP/IP architecture is independent of any particular form of networking technology.

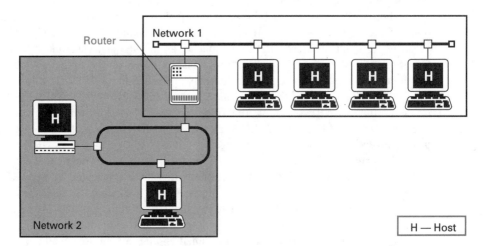

Figure 1.1   TCP/IP networking software.

*In this book, we use the term *internet* with a lowercase *i* to refer generically to any TCP/IP internet; we use the term *Internet* with an uppercase *I* to refer to the Worldwide Internet.

One of the powers of the TCP/IP architecture is its ability to accommodate new forms of network technology as they become available.

- **Routers.** A *router* is a device that provides connectivity between the various individual networks making up the internet.* The function of a router is to move network traffic from one physical network to another when a program running in a host attached to one physical network has to communicate with a host attached to some other physical network. The routing function can be performed by an ordinary host that runs routing software, or it can be performed by a specialized device that is dedicated to the routing function. In large internets, routing is generally performed by dedicated routers.

The individual networks making up the internet and the routers that interconnect them are hidden from the user. Users view the internet as simply one unified network in which any host can send data traffic to any other host.

PHYSICAL NETWORK TECHNOLOGIES

In an internet, data units are passed from one device to another across physical circuits. The transmission of data across a physical circuit is controlled by a *data link protocol*. A data link protocol defines the formats of the data units—typically called *frames*—that are transferred across the physical circuit.

A data link protocol also defines the rules that govern how those frames are exchanged. A physical circuit in conjunction with a data link protocol forms a *data link* over which data can be transmitted in an error-free fashion. Each physical network in a TCP/IP internet takes the form of a data link.

The physical network technologies that can be used to implement the data links in an internet can be divided into two categories—*local area network* data links and *wide area network* data links.

Local Area Network Data Links

A local area network (LAN) implements a form of data link technology that is designed to meet the requirements for high-speed, relatively short-distance communication among intelligent devices. The majority of local area networks that are in use today connect personal computers and workstations to one another and to larger systems, often called *servers*.

LAN data links are normally constrained to being within a single building or within a campus of buildings. They do not ordinarily cross public thoroughfares and normally operate over private cabling. Typical data transfer speeds provided by LAN data links range from 4 Mbps to 100 Mbps. LAN data link technology is generally used to create peer networks in which any device on the LAN data link can communicate with any other device on the LAN.

---

*Much of the TCP/IP literature uses the term *gateway* to refer to a device functioning as a router. It is more common in computer networking to use the term gateway to refer to a device that performs a protocol conversion function, and most TCP/IP authorities now use the term router instead of gateway.

A wide variety of LAN data link technologies are in common use. Box 1.1 describes some of the most commonly used LAN data link technologies that are used in the TCP/IP environment.

Wide Area Network Data Links

Many of today's computer networks use public telecommunications facilities to implement *wide area network* (WAN) data links for communicating over large geographic areas. Commonly used data transfer speeds in the wide area networking environment range from 2400 bits per second (bps) using low-cost modems and ordinary dial-up telephone connections to as high as 45 megabits per second (Mbps) over a leased T3 digital telecommunications facility. Higher speeds are also possible and will become more common in the 1990s. Wide area networking facilities are most often used to implement point-to-point connections between pairs of devices.

Most WAN data links take the form of various types of analog or digital telecommunications circuits provided by common carriers or government telecommunications administrations. These range from ordinary telephone circuits that are provided via the switched telephone network to specialized, high-speed digital telecommunications circuits that can be leased on a month-to-month basis from a common carrier.

BOX 1.1   Local Area Network (LAN) data link technologies.

- **Ethernet.** A LAN data link technology in which systems are attached to a common transmission facility, such as a coaxial cable or twisted-pair cable. A system typically attempts to transmit whenever it has data to send. Ethernet is the most widely used form of LAN data link technology.

- **Token Ring.** A LAN data link technology in which systems are connected to one another using point-to-point twisted-pair cable segments to form a ring structure. A system is allowed to transmit only when it has a special data unit, called the *token,* which is passed from one system to another around the ring.

- **Token Bus.** A LAN data link technology in which systems are connected to a common transmission medium in a similar manner as an Ethernet LAN. A system is allowed to transmit only when it has the token, which is passed from one system to another. Token Bus LANs are sometimes used in factory automation environments.

- **ARCnet.** A relatively low-speed form of LAN data link technology in which all systems are attached to a common coaxial cable. As with the Token Bus form of LAN, a system transmits when it has the token.

- **Fiber Distributed Data Interface (FDDI).** A high-speed LAN data link technology in which systems are connected to one another using point-to-point fiber-optic cable segments to form a ring structure. A system is allowed to transmit only when it has the token.

- **LocalTalk.** A low-speed LAN data link technology—part of Apple Computer's AppleTalk networking scheme—in which systems are attached to a common cable. LocalTalk technology has been built into most of the computing devices that Apple Computer manufactures.

Some of the wide area network data link technologies that can be used in constructing TCP/IP internets are described in Box 1.2.

The LAN and WAN data link technologies that are most often used in constructing
TCP/IP internets are described further in Appendix A.

BOX 1.2   Wide Area Network (WAN) data link technologies.

- **HDLC Data Links.** *High-Level Data Link Control* (HDLC) is an international standard
  data link protocol that can be used to control transmission over point-to-point telecommunications circuits. Many other data link protocols are based on the HDLC standard. The
  HDLC protocol has its roots in the *Synchronous Data Link Control* (SDLC) protocol
  developed by IBM in the early 1970s for use in SNA. HDLC is a bit-oriented protocol in
  which data is transported over the link a frame at a time.

- **Point-to-Point Protocol Data Links.** The *Point-to-Point Protocol* (PPP) is an adaptation
  of HDLC that is oriented to long-distance communication in a TCP/IP internet. The Point-
  to-Point Protocol improves on HDLC by adding a protocol identification mechanism. The
  Point-to-Point Protocol allows a point-to-point connection to be established between two
  network devices that allows frames associated with multiple communication protocols to
  flow over the data link without interfering with one another.

- **X.25 Data Links.** An alternative to using conventional common carrier telecommunications circuits in a computer network is to use a public packet-switched data network
  (PSDN). X.25 PSDNs are generally operated by either a common carrier or a private
  telecommunications service provider and provide virtual circuits that are used in the same
  manner as ordinary telecommunications point-to-point links. CCITT *Recommendation
  X.25* defines a standard way for attaching a computer or other intelligent device to a
  PSDN.

- **Frame Relay Data Links.** *Frame Relay* networks supply services that are similar to those
  provided by X.25 packet-switching networks. However, routing decisions in a Frame
  Relay network are relatively simple and are made more quickly in order to support higher
  transmission speeds. Frame Relay data links support a variety of transmission speeds, but
  the target speed is generally in the neighborhood of the speeds supported by T1 facilities.
  Like X.25 networks, Frame Relay networks are generally operated by a common carrier
  and provide users with virtual circuits.

- **ISDN Data Links.** An *Integrated Services Digital Network* (ISDN) is a public telecommunications network that supplies end-to-end digital telecommunications services that
  can be used for both voice and nonvoice purposes. ISDN services include both packet-
  mode services and circuit-mode services. Packet-mode ISDN services offer services that
  are similar to those provided by an X.25 PSDN. Circuit-mode services can be used as
  replacements for conventional telecommunications circuits.

- **Broadband ISDN Data Links.** *Broadband ISDN* (B-ISDN) represents a possible future
  direction of the telephone industry and will require that the conventional copper-wire
  local loops that now go into subscriber premises be replaced by optical fiber cables. B-
  ISDN services are built on top of a Physical layer specification called SONET, which
  includes specifications for transmission speeds ranging from 51 megabits per second
  (Mbps) through 2.4 gigabits per second (Gbps).

(Continued)

BOX 1.2 *(Continued)*

- **Distributed Queue Dual Bus Data Links.** *Distributed Queue Dual Bus* (DQDB) data links can be used to provide LAN-like services over a wider geographic area. The type of network that the DQDB protocol operates over is generally referred to as a *Metropolitan Area Network* (MAN). The DQDB protocol is relatively independent of the underlying physical transmission medium and can operate at SONET speeds.

- **Switched Multi-Megabit Data Service Data Links.** The *Switched Multi-Megabit Data Service* (SMDS) is a wide area packet-switching service implemented by many telecommunications providers that supports packet-switching services similar to an X.25 network. However, SMDS provides services at very high speeds rather than the relatively slow speeds provided by a typical X.25 PSDN.

- **Asynchronous Transfer Mode Data Links.** *Asynchronous Transfer Mode* (ATM) is a high-speed networking technology that has the potential for better integrating different types of LAN and WAN communication technologies. ATM uses a high-speed form of packet switching called *cell switching* that carries data in 53-octet cells.* ATM technology can be used in conjunction with private cabling or with common carrier circuits.

PHYSICAL NETWORK IMPLEMENTATION

TCP/IP internets are physically implemented by interconnecting individual physical networks that may employ the same or different data link technologies. The specific components used to implement the physical networks making up a typical TCP/IP internet, shown in Fig. 1.2, include computing devices, network interface cards, a cabling system, hubs or concentrators, and networking software.

Computing Devices

Physical networks are typically used to interconnect general-purpose computing devices, such as personal computers or workstations, which may be of the same or of different types. Special-purpose devices, such as intelligent printers, may also be directly attached to a network. Simple peripheral devices, such as hard disks and simple line printers, are not typically attached directly to a computer network. Instead, such peripheral devices are attached to one of the networked computer systems. Peripheral devices can, however, be made accessible to other systems on the network and can be shared by all network users.

As we discussed earlier, in a TCP/IP internet, the computing devices that end users perceive and that run application programs are called *hosts*. The computing devices that are used to interconnect physical networks are called *routers*.

*International standards for computer networking typically use the term *octet* to refer to a collection of 8 bits. Even though the term *byte* is today more common than *octet*, we will adopt the international standard terminology and use the term *octet* to refer to an arbitrary collection of 8 bits, such as when describing a communication protocol. But we will continue to use the term *byte* when referring to a collection of 8 bits in a storage system.

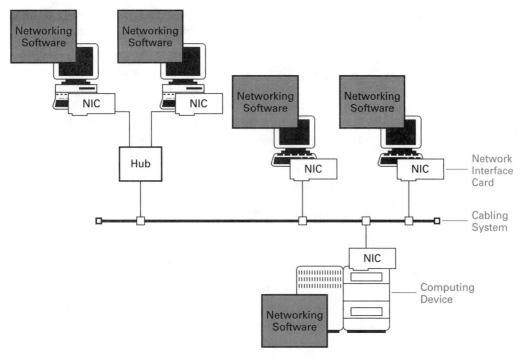

Figure 1.2   Physical network components.

Network Interface Cards

A *network interface card* (NIC), sometimes called a *network adapter,* is typically installed in each computing device that is directly attached to a physical network. On a local area network, the NIC is sometimes called a *LAN adapter.* A NIC performs the hardware functions that are required to provide a computing device with physical communication capabilities.

Some types of computing devices that are designed for use on specific types of physical networks, such as a network printer, may have the functions of a NIC integrated directly into them. Other types of computing devices, such as the host computers employed by end users, allow various types of NICs to be installed in them.

Cabling Systems

Cabling systems are particularly important on physical networks that use privately-installed cabling, such as a typical local area network. A LAN cabling system includes the cable used to interconnect the NICs installed in the networked computing devices. Various types of electrical cable or fiber-optic cable are used to implement LANs. The cabling system also typically includes *attachment units* that allow the devices to attach to the cable. In some cases, the cabling system is replaced with some form of wireless communication, such as radio, microwave, or infrared signaling. With wide area network data links, the cabling system is implemented by a telecommunications provider.

Access Units or Concentrators

Some physical network implementations use devices called *access units, concentrators,* or *hubs* that allow multiple network devices to be connected to the network through a central point. Attaching devices through a central concentrator often simplifies the installation and maintenance of the network.

TCP/IP Networking Software

Network interface cards (NICs) perform low-level functions that allow physical communication to take place over a physical network between interconnected devices. High-level functions that end users employ for doing useful work are generally handled by TCP/IP networking software that accesses a NIC on behalf of an end user.

In the personal computer environment, software products that provide end user communication facilities are often called *network operating systems.* Network operating systems augment a computer system's conventional system software by providing networking facilities, such as remote file and printer access. Some personal computer network operating systems provide support for TCP/IP communication facilities.

TCP/IP NETWORKING SOFTWARE

An important role of the TCP/IP protocol suite is to define a set of universal communication services. These services can then be implemented in a standardized manner in the networking software that runs on a wide variety of different types of computer systems. TCP/IP users, which can be either end users or application programs, employ the TCP/IP networking software to communicate over an internet with other users. The TCP/IP networking software sits between the user and the physical network to which the user's host is attached, as shown in Fig. 1.3. The TCP/IP networking software provides a unified interface that is independent of the underlying networking technology.

The TCP/IP protocol suite has been implemented in networking software that is available for a great many widely used operating systems, including most UNIX variations. TCP/IP networking software is also available for use with personal computers and workstations running MS-DOS, Windows, Windows/NT, and OS/2 system software. Many network operating systems for personal computers, such as NetWare, LAN Manager, LAN Server, and PATHWORKS incorporate support for the TCP/IP protocols as well as support for their own native communication protocols. TCP/IP implementations are available for IBM's AIX, OS/400, VM, and MVS platforms and for Digital Equipment Corporation's OpenVMS and Ultrix platforms. Most of the systems in Apple's computer system family can also run TCP/IP networking software.

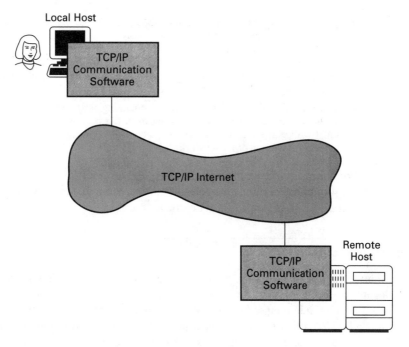

Figure 1.3   TCP/IP networking software.

In some environments, the TCP/IP networking software is bundled with the operating system, as it is with many types of graphics workstations that run a UNIX variation. In other cases, the TCP/IP networking software is available separately.

A major benefit of the TCP/IP protocol suite is that it allows internets to be constructed that connect diverse types of computer systems—that may be running a great many different types of operating systems—in a heterogeneous computer networking environment. A workstation running a variation of UNIX, for example, can successfully communicate over a TCP/IP internet with a large IBM mainframe running MVS and with a small personal computer running MS-DOS as long as all the systems run networking software that implements the TCP/IP protocols.

ADMINISTRATION FUNCTIONS

As an organization begins to make heavy use of computer networking technology, two personnel roles tend to emerge, either formally or on an ad hoc basis—*system administrator* and *network administrator*. These two roles may be performed by different individuals (or groups in large organizations), or they may be fulfilled by the same individual. Some of the responsibilities associated with each of these two important personnel roles are as follows:

- **System Administrator.** An individual operating in the role of *system administrator* is responsible for installing and maintaining software on host computers that are designated as servers and for helping individual workstation or personal computer users install and maintain software on their own individual computers. There is often a need for a system administration role even when a group of workstations or personal computers used by an individual organization are not networked.

- **Network Administrator.** An individual operating in the role of *network administrator* assists system administrators by helping to install networking software on servers, individual workstations, and personal computers and performs network-wide tasks to ensure the proper operation of the network.

For simplicity, this book will often use the term *administrator* to refer to an individual or group that performs the roles of either system administrator or network administrator in a TCP/IP networking environment.

TCP/IP INTERNETWORKING

Many computer networks are made up of LAN data links that tie together the equipment located at each particular site in an organization. The LAN data links at the different sites are then often interconnected using WAN data link facilities. A TCP/IP internet typically uses a LAN/WAN configuration in which individual LAN data links connect the hosts at a particular site, and WAN data links tie together the various sites.

A small TCP/IP internet using both LAN and WAN data links is shown in Fig. 1.4. Notice that in this internet the hosts are connected to the LAN data links, and routers are used to interconnect the two LANs. However, TCP/IP also permits an individual host to be directly connected to a router using a point-to-point link.

An interesting characteristic of the TCP/IP internetworking environment is that few TCP/IP internets are explicitly designed. Instead, they simply evolve over time. In a typical scenario, an individual department in an organization acquires a number of workstations and appoints an individual to operate in the role of the system administrator. The system administrator hooks the workstations together with LAN hardware and cabling and installs the TCP/IP networking software in each of the hosts. Such a LAN tends to grow as more workstations and server systems are added to it.

Another department close by might at the same time be acquiring workstations and might also be hooking them together using TCP/IP networking software. The two departments may then decide that it would be beneficial to connect the networks together so they can exchange information between them. If the departments are located close to one another, they can connect their two LANs using a single router.

A department in some remote location might also acquire some workstations that they connect together using LAN technology. They want to communicate with the other two departments, so they connect their network with the first two using a second router and a leased telecommunications line. The three departments could later find it necessary to connect a large mainframe in their own information systems department to the entire private internet. At some point, the organization may choose to connect their private

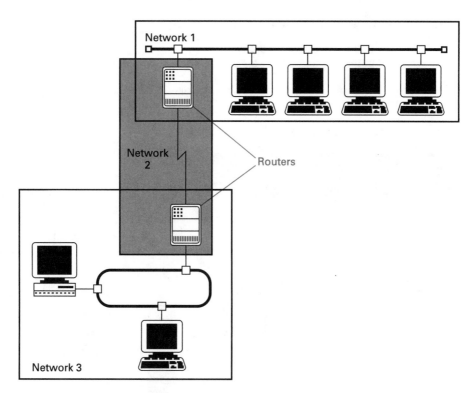

Figure 1.4   Small internet using both local area networking and wide area networking facilities.

internet to the Worldwide Internet and begin communicating worldwide with other organizations on the Internet, as illustrated in Fig. 1.5.

SUMMARY

TCP/IP is a protocol suite defining the rules that govern how messages are exchanged in a peer-to-peer computer network. The TCP/IP protocols allow a system of interconnected LAN and WAN data links to form an integrated internet in which all attached computer systems can freely exchange information.

A TCP/IP internet is made up of three major categories of components—host computers, physical networks to which hosts are attached, and routers that interconnect physical networks. TCP/IP supports physical networks implemented using a wide range of wide area network and local area network data link technologies. A typical TCP/IP internet consists of a collection of LAN data links that are interconnected using routers and WAN telecommunication facilities. The physical networks that are used to construct TCP/IP internets are made up of components that include computing devices, network

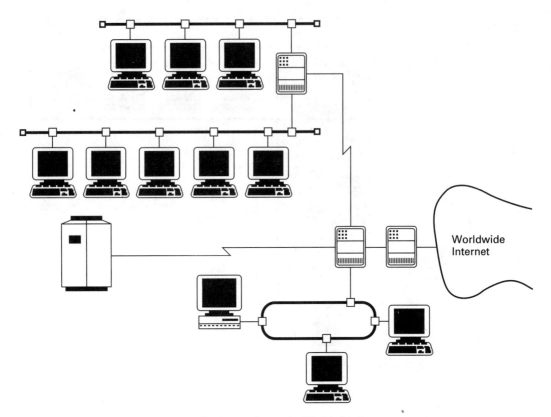

Figure 1.5   Connecting to the Worldwide Internet.

interface cards, cabling systems, access units or concentrators, and TCP/IP networking software.

The users of a TCP/IP internet employ TCP/IP communication software that sits between the user and the physical network to which the user's host is attached. The TCP/IP networking software presents a unified interface that is independent of the underlying networking technology. TCP/IP communication software is implemented on a wide range of computing systems of all sizes.

Chapter 2 describes the Worldwide Internet, the world's largest TCP/IP internet, connecting thousands of networks containing millions of computers in universities, research facilities, and commercial organizations.

Chapter **2**

The Worldwide Internet

As we introduced in Chapter 1, the Worldwide Internet is the world's largest TCP/IP internet, linking millions of computers throughout the world. The Internet has seen staggering growth due to two factors—the ease with which TCP/IP networks can be interconnected and the open-door policy that allowed organizations of all types to gain easy access to the Internet.

For a number of years, the ARPANET served as the long-haul backbone network for the Internet. An experimental, four-node version of the ARPANET first began operation in 1969. The experiment was successful, and the network quickly grew into a network spanning the United States. In 1975, the Defense Communication Agency (DCA) assumed responsibility for operating the ARPANET.

The initial protocols used on the ARPANET were slow, and software implementations of them were prone to error. In 1974, a new set of protocols was proposed by Vinton G. Cerf and Robert E. Kahn. The Cerf/Kahn protocols formed the basis of what eventually evolved into today's Internet Protocol (IP) and Transmission Control Protocol (TCP), the two major TCP/IP protocols after which the protocol suite derives its name.

By 1983, the ARPANET had expanded to include over 300 computers that were shared by government and research installations across the United States. In 1984, the ARPANET was split into two pieces—the ARPANET, devoted primarily to research, and MILNET, an unclassified military computer network. The term *Internet* was coined at that time to refer to both ARPANET and MILNET.

The ARPANET eventually formed the backbone for what has evolved into today's Internet. Today, the Internet serves the needs not only of government and research organizations but is used by a wide variety of commercial organizations as well. In 1990, the ARPANET was officially shut down.

INTERNET HIERARCHICAL STRUCTURE

The Internet is organized as a three-level hierarchy, as illustrated in Fig. 2.1. Individual host computers are typically connected to local networks that are operated by universities, research centers, federal and state agencies, and individual commercial organizations.

Local neworks are connected to a number of regional, midlevel networks that are operated by large universities and some commercial enterprises. Each of the regional networks is connected to the NSFNET backbone network.

NSFNET Backbone Network

The role of the Internet backbone in the United States today has been taken over by the *NSFNET,* a high-speed network run by the National Science Foundation (NSF). NSFNET consists of a number of computers called *nodal switching systems* (NSSs) that are interconnected by leased T3 digital telecommunication facilities that support a bit rate of 45 Mbps. Each of the Internet regional networks is connected to at least one of the NSFNET nodal switching systems.

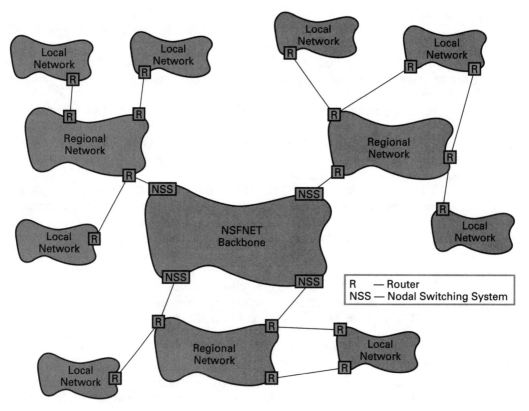

Figure 2.1   Internet hierarchical logical structure.

National Research and Education Network (NREN)

It is possible that the role of the NSFNET will be taken over in the future by a higher-speed network, called the National Research and Education Network (NREN), that is undergoing development by the U. S. government. The NREN is likely to be a test bed for new information services that require a very-high-capacity digital network.

INTERNET ADMINISTRATION

The Defense Data Network (DDN) is the governmental organization that has overall responsibility for administering the Internet. A large number of organizations help DDN in its administration tasks. The following sections describe some of them.

DDN Network Information Center

The DDN *Network Information Center* (NIC) is the organization responsible for collecting and distributing information about TCP/IP protocols. The NIC is also responsible for assigning unique names and addresses to the networks and systems that are connected to the Internet by individual organizations. The NIC is operated by Government Systems, Inc. (GSI). At the time of writing the address and telephone numbers for the NIC are as follows:

> DDN Network Information Center
> 14200 Park Meadow Drive
> Suite 200
> Chantilly, VA 22021
> (800) 365-3642; (703) 802-4535

Many organizations apply to GSI for network IDs to use in their own private internets to ensure uniqueness should their private internets ever have to be connected to the Worldwide Internet.

Internet Assigned Numbers Authority

The *Internet Assigned Numbers Authority* (IANA) is responsible for assigning values for network parameters, special network addresses, names of services, and various types of standard identifiers. At the time of writing, the role of the IANA is performed by the University of Southern California Information Services Institute.

Network Operations Center

The *Network Operations Center* (NOC) manages the telecommunications links and the NSSs making up the NSFNET backbone network. The NOC is operated by Merit, Inc. on behalf of the National Science Foundation.

Internet Activities Board

The *Internet Activities Board* (IAB) is the organization that coordinates the development and evolution of the TCP/IP protocol suite. The IAB began as an organization funded by DARPA. It has since evolved into an autonomous organization that is staffed by volunteers, recruited from a variety of government and commercial organizations, who serve on a variety of task forces. The chairman of the IAB is called the *Internet Architect*.

Internet Engineering Task Force

The *Internet Engineering Task Force* (IETF) is an organization staffed by volunteers from the TCP/IP community that studies Internet technical issues and recommends Internet standards to the IAB.

CONNECTING TO THE INTERNET

In the early years of the operation of the Internet, only academic and research organizations could gain access to the network. Today, however, any organization can apply to the NIC for name and address assignments and can connect its own private network to the Internet. A commercial organization, or an individual, can gain access to the Internet through either a dedicated or dial-up connection. Access to the Internet is typically made through one of a number of companies that provide Internet access services on a fee basis. The NIC maintains a list of companies that provide Internet access services.

INTERNET INFORMATION RESOURCES

Various organizations that have computers attached to the Internet make an astonishingly wide range of information and services available to anyone who can access the Internet. The book *The Whole Internet User's Guide & Catalog* contains listings of some of the sources of information that are available.[1] Box 2.1 lists a few representative examples of the resources on the Internet that can be accessed.

LOCATING INTERNET RESOURCES

Once a particular public information resource has been located on the Internet, it is a relatively simple matter to obtain access to it. In many cases, the TCP/IP File Transfer Protocol (FTP), described in Chapter 5, can be used to download a copy of the desired information to the user's own host. However, the Internet is so vast, and there are so many sources of information, that locating a desired resource can be quite difficult.

The Internet supports a number of different software tools that can be used to navigate through the Internet and to help in locating those sources of information that are of interest. Box 2.2 describes some of the available information access tools.

BOX 2.1   Representative Internet information resources.

- **Agriculture.** Among the agriculturally-oriented resources is AGRICOLA, an online database containing citations to agricultural literature in the National Agriculture Library and related institutions on nutrition, agricultural economics, and parasitology.

- **Alcoholism.** Among the resources devoted to health is an online database containing articles and other information pertaining to alcoholism and other forms of substance abuse.

- **Anthropology.** Among the resources devoted to anthropology, the Thai-Yunnan Project maintains a database of annotated bibliographical and research notes collected by the Thai-Yunnan Project, Department of Anthropology, Australian National University. The database contains extensive information on ethnic groups of southeast Asia, including languages, religions, and customs.

- **Chinese Literature.** Among the many resources devoted to literature is an online database containing a library of Chinese classics, as posted on the Chinese Poem Exchange Network. The database includes texts ranging from the ancient Chinese philosophers to the present.

- **Cooking.** Among the cooking-oriented resources is an online database maintained by the University of Stuttgart that contains a general information server providing access to a collection of recipes and an online cookbook. Recipes are presented in both German and English.

- **Drosophila Stocks.** Among the resources devoted to the biological sciences is a database containing a list of sources for Drosophila (fruit flies) with various traits.

- **Genealogy.** An extensive database containing genealogical information of various types includes various genealogy database programs and lists of genealogy societies, magazines, and newsletters.

- **Indian Classical Music.** Among the music-related resources is an online database of Indian Compact Discs (CDs), including Hindustani and Karnatic CDs.

- **Library Catalogs.** The card catalogs for hundreds of libraries are available through various online databases.

- **Molecular Graphics.** A variety of 3D raster software is available for viewing molecular graphics.

- **NSF Publications.** The National Science Foundation maintains a database containing NSF publications.

- **PC Magazine.** Ziff Davis maintains electronic versions of back copies of PC Magazine.

- **Space Information.** The National Aeronautics and Space Administration (NASA) maintains entries about the history, current status, and future of NASA and space flight in general. Files are also available for downloading that contain photographs and other images taken from Space Shuttle, Magellan, and Viking missions.

- **Supercomputers.** The San Diego Super Computer Documentation is a database containing various information about supercomputers, including the documentation for Cray supercomputers.

- **Teaching.** The many resources of interest to teachers includes a collection of software to aid in the teaching of mathematics at the college level.

BOX 2.2   Internet information access tools.

- **The Finger Facility.** The *Finger* facility is implemented by a UNIX program that allows the user to determine a person's login name given the name of that person's host computer. The **finger** program can be used to generate a list of all the users who are logged into a particular Internet host computer.

- **The Whois System.** The *Whois* system implements an Internet directory that is similar to a white pages telephone directory. The Whois directory is maintained by the DDN NIC and lists people who are responsible for operating the Internet and who are doing Internet research. The Whois service has become a model for other directory services.

- **The Archie System.** The *Archie* system is implemented on a number of servers on the Internet, designated as *Archie servers,* that provide indexes to a large number of public information servers on the internet. A user can log into an Archie server and use the **archie** program to ask for a variety of different types of keyword searches to locate hosts that have information matching the search criteria. A variety of different types of searches can be requested, including searches on the basis of file names and searches on the basis of descriptive indexes that the Archie system maintains.

- **The Internet Gopher.** The *Internet gopher* is a system that allows a user to browse through a set of indexed resources by selecting choices in menus.

- **The WAIS Service.** The *WAIS* service is a distributed text searching system that allows the user to make various types of searches based on the contents of one or more indexed text databases. A number of WAIS-structured databases are available on the Internet.

- **The Worldwide Web.** The *Worldwide Web* (WWW) is a retrieval system that is under development at the time of writing. The Worldwide Web is based on hypertext technology that attempts to organize Internet information resources as a set of hypertext documents. The user traverses the network by moving from one hypertext document to another via links that are implemented between them.

REQUESTS FOR COMMENTS

TCP/IP standards are published in a series of documents called *Requests for Comments* (RFCs), each of which is assigned a unique 4-digit number. RFCs can be downloaded in machine-readable form from the Internet, or they can be obtained in hard-copy form from GSI. Most of the RFCs are stored in ASCII form and can be printed out on almost any printer. Some RFCs are also available in PostScript format and can be printed out, complete with formatting, on any printer that supports the Adobe PostScript page description language.

The NIC publishes an RFC, called IAB Official Protocol Standards, that describes the current status of TCP/IP protocols. This document is re-released from time to time with a new RFC number. At the time of writing, this document is published as RFC 1250. Appendix D provides a list of some of the RFCs that are available on the Internet or through the NIC.

A set of two RFCs constitute important reference sources concerning the protocols that are typically implemented in TCP/IP systems:

- **RFC 1122—Requirements for Internet Hosts—Communication Layers.** This RFC concentrates on protocols that concern communication between TCP/IP hosts.

- **RFC 1123—Requirements for Internet Hosts—Application and Support.** This RFC concentrates on protocols that provide services to end users.

These two RFCs identify the specific RFC that is the original source that defines each TCP/IP protocol, corrects errors that were detected in the original protocol description since its publication, and supplements the original protocol specifications in various ways.

PROTOCOL STATES AND STATUS LEVELS

The IAB Official Protocol Standards RFC defines TCP/IP protocols as being in one of four *states* and having one of five *status levels.*

Protocol States

The state of a TCP/IP protocol refers to its progress in making its way through the TCP/IP standardization process. The four possible states of a protocol at any given time are as follows:

- Experimental
- Proposed
- Draft
- Standard

Protocol Status Levels

Some of the TCP/IP protocols must be implemented in any system that uses the TCP/IP protocol suite, especially for connection to the Internet; others are used only where there is some special need; and still others are no longer used in practice. All TCP/IP protocol have one of the following five status levels:

- Required
- Recommended
- Elective
- Limited Use
- Not Recommended

SUMMARY

The Worldwide Internet, the world's largest TCP/IP internet, has seen rapid growth because of the ease with which TCP/IP networks can be interconnected and the open-door policy that has allowed organizations of all types to gain easy access to the Internet.

The Internet is organized as a three-level hierarchy with the NSFNET, a high-speed network run by the National Science Foundation, playing the role of the backbone network. The Defense Data Network (DDN) is the governmental organization responsible for Internet administration. Some of the organizations that help in the administration task are the DDN Network Information Center (NIC), the Internet Assigned Numbers Authority (IANA), the Network Operations Center (NOC), the Internet Activities Board (IAB), and the Internet Engineering Task Force (IETF).

The Internet provides access to a wide variety of public information sources. Some of the tools available for locating Internet information include the Finger facility for determining login names, the Whois directory service maintained by the DDN NIC, the Archie system for searching indexes of public information, the Internet Gopher for browsing resources using menus, the WAIS system for searching text databases, and the Worldwide Web for accessing Internet resources using hypertext technology.

TCP/IP standards are described in Requests for Comments (RFCs) that can be downloaded from the Internet or can be obtained in hardcopy from the DDN NIC.

Chapter 3 describes the architecture underlying the TCP/IP protocol suite and describes how TCP/IP networking software can be divided into functional layers.

REFERENCE

1. Ed Krol, *The Whole Internet User's Guide and Catalog,* O'Reilly & Associates, Inc., Sebastopol, CA, 1992.

Chapter 3

TCP/IP Architecture

Part of the power of the TCP/IP protocol suite comes from its ability to allow a wide variety of different types of devices, from different vendors, to interoperate with one another. Supporting a wide variety of devices, however, can present substantial compatibility problems. For widely varying devices to be linked together, the hardware and software of these devices need to be compatible or else complex interfaces have to be built for meaningful communication to take place. In order to facilitate this compatibility, *network architectures* have been developed that allow complex networks to be built using a variety of equipment. The TCP/IP protocols together make up one such network architecture.

In modern computer networks, data transmission functions are performed by complex hardware and software in the various devices that make up a network. In order to manage this complexity, the software functions performed in network devices are divided into independent *functional layers*. The TCP/IP suite of protocols together make up a layered architecture having the four software layers illustrated in Fig. 3.1. The four TCP/IP

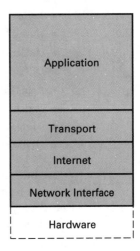

Figure 3.1   TCP/IP architectural layers.

software layers build on the underlying networking hardware that operates below the TCP/IP software layers. The functions of each of the TCP/IP functional layers are described later in this chapter.

TCP/IP communication software is divided into layers so that the highest layer—the one supporting application programs and end users—is shielded from the lower layers that handle the details concerning network communication.

TCP/IP makes it possible for an application running in one host in the internet to easily communicate with an application running in another host as if the two hosts were directly connected. Communication appears simple, even though there may be a complex internet consisting of many physical networks and many routers between the two hosts running the communicating programs. Each of the two communicating hosts runs software that implements all four layers of the TCP/IP architecture to handle communication functions.

NETWORK ARCHITECTURES

A *network architecture* is a comprehensive plan and a set of rules that govern the design and operation of the hardware and software components used to create computer networks. Network architectures define sets of *communication protocols* that govern how communication takes place.

A software system for communicating in a computer network generally conforms to a particular network architecture, such as TCP/IP, and uses a particular set of communication protocols. There are many different network architectures and systems of communication protocols that are in use today in computer networks.

The following are some of the most commonly used computer networking schemes, in addition to the TCP/IP protocol suite, that are used in constructing computer networks:

- Xerox Networking System (XNS)
- Novell NetWare
- DECnet Phase IV
- DECnet/OSI
- AppleTalk
- NetBIOS
- Systems Network Architecture (SNA) Subarea Networking
- SNA Advanced Peer-to-Peer Networking (APPN)

Figure 3.2 illustrates a general model for a layered network architecture. There is an *interface* between each pair of layers, and each functional layer provides a set of *services* to the layer above it. The services defined by layer interfaces are represented by the vertical arrows in Fig. 3.2.

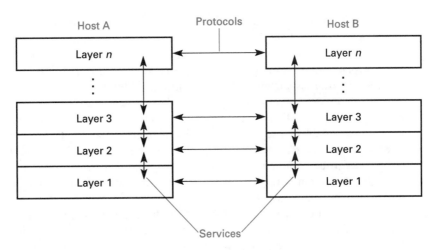

Figure 3.2   Layer services and communication protocols.

COMMUNICATION PROTOCOLS

A network architecture also defines *communication protocols* that are used by a pair of corresponding layers in different systems in providing that layer's services. Protocols are represented by the horizontal arrows in Fig. 3.2. A communication protocol defines the formats of the data units that are exchanged by two complementary layers in different machines and documents the rules that govern how those data units are exchanged.

In a layered architecture, such as TCP/IP, the user of a protocol running in a particular layer is generally a process running in the layer above. For example, the user of a protocol running in the TCP/IP Internet layer is typically a process running in the Transport layer, and the user of a protocol running in the Transport layer is typically a process running in the Application layer. The user of a protocol running in the Application layer is typically the person or application program employing the internet for communication.

An important set of protocols operating in the Internet and Transport layers of the TCP/IP architecture provide basic data transfer services. A communication protocol that provides a data transfer service can provide either a *connection-oriented* service or a *connectionless* service to a user of that protocol.

Connection-Oriented Protocols

A process implementing a connection-oriented protocol provides a service similar to that provided by the telephone system. It consists of three distinct phases:

- Connection establishment (dial a call)
- Data transfer (talk over the connection)
- Connection release (hang up the phone)

A three-party agreement must be established before communication can take place. The three parties include the two communicating partners and the data transfer service itself. An exchange of messages that implements a procedure called a *handshake* generally takes place between the processes implementing the protocol in each of the hosts in order to set up an association, called a *connection,* between them.

With a connection-oriented protocol, data transfer always involves a *pair* of communicating partners. If a process wishes to transmit a message to two or more other partners, it must establish a separate connection with each, and it must transmit the message to each partner in a separate operation. With a connection-oriented protocol, the recipient only needs to be completely identified at the time that the connection is established. Enough information is required when transferring data only to identify the connection with which the data is associated.

A connection-oriented protocol is often described as providing a *reliable* and *sequential* data transfer service. As long as the connection remains established, the sender can assume that each message is successfully received and that the messages are received in the same order sent. If something goes wrong, the connection is released, and all parties are informed of the release. The connection can be released at any time by either of the communicating parties or by the protocol itself. This is an inherent property of a connection-oriented protocol because any of the three parties can independently fail at any time.

Connectionless Protocols

A connectionless protocol works more like the postal system. A process implementing a connectionless protocol accepts each message for transmission and tries its best to deliver it, just as the postal system accepts addressed letters and attempts to deliver them to their intended recipients. With a connectionless protocol, communication takes place in a single phase, and there is no need to establish a logical connection between the sending and the receiving processes. The user process hands a message to the process implementing the protocol and identifies the destination process to which the message is to be sent. The process implementing the protocol then attempts to deliver the message to its destination. Each message must completely specify its intended recipient and is handled independently from all other messages.

A connectionless protocol may incur less protocol overhead than a connection-oriented protocol, especially when small amounts of data must be transferred. The delay involved in sending small amounts of data is also often less with a connectionless protocol because no time is spent in setting up a connection before the message is sent. With a connectionless protocol, a multicast facility can be implemented in which a message can be sent to several destinations using the same request.

However, with a connectionless protocol, nothing is done to ensure that messages are received in the same sequence sent, the receiver sends no acknowledgment that it has received a message, and no error recovery procedures are provided. Any required error recovery services must be provided by a higher-level protocol or by the programs that are communicating.

A connectionless protocol typically provides a *best-effort* delivery service, sometimes called a *datagram* service. The sender does not know for sure that a message being sent will actually be received by its intended recipient. A connectionless protocol does not provide a reliable service.

Connectionless versus Connection-Oriented Protocols

It is important to point out that the term *reliable* used in describing the difference between a connectionless and a connection-oriented protocol is perhaps not the best term that could be used. *Reliable* has a *good* connotation that may cause the reader to infer that a connection-oriented protocol is in some way *better* than a connectionless protocol. The point is, however, that connectionless protocols are better for some purposes, and connection-oriented protocols are better for others.

For example, a connection-oriented protocol, although it may provide a reliable service, may provide a very poor service if frequent failures cause the connection to be constantly broken, thus requiring new connections to be established to continue data transfer. On the other hand, a connectionless protocol may provide a very good service that delivers 999,999 messages out of every 1,000,000 sent, even though we may not be able to consider it completely reliable.

A connectionless protocol is often appropriate for an application that does not require that 100 percent of the messages get through. A connectionless protocol is also often appropriate in a lower layer, even when reliability is important. In such a case, the required reliability controls are simply provided by a process operating in a layer above the one in which the unreliable connectionless protocol is operating. Errors are detected by the higher-layer process and are corrected there, possibly by requesting that lost messages be retransmitted.

Connectionless and Connection-Oriented Protocols in TCP/IP

The TCP/IP protocol suite is based on the *Internet Protocol* (IP), a connectionless protocol operating in the Internet layer. The service it provides is used by either the *User Datagram Protocol* (UDP), a connectionless Transport layer protocol, or by the *Transmission Control Protocol* (TCP), a connection-oriented Transport layer protocol. The decision to use UDP or TCP is based on whether the application requires the Transport layer protocol to provide reliability controls. IP, UDP, and TCP are discussed further in this chapter and are described in detail in later chapters in this book.

OSI REFERENCE MODEL

During the time that the TCP/IP protocol suite was being developed, an ambitious project was underway in the International Organization for Standardization (ISO) to develop a single international standard set of communication protocols that could be used in a computer network. By 1984, ISO had defined an overall model of computer communication called the *Reference Model for Open Systems Interconnection,* or *OSI model* for short. The OSI model, described in international standard ISO 7498, documents a generalized model of system interconnection.

By the time the OSI model was finally adopted as an international standard, the TCP/IP protocol suite, which does not conform entirely to the OSI model, was well established as a working computer networking scheme.

Purpose of the OSI Model

The OSI model was designed to provide a common basis for the coordination of standards development for the purpose of interconnecting *open systems.* The term *open* in this context means systems open to one another by virtue of their mutual use of applicable standards.

The OSI model describes how machines can communicate with one another in a standardized and highly flexible way by defining the functional layers that should be incorporated into each communicating machine. The OSI model does not define the networking software itself, nor does it define detailed standards for that software; it simply defines the broad categories of functions each layer should perform.

OSI Network Architecture

ISO has also developed a comprehensive set of standards for the various layers of the OSI model. These standards together make up the *OSI network architecture.* The protocols in the TCP/IP protocol suite influenced the development of many of the standards making up the OSI architecture.

The standards making up the OSI network architecture are not today widely implemented in commercial products for computer networking. However, the OSI model is still important. The concepts and terminology associated with the OSI model have become widely accepted as a basis for discussing and describing network architectures. The OSI model is often used in categorizing the various communication protocols that are in common use today and in comparing one network architecture with another. TCP/IP is often compared with the OSI model in discussing the layering structure of the TCP/IP protocol suite. We next introduce the seven layers of the OSI model before further examining the TCP/IP functional layers.

OSI Model Functional Layers

The OSI model defines seven functional layers. Each layer performs a different set of functions, and the intent is to make each layer as independent as possible from all the others.

There is a fundamental difference in orientation between the top three layers of the OSI model and the bottom four layers. The top three layers are concerned with services that are oriented to the application programs themselves. The bottom four layers are concerned more with the network and provide a general data transport service useful to any application.

The seven functional layers of the OSI model are illustrated and described in Box 3.1.

BOX 3.1   OSI model functional layers.

Application
Presentation
Session
Transport
Network
Data Link
Physical

- **The Application Layer.** The topmost layer, the one user processes plug into, is the Application layer. The Application layer provides a means for application programs to access the system interconnection facilities to exchange information. Communication services provided by the Application layer hide the complexity of the layers below from the communicating programs. As far as the Application layer is concerned, a program running in one computer sends a message, and a program running in some other computer receives it. The Application layer is not concerned with any of the details concerning how the message gets from the source computer to the destination computer.

- **The Presentation Layer.** The Presentation layer is the lowest layer interested in the *meaning* of the streams of bits that are exchanged between communicating programs. It is concerned with preserving the *information content* of data transmitted over the network. The OSI model defines two major functions for the Presentation layer. First, the Presentation layer in the two communicating systems must negotiate a common syntax for transferring the messages exchanged by two communicating programs. Second, the Presentation layer must ensure that one system does not need to care what form of internal data representation the other system is using. If both systems are personal computers running BASIC programs, the Presentation layer has little to do because both programs use a common form of internal data representation. However, if a FORTRAN program running in a VAX minicomputer is communicating with a COBOL program running in an IBM mainframe, the Presentation layer becomes more important. The FORTRAN program may represent an integer using a 32-bit binary number; the COBOL program may represent an integer using packed-decimal notation. The Presentation layer performs the necessary conversions that allow each program to work with data in its own preferred format without having to be aware of the data formats that its partner uses.

- **The Session Layer.** The Session layer is responsible for organizing the dialog between two communicating programs and for managing the data exchanges between them. To

(Continued)

BOX 3.1 *(Continued)*

do this, the Session layer imposes a structure on the interaction between two communicating programs. The Session layer defines three types of dialogs: two-way simultaneous interaction, where both programs can send and receive concurrently; two-way alternate interaction, where the programs take turns sending and receiving; and one-way interaction, where one program sends and the other only receives. In addition to organizing the dialog, Session layer services include establishing synchronization points within the dialog, allowing a dialog to be interrupted, and later resumed from a synchronization point.

- **The Transport Layer.** The OSI model classifies each system in the network as one of two types: *end systems* act as the source or the final destination of data, and *intermediate systems* perform routing and relaying functions. The Transport layer is the lowest layer required *only* in two end systems that are communicating. Intermediate systems between two end systems that perform only routing and relaying functions may only implement the bottom three layers. The Transport layer forms the uppermost layer of a reliable end-to-end data transport service. The Transport layer hides from the higher layers all the details concerning the actual moving of streams of bits from one computer to another and shields network users from the complexities of network operation. The functions performed in the Transport layer include end-to-end integrity controls that are used to recover from lost, out-of-sequence, or duplicate messages.

- **The Network Layer.** The *Network* layer is concerned with making routing decisions and relaying data from one system to another through the network. The facilities provided by the Network layer supply a service that higher layers employ for moving data units, often called *packets,* from one end system to another, where the packets may flow through any number of intermediate systems over any number of data links. The application programs running in two end systems that wish to communicate should not need to be concerned with the route packets take. The Network layer functions operating in end systems and in intermediate systems together handle these routing and relaying functions.

- **The Data Link Layer.** The *Data Link* layer is responsible for providing data transmission over a single link from one system to another. Control mechanisms in the Data Link layer handle the transmission of data units, often called *frames,* over a physical circuit. Functions operating in the Data Link layer allow data to be transmitted, in a relatively error-free fashion, over a sometimes error-prone physical circuit. This layer is concerned with how bits are grouped into frames and implements error-detection mechanisms that identify transmission errors. With some types of data links, the Data Link layer may also perform procedures for flow control, frame sequencing, and recovering from transmission errors.

- **The Physical Layer.** The *Physical* layer is responsible for the actual transmission of signals, such as electrical signals, optical signals, or radio signals, between communicating machines. Physical layer mechanisms in each of the communicating machines typically control the generation and detection of signals that are interpreted as 0 bits and 1 bits. The Physical layer does not assign any significance to the bits. For example, it is not concerned with how many bits make up each unit of data, nor is it concerned with the meaning of the data being transmitted. In the Physical layer, the sender simply transmits a signal and the receiver detects it.

TCP/IP FUNCTIONAL LAYERS

Figure 3.3 shows how the functional layers of the TCP/IP architecture compare with the layers of the OSI model. The TCP/IP architecture does not separate out application-oriented functions into three distinct layers as in the OSI model. Therefore, the TCP/IP Application layer is roughly equivalent to the OSI Application, Presentation, and Session layers. The TCP/IP Transport layer is equivalent to the OSI model Transport layer, and the TCP/IP Internet layer is equivalent to the OSI model Network layer. The lowest layer of the TCP/IP architecture, the Network Interface layer, is roughly equivalent to the OSI model Data Link layer. The physical equipment used to implement data links, which is addressed by the OSI model Physical layer, is outside the scope of the TCP/IP architecture. Any type of physical communication circuit can be used in a TCP/IP internet as long as a Network Interface layer function can be implemented for it.

The following sections describe the functions of each of the layers making up the TCP/IP architecture and introduces the major protocols that operate in each layer. Figure 3.4 shows how the major components and protocols defined in the TCP/IP protocol suite map against the TCP/IP functional layers.

APPLICATION LAYER

The TCP/IP Application layer is where the application programs that use the internet for communication reside. Some Application layer software for the TCP/IP environment implements a set of standardized *Application layer protocols* that provide services directly to the users of terminals or workstations. Other Application layer software provides

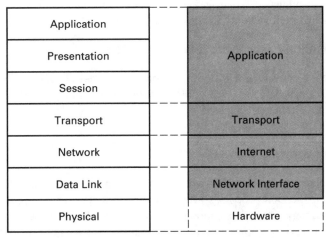

OSI Model Functional Layers   TCP/IP Functional Layers

Figure 3.3   TCP/IP and OSI architectural layer comparison.

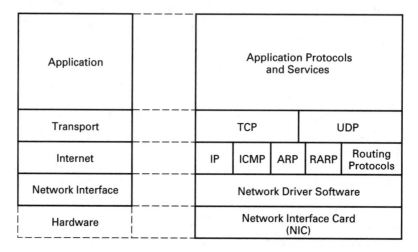

Figure 3.4   TCP/IP components and major protocols.

application programming interfaces (APIs) that can be used to create user-written application programs that communicate over the internet.

TCP/IP defines a wide range of Application layer protocols that provide services to internet users, including remote login, file copying and sharing, electronic mail, directory services, and network management facilities. Some application protocols are widely used; others are employed only for specialized purposes.

Application Layer Protocols and Services

Figure 3.5 shows some of the most commonly used TCP/IP Application layer protocols and services, and Box 3.2 contains brief descriptions of them. These protocols are described further in Chapter 5.

TRANSPORT LAYER

Most computing systems on which TCP/IP communication software typically runs allow many application processes to execute concurrently. Therefore, on a given host, there may be many active application processes, all of which may wish to use TCP/IP communication services at the same time. The function of a Transport layer protocol is to provide an end-to-end data transport service whose users are the individual application processes running in TCP/IP hosts.

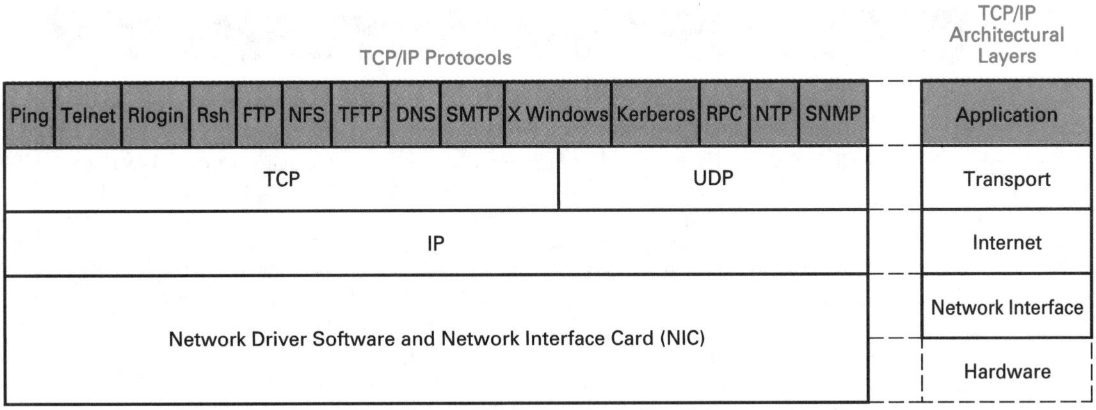

TCP/IP Protocols

Ping	Telnet	Rlogin	Rsh	FTP	NFS	TFTP	DNS	SMTP	X Windows	Kerberos	RPC	NTP	SNMP		Application
TCP								UDP							Transport
IP															Internet
Network Driver Software and Network Interface Card (NIC)															Network Interface
															Hardware

Figure 3.5 Representative Application layer protocols and services.

BOX 3.2 Representative Application layer protocols and services.

End User Services

- **Ping Connectivity Testing.** *Ping,* which is short for *Packet InterNet Groper,* can be used to test for connectivity between any two hosts in the internet. Ping uses an Internet layer protocol called the *Internet Control Message Protocol* (ICMP) in performing its functions. ICMP is introduced later in this chapter and discussed further in Chapter 12. In using Ping, a user typically executes a program named **ping** that sends an ICMP Echo Request message to another host. When a host receives an ICMP Echo Request message, it sends an ICMP Echo Reply message back to the original sender. For each Echo Reply message that it receives, Ping calculates the amount of time elapsed since it sent the original Echo Request message. This provides the Ping user with an estimate of the round-trip delay that is being experienced in exchanging data with the specified host.

- **Telnet Remote Login.** Telnet allows a user to login to some other host in the internet. The Telnet protocol establishes a client-server relationship between the local Telnet software (the client) and the remote Telnet software (the server). Telnet handles the data transfers that are required between the host implementing the client and the host implementing the server. These data transfers make it appear as if the user is logged into the remote host directly, even though the user is actually employing the user interface device to communicate with the local host.

- **Rlogin Remote Login.** The Rlogin service is a service that is related to Telnet but is typically provided only by variations of the UNIX operating system. Telnet allows a user at any type of TCP/IP host to login to any other type of TCP/IP host. The local host and remote host may be running entirely different operating systems. The Rlogin service is normally used when a user at a local UNIX host wants to

(Continued)

BOX 3.2   *(Continued)*

login to a remote UNIX host. For the UNIX user, Rlogin is somewhat easier to use than Telnet and provides a few additional services.

- **Rsh Remote Execution.** The *Rsh* remote execution service allows the user to issue, at the local host, a command to request an operating system function or to request the execution of an application program on some other host in the internet. When using the Rsh service, the user enters a command at the local host, and the command is then sent to and executed on the remote host. The results of the command or the results of the application program execution are then returned to the user at the local host. A similar service to Rsh called *Rexec* is available on some TCP/IP hosts as well.

- **FTP File Transfer.** The *File Transfer Protocol* (FTP) implements a user-oriented file transfer service. FTP allows the user to transfer data in both directions between the local host and a remote host. FTP can be used to transfer files that contain either binary data or ASCII text. Certain versions of FTP also allow for the transfer of files containing EBCDIC data. Files can be transferred one at a time, or a single request can cause multiple files to be transferred. FTP also provides ancillary functions, such as listing the contents of remote directories, changing the current remote directory, and creating and removing remote directories. FTP typically uses a connection-oriented Transport layer protocol, such as TCP, in providing its services.

- **NFS Remote File Access.** The *Network File System* (NFS) implements a number of high-level services that provide authorized users with access to files located on remote hosts. System administrators generally designate one or more hosts in the internet to play the role of NFS file servers. These hosts run NFS server software that make certain designated directories on their disk storage devices available to other hosts. A user accesses an NFS-mounted directory in the same manner as accessing a directory on a local disk. The fact that a directory is an NFS-mounted directory on a remote host is typically transparent to the user of the local host.

Support Services

- **TFTP File Transfer.** The *Trivial File Transfer Protocol* (TFTP) is a simple file transfer facility that also provides the ability to transfer data in both directions between the local host and a remote host. TFTP is generally used only by system software that performs such functions as downline loading of program code and is not intended to be employed directly by end users. TFTP implements its own reliability controls and can run on top of any type of transport service. Most implementations of TFTP use the connectionless UDP Transport layer protocol.

- **DNS Name Resolution.** Each host attached to a TCP/IP internet has at least one 32-bit internet address assigned to it. (See Chapter 4.) Each host also typically has a unique name to make it possible for users to easily refer to the host without knowing its internet address. Since the underlying TCP/IP protocols all refer to individual hosts using their internet addresses, each host must implement a *name resolution* function that translates between host names and internet addresses. In small TCP/IP internets, the function of translating between a host name and the internet address associated with that host can be performed by the host itself through a configuration file typically named **hosts.** In a large internet, it is unwieldy to try to maintain name-to-address mappings for each individual host in local **hosts** files. The *Domain Name System* (DNS) is a directory service that can be

BOX 3.2 *(Continued)*

used to maintain the mappings between names and internet addresses in a limited number of places in the internet rather than at the location of each host.

- **SMTP Electronic Mail.** The *Simple Mail Transfer Protocol* (SMTP) is a protocol used for the transfer of electronic mail messages. SMTP is designed to be used by electronic mail software that provides the user with access to messaging facilities; it is not designed to be employed by end users directly. Mail facilities allow the user to send messages and files to a user connected to the local network, to a user connected to some other network in the internet, or to a user connected to a non-TCP/IP network that has a connection to the TCP/IP internet. Many types of electronic mail systems have been implemented for the TCP/IP environment, some of which can be interconnected with the electronic messaging systems of other types of networks, such as PROFS and DISOSS in the IBM environment, and with public electronic mail services, such as MCI Mail and CompuServe.

- **X Window System Presentation.** The *X Window System* is a set of distributed graphical presentation services that implement a windowing system on a graphics display. It implements a client-server relationship between an application program (the client) and the windowing software in a workstation or terminal that controls a window on the graphical display (the server). The client and server can be running in different computing systems or in the same computing system. The X Window System allows a user at a graphics workstation to have multiple windows open on the screen, each of which might be controlled by a separate client application program. The X Window System defines a protocol that is used to transmit information between the client application program and the server windowing software.

- **Kerberos Security.** Kerberos is an encryption-based security system that provides mutual authentication between a client component and a server component in a distributed computing environment. It also provides services that can be used to control which clients are authorized to access which servers. In the Kerberos system, each client component and each server component is called a *principal* and has a unique *principal identifier* assigned to it. These principal identifiers allow clients and servers to identify themselves to each other to prevent fraudulent exchanges of information. Authorization of a client to access a particular server can be implemented independently from the authentication service.

- **Remote Procedure Call.** *Remote procedure call* (RPC) mechanisms allow a procedure running in the local host to call a procedure that is running in a remote host. Procedure argument and result values are transferred across the internet in a transparent fashion.

- **NTP Distributed Time.** The Network Time Protocol (NTP) implements algorithms that permit networked computing systems to maintain common, correct values for the date and time of day.

- **SNMP Network Management.** Network management services are typically provided in a TCP/IP internet through software that implements the *Simple Network Management Protocol* (SNMP). SNMP defines a *Management Information Base* (MIB), which is a database that defines all the objects that can be managed in the internet. SNMP also defines the formats of a set of network management messages and the rules by which the messages are exchanged. The network management messages are used to make requests for performing network management functions and to report on events that occur in the network.

Transport Layer Protocols

Two major TCP/IP protocols operate in the Transport layer. These are briefly described in Box 3.3.

An application process can use either UDP or TCP to request data transfer services. The protocol that an application uses depends on whether it requires only a best-effort, datagram data delivery service or whether it requires the reliability controls provided by a connection-oriented data transfer service.

BOX 3.3   Transport layer protocols.

- **UDP.** The *User Datagram Protocol* (UDP) is the simplest transport protocol. It is a best-effort, connectionless Transport layer protocol that adds little to the underlying IP datagram delivery service.
- **TCP.** The *Transmission Control Protocol* (TCP) is a connection-oriented Transport layer protocol that provides for reliable, sequenced stream data delivery.

Transport Layer Protocol Ports

Each host in the internet is assigned at least one unique internet address. An internet address uniquely identifies a particular point of attachment to the internet. The job of a Transport layer protocol is to deliver data from a particular process running in the source host to a particular process running in the destination host. Therefore, the TCP/IP Transport layer requires a level of addressing above that provided by the internet address assigned to a host. This higher level of addressing is provided by *Transport layer protocol ports.*

Each application process running in a host must be assigned a 16-bit Transport layer protocol *port number* to differentiate it from other users of the same Transport layer protocol in a host. Each application process that is using TCP/IP communication services is assigned one or more port numbers on its host. When a source application process sends data to a destination application process using a Transport layer protocol, it must provide three pieces of information to the Transport layer protocol:

- The data to be sent.
- The internet address of the host on which the destination application process is running.
- The number of the port on the destination host that is assigned to the destination application process.

Each Transport layer protocol in the TCP/IP protocol suite has its own set of port number assignments. For example, the TCP port number assignments are separate from the UDP port number assignments, and data sent to TCP port 27 is separate from data sent to UDP port number 27.

Client-Server Relationship

Most distributed applications that use TCP/IP for communication implement the client-server model of distributed computing, discussed further in Chapter 17. Transport protocol ports can be used in implementing client-server applications. In a client-server application, one application component, called the *server,* provides a well-defined service for application components running in other hosts, called *clients.* In a client-server application, the client is responsible for establishing communication with the server. The client then makes a request for a service by transmitting data to the server. The server then carries out the service and replies by sending data back to the client.

In such an application, the client needs to know the port number that the server is using. The client then sends the server the client's own port number to which the server can reply.

Port Assignments

TCP/IP defines the use only of port numbers 0 through 255 and leaves the assignment of other ports up to TCP/IP users. In order to provide some structure to the way in which port numbers are assigned to client and server processes, port numbers are generally allocated by convention in the following manner:

- Port 0—Not used
- Ports 1-255—Reserved ports for well-known services
- Ports 256-1,023—Other reserved ports
- Ports 1,024 - 4,999—Ephemeral client ports
- Ports 5,000 - 65,535—User-defined server ports

Reserved Ports for Well-Known Services

To support the needs of certain types of servers that are of general usefulness in most internets, the reserved port numbers from 1 through 255 are used by certain *well-known services* to which specific port assignments have been made. The port assignments for well-known services are considered standard and are typically used by any host that supports TCP/IP. For example, the Trivial File Transport Protocol (TFTP) uses well-known UDP port number 69. A TFTP client application that wishes to access the services of a TFTP server must know the internet address of the host running the TFTP server and then uses UDP port number 69 to establish communication with the TFTP server on that host. Reserved ports, including those used for well-known services, are assigned by the *Internet Assigned Numbers Authority* (IANA) and are documented in an RFC.

Other Reserved Ports

The port numbers from 256 through 1,023 are reserved port numbers that were originally used for UNIX-related services. Some of these port numbers are now used for general-purpose services, such as certain routing functions.

Ephemeral Client Ports

In a client-server application, a client process uses one of the *ephemeral* client port numbers in establishing communication with a server. As part of the dialog that takes place between the client and server processes, the client sends to the server the ephemeral port number that it is using. Most TCP/IP communication software implements a function that a client process can use to obtain the port number of an unused ephemeral port on that host.

User-Defined Server Ports

User-written client-server applications employ the user-defined server port numbers for server processes. The port number that a user-defined server accesses is established by convention between the server and its clients.

INTERNET LAYER

The *Internet* layer of the TCP/IP architecture provides routing and relaying functions that are used when data must be passed from a host in one network to a host in some other network in the internet. The TCP/IP Internet layer is sometimes called the *Network* layer or the *Internetworking* layer in some TCP/IP literature. The Internet layer operates in the source and destination hosts and in all the routers along the path between the hosts. It is the layer in which routing decisions are made that determine the path over which each message travels through the internet.

Internet Layer Protocols

Box 3.4 briefly describes the TCP/IP protocols that operate in the Internet layer.

NETWORK INTERFACE LAYER

The main function of the Network Interface layer is to handle hardware-dependent functions and to present a standardized interface to the Internet layer of TCP/IP.

The TCP/IP suite of protocols does not specify details concerning the protocols to be used in the Network Interface layer and below. The Network Interface layer of TCP/IP is responsible for accepting messages from the Internet layer and preparing them for transmission across any desired type of data link technology.

An individual TCP/IP network may be a local area network, using a LAN data link technology such as Ethernet, Token Ring, or FDDI. An individual TCP/IP network may also be implemented using a wide area network data link technology, such as a point-to-point leased or dial-up line, satellite link, or specialized digital circuit. One of the reasons TCP/IP has become widely used is that it can be used in conjunction with almost any type of underlying physical circuit and data link technology.

One important function of the Network Interface layer is to examine each frame that the network interface card (NIC) installed in the host computer receives and to deter-

---

BOX 3.4   Internet layer protocols.

- **Internet Protocol.** The *Internet Protocol* (IP) is the core protocol of the TCP/IP protocol suite. It provides a connectionless, best-efforts data delivery service that is used in moving packets from one host to another through the internet.

- **Internet Control Message Protocol.** The *Internet Control Message Protocol* (ICMP) employs the services of IP to allow hosts to report on error conditions and to provide information about unexpected circumstances.

- **Address Resolution Protocol.** The *Address Resolution Protocol* (ARP) helps a source host deliver data directly to a destination host when the two hosts are on the same physical network. It allows the source host to determine the destination host's physical hardware address given the destination host's internet address. TCP/IP internet addresses are discussed in Chapter 4.

- **Reverse Address Resolution Protocol.** The *Reverse Address Resolution Protocol* (RARP) allows a host that does not yet have its internet address to obtain it. RARP is typically used to support workstations and intelligent terminals that do not have their own disk storage.

- **Routing Protocols.** The basic routing function in a TCP/IP internet is performed by IP. However, in internets that employ routers, the routers often run additional routing protocols that allow them to exchange routing information with each other. Routing protocols are discussed in Chapter 13.

---

mine, from the way in which control bits in the frame are set, for which of the Internet layer protocols the frame is intended. This is called a *demultiplexing* function.

HARDWARE LAYER

A *Hardware* layer can be identified below the Network Interface layer. However, the Hardware layer is actually outside the scope of the TCP/IP architecture. The layers above the hardware layer all consist of software running in the host computers attached to the internet. The hardware layer is concerned with physical entities, such as the NICs, transceivers, hubs, connectors, and cables that are used to physically hook hosts together.

Any physical networking technology can be employed in a TCP/IP internet, using any supported transmission medium, such as twisted-pair cable, coaxial cable, or fiber-optic cable. All that is needed is appropriate software operating in the Network Interface layer to provide the computing system with access to the physical network.

SUMMARY

TCP/IP is one of a number of network architectures that constitutes a comprehensive plan and set of rules that govern the design and operation of computer networks. A network architecture defines the interfaces between functional layers of the architecture and communication protocols that govern how messages are exchanged via the network.

Network architectures, including TCP/IP, are often compared with the Reference Model for Open Systems Interconnection (OSI) model, which forms the basis of an international standard architecture for networking. The seven functional layers of the OSI model are the Application layer, the Presentation layer, the Session layer, the Transport layer, the Network layer, the Data Link layer, and the Physical layer.

The TCP/IP architecture constitutes four functional layers. The TCP/IP Application layer, which corresponds to the OSI Application, Presentation, and Session layers, is where the application programs that use the internet reside. The Transport Layer, which corresponds to the OSI Transport layer, provides an end-to-end data transport service. The Internet layer, which corresponds to the OSI Network layer, provides routing and relaying functions. The Network Interface layer, which corresponds to the OSI Data Link layer, provides an interface to the physical networking facilities. A Hardware layer, which corresponds to the OSI Physical layer, can be identified below the Network Interface layer but is considered to be outside the scope of the TCP/IP architecture.

Chapter 4 describes the mechanisms that are used in TCP/IP internets for addressing host computers and routers.

Chapter **4**

TCP/IP Addressing

As we have seen in earlier chapters, a TCP/IP internet is a virtual network built by interconnecting a number of individual physical networks—each of which might employ a different form of data link technology—using a system of routers. An internet supplies a universal communication service that allows any host on the internet to communicate with any other host as easily as if they were directly connected with a point-to-point link. The system of interconnected physical networks and routers are transparent to the users of the internet.

An internet can supply a universal communication service only if there is a way of unambiguously identifying each host that is attached to the network. This chapter discusses the important topic of internet addressing.

THREE LEVELS OF IDENTIFIERS

There are three types of identifiers, illustrated in Fig. 4.1, that are important in the TCP/IP environment—host names, internet addresses, and physical hardware addresses. The following sections describe each of these types of identifiers.

Host Names

Users of a TCP/IP internet, both human users and application programs, often refer to hosts in the internet using a *host name* that consists of a string of alphanumeric characters. A small internet can use host names that form a flat namespace in which the names have no internal structure. Each host is simply given a 1- to 8-character alphanumeric name that is chosen to be easy to remember.

In a large internet, the job of administering a flat namespace eventually becomes too large, and a hierarchical system based on the conventions established for the Worldwide Internet is typically used. In the Internet, a tree-structured namespace is used that contains sets of *domain names*. A domain name consists of a sequence of simple names

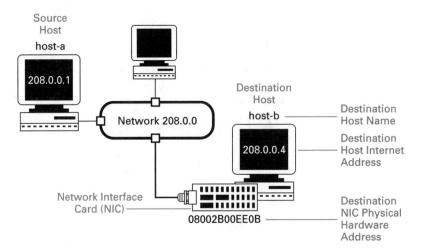

Figure 4.1   Three levels of identifiers.

separated by periods. Each simple name, or set of simple names, identifies a *domain* under the control of some authority. A typical domain name using the naming conventions established for the Worldwide Internet looks like the following:

```
training.lebeninc.com
```

Domain names are read from left to right with the most local domain first and the most global domain last. The domain name **com** identifies the network as being administered by a commercial organization, the domain name **lebeninc.com** might identify the set of hosts administered by the organization named Leben, Inc., and the domain name **training.lebeninc.com** might identify a set of hosts administered by Leben, Inc.'s training department. Leben, Inc.'s training department might then assign a unique *fully-qualified domain name* (FQDN) to an individual host as follows:

```
joespc.training.lebeninc.com
```

A host name must be unique within its own domain; therefore, a combination of the host name and the name of the domain itself gives each host a unique identifier that can be used to distinguish it from all other hosts in an internet.

Users generally refer to a host in their own domain using a simple name consisting of the first qualifier of the name alone, while they refer to hosts in other domains using a fully-qualified domain name. For example, we can refer to the host having the above fully-qualified domain name as **joespc** from within the **training.lebeninc.com** domain.

Naming conventions for host identification are described further in Chapter 7.

Internet Addresses

Each host in a TCP/IP internet is also assigned at least one unique *internet address*. An internet address is a 32-bit binary number that TCP/IP protocols use to uniquely identify points of attachment to the internet. The internal structure of an internet address is described later in this chapter. An important characteristic of an internet address assigned to a host is that it unambiguously identifies to which of the physical networks making up an internet the particular host is attached.

Physical Hardware Addresses

On a typical physical network, such as a LAN data link, each device attached to the LAN is assigned a unique *hardware address,* or *station address.* The hardware address is typically assigned when the network interface card (NIC) is manufactured and is of no concern to the user. LAN data links that conform to international standards typically use a 48-bit *station address* to uniquely identify each station on the LAN. However, international standards for LANs also permit the use of 16-bit station addresses, and a LAN data link that implements proprietary LAN technology may define its own station addressing schemes using any number of bits for physical hardware addresses.

IDENTIFIER CONVERSIONS

There are two different identifier conversions that must routinely take place during the operation of the internet. These are shown in Fig. 4.2 and are described in the following sections.

Host Name to Internet Address Conversion

When a user requests that communication be set up between a local host and some remote host, the local user generally refers to the remote host using its host name. The protocols operating in the TCP/IP Transport and Internet layers work only with internet addresses and are not concerned with host names. Therefore, a *name resolution* function must be performed in the Application layer to translate a host name to its associated internet address. Name resolution can be performed by the host itself using a **hosts** configuration file that maintains a list of name-to-address mappings for the host. Alternatively, the *Domain Name System* (DNS) can be used to perform name resolution operations.

Name resolution, using both **hosts** files and the Domain Name System, is described in detail in Chapter 7.

Internet Address to Physical Hardware Address Conversion

A host that is attached to a LAN data link must often deliver data to other hosts on its own LAN. As we introduced in Chapter 3, the data unit handled in the TCP/IP Internet layer by the Internet Protocol (IP) is called an *IP datagram.* An IP datagram contains only the internet address of the destination host and not that host's physical hardware address. A source host must be able to determine from the internet address the physical hardware address of the station on the LAN that is associated with the destination host. The Address Resolution Protocol (ARP) is responsible for translating from internet

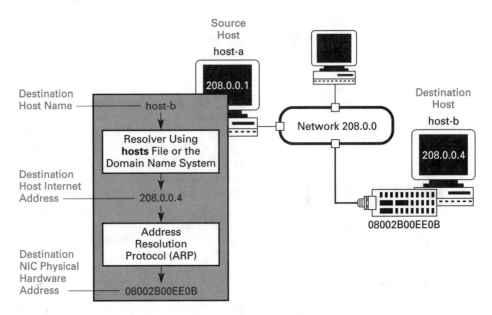

Figure 4.2   Converting between identifiers.

addresses to physical hardware addresses to support data delivery within a physical network. ARP is typically implemented on any host that is attached to a LAN data link.

The Reverse Address Resolution Protocol (RARP) is responsible for the opposite conversion—from a physical hardware address to an internet address. RARP is typically used by a diskless computer that does not know its internet address when it is first powered on. RARP allows the diskless host to contact a RARP server to obtain its internet address.

The operation of ARP and RARP are described in Chapter 11.

INTERNET ADDRESSING

One of the tasks that IP performs during the operation of a TCP/IP internet is to perform a routing function that determines the path IP datagrams travel from a source host to a destination host. The routing function is examined in detail in Chapters 10 and 13. The header of each IP datagram that travels through the internet contains the internet address of the source host and the internet address of the destination host. In order to perform the routing function, IP examines the destination internet address field in each IP datagram that it handles to determine to which network the datagram must be delivered.

Internet Address Formats

Internet addresses are 32 bits in length and contain two parts—a *network identifier* and a *host identifier*. The initial bits of the network identifier identify what class the address

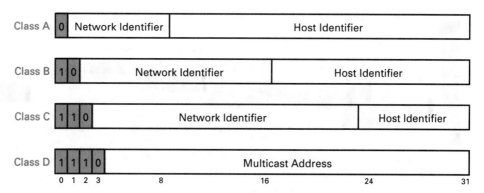

Figure 4.3   Four primary forms of internet addresses.

belongs to. The formats of the internet addresses for the four most commonly used address classes are shown in Fig. 4.3 and are described below:

- **Class A Addresses.** An address with the first bit set to 0 is a *class A address.* A class A address provides 7 bits to identify the physical network and 24 bits to identify hosts. In any internet there can be up to 126 networks that use class A addresses. Since a class A address provides 24 bits for uniquely identifying hosts, a class A network can, for practical purposes, contain an almost unlimited number of hosts.

- **Class B Addresses.** An address with the first two bits set to 10 is a *class B address.* A class B address provides 14 bits to identify the network and 16 bits to identify hosts. A class B address allows for up to $2^{14}-2$ different physical networks and up to $2^{16}-2$ different hosts on each network.

- **Class C addresses.** An address with the first three bits set to 110 is a *class C address.* A class C address provides 21 bits to identify the network and 8 bits to identify hosts. A class C address allows for up to $2^{21}-2$ different physical networks but only up to 254 different hosts on each network.

- **Class D Addresses.** An address with the first four bits set to 1110 is a *class D address.* A class D address is used to implement a form of multicasting in which an address refers to some collection of hosts in an internet, all of which receive the IP datagrams having the specified multicast address.

The internet addressing scheme allows for relatively few class A networks. For example, in the Worldwide Internet, very few class A addresses still remain unallocated, and it is no longer possible for an individual organization to get a class A address assignment. Class B and class C addresses are the only types of addresses available for assignment to individual organizations.

Dotted-Decimal Notation

When writing down internet addresses, or when software displays them to human users, a form of notation called *dotted-decimal notation* is typically used to represent 32-bit internet addresses. For example, assume a host has the following internet address:

        10000000 00001011 00000011 00011111

The above class B internet address would be written down or displayed in dotted-decimal notation as 128.11.3.31.

In dotted-decimal notation, a separate decimal number is used to represent the value of each individual octet of the address, and the address octet values are separated with periods. Class A addresses range from 0.0.0.1 to 127.255.255.254, class B addresses range from 128.0.0.1 to 191.255.255.254, and class C addresses range from 192.0.0.1 to 223.255.255.254. Internet addresses expressed in dotted-decimal notation, instead of host names, can be used in most TCP/IP commands to refer to hosts in an internet.

INTERNET ADDRESSING AUTHORITY

An organization constructing a private internet is free to assign internet addresses to hosts and routers using any assignment scheme it chooses to use. An individual organization is also free to decide whether class A, B, or C addresses are appropriate for each physical network that makes up its own private internet.

The best approach to follow in assigning internet addresses is to assign a globally unique network identifier to each physical network. You can do this by applying to the DDN *Network Information Center* (NIC) to obtain one or more unique network identifier assignments. By assigning globally-unique network identifiers to your own physical networks, you can ensure that your organization will be able to interconnect its own physical networks with those of other organizations and with the Worldwide Internet itself should that become necessary or desirable.

The NIC assigns values to use for the network identifier portion of the address. The individual organization is responsible for assigning host identifier values so that each network connection has a unique internet address. Most network address values that the NIC assigns are for class C addresses that can attach only up to 254 hosts. An organization requesting a class B address assignment must be able to justify why it needs one.

SUBNETTING

The original TCP/IP addressing scheme allowed for only a two-level hierarchy of identification—*network* identification and *host* identification within an individual network. This is sufficient when the number of physical networks making up an internet is relatively small. However, there are now many very large internets in existence. The Worldwide Internet contains thousands of physical networks and millions of hosts. In order to allow the TCP/IP internet addressing scheme to accommodate large numbers of physical networks, the notion of *subnetting* was devised.

Subnet Identifier

The system of subnetting adds a third level to the hierarchy of addressing provided by the internet addressing scheme. To use subnetting, some number of bits from the host identi-

Standard Class B Address

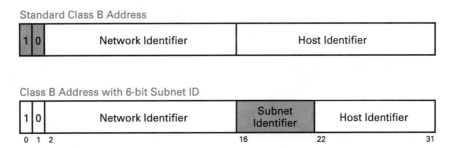

Class B Address with 6-bit Subnet ID

Figure 4.4   Class B internet address using a 6-bit subnet identifier.

fier portion of the internet address is designated as a *subnet identifier*. For example, Fig. 4.4 shows how an organization that has been assigned a class B internet address can use that class B address to identify a number of individual physical networks.

Figure 4.4 shows that six bits of the host identifier portion of the address have been designated for use as a *subnet identifier*. Each value of the 6-bit subnet identifier can be assigned to a separate physical network, thus allowing that organization to create up to 62 separate networks, each of which uses the same class B network identifier value but a different subnet ID value.

Subnet Mask

During the installation of the TCP/IP networking software a subnet mask is specified that indicates how many bits of the address are used to identify the network and how many are to identify individual hosts. A subnet mask is a 32-bit data structure that contains a 1 in each bit position that indicates a bit that is used to identify the network and subnet and a 0 in each bit position that is used to identify a host.

For class B addresses with subnetting, in which the first 6 bits of what is ordinarily the host ID field of the address contains the subnet identifier, the subnet mask using dotted-decimal notation would be 255.255.252.0. This subnet mask is shown in Fig. 4.5.

Class B Address with 6-bit Subnet ID

Subnet Mask for Class B Address with 6-bit Subnet ID

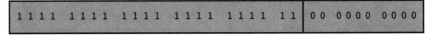

Figure 4.5   Subnet mask for Class B internet address using a 6-bit subnet identifier.

A subnet mask must typically be provided during TCP/IP networking software installation whether or not subnetting is used. For example, using dotted-decimal notation, the subnet masks for class A, B, and C addresses, with no subnetting, are as follows:

- Class A: 255.0.0.0
- Class B: 255.255.0.0
- Class C: 255.255.255.0

Choosing Subnet Identifiers

The length of the subnet identifier field, and the appropriate subnet mask to use, is chosen based on how many networks you expect to create using the same internet address assignment and how many hosts you expect to attach to each of those networks. For example, as previously shown, a class B address with a 6-bit subnet identifier allows for up to 62 different networks using the same class B address assignment and up to 1022 hosts per network.

In making individual subnet address and host assignments, you should assign subnet identifiers starting at the high end of the range of subnet ID values and should make host assignments starting at the low end of the range of host ID values. This provides the most flexibility should it later become necessary to change the subnet mask. For example, you may find that it becomes necessary to create more individual networks than originally anticipated, or it may become necessary to add more hosts to one or more networks than originally anticipated. Starting subnet IDs at the high end of the range and host IDs at the low end results in internet address assignments that are likely to have all 0 bits in the region between subnet ID values and host ID values. Hopefully, the two will never meet, thus allowing the dividing line between subnet ID and host ID values to be easily moved. This allows the subnet mask to be modified without having to change any actual address assignments.

ROUTERS AND MULTIHOMED HOSTS

Although an internet address is often interpreted as uniquely identifying a host in an internet, such an interpretation is not strictly accurate. An internet address actually uniquely identifies a particular point of attachment to one of the physical networks in an internet. Therefore, it is possible for a host to have multiple internet addresses, one for each NIC that it implements for attachment to a physical network in the internet. A router must have at least two network attachments and, thus, have at least two internet addresses. A host can also implement multiple network attachments, thus allowing it to send traffic directly to different physical networks. Such a host is often called a *multihomed host.*

INTERNET ROUTING

An important characteristic of an internet address, from the viewpoint of routing efficiency, is that the address of the physical network to which a destination host is attached can be extracted from the full internet address using very few machine instructions. An internet may contain a large number of hosts, but all but the largest internets contain relatively few individual physical networks.

TCP/IP routing decisions are made based only on the network identification portion of internet addresses and not on the host identification portion. In other words, the routing function is concerned only with delivering IP datagrams to the appropriate destination network.

A router that receives an IP datagram for routing can tell immediately whether the IP datagram is destined for one of the networks to which it is physically attached. If the network identifier in the destination address does not match one of the router's own network addresses, the router sends the IP datagram on to another router that is closer to the IP datagram's final destination. Only if the network identifier matches one of its own network addresses does the router examine the host identifier portion of the address. The router then either accepts the datagram if the datagram is addressed to it or forwards the datagram to the appropriate host, possibly using ARP to determine the appropriate physical hardware address to use.

LOCAL HOST NAME AND ADDRESS

A command that a user issues can refer to his or her own host using that host's own name or internet address. The name **localhost** and the class A internet address 127.0.0.1 also usually refers to the local host. So a user can alternatively refer to his or her own host by issuing a command specifying either the host name **localhost** or the internet address 127.0.0.1, no matter what the host's actual name and address assignment is. The local **hosts** file on any TCP/IP host typically contains an entry that assigns the host name **localhost** to internet address 127.0.0.1 in addition to having an entry for that host's actual name and internet address assignment.

SUMMARY

There are three levels of identifiers that are important in the TCP/IP environment—host names, internet addresses, and physical hardware addresses. There are two different identifier conversions that must take place during the operation of the internet—host name to internet address conversion and internet address to physical hardware address conversion.

Internet addresses are 32 bits in length and contain a network identifier and a host identifier. When writing down internet addresses, or when software displays them, dotted-decimal notation is typically used, in which a decimal number is used to represent the value of each individual internet address octet. There are four commonly used internet address classes—class A addresses (0.0.0.1 to 127.255.255.254) provide 7 bits to identify the physical network and 24 bits to identify hosts, class B addresses (128.0.0.1 to 191.255.255.254) provide 14 bits to identify the network and 16 bits to identify hosts, class C addresses (192.0.0.1 to 223.255.255.254) provide 21 bits to identify the network and 8 bits to identify hosts, and class D addresses (initial bits 1110) that are used to implement a form of multicasting. Subnetting can be used to augment the original TCP/IP addressing scheme, in which some number of bits from the host identifier portion of the internet address are used as a subnet identifier. The subnet mask defines which portion of the host ID value is used as a subnet ID.

TCP/IP routing decisions are made based only on the network identification portion of internet addresses and not on the host identification portion. A router that receives an IP datagram can tell immediately whether an IP datagram that it receives is destined for one of the networks to which it is physically attached.

Chapter 5 begins Part II of this book and describes the services and protocols that are provided in the Application layer of the TCP/IP architecture. Chapter 5 describes the broad range of application services that TCP/IP networking software makes available to end users.

APPLICATION LAYER PROTOCOLS AND SERVICES

Chapter 5   Application Services

Chapter 6   Network File System

Chapter 7   Domain Name System

Chapter **5**

Application Services

The services that are provided in the TCP/IP Application layer are the services that end users perceive. These are the services that a computing system user employs to perform useful work on a TCP/IP internet. Application layer services are the subject of this chapter.

A wide variety of TCP/IP Application layer services and protocols are defined. Some application protocols are widely used; others are employed only for specialized purposes. Figure 5.1 shows the most commonly used TCP/IP application-level protocols and illustrates how they relate to the other layers in the TCP/IP architecture.

Most of the application protocols are defined by RFCs in the same manner as for the lower layer protocols, but some of the application protocols have been developed by independent organizations that have made them generally available to the TCP/IP networking community.

Many of the application-level protocols and services described in this chapter are available in a number of different computing environments. For example, all of them

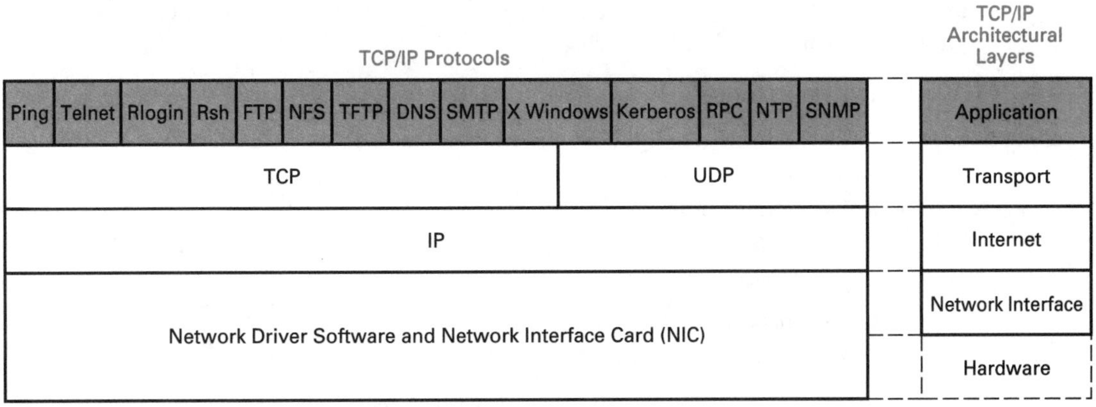

TCP/IP Protocols														TCP/IP Architectural Layers
Ping	Telnet	Rlogin	Rsh	FTP	NFS	TFTP	DNS	SMTP	X Windows	Kerberos	RPC	NTP	SNMP	Application
TCP								UDP						Transport
IP														Internet
Network Driver Software and Network Interface Card (NIC)														Network Interface
														Hardware

Figure 5.1 Representative Application layer protocols and services.

are provided by most UNIX operating systems that are based on the BSD implementation. Most of them are also provided by other operating systems that support TCP/IP communication software. The command and command response examples provided in this chapter are based on a 4.3BSD implementation. However, the commands and responses found in TCP/IP implementations in other environments are similar to those shown.

APPLICATION LAYER SERVICE CATEGORIES

The services and protocols that operate in the TCP/IP Application layer can be divided into two categories—end user services and protocols and support services and protocols.

End User Services and Protocols

The services and protocols in the end user category are the services and protocols that users employ directly. The following are the end user services and protocols that are described in this chapter:

- Ping Connectivity Testing
- Telnet Interactive Login
- Rlogin Interactive Login
- Rsh Remote Execution
- FTP File Transfer
- NFS Remote File Access

Support Services and Protocols

The services and protocols in the support category are services and protocols that are used to support the services that users request. The following are the support services and protocols that are described in this chapter:

- TFTP File Transfer
- Name Resolution
- SMTP Electronic Mail
- X Windows Presentation
- Kerberos Security
- Remote Procedure Calls
- NTP Distributed Time
- SNMP Network Management

The following sections describe the TCP/IP application services and protocols in each of the two above categories, beginning with the services in the end user category.

PING CONNECTIVITY TESTING

Ping is an Application layer service that can be used to test for connectivity between any two hosts in an internet. Ping is short for *Packet InterNet Groper*, and **ping** is the name of a program originally used in the Internet to test the reachability of remote destination hosts. Ping is now generally available in most TCP/IP implementations. A user employs Ping by entering the **ping** command that references some other host either by name or internet address. Ping then displays information concerning the reachability of the referenced host.

Ping Operation

Ping uses a characteristic of the Internet Control Message Protocol (ICMP), which is described further in Chapter 12. When a host receives an ICMP Echo Request message, it sends an ICMP Echo Reply message back. Along with each ICMP Echo Reply message that it receives, Ping calculates the amount of time elapsed since it sent the original Echo Request message. This provides the Ping user with an estimate of the round-trip delay that is being experienced in exchanging data with the specified host.

Ping Examples

Suppose we wanted to find out if the host named **joeshost** was reachable. We might enter the following **ping** command at the dollar sign prompt:

```
$ ping joeshost
```

As a result of the above command, we might receive the following results:

```
$ ping joeshost
Ping joeshost: 56 data bytes
64 bytes from joeshost.lebeninc.com (141.131.1.2): icmp_seq=0. time=2849. ms
64 bytes from joeshost.lebeninc.com (141.131.1.2): icmp_seq=1. time=2042. ms
64 bytes from joeshost.lebeninc.com (141.131.1.2): icmp_seq=2. time=1118. ms
64 bytes from joeshost.lebeninc.com (141.131.1.2): icmp_seq=3. time=446. ms
64 bytes from joeshost.lebeninc.com (141.131.1.2): icmp_seq=4. time=440. ms
64 bytes from joeshost.lebeninc.com (141.131.1.2): icmp_seq=5. time=445. ms
64 bytes from joeshost.lebeninc.com (141.131.1.2): icmp_seq=6. time=430. ms
64 bytes from joeshost.lebeninc.com (141.131.1.2): icmp_seq=7. time=410. ms
```

The **ping** command continues to execute and sends a continuous sequence of ICMP Echo Request messages to the specified host, and the referenced host will continue replying with ICMP Echo Reply messages until we interrupt the command. Ping then displays summary information regarding the reachability of **joeshost:**

```
^?
----joeshost.lebeninc.com Ping Statistics----
8 packets transmitted, 8 packets received, 0% packet loss
round-trip (ms) min/avg/max = 410/1022/2849
$
```

For a reachable host, the Ping service ends by indicating the minimum, average, and maximum round-trip delay that results from sending data to the referenced host.

If we enter a **ping** command for a host that is currently unreachable, Ping displays messages that tell us that fact:

```
$ ping samshost
ICMP Host Unreachable from gateway 192.43.235.2
 for icmp from myhost.simul.com (140.252.1.54) to
  samshost.lebeninc.com(141.131.1.11)
no answer from samshost.lebeninc.com
$
```

TELNET INTERACTIVE LOGIN

Telnet allows the user on the local host to login to a remote host. The Telnet protocol establishes a client-server relationship between the Telnet client software running on the local user's host and the remote Telnet server software running on the remote host. The Telnet client and server software together handle the data transfers that are required between the local host and the remote host. These data transfers make it appear as if the user is logged into the remote host directly, even though the user is actually communicating with the local host.

Telnet Functions

The Telnet protocol performs three important functions that are used in implementing the remote login service:

- **Network Virtual Terminal.** Telnet defines a *network virtual terminal* (NVT) that provides an interface to remote hosts against which all Telnet client software is built. NVT defines an imaginary terminal device that the Telnet client software emulates.
- **Option Negotiation.** Telnet defines a mechanism by which a Telnet client and a Telnet server negotiate options that they both agree to use during a Telnet session.
- **Symmetric Session View.** Both ends of a Telnet session are treated symmetrically, and either end of the connection can be implemented by an application program.

Telnet Operation

Figure 5.2 shows how a Telnet client and a Telnet server conduct a Telnet session on behalf of a real user. The Telnet server conducts a conversation and supplies services to the network virtual terminal. The Telnet client software accepts user commands at a real user interface device and converts these to network virtual terminal commands. The Telnet client also accepts responses that the Telnet server makes to the network virtual terminal and converts them to responses acceptable to the real user interface device. When using Telnet, the Telnet service generally prompts the user for a login name and a password each time the **telnet** command is issued.

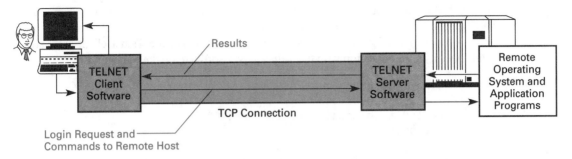

Figure 5.2   Telnet remote login protocol operation.

The Telnet software implements the login session using the TCP Transport layer protocol via a TCP connection between the Telnet client process and the Telnet server process. A Telnet server is typically capable of accepting TCP requests for the establishment of concurrent transport connections from a number of Telnet clients.

The Telnet software can operate in one of two modes—*command mode* and *input mode.*

Telnet Command Mode

To enter the command mode, we enter the **telnet** command with no arguments:

```
$ telnet
```

The Telnet client software on our own host then prompts us to enter subcommands that describe the specific task we want to perform:

```
$ telnet
telnet> _
```

The Telnet subcommands that we can enter vary from one implementation to another. In general, they specify such things as the type of terminal being emulated, whether information should be sent a character at a time or a line at a time. Subcommands are also generally available to explicitly open and close the connection to the remote host.

Telnet Input Mode

Telnet is more often used in input mode in which default values are used for much of the information that can be explicitly specified in command mode. To use Telnet in input mode, we include an argument in the **telnet** command that specifies the name of the host to which we would like to login.

```
$ telnet joeshost
```

If we are logging into a remote host that is not on our own internet, we need to specify a fully-qualified domain name. If we are logging in to a host on our own internet, we need not specify the high-level qualifiers of the domain name. We can also issue the **telnet** command specifying an internet address instead of a domain name using dotted-decimal notation.

After we enter a valid **telnet** command in input mode, the Telnet client software establishes a TCP connection with the Telnet server software on the remote host.

```
$ telnet joeshost
Trying 208.0.0.3 ...
Connected to bighost.lebeninc.com.
Escape character is '^]'.

4.3 BSD Unix (bighost.lebeninc.EDU) (ttype)

login:
```

After the connection is established, we will be allowed to login in the same manner as a user at a user interface device that is directly attached to the remote host:

```
login: leben
password:

Warning: no Kerberos tickets issued.
Copyright (c) 1980,1983,1986,1988,1990,1991 The Regents of the
 University of California.

All rights reserved.

4.3 BSD Reno Unix #8

Erase is Delete
Kill is Ctrl-U
Interrupt is Ctrl-C
$
```

After we enter a valid login sequence, we are then able to enter any command that we would be able to enter had we logged in to a local user interface device attached to the remote host.

Notice that the normal UNIX dollar sign prompt is displayed. However, it is being displayed by the remote host rather than by our local host. The commands we can enter may be restricted due to authorization procedures that may be implemented on the remote host.

The following is an example of the output we might see if we entered a UNIX **ls** command to the remote host:

```
$ ls
a.out*       buf.c      error.o    std.err         typescript
bigfwrite.c  conf.c     ourhdr.h   std.out         wait1.c
bin/         error.c    prexit.c   testsymlink.c
$
```

To terminate the Telnet connection with the remote host, we enter the **logout** Telnet subcommand:

```
$ logout
Connection closed by foreign host.
$
```

Notice that we again have the dollar sign prompt, but this time it is displayed by the local host software and we now have access to the services of our local host.

RLOGIN INTERACTIVE LOGIN

The *Rlogin* service is related to Telnet but is typically provided only by variations of the UNIX operating systems. Telnet allows a user at any type of TCP/IP host to log into any other type of TCP/IP host. The local host and remote host may be running entirely different operating systems. The Rlogin service, on the other hand, is normally used when a user at a local UNIX host wants to login to a remote UNIX host.

For the UNIX user, Rlogin is somewhat easier to use than Telnet and provides a few additional services. For example, Rlogin allows the user to maintain a list of hosts in an **rhosts** file so the user need not enter the login name and password at the time of each login, as with Telnet.

RSH REMOTE EXECUTION

The *Rsh* remote execution service is implemented on most UNIX and non-UNIX TCP/IP hosts. The Rsh service allows the user to issue, at the local host, a command to request an operating system function or to request the execution of an application program on some other host in an internet. A similar service to Rsh called *Rexec* is available on some TCP/IP hosts as well.

When using the Rsh service, the user enters the applicable command at the local host, but the command is actually executed on the remote host. The results of that operating system command or the results of the application program execution are then returned to the user at the local host. The Rsh facility implements a client-server relationship between the Rsh software in the local host (the Rsh client) and the Rsh software in the remote host (the Rsh server).

Figure 5.3 shows how the Rsh facility operates. The Rsh remote execution service is typically provided on the user's host by a client process called **rcmd.** The remote host typically runs a daemon server process called **rshd.*** The **rshd** daemon accepts commands that are entered by the user of the Rsh client software.

*On UNIX systems, processes that run in the background are called *daemons* and have names that end in the letter "d". In the UNIX environment, TCP/IP server processes are normally implemented in the form of daemons.

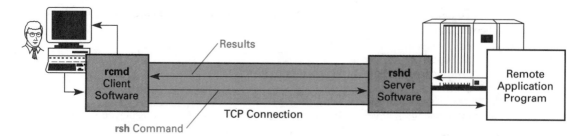

Figure 5.3   Rsh remote execution protocol operation.

FTP FILE TRANSFER

The *File Transfer Protocol* (FTP) is the file transfer protocol that is typically employed by TCP/IP end users. An implementation of FTP allows the user to transfer data in both directions between the local host and a remote host. FTP can be used to transfer files that contain either binary data or ASCII text. Certain versions of FTP also allow for the transfer of files containing EBCDIC data.

FTP allows files to be transferred one at a time, or a single request can cause multiple files to be transferred. FTP also provides ancillary functions, such as listing the contents of remote directories, changing the current remote directory, and creating and removing remote directories.

FTP uses the TCP Transport layer protocol to transfer data and uses the reliability controls that are automatically provided by a TCP connection to ensure that data is transferred reliably and that a transferred file is an exact copy of the original. FTP is designed to operate across computing systems of different types and accommodates a variety of differences in how files are stored, accessed, and protected. The way in which FTP accommodates these differences is by allowing file attributes to be specified as part of the file transfer request. These attributes include *data type, file type,* and *transmission mode.*

Data Types

FTP defines four possible data types:

- **ASCII.** The ASCII data type denotes data represented using the 7-bit ASCII coding system with each ASCII character stored in an 8-bit octet.

- **EBCDIC.** The EBCDIC data type denotes data represented using the IBM EBCDIC 8-bit encoding system.

- **Image.** The Image data type denotes data treated as a continuous bit stream.

- **Logical Octet Size.** With the Logical Octet Size data type, the number of bits in each octet is explicitly specified. This logical grouping of bits into octets is preserved across the file transfer operation.

The ASCII and EBCDIC data types are most often used with text files; Image and Logical Octet Size data types are typically used for binary program images and for encoded and tabular data that cannot be handled in the form of text.

File Types

The file types defined by FTP are as follows:

- **File Structure.** A file having the *file structure* file type consists of a string of octets terminated by an End of File marker.
- **Record Structure.** A file having the *record structure* file type consists of a set of records. When a record structured file is transferred, the end of each record is indicated by an End of Record marker.
- **Page Structure.** The *page structure* file type was defined for a file structure used with DEC's TOPS-20 systems, used extensively in the early days of the ARPANET. This file type is no longer commonly used.

Although the number of file types defined is limited, they have proven sufficient to accommodate the majority of file transfer operations typically required in the TCP/IP environment.

Transmission Modes

The data type and file type attributes address the way a file is stored in the source and destination hosts. The *transmission mode* attribute is concerned with the way in which a file is transferred across the internet. Transmission mode options are designed to deal with restarting an interrupted data transfer operation and with enhancing file transfer efficiency. Possible transmission modes include the following:

- **Stream.** With the *stream* transmission mode, data is sent over the network with no specialized processing. The stream transmission mode can be used with all file types.
- **Block.** With the *block* transmission mode, data is encapsulated into records. Each record contains a count field, the data, and an End of Record marker. With the block transmission mode, the source and destination hosts keep track of the progress of the transfer, and if the transfer is interrupted, the transfer can be restarted from the last correctly received record.
- **Compressed.** With the *compressed* transmission mode, data is compressed before transmission by replacing contiguous sequences of the same character with a single occurrence of the character and a count of the number of times the character occurs. The destination FTP process expands the data back to its original form.

FTP Operation

FTP employs two separate TCP connections to accomplish a file transfer. A *control connection* is used to pass control information, in the form of commands and replies, back and forth between the FTP processes running in each host. A *data transfer connection* is used for the actual transmission of file data and acknowledgments.

The FTP process in the host that is making the file transfer request is called the *FTP client*. The FTP process in the host receiving the request is the *FTP server*. The process involved in executing a file request is as follows:

1. A user (person or application program) invokes FTP services and passes the FTP client the name of the host to receive the request. The FTP client opens a TCP connection with the FTP server on the designated host using TCP port number 21, the standard TCP port number associated with FTP control procedures. This connection is the control connection.

2. The FTP client sends commands to the FTP server with the account name and password of the user. The FTP server allows the receiving host to perform any necessary authentication of the user's access rights and sends replies back to the FTP client indicating whether authentication was successful.

3. The FTP client sends commands indicating the file name, data type, file type, and transmission mode to be used for the transfer and whether the FTP client will send a file to the FTP server or receive a copy of a file from the FTP server. The FTP server sends replies indicating whether or not the transfer options are acceptable.

4. The FTP server opens another TCP connection with the FTP client to use for data transfer, using TCP port number 20 on the server host and a destination port number previously sent to it by the FTP client.

5. The sending FTP process packages data as agreed upon in the options and sends it to the receiving FTP process using the data transfer connection. Standard TCP flow control, error checking, and retransmission procedures are used to ensure that the file is transferred correctly and completely.

6. When the entire file has been transferred, the sending FTP process closes the data transfer connection. The control connection can then be used to begin another data transfer operation, or it also can be closed.

Commands and Replies

FTP defines the formats to be used for the commands and replies sent across the control connection. A command consists of a four-octet ASCII character string. A reply consists of a three-digit numeric code followed by an optional text string. The first digit of the numeric code indicates the general status of the reply, as follows:

    1—Positive preliminary reply

    2—Positive completion reply

    3—Positive intermediate reply

    4—Transient negative reply

    5—Permanent negative reply

A complete list of the defined commands and replies is included in the FTP specification.

FTP Subcommands

To start an FTP file transfer session, we typically enter an **ftp** command that specifies the name or internet address of the remote host with which we would like to begin a file transfer session. The FTP session normally operates on the files contained in a working directory on the local host and a working directory on the remote host. The working directory of the local host begins as the directory that is the current directory when the **ftp** command is issued. The working directory of the remote host begins as a directory established by the remote host FTP implementation.

After we enter the **ftp** command and the file transfer session is started, we then enter subcommands to specify the file operations we would like executed. The subcommands that we can enter depend on the FTP implementation. The subcommands used most often and that are provided by all FTP implementations are listed in Box 5.1.

NFS REMOTE FILE ACCESS

The *Network File System* (NFS) is a widely implemented TCP/IP service that was initially developed by Sun Microsystems. Sun made the NFS specification, along with source code that implements it, publicly available, and NFS is now available for use with a wide variety of UNIX and non-UNIX operating systems. NFS defines a number of high-level services that provide authorized users with transparent access to files located on remote hosts.

NFS is typically employed to provide users with access to the files maintained on one or more computing systems that are designated as file servers. The file servers run NFS server software that make certain designated directories on their disk storage devices available to other hosts. A user host runs NFS client software to provide the user with access to the files maintained on NFS servers. The NFS client software allows the user to assign one or more drive letters to remote directories. These drive letters can then be used to refer to the remote directories in operating system commands and application programs as if they were directories located on local disk drives.

NFS is described further in Chapter 6.

TFTP FILE TRANSFER

The *Trivial File Transfer Protocol* (TFTP) is a very simple file transfer facility that provides the ability to transfer data in both directions between the local host and a remote host. TFTP is the first of the protocols we discuss that are in the support services category.

TFTP implements its own reliability controls and can run on top of any type of transport service. The UDP datagram Transport layer protocol is used by most TFTP implementations. The end-to-end reliability controls that TFTP implements take the form of a message sequencing system, timeouts, and retransmissions to ensure that files are transferred intact.

TFTP is generally used only by system software that performs such functions as downline loading of program code. It is not intended to be employed directly by the users of TCP/IP communications software.

BOX 5.1   FTP subcommands.

- **ls.** Displays a listing of the files in directory on the remote host. Syntax:

```
ls [dir]
```

If no directory name is specified in an **ls** command, the contents of the directory is changed to the current working directory.

- **lcd.** Changes the local host's working directory. Syntax:

```
lcd [dir]
```

If no directory name is specified in an **lcd** command, the directory is changed to the local host's home directory.

- **cd.** Changes the remote host's working directory. Syntax:

```
cd <dir>
```

- **get, rcve.** Transfers a file from the working directory of the remote host to the working directory of the local host. Syntax:

```
get <remote-file> [local-file]
rcve <remote-file> [local-file]
```

Either **get** or **rcve** can be used to transfer a file from the remote host to the local host. If no **local-file** name is specified, the copied file is given the same name as the original file.

- **put, send.** Transfers a file from the working directory of the local host to the working directory of the remote host. Syntax:

```
send <local-file> [remote-file]
send <local-file> [remote-file]
```

Either **put** or **send** can be used to transfer a file from the local host to the remote host. If no **remote-file** name is specified, the copied file is given the same name as the original file.

- **delete.** Deletes the specified file from the working directory of the remote host. Syntax:

```
delete <filename>
```

- **quit.** Ends the FTP session. Syntax:

```
quit
```

NAME RESOLUTION

As described in Chapter 4, the hosts attached to an internet each have one or more unique 32-bit internet addresses assigned to them, one for each physical network attachment. In a TCP/IP internet, each host is also assigned a unique name to make it easy for users to refer to hosts without needing to know their internet addresses. Since the underlying TCP/IP protocols, such as IP, TCP, and UDP all refer to individual hosts using their 32-bit internet addresses, each host must implement a *name resolution* function that can translate between host names and internet addresses.

The name resolution function allows the user to enter commands that refer to a remote host by its unique name. The name resolution function accepts the host name and returns the 32-bit internet address that is associated with it. This process is illustrated in Fig. 5.4.

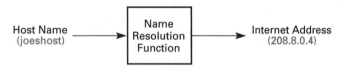

Figure 5.4   The name resolution function.

There are two methods that can be used for name resolution in a TCP/IP internet—**hosts** files and the Domain Name System (DNS). Each of these name resolution methods is described next.

Name Resolution with hosts Files

In small TCP/IP internets, the function of translating between a host name and the internet address associated with that host can be performed by the host itself through a configuration file typically named **hosts.** Most implementations of TCP/IP software provide a **hosts** file facility that maintains a local database of host name to internet address mappings. The **hosts** file must contain a name-to-address mapping for each host that the user of that host wishes to contact. Local **hosts** files are typically used for name resolution only in small internets in which it is relatively easy for the system administrator to maintain the **hosts** file on each host. Local **hosts** files are generally maintained using an ordinary text editor, although some implementations of TCP/IP communications software provide for the semiautomated maintenance of **hosts** files on a networkwide basis.

Name Resolution with the Domain Name System

In a large internet, it is unwieldy to try to maintain local **hosts** files with name-to-address mappings for each individual host. The *Domain Name System* (DNS) is a hierarchical naming facility that can be used to maintain the mappings between names and internet addresses in a limited number of places in an internet rather than at the location of each host.

The Domain Name System works with domain names. As we introduced in Chapter 4, domain names are names that each consists of a series of simple names connected with periods. Each of the simple names refers to a *domain,* which consists of some subset of the hosts in an internet.

DNS defines a client-server relationship between an application that is making a request for a name translation service and a host attached to an internet that is providing a name translation service. The DNS client software is called the *resolver* and the DNS server software is called the *nameserver.* When DNS is used, all hosts in an internet run the resolver DNS client process. This is shown in Fig. 5.5.

In a small internet, there might be a single host that is designated as the nameserver and is responsible for supplying name translation services to all the resolvers. In a large internet, requiring a single host to provide all name translation services would create a resource bottleneck. Therefore, DNS allows the naming database to be distributed among multiple nameservers. Depending on the location of the host that is making a request for a name resolution service and the location of the requested resource, it might be necessary for a number of nameservers to be accessed to perform a name resolution operation.

The operation of DNS is described in detail in Chapter 7.

SMTP ELECTRONIC MAIL

One of the most commonly used networking applications in any computer network is electronic mail, and TCP/IP internets are no exception. Many types of electronic mail systems have been implemented for the TCP/IP environment, and the electronic mail facilities of TCP/IP internets are often interconnected with the electronic messaging systems of other types of networks. For example, TCP/IP electronic mail facilities can be interconnected with PROFS and DISOSS messaging systems commonly employed in the IBM large-system environment. The electronic mail facilities of individual internets can also be interconnected with public electronic mail services, such as those operated by MCI Mail and CompuServe.

TCP/IP defines an electronic messaging protocol, called the *Simple Mail Transfer Protocol* (SMTP). SMTP is designed to be used by electronic mail software that provides users with access to messaging facilities. Mail facilities allow a user to send messages

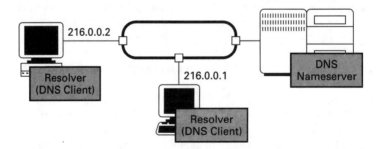

Figure 5.5   Resolver DNS clients and a DNS nameserver.

and files to a user connected to the local network, to a user connected to some other network in the internet, or to a user connected to a non-TCP/IP network that has a connection to your network or internet.

SMTP does not define how mail to be sent is passed from a user to SMTP, nor does it specify how SMTP delivers mail to a receiving user. SMTP also does not define the internal format of mail messages. SMTP deals only with the exchanges that occur between the two SMTP processes. The SMTP process with mail to send is called the *SMTP client,* and the SMTP process that receives mail is the *SMTP server.*

SMTP Operation

An SMTP operation consists of three steps:

1. A connection between the SMTP client and the SMTP server is established.
2. Mail is transferred across the connection.
3. The connection is closed.

The following sections describe each of these three steps.

Connection Setup

When there is mail to send, the SMTP client opens a TCP connection with the SMTP server at the destination host using TCP port number 25, the TCP port number that is associated with SMTP servers. The client then sends a Hello command containing the name of the sending user. The SMTP server returns a reply indicating its ability to receive mail.

Mail Transfer

Mail transfer begins with a Mail command containing the name of the user sending the message. This is followed by one or more Rcpt commands that identify the intended recipients of the message. A Data command begins the transfer of the actual message text. The Data command is followed by a series of data units that contain the message text. The SMTP server responds to each command with an appropriate reply.

TCP mechanisms for error detection and retransmission are used to ensure successful transfer of mail messages. When the SMTP server has successfully received the message for a given destination user, the client SMTP process removes that user from the list of destinations for the message. When all destinations have been sent copies of the message, the message and its list of destinations are removed from the sending message queue. SMTP can be considered a reliable delivery service in that it ensures that a message reaches the destination host. However, SMTP defines no procedures to guarantee that the message is successfully delivered to the destination *user* at that host.

When message transfer operations for a given message have been completed, the TCP connection can be used to transfer another message, the direction of transfer can be changed to allow the destination host to send messages back, or the connection can be closed.

Connection Closing

The SMTP client closes the connection by issuing a Quit command. Both sides then execute a TCP Close operation to release the TCP connection.

Data Formats

The commands used with SMTP begin with a four-octet command code, encoded in ASCII, which can be followed by an argument. Box 5.2 lists the basic SMTP commands. SMTP replies use the same format as FTP—a three-digit numeric value followed by a text string.

BOX 5.2   SMTP commands.

- HELO
- MAIL FROM:
- RCPT TO:
- DATA
- RSET
- SEND FROM:
- SOML FROM:
- SAML FROM:
- VRFY (string)
- EXPN (string)
- HELP (string)
- NOOP
- QUIT
- TURN

X WINDOWS PRESENTATION

Windowing presentation facilities are provided in the TCP/IP environment by a facility called the *X Window System,* often called simply *X Windows* for short. X Windows is a comprehensive windowing facility developed by Project Athena, a cooperative effort among MIT, IBM, and Digital Equipment Corporation. The X Window System is a set of distributed graphical presentation services that implement a windowing system on a graphics display. It implements a client-server relationship between an application program (the client) and the windowing software in a workstation or terminal that controls a window on the graphical display (the server). As shown in Fig. 5.6, a client application program can run on the same host as the server window or it can run in some other host in the internet.

The X Window System allows a user at a graphics workstation to have multiple windows on the screen, each of which might be controlled by a separate client application program. The X Window System defines a protocol that is used to transmit information between the client application program and the server windowing software. The X Window System also defines an application programming interface that client application programs can use to access the services of the display in a standardized manner.

Note that with X Windows, the client/server relationship between the workstation and the host is different from what one might expect on first glance. The windowing soft-

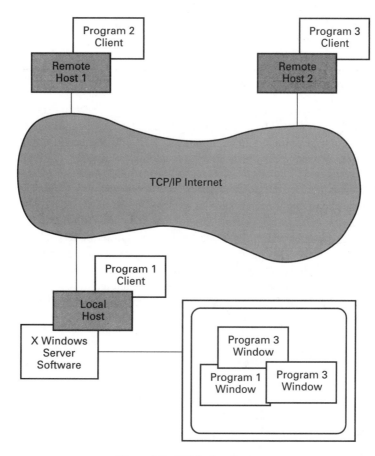

Figure 5.6   X Window System.

ware running in the workstation plays the role of the server that is providing the services that give windowing capabilities. The application program running in what might be a large-system host plays the role of the client that is accessing those windowing services.

KERBEROS SECURITY

Authentication and authorization services can be provided in a TCP/IP internet by a facility called *Kerberos*. Kerberos is an encryption-based security system that provides mutual authentication between a client application component and a server application component in a distributed computing environment. It also provides services that can be used to control which clients are authorized to access which servers.

In the Kerberos system, each client component and each server component is called a *principal* and has a unique *principal identifier* assigned to it. These principal identifiers allow clients and servers to identify themselves to each other to prevent fraudulent exchanges of information between principals. Authorization of a client to access a particular server can be implemented independently from the authentication service.

REMOTE PROCEDURE CALLS

A *remote procedure call* (RPC) facility provides an easy-to-use method that application developers can use to implement communication applications. An RPC facility allows application components to communicate with one another in a transparent fashion over the internet using an ordinary procedure call mechanism.

Figure 5.7 illustrates a typical RPC functional model. A module called a *stub* in the local host mimics the presence of the actual procedure to which the client calling procedure is attempting to pass control. The client stub, in turn, requests the services of the RPC facility on behalf of the client. The RPC facility uses TCP/IP communication services to transmit argument information and results to and from the RPC facility in the remote host.

When the RPC facility in the server host receives the parameter information generated as a result of the procedure call, it loads the server module containing the requested procedure and passes control to it, using a stub unique to that procedure. The called server procedure then passes results information back to its stub. The RPC facility then transmits the results back to the client.

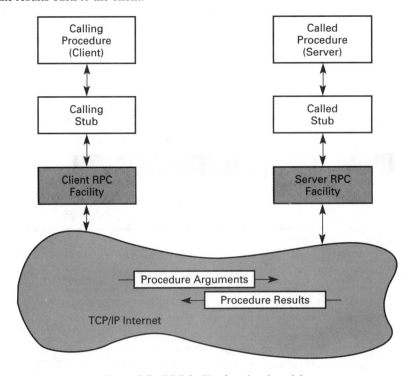

Figure 5.7   RPC facility functional model.

The client and server procedures exchange parameter information and results as if they both resided in the same host, and the fact that an internet is being used to communicate argument information and results is hidden from them.

There are two major software subsystems that are typically used to provide remote procedure call facilities in the TCP/IP environment:

- **Sun RPC.** An implementation of the *Sun RPC* facility is provided in most operating systems that are based on BSD UNIX. The Sun RPC facility is also provided on a number of other UNIX and non-UNIX operating systems and is available with any implementation of Sun's Network File System (NFS). The source code for the Sun RPC facility is available from Sun Microsystems for a nominal charge. The Sun RPC facility is examined in detail in Chapter 20.

- **Hewlett-Packard RPC.** The *Hewlett-Packard (HP) RPC* facility was originally developed by Apollo Computer Inc., which was subsequently acquired by Hewlett-Packard. The HP RPC facility is provided as part of a software subsystem called the Network Computing System (NCS). The HP NCS is a programmer toolkit that allows programmers to access the HP RPC facilities in a similar manner to Sun RPC. Like Sun RPC, the NCS software subsystem is implemented on a wide variety of UNIX and non-UNIX operating systems.

TIME SERVICES

The notion of time is taken for granted in most of today's centralized computer systems. However, the mechanisms used to provide time in these systems are inadequate when applied to distributed systems. Even if all the computers in the network have accurate clocks, we cannot expect a diverse group of computer operators to all set the clocks correctly on a large number of computers. So in a networking environment, mechanisms are required for consistently setting the clocks on all the computers and for maintaining their accuracy. A time service must be available that allows users to obtain consistent time values no matter where they reside in the network. This is not possible if each node in the network is responsible for independently maintaining its own internal clock.

Time Service

TCP/IP defines a simple *Time* service that a host can use to contact another host to obtain a date and time-of-day value. A host that operates in the role of a time server ordinarily implements the Time service through TCP or UDP port number 37. (TCP/IP defines two separate Time services, one that is accessed via UDP and another that is accessed via TCP.) An implementation returns a time value in the form of a 32-bit integer that represents the number of seconds that have elapsed since January 1, 1900.

Maintaining Synchronized Time Values

The Time service defines the means by which one host can provide another host with a value for the date and time of day but does not define the means by which the networked computers maintain a consistent notion of time. TCP/IP software offers two solutions for maintaining date and time-of-day values that are correct on a networkwide basis—the **timed** daemon and the *Network Time Service* (NTS) protocol.

timed Daemon

The **timed** daemon is a UNIX program that can be run on all the computers attached to a UNIX local area network. The **timed** daemon runs in the background on each host and exchanges clock values with other hosts that are also running **timed.** Each host's copy of **timed** makes clock value comparisons, and based on the results, slowly adjusts its clock. This process is repeated periodically so that all the clocks in the networked computers eventually reach and maintain a value that is essentially the same on all the computers.

Network Time Service Protocol

The *Network Time Service* (NTS) protocol is a more complex protocol for maintaining consistent date and time-of-day values among a set of networked computers. NTS is better suited than the **timed** program for maintaining consistent clock values when long distances may separate some of the networked computers. NTS runs complex algorithms that take into account the propagation delays on long-distance links.

With NTS, certain hosts in the internet are designated time servers that are responsible for maintaining correct clock values. Some or all of the time servers may have access to a time provider, such as software that contacts the radio stations WWV in Colorado and WWVH in Hawaii that periodically broadcast correct time values.

SNMP NETWORK MANAGEMENT

Network management services are typically provided in a TCP/IP internet through software that implements the *Simple Network Management Protocol* (SNMP). SNMP defines a *Management Information Base* (MIB), which is a database that defines all the objects that can be managed in the internet. SNMP also defines the formats of a set of network management messages and the rules by which the messages are exchanged. The network management messages are used to make requests for performing network management functions and to report on events that occur in the network. Network management is described further in Chapter 14.

SUMMARY

The services and protocols that operate in the TCP/IP Application layer are the services that end users perceive. These services and protocols can be divided into two major categories—end user services and protocols, and support protocols and services.

The services and protocols in the end user category are those that end users invoke directly, typically employing a user interface device. The Ping service is used for testing the connectivity between two systems. Telnet allows a user on a local host to login to a remote host. The Rlogin facility is similar to Telnet but is provided only in the UNIX environment. The Rsh remote execution facility allows a user at a local host to specify that an operating system command or application program be run on a remote host. The File Transfer Protocol (FTP) allows a user to transfer files between a local host and a remote host. The Network File System (NFS) provides users at a local host with access to a remote host's file system.

The services and protocols in the support category are used to provide support functions that are invoked by the services that users request. The Trivial File Transfer Protocol (TFTP) is a simple file transfer facility that is sometimes used for support functions, such as downline loading of program code. Name resolution facilities, provided by local **hosts** files or by the Domain Name system, translate between host names and internet addresses. The Simple Mail Transfer Protocol (SMTP) is used to implement electronic messaging systems. The X Windows System provides windowing presentation services to support user interface devices with a graphics display. The Kerberos security facility provides authentication and authorization services. Remote procedure call facilities allow programs to communicate over an internet using an ordinary procedure call mechanism. Time services provide facilities for supplying programs with date and time-of-day values and for synchronizing the clocks on networked computing systems. The Simple Network Management Protocol defines how distributed resources can be monitored and controlled in the TCP/IP environment.

Chapter 6 describes the Network File System (NFS) that is widely used in the TCP/IP environment for providing user hosts with access to other hosts that are functioning in the role of file servers.

Network File System

The growth of local area networks in the computing environment has been driven largely by the need for sharing resources among personal computer users. A number of personal computer network operating systems have been developed that provide print and file server support for personal computers, such as the Novell NetWare network operating system products.

In the workstation and TCP/IP internetworking environment, file sharing services that are similar to those provided by a networking operating system, such as NetWare, are provided by Application layer services like the Network File System (NFS). NFS provides local hosts with access to the file systems on remote hosts that are operating as file servers. NFS was developed by Sun Microsystems and is available for use with a wide variety of UNIX and non-UNIX operating systems.

NFS CLIENT-SERVER ARCHITECTURE

NFS implements a client-server architecture, as illustrated in Fig. 6.1. System and network administrators generally designate one or more hosts in the internet to play the role of NFS file servers. These hosts run NFS server software that make certain designated directories on their disk storage devices available to other hosts in an internet. Making a directory on an NFS server available to NFS clients is called *exporting* the directory.

A user accesses the files on an NFS server using NFS client software. An NFS client attaches a remote NFS directory to the local file system by *mounting* it. A user accesses an NFS-mounted directory in the same manner as accessing a directory on a local disk. The NFS-mounted directory becomes logically a part of the client's local file

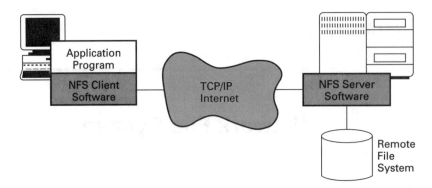

Figure 6.1   NFS client-server architecture.

system and is indistinguishable to application software from the directories in the local file system. The fact that a directory is an NFS-mounted directory on a remote host is typically transparent to the user of the local host.

NETWORK INFORMATION SERVICE

NFS is often employed together with a companion set of Application layer services from Sun called the *Network Information Service* (NIS). NIS provides simple directory services that allow system administrators to maintain configuration information in a central NFS server.

NIS provides some services that are similar to those provided by the Domain Name System (DNS), such as mapping between host names and internet addresses. However, NIS and DNS are often employed together, and when NIS does not have a required name-to-address mapping, a call is typically automatically sent to DNS for name resolution.

REMOTE PROCEDURE CALLS

Included as part of NFS is the Sun RPC facility that allows program components to communicate over an internet using an ordinary procedure call mechanism. Many of the facilities of NFS that users perceive run on top of the Sun RPC facility. The Sun RPC facility is described further in Chapter 20.

NFS FILE SYSTEM MODEL

NFS was developed for the UNIX operating system environment and is based on the UNIX file system model. In a typically UNIX file system, files are stored in directories that are arranged in a hierarchical structure on the computer system's disk storage devices. UNIX file system directories and files are referenced using *path names* that list all the names from the root of the directory to the file in question. An example of a UNIX path name might be

```
/usr/lebeninc/source/prog1
```

Implementations of NFS are also available for the personal computer MS-DOS environment, which uses a different system for file names. Facilities are typically provided in NFS implementations for personal computers to allow a mapping between UNIX file names and MS-DOS file names so that NFS client software running on personal computers can access the files stored on UNIX NFS servers.

NFS implements two protocols that are used together to provide users with access to remote files—the mount protocol and the NFS protocol.

MOUNT PROTOCOL

The NFS *mount protocol* provides the facilities that are required to connect directories on NFS servers to the directory structure of hosts running NFS client software. The Mount protocol runs over both the UDP and TCP Transport layer protocols.

An NFS file server makes the files in a particular directory structure available to other hosts by exporting the directory. The directories that are exported by a particular server are generally specified in an **exports** configuration file. The **exports** file lists the specific directories on the server that are to be made available to NFS clients. The **exports** file can specify the type of access rights clients can be given to each directory, such as read only, read/write, and so on.

Before an NFS client host can access an NFS server, it must specify which directories that have been exported by the server it would like to access. A client typically does this by issuing a **mount** command for each directory it would like to access. An NFS **mount** command can specify a number of parameters that specify options such as the following:

- The desired access rights for the files in the specified directory.
- The number of times a **mount** command should be reissued should it fail.
- Whether an NFS function can be interrupted.
- Security requirements.

NFS PROTOCOL

The NFS protocol handles the actual network transmission that is required to provide the user with local access to remote files. The NFS protocol is built on top of the UDP Transport layer protocol and implements its own reliability controls. The NFS protocol defines a number of mechanisms that allow NFS client software to access, read, and write files stored on NFS servers. Box 6.1 lists some of these mechanisms.

> ### BOX 6.1   NFS protocol mechanisms.
>
> - Test for server response and timing.
> - Obtain the attributes of a file.
> - Set the attributes of a file.
> - Obtain a file handle for a file.
> - Obtain information about a symbolic link (alias) for a file.
> - Read a specified number of octets from a file.
> - Write a specified number of octets to a file.
> - Create a new file in a specified directory.
> - Delete an existing file from a specified directory.
> - Rename an existing file.
> - Create a file that is linked to an existing file.
> - Create a symbolic link (alias) for an existing file.
> - Create a new directory.
> - Delete an empty directory.
> - Obtain directory entries.
> - Obtain information concerning the remote file system.

NFS IMPLEMENTATION

In the UNIX environment, NFS client and server software is implemented in the form of UNIX daemon processes that run on the client and server hosts. NFS daemons are generally started on the client and server machines through boot scripts that cause the required software to be started up when the operating system is loaded. Box 6.2 lists the UNIX daemons that make up a typical NFS implementation.

SUMMARY

The Network File System (NFS), developed by Sun Microsystems, provides local hosts with access to the file systems on remote hosts. NFS implements a client-server architecture in which application programs on a local host use NFS client software to access NFS server software running in hosts operating in the role of file servers. NFS runs on top of the Sun RPC facility and is often employed in conjunction with the Sun Network Information Service (NIS) that provides simple directory facilities.

An NFS server makes a file system directory available to NFS clients by exporting it. Directories to be exported are typically specified in an **exports** file maintained on the server. NFS clients access directories on NFS servers by mounting them. NFS clients issue **mount** commands naming the specific directories they would like to access.

BOX 6.2   NFS daemon processes.

- **rpc.mountd.** The **rpc.mountd** daemon runs on an NFS server host and processes the **mount** requests that NFS clients make.

- **nfsd.** The **nfsd** daemon runs on an NFS server host and services the file access requests that arrive from NFS clients.

- **biod.** The **biod** daemon runs on an NFS client host and handles the requests that software on the client host makes for access to NFS-mounted directories.

- **rpc.lockd.** The **rpc.lockd** daemon runs on both client and server hosts and handles file locking operations.

- **rpc.statd.** The **rpc.statd** daemon runs on both client and server hosts and provides monitoring services required by the **rpc.lockd** daemon.

NFS implements two major protocols that are used to provide users with access to remote files. The mount protocol provides the facilities that are required to connect directories on NFS servers to the client host's local directory structure. The NFS protocol implements the network communication mechanisms that are required to allow clients to access the files on NFS servers.

Chapter **7**

Domain Name System

As we introduced in Chapter 4, in a TCP/IP internet, each host has both a name and an internet address. A resolver process in each user host handles the translation between a host name and its internet address. The *Domain Name System* (DNS) is a hierarchical naming facility in which hosts running a DNS *nameserver* process maintain mappings between names and internet addresses. When DNS is used for name resolution, a user host's resolver process contacts a DNS nameserver to satisfy name resolution requests. This chapter examines name resolution, concentrating on how name translations are performed using DNS.

Most TCP/IP user commands allow remote hosts to be referenced using either their names or their internet addresses. For example, if a user knows the internet address of a host, the user can log onto that host by entering a **telnet** command referencing a dotted-decimal internet address:

```
telnet 190.128.1.1
```

Since host names are easier to remember than internet addresses, most users prefer to use names in TCP/IP commands. A *resolver* process running on each host in the internet performs the processing that is required to translate the host names of destination systems into their associated internet addresses. The user automatically requests a name resolution operation simply by referring to the host's name in a command:

```
telnet bigvax
```

The previous command makes a request to login to a host in which the host name is **bigvax.** The name resolution function in the user's host is automatically invoked by the TCP/IP communication software to translate the host name **bigvax** into the internet address associated with it.

NAME RESOLUTION USING hosts FILES

As we introduced in Chapter 5, in a small internet, simple 1 to 8 character names are typically used to name hosts, and the mappings between names and addresses are maintained in a local file, often called **hosts,** that is maintained by each host. The resolver process in each host translates a host name into its corresponding internet address by looking up the name in the local **hosts** file, as shown in Fig. 7.1.

When local **hosts** files are used for name resolution, the network administrator must ensure that the **hosts** files in all the hosts in the internet are updated each time a host is added to or deleted from the network. In a large internet that changes frequently, keeping **hosts** files up-to-date can become a cumbersome process.

NAME RESOLUTION USING THE DOMAIN NAME SYSTEM

The *Domain Name System* (DNS) provides a networkwide directory service that maps between host names and internet addresses. When DNS is used for name resolution, each host still runs a resolver process. However, instead of consulting a local **hosts** file, the DNS resolver contacts a nameserver system somewhere in the internet. The nameserver uses a directory database to perform the name translation operation and sends the results back to the resolver on the local host, as shown in Fig. 7.2.

There is typically more than one nameserver in an internet, and the directory database may be distributed among them. Where an individual nameserver does not have direct access to the entire directory database, a host's resolver process may have to contact more than one nameserver. In some cases the nameservers may also exchange information with one another to satisfy name resolution requests.

Each DNS nameserver maintains a tree-structured directory database. The collection of all the names stored in the DNS directory databases maintained by all the nameservers form a global *namespace* containing the names of all the hosts that can be referenced anywhere in the internet.

For the average user, the operation of the name resolution function is transparent. A user does not ordinarily care whether **hosts** files or the Domain Name System is used for name resolution. The remainder of this chapter assumes that DNS is used for name resolution.

INTERNET NAMING SCHEME

The naming scheme used in the Worldwide Internet provides an example of how DNS can be used to provide a comprehensive solution to the naming problem in a large internet. Although private internets can adopt any desired naming convention, most private internets use a naming scheme that is consistent with the conventions used in the Internet.

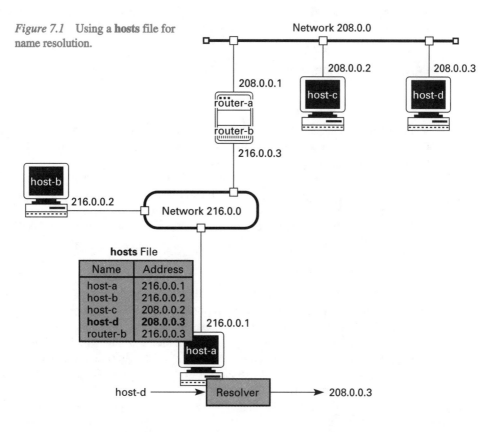

Figure 7.1 Using a **hosts** file for name resolution.

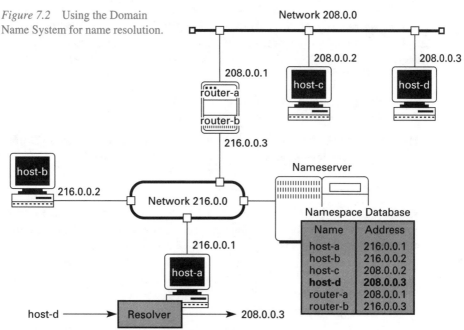

Figure 7.2 Using the Domain Name System for name resolution.

Hierarchical Namespace

The original set of host names that were used in the Worldwide Internet formed a flat namespace in which the names had no internal structure. In the original scheme, the Network Information Center (NIC) assigned names to those requesting them. The job of administering a flat namespace eventually became too large, and the present hierarchical system was eventually adopted in which a tree-structured namespace is used.

The present hierarchical system used in the Internet to name hosts is based on domain names. As we introduced in Chapter 5, a domain name consists of a sequence of simple names separated by periods. Each simple name, or set of simple names, identifies a *domain* under the control of some authority. A typical domain name in the Worldwide Internet looks like the following:

```
training.lebeninc.com
```

In a domain name, the most local domain is first and the most global domain is last. The domain name **com** identifies the network as being administered by a commercial organization, the domain name **lebeninc.com** might identify the set of hosts administered by the organization named Leben, Inc., and the domain name **training.lebeninc.com** might identify a set of hosts administered by Leben, Inc.'s training department. Leben, Inc.'s training department might then assign a unique fully-qualified domain name (FQDN) to an individual host as follows:

```
joespc.training.lebeninc.com
```

If a user is referring to a host that is located in a network administered by the user's own organization, high-level domain name qualifiers can be omitted when referring to hosts. For example, if an individual is using a host that is attached to the network administered by Leben, Inc.'s training department, the following two **telnet** commands would be equivalent:

```
telnet joespc.training.lebeninc.com
telnet joespc
```

The DNS resolver software automatically supplies the missing high-level domain name qualifier **training.lebeninc.com** if it is omitted from a command.

Internet Standard Domain Names

The NIC has specified a set of standard top-level domain names that form the basis of both a geographical and nongeographical naming system. The following are some commonly used top-level domain names that have been assigned by the NIC:

- com—Commercial organizations
- edu—Educational institutions
- gov—Government institutions

- mil—Military groups
- net—Major network support centers
- org—Organizations other than the above
- int—International organizations
- *country code*—Two-character identifier identifying a country in the geographical scheme

All country codes in the geographical scheme are two characters in length, and all the domain names in the nongeographical scheme are three characters in length. Therefore, the length of the final qualifier in a name identifies whether the name conforms to the geographical or the nongeographical scheme.

Figure 7.3 shows a portion of the Internet namespace, showing how it is structured hierarchically.

When an organization connects its own private internet to the Worldwide Internet, it applies to the NIC for a high-level domain name to use in assigning names to hosts in its own networks. The organization can elect to use either the geographical or the nongeographical scheme.

For example, if a commercial organization in the United States elects to use the nongeographical scheme, it would use the high-level domain name **com** and is assigned a next-level domain name that is different from all others that the NIC has assigned to commercial organizations in the United States. The individual organization is then responsible for assigning domain names beneath the first two levels of qualification.

An organization in the United States can, alternatively, elect to use the geographical scheme. Leben, Inc., located in the Chicago area, might use the high-level domain name **lebeninc.chi.il.us** to identify the hosts on its own internet. This name identifies an organization named Leben, Inc., in the city of Chicago, in the state of Illinois, in the United States. In the geographical scheme, Western Union city codes and U.S. Postal Service

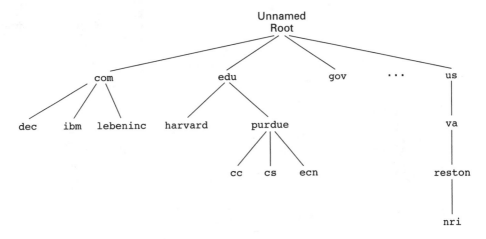

Figure 7.3   A portion of the Internet namespace tree structure.

two-character state codes are used to identify the city and state in the United States. Since names constructed using the geographical scheme can become long, the nongeographical scheme is more commonly used today by organizations in the United States.

DNS CLIENT AND SERVER SOFTWARE

DNS implements software components that have a client-server relationship. Each host in an internet that uses the Domain Name System runs *DNS client* software, which implements the resolver function, that can be used to request name resolution services. Certain designated servers implement *DNS nameserver* functions that perform name resolution operations on behalf of the DNS resolver clients, as illustrated in Fig. 7.4.

In processing a command that references a domain name rather than an internet address, the TCP/IP software automatically invokes the DNS resolver function. The resolver then accesses one or more nameservers to perform the function of translating the domain name into its associated internet address before actually executing the command containing the domain name reference. The name resolution operation is transparent to the user entering the command.

In a small internet, it is possible for the function of the nameserver to be provided by a single, centralized computer that performs all required name lookup operations. The nameserver software might be run in one of the hosts already designated as a server, such as a file server. In a larger internet, the use of a single nameserver might result in a com-

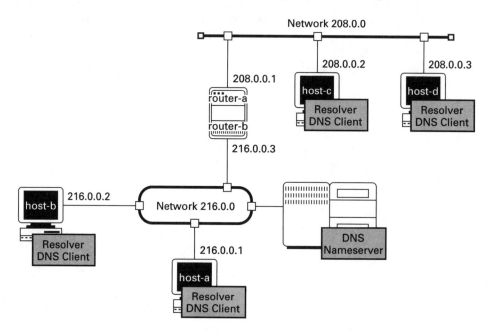

Figure 7.4   Domain Name System client and server software.

munication bottleneck due to the need for all users to access a single facility to perform name resolution operations. Using only one nameserver also results in a single point of failure that could disable the entire network should the nameserver fail.

It is generally desirable to implement at least two nameservers, one designated the primary nameserver and the other the secondary. The secondary nameserver takes over name resolution operations should the primary nameserver fail. In larger internets, it is common to use several nameservers, each of which maintains only a portion of the namespace. It is also possible to replicate portions of the namespace among multiple nameservers to increase availability.

An organization that connects its individual internet to the Worldwide Internet must provide at least one primary nameserver and a secondary nameserver that are both capable of performing naming operations for the domain names under that organization's control.

NAME RESOLUTION OPERATIONS

In performing a name resolution operation, a host's resolver process formats a name resolution request message and sends it to a nameserver. The DNS protocol requires each resolver to know how to reach at least one nameserver. The resolver sends the request to the nameserver using standard TCP transmission facilities.

Nameservers are linked hierarchically, reflecting the hierarchical structure of domain names. Root servers are able to recognize top-level domain names and know which server resolves each top-level name. The server for a top-level domain name knows the servers that can resolve subdomains under that domain name, and so on proceeding down.

Figure 7.5 shows an example of a possible hierarchy of nameservers. Given a request to resolve the name **joeshost.training.lebeninc.com,** the root server would know the name-

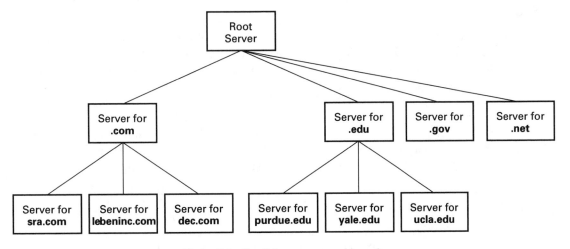

Figure 7.5 Possible name server hierarchy.

server for **.com,** and the nameserver for **.com** would know the server for **lebeninc.com,** which would be able to resolve all full names with the **lebeninc.com** high-level qualifier.

DNS client software can request name resolution services in two ways—through recursive resolution or through iterative resolution. TCP/IP internets typically employ both types of name resolution operations.

Recursive Resolution

With *recursive resolution,* the DNS resolver client software requests a name translation service of a DNS nameserver that it knows about. That nameserver contacts other nameservers, as required, to completely perform the name resolution operation. The nameserver originally contacted by the resolver then passes the internet address back to the user host's resolver process.

With recursive resolution, all the computational complexity of name resolution lies in the nameservers, and the resolver software simply makes requests for name resolution services that the nameservers satisfy. Recursive resolution is often employed by simpler hosts, such as personal computers and workstations.

Iterative Resolution

With *iterative resolution,* the resolver client requests a name resolution service of a DNS nameserver that it knows about. That nameserver either performs the service or informs the resolver of some other nameserver that it should contact. The resolver client iteratively contacts nameservers until the name resolution operation has been completed.

With iterative resolution, the computational complexity of name resolution is split between the resolver software and the nameservers. Iterative resolution is typically performed by more capable minicomputers and mainframes.

CACHING

DNS client resolver software often implements a caching function that minimizes the interaction that must take place between the client and the nameservers. Each time a user host's resolver process performs a name resolution operation, it stores the results of that operation in an internal cache. The cache maintains the results of the most recently performed name resolution operations. If the DNS resolver receives a request for the resolution of a name for which it already maintains a cache entry, it can resolve the name using the cache entry rather than having to contact a nameserver. Cache entries are given a *time to live* value to prevent them from remaining in the cache beyond a reasonable amount of time. This handles the situation where hosts are moved from one location to another in the internet.

DNS MESSAGE FORMAT

The resolver process in a host sends requests for name resolution to a nameserver process using DNS messages. DNS messages are also used for responses flowing from a nameserver back to the resolver. Box 7.1 shows the format of a DNS message and describes its fields.

BOX 7.1   Domain Name System (DNS) message format.

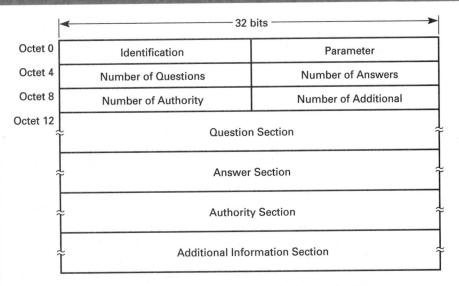

- **Identification.** A value used to correlate a response with its associated request.
- **Parameter.** Identifies the type of query and certain processing options to be applied.
- **Number of Questions.** Specifies the number of queries in this request. The Question Section of a request can contain information about multiple queries.
- **Number of Answers.** Specifies the number of answers in the response. The Answer Section of a response can contain information about multiple answers.
- **Number of Authority.** Specifies the number of authority resource records in the response. The Authority Section of a response can contain multiple resource records.
- **Number of Additional.** Specifies the number of additional information resource records in the response. The Additional Information Section of a response can contain multiple resource records.
- **Question Section.** Contains queries in the format shown below. A query consists of a Query Domain Name field containing the fully-qualified domain name about which information is required, a Query Type field specifying the type of information required, and a Query Class field identifying the protocol suite with which the name is associated.

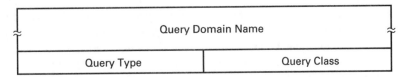

- **Answer Section.** Contains information returned in response to a query in the format shown below. The Resource Domain Name, Type, and Class fields are from the original

(Continued)

BOX 7.1   *(Continued)*

query. The Time To Live field specifies how long this information can be used if it is cached at the local host. The format of the Resource Data field depends on the type of information requested.

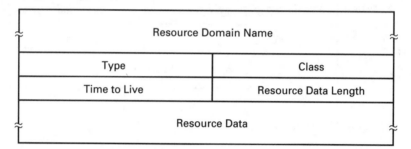

- **Authority Section.** Identifies the server that actually provided the information if a name-server has to contact another nameserver to provide a response. The format for this field is the same as for the Answer Section.

- **Additional Information Section.** Contains additional information related to the name in a query. For example, for a type MX query, the name of a host that is a mail exchanger is returned as the answer. The Additional Information Section contains the internet address associated with that name.

DNS Query Types

A naming database maintains different types of information, and each query specifies the particular type of information that is requested. Some of the different query types are shown in Box 7.2. The naming database can also contain different sets of information for use with protocol suites other than TCP/IP. The query identifies the protocol suite for which the query is being made.

SUMMARY

Each host in a TCP/IP internet runs a resolver process that performs a translation between host names and internet addresses. The resolver is generally invoked by an Application layer service on behalf of the end user. The resolver can perform name translation operations using local **hosts** files or through the use of the Domain Name Service (DNS).

When DNS is used for name resolution, the naming scheme implemented in the Internet is typically used to assign host names. The Internet naming system is based on the use of domain names that consist of simple names separated by periods. The NIC has assigned a set of high-level domain name qualifiers that can be used in assigning global-ly-unique names.

BOX 7.2 DNS query types.	
Type	**Contents**
A	32-bit IP host address.
CNAME	Canonical Domain Name for an alias.
HINFO	Name of CPU and operating host.
MINFO	Information about a mailbox or mail list.
MX	Name of a host that acts as mail exchanger for a domain.
NS	Name of the authoritative server for a domain.
PTR	Domain name.
SOA	Multiple fields that specify which parts of the naming hierarchy a server implements.
TXT	Uninterpreted string of ASCII text.

DNS software implements a client-server relationship between resolver client software operating in individual hosts and DNS server software operating in hosts designated as nameservers. Any number of hosts in an internet can function as nameservers, but typically at least two are required—a primary nameserver and one or more secondary nameservers. In large internets, the namespace can be partitioned and replicated to increase performance and availability.

DNS name translation operations can be either recursive or iterative. With recursive name resolution, a DNS client makes a request of a single nameserver for a name translation operation, and all the nameservers work together to satisfy it. With iterative name resolution, the DNS client resolver software is responsible for contacting all the nameservers that are required to resolve a name.

Chapter 8 begins Part III that discusses the protocols that operate in the TCP/IP Transport layer. Chapter 8 describes the User Datagram Protocol (UDP) that provides an unreliable, datagram data delivery service.

PART III

TRANSPORT LAYER PROTOCOLS

Chapter 8   User Datagram Protocol   Chapter 9   Transmission Control Protocol

User Datagram Protocol

Some TCP/IP applications require few services beyond the basic best-effort datagram delivery service that is provided by IP. Such an application can employ the *User Datagram Protocol* (UDP) Transport layer protocol.

UDP adds a Transport layer addressing mechanism to the underlying best-effort IP data delivery service provided by the TCP/IP Network layer. UDP delivers a data unit called a *user datagram* from an application process in the source host to an application process in the destination host. UDP uses the services of the underlying IP Network layer service to make a best-effort attempt to deliver each user datagram to its destination. UDP also adds a minimal reliability mechanism to the underlying connectionless IP delivery service in the form of an optional checksum. However, UDP makes no attempt to ensure that user datagrams are successfully delivered. Each user datagram is transported through an internet in a single IP datagram.

UDP CONNECTIONLESS SERVICE

The service that UDP provides is a connectionless data delivery service that can be thought of as a black box. The UDP user at one end inserts a user datagram into the black box. Then, if nothing goes wrong, an identical copy of the user datagram emerges from the black box at the other end and is received by the UDP user there, as illustrated in Fig. 8.1.

It is possible for the UDP service to lose user datagrams, to deliver them in a sequence different from that in which they were sent, or to duplicate them. Because it is possible for these errors to occur, UDP cannot be considered to provide a reliable service. The application itself must implement any required reliability controls when it uses the UDP Transport layer protocol.

An application that uses UDP is one that simply sends messages into the internet and does not need the TCP/IP communication software to tell it whether the messages were successfully received. Such an application may not care whether the message was received, or it might implement its own procedures for implementing end-to-end controls.

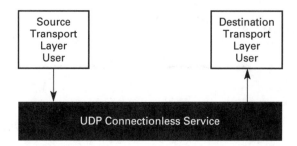

Figure 8.1   The UDP connectionless, best-efforts data transfer service.

UDP APPLICATIONS

Many types of applications can make use of the UDP connectionless data transfer service and have no need for the reliability controls implemented by TCP. Any type of distributed, client-server application that employs a simple request-response protocol is a candidate for UDP. The client application component makes a request, and the server application component sends back a response to the request. The fact that the server sends back a response is itself an acknowledgment that the server received the request. If the client does not receive a response within a period of time, it can resend the request.

An example of a client-server application that might make use of a connectionless data delivery service is one in which the client asks the server to send it the current date. Such a client-server application might use UDP to provide it with the data transfer services it requires. The client process asks for the date, and the server process sends it. The message containing the date itself functions as a positive acknowledgment. If the client receives the date, all is well; if the client does not receive the date after a certain time period, the client can request the date again. After a certain number of time-outs, the client might assume that the date server is not available. The reliability controls provided by a connection-oriented Transport layer protocol are not needed for such an application.

A number of application services employ UDP in performing their functions. Some of these, with their UDP port assignments, are listed in Box 8.1.

UDP USER DATAGRAM FORMAT

Box 8.2 shows the format of a UDP datagram and describes the fields in the UDP header. UDP datagrams are often called *user datagrams* to distinguish them from IP datagrams. UDP datagrams are carried through the internet encapsulated within IP datagrams.

UDP PROTOCOL MECHANISMS

A distinguishing feature of UDP is that it implements very few mechanisms over and above those provided by the underlying IP connectionless data transfer service. The following sections describe some of the mechanisms that are associated with UDP.

BOX 8.1   Application services that use UDP.

Service	Port	Service Description
Echo	7	Echos a received user datagram back to the sender.
Discard	9	Discards any user datagram that is received.
Daytime	13	Returns a date and time of day value.
Quote	17	Returns a character string containing a "quote of the day."
Chargen	19	Returns a character string of random length.
Nameserver	53	Domain Name Service nameserver process.
Bootps	67	Server port used to download configuration information.
Bootpc	68	Client port used to receive configuration information.
TFTP	69	Trivial File Transfer Protocol (TFTP) server process.
SunRPC	111	Used to implement the Sun RPC service.
NTP	123	Used to implement the Network Time Protocol (NTP).
SNMP	161	Used to receive SNMP network management queries.
SNMP	162	Used to receive SNMP problem reports.

BOX 8.2   User Datagram Protocol (UDP) user datagram format.

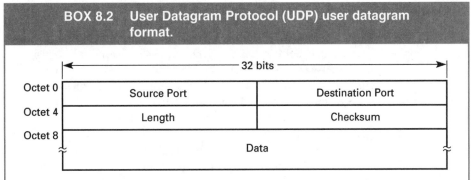

- **Source Port.** The number of the UDP port used by the process in the source host that originated the user datagram.
- **Destination Port.** The number of the UDP port used by the process in the destination host that is to receive the user datagram.
- **Length.** The total length, in octets, of the user datagram, including the header and the Data field.
- **Checksum.** A checksum value used in validating the fields in the user datagram.

UDP Error Checking

The only error checking provided by UDP is via the Checksum field. If the checksum value calculated by the receiving host does not agree with the checksum contained in the user datagram, the receiving host discards the user datagram.

UDP Overflows

A process that uses UDP for data transfer operations typically reserves buffer storage to hold a queue of user datagrams that arrive at the port used by the process. Typically, a server process that uses UDP to communicate with clients does not know how many user datagrams may be sent to it at any given time. If more user datagrams arrive at the server's port than the server is designed to handle, user datagrams are discarded.

A server component that uses UDP is not aware that user datagrams are overflowing its buffers, but the network administrator can issue the **netstat** command to determine if user datagrams are being discarded. The following is an example of such a **netstat** display:

```
netstat -s
udp:
     2 incomplete headers
     0 bad data length fields
     0 bad checksums
     27 socket overflows
```

SUMMARY

The User Datagram Protocol (UDP) is a Transport layer protocol that provides a connectionless, datagram data delivery service. UDP provides what must be considered an unreliable service because it is possible for user datagrams to be lost, duplicated, or delivered in a sequence different from that sent. Applications that implement a simple request-response protocol are possible candidates for UDP.

UDP delivers data units called user datagrams from a source Application layer process to a destination Application layer process. The fields in the header of a user datagram include the source port, the destination port, the length of the user datagram, and a checksum. UDP employs simple protocol mechanisms that add addressing mechanisms on top of the underlying connectionless IP data delivery service.

Chapter 9 examines TCP, UDP's companion Transport layer protocol, that provides a reliable, connection-oriented data delivery service.

Chapter 9

Transmission Control Protocol

While UDP is useful for some types of networking applications, many other applications require the communication software to accept the burden of providing a reliable, sequenced data transfer service. *Reliable* in this context means that the destination process either receives all messages sent or receives an indication that an error has occurred. *Sequenced* means that the service delivers octets to the receiver in the same sequence in which they were sent.

A reliable, sequenced data delivery service is often called a *connection-oriented* service. A connection-oriented data transfer service is one in which a logical association, called a *connection,* is formed between the Transport layer process in the source host and the Transport layer process in the destination host. The Transport layer protocol then performs all the end-to-end controls that are required to provide a reliable, sequenced data transfer service.

TCP CONNECTION-ORIENTED SERVICE

The *Transmission Control Protocol* (TCP) Transport layer protocol provides a connection-oriented data transfer service that transmits an unstructured stream of octets from a TCP port in the source host to a TCP port in the destination host. The TCP user at one end requests a connection, both the TCP protocol itself and the TCP user at the other end agree, and TCP establishes the connection.

The TCP data transfer service is a full-duplex data transfer service in which data can concurrently flow in both directions between the two communicating processes. The data transfer service provided by TCP can be viewed as a set of two pipes connecting the two TCP users—one pipe for a stream of octets flowing in one direction and the other for a stream of octets flowing in the opposite direction, as shown in Fig. 9.1.

The TCP user at one end inserts data into the appropriate pipe, and an identical copy of that data emerges at the other end. The user can hand the data to TCP in units of any desired size. For example, data can be passed one octet at a time or in the form of

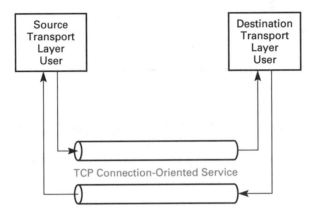

Figure 9.1   The TCP reliable, full-duplex data transfer service.

long messages. TCP does not assume that there is any structure to the data being transmitted. Octets inserted into the pipe simply emerge from the other end in the same sequence in which they were sent. With TCP, either an identical copy of the octet stream emerges from the pipe or the connection is released and the two TCP users are informed that a failure has occurred.

TCP APPLICATIONS

Many applications require the reliability controls that are provided by a connection-oriented data transfer protocol like TCP. For example, an application that implements a file transfer operation is well-suited for a connection-oriented Transport layer protocol. Two processes running in different hosts establish a connection, the data contained in a file flows over the connection from one process to the other, and the two processes then release the connection. A large amount of data flows between the two processes, and the reliability controls implemented by a connection-oriented Transport layer protocol are useful in ensuring the reliability of the data transfer operation.

A number of application services employ TCP in performing their functions. Some of these, with their TCP port assignments, are listed in Box 9.1. Note that TCP port number assignments are separate from the port assignments for UDP.

TCP SEGMENT FORMAT

TCP provides a stream-oriented data transfer service in which the application processes that are communicating view the data being transferred as a continuous stream of octets. However, the TCP protocol breaks the octet stream for transmission into a series of data units called *segments*. Segments are encapsulated in IP datagrams for transmission using the services of IP. TCP itself does not impose any structure on the data being transmitted,

BOX 9.1 Application services that use TCP.		
Service	**Port**	**Service Description**
Discard	9	Service that discards any user data that is received.
Chargen	19	Service that returns a character string of random length.
FTP	20	Used to implement FTP file transfer operations.
FTP	21	Used to implement FTP control procedures.
Telnet	23	Used to implement the Telnet remote login service.
SMTP	25	Used to implement the SMTP Email service.
X400	103	Used to implement the X400 Email service.

and the segment structure of the data is transparent to the two TCP users, who can view the transmitted data as a continuous stream.

Box 9.2 shows the format of a TCP segment and describes the fields in the segment header. Segments can be of any desired size. Octets that are transferred from one TCP user to another appear at the destination host in the same sequence in which they were sent. With TCP, either an identical copy of the data stream appears at the destination, or the connection is released and the two TCP users are informed that a failure has occurred.

TCP PROTOCOL MECHANISMS

There are a number of mechanisms that TCP uses in providing a reliable, sequenced data transfer service. Some of these are described in the sections that follow.

Connection Establishment

When a TCP user in the source host requests a connection with a TCP user in the destination host, the TCP process in the source host sends a connection request message to the TCP process in the destination host. This begins a procedure called a *handshake,* in which the characteristics of the connection are specified and the connection is established.

In order for TCP to establish a connection, the source TCP user must specify the internet address of the destination host and the port number associated with the destination TCP user. Assuming the TCP process in the destination host can accept the connection, it continues the handshake procedure by sending back an acknowledgment message. The source host then sends its own acknowledgment message to confirm that the connection has been established. As part of the handshake procedure, the two hosts agree on initial sequence numbers to use, based on sequence numbers included in the connection request and acknowledgment messages.

Data Transfer

Once a TCP connection has been established, TCP implements a full-duplex path between a pair of users of the TCP protocol. TCP transfers data from transmit buffers in

BOX 9.2   Transmission Control Protocol (TCP) segment format.

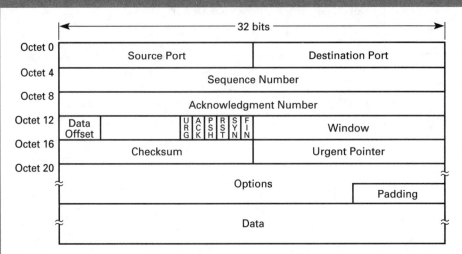

- **Source Port.** The number of the TCP port assigned to the process in the source host that originated the segment.

- **Destination Port.** The number of the TCP port assigned to the process in the destination host that is to receive the segment.

- **Sequence Number.** Indicates the octet sequence number of the first octet of data contained in the Data field.

- **Acknowledgment Number.** Indicates the octet sequence number of the data octet that is expected to be received from the partner host.

- **Data Offset.** The length of the TCP header measured in 32-bit words. Padding is used between the TCP header and the Data field to ensure that the Data field begins on a 32-bit word boundary.

- **Flags.** Bits used to control the operation of the protocol.

- **Window.** A receive window size value used to implement flow control procedures.

- **Checksum.** A checksum value used in validating the fields in the segment.

- **Options.** Fields used to implement protocol options. The only option field defined at the time of writing is a 32-bit maximum segment size field. This field is encoded in the form of a 16-bit introducer followed by a 16-bit maximum segment size value, thus allowing for a segment size up to 65,535 octets.

the sending host to receive buffers in the destination host over a TCP connection. The source and destination TCP processes use the services of the underlying IP protocol to exchange TCP segments, and segments are encapsulated in IP datagrams for transmission. As described earlier, TCP provides its users with a stream-oriented data transfer service, and the segment structure of the information that is actually transferred over a TCP connection is transparent to the two TCP users.

Error Detection and Retransmission

TCP provides detection and recovery from loss, duplication, corruption, and misordering of IP datagrams that might occur in lower layers. It employs send sequence numbers and an acknowledgment mechanism to ensure that all segments are delivered without error and in the proper sequence.

Each segment sent contains a Sequence Number field that indicates the octet position in the overall data stream of the data contained in that segment. The TCP process in the receiving host checks the Sequence Number field value in each received segment to ensure that there are no missing, duplicated, or out-of-sequence segments.

As the recipient sends data back, it includes an Acknowledgment Number field value in each segment that indicates the sequence number of the octet position of the next octet it expects to receive. This acknowledges successful receipt of all octets in the data stream prior to the octet identified in the Acknowledgment Number field.

TCP also employs a retransmission timer to detect lost segments that are caused by errors occurring in lower layers. When each segment is sent, the TCP process in the sending host starts the retransmission timer. If the timer expires before that segment is acknowledged, the sender retransmits the segment. Since TCP transmission is full duplex, each TCP user keeps track of sequence numbers for data it is sending and for data it has received.

TCP also uses checksums for error detection. A checksum value is calculated and included in each segment that is sent. When a segment is received, the recipient calculates a checksum value. If the calculated value does not agree with the value contained in the segment, the segment is discarded. Since the erroneous segment is not acknowledged, the sender eventually times out and retransmits the segment.

Flow Control

TCP also uses acknowledgments to implement flow control procedures to balance the relative speeds of the sender and the receiver. The flow control mechanism is imposed on the sending TCP process by the receiving TCP process. When a connection is established, a window size is agreed upon for transmission in each direction. The window size specifies the number of octets that the sender is allowed to transmit before receiving an acknowledgment. Each acknowledgment that is returned also contains a new window size value that determines the number of octets that can be sent before the next acknowledgment. The window values in acknowledgments can be adjusted upward or downward to respond to changing conditions in the network.

Congestion Control

Congestion occurs when an internet, or part of an internet, is overloaded and has insufficient communication resources for the volume of traffic it is experiencing. TCP contains mechanisms that reduce the load on an internet to prevent congestion from occurring and to reduce congestion should it occur. The congestion control mechanisms are imposed on the receiving TCP process by the sending TCP process.

Connection Release

A TCP connection can be released at any time by either of the TCP users or by the TCP service itself. When a TCP user requests the connection release, it should ensure that any data octets in transit have been successfully received before requesting the connection release. To release the connection, a host sends a message indicating that it has no more data to send. The other host returns an acknowledgment message, and no further data can be sent in that direction. When the other TCP user is finished sending data, it closes its end of the connection in a similar manner.

SUMMARY

The Transmission Control Protocol (TCP) is a Transport layer protocol that provides a full-duplex, connection-oriented, stream data delivery service. TCP provides a reliable service that detects and recovers from lost, duplicated, and missequenced data. Applications that require the Transport layer to handle reliability controls are possible candidates for TCP.

TCP delivers data units called segments from a source TCP Transport protocol port to a destination TCP Transport protocol port. The Application layer processes employing TCP are not aware of the segment structure of the data and perceive a continuous octet stream. The fields in the header of a TCP segment include the source port, the destination port, a sequence number, an acknowledgment number, a data offset, flag bits, the window size, checksum, and option fields. TCP employs protocol mechanisms to detect and recover from transmission errors, including connection establishment, data transfer, error detection, retransmission, flow control, congestion control, and connection release.

Chapter 10 begins Part IV that examines the TCP/IP protocols operating in the Internet layer. Chapter 10 looks at the Internet Protocol (IP) that provides the routing and relaying functions required to deliver data from a source host to a destination host.

PART IV

INTERNET LAYER PROTOCOLS

Chapter 10   Internet Protocol

Chapter 11   ARP and RARP Address
             Resolution

Chapter 12   Internet Control Message
             Protocol

Chapter 13   Routing Protocols

Internet Protocol

The *Internet Protocol* (IP) is one of the major protocols after which the TCP/IP protocol suite is named. IP runs in the TCP/IP Internet layer and is responsible for moving data units from a source host to a destination host. The source and destination hosts can be on the same physical network, or they can be on different physical networks that are connected via routers. IP is responsible for making what might be a complex internet look to all the hosts as if the internet were a single, integrated network rather than a collection of individual physical networks. This chapter describes the functions of IP in a TCP/IP internet.

An IP process operates in each host and router that lies in the path over which a message travels from the source host to the destination host. The main job of IP is to make the topology of the internet, and the physical characteristics of each of the individual networks making up the internet, transparent to the hosts that are exchanging data. A host can send data units any other host in an internet without having to be aware of the physical details concerning the routers and data links that each data unit must traverse in reaching its destination.

IP USERS

A user of IP is typically a higher-level data transfer service implemented by one of the protocols running in the TCP/IP Transport layer. The unit of data that a Transport layer process passes down to IP is called an *IP datagram*. An IP datagram is sometimes called a *packet*. Among other things, the header attached to an IP datagram contains the internet address of the source host and the internet address of the destination host. The main function of IP is to move an IP datagram from the source host to the destination host.

IP CONNECTIONLESS SERVICE

IP provides a connectionless, best-effort data delivery service. The Transport layer process running in the source host passes an IP datagram down to IP. The IP datagram contains the internet address of the destination host to which the IP datagram is to be sent. IP processes running in the source host and in all the routers in the path that lies between the source host and the destination host cooperate in delivering the IP datagram to the destination host. If the IP datagram is successfully delivered, the IP process running in the destination host passes the IP datagram up to a Transport layer process there.

No sequence checking is done to ensure that IP datagrams are received in the same sequence in which they were sent, and the receiving host sends no acknowledgment that it has received an IP datagram. No flow control or error recovery is provided as part of the IP datagram delivery service. IP makes routing decisions *independently* for each IP datagram, and each IP datagram may possibly flow over a different path through the internet.

The service that IP provides to its users can be thought of as a black box. The Transport layer process at one end inserts an IP datagram into the black box. Then, if nothing goes wrong, an identical copy of the IP datagram emerges from the black box at the other end and is received by the Transport layer process there, as shown in Fig. 10.1. IP provides a service to a Transport layer protocol that is similar to the service that UDP provides to an application program.

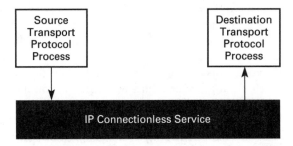

Figure 10.1 The IP connectionless, best-efforts data transfer service.

As with any connectionless data transfer service, there are three things that can go wrong during the operation of IP, as shown in Fig. 10.2.

- **Lost IP datagrams.** It is possible for IP to occasionally lose an IP datagram. For example, a router may become congested and may temporarily begin discarding IP datagrams. Or a transmission error may occur in transmitting an IP datagram, causing the datagram to be lost. When IP discards or loses an IP datagram neither the source nor the destination Transport layer process is explicitly notified of the lost IP datagram; the IP datagram simply does not arrive at the destination.

- **Out-of-Sequence IP datagrams.** It is possible for each IP datagram to take a different path through the internet, and each IP datagram may take a different amount of time to arrive at its destination. If the Transport layer process in the source host sends a number

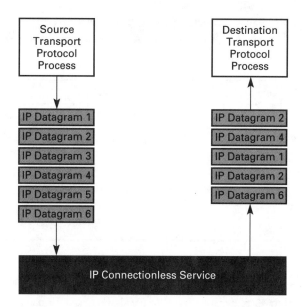

Figure 10.2   Losing, missequencing, and duplicating IP datagrams.

of IP datagrams, they may arrive at the other end in a sequence different from the sequence in which they were sent.

- **Duplicate IP datagrams.** Duplicate IP datagrams can also be received. For example, a sending Transport layer process might employ a timer to help determine if an IP datagram that it has sent has been received. If the timer expires before the sending Transport layer process receives an acknowledgment, it might send the IP datagram again. In some cases, the timer might expire while an acknowledgment is still in transit, thus causing duplicate IP datagrams to arrive at the destination.

Because it is possible for the above errors to occur, IP cannot be considered to provide a reliable service. If a reliable data transfer service is required by the application, a protocol running in the Transport layer (such as TCP) must be responsible for detecting lost IP datagrams and requesting their retransmission, placing the IP datagrams into their proper sequence, and detecting and discarding duplicate IP datagrams.

IP DATAGRAM FORMAT

Box 10.1 shows the format of the IP datagram and describes the fields in the IP datagram header.

IP PROTOCOL MECHANISMS

The Internet protocol employs two important protocol mechanisms in moving an IP datagram from a source host to a destination host—*routing* and *segmentation*. The following sections describe these two mechanisms.

BOX 10.1   IP datagram format.

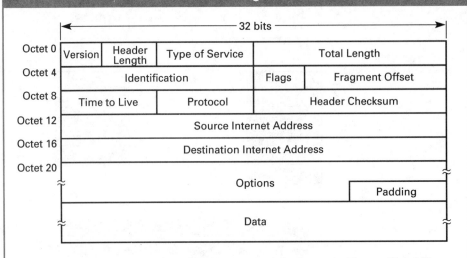

- **Version.** Identifies the version of IP that generated the datagram. The version of IP current at the time of writing is 4. A datagram having a version number different from 4 is discarded.

- **Header Length.** The length, in octets, of the IP header.

- **Type of Service.** An 8-bit code that indicates the quality of service that is desired for the datagram.

- **Total Length.** The length, in octets, of the entire datagram, including the header and the Data field.

- **Identification, Flags, and Fragment Offset.** Fields used to handle segmentation and reassembly if it is required.

- **Time to Live.** A value that indicates how long the datagram can remain in the internet before being discarded. This value is decremented by each router that processes the datagram. If the value reaches 0 before the datagram reaches the destination host, the datagram is discarded.

- **Protocol.** Identifies the higher-level protocol with which the datagram is associated. The following are some common values for the Protocol field:
  — 1 = The IP datagram carries an ICMP message
  — 6 = The IP datagram carries a TCP segment
  — 17 = The IP datagram carries a UDP user datagram

- **Header Checksum.** Used to check the data in the IP header itself in a received packet to ensure that the header was not damaged during transmission.

- **Source and Destination Internet Addresses.** Address fields that identify the source and destination hosts. The source and destination internet addresses are passed to IP along with the packet to be transmitted and are used by IP for routing.

- **Options.** Up to 40 octets of additional information used to control functions such as routing and security.

Routing

IP runs a distributed routing algorithm, functions of which operate in all the hosts and routers in the internet. The Internet protocol routing function is responsible for moving each IP datagram from the source host to the destination host, no matter how many routers the IP datagram may have to traverse in getting to the correct destination host. Each router that processes an IP datagram during its trip through the internet must decide the next hop the IP datagram should take in traveling to its final destination. The IP routing function is described further later in this chapter.

Segmentation

An individual physical network may place an upper limit on the size of the transmission frame that it can support. For example, an Ethernet LAN limits the data portion of a frame to 1500 octets. The IP *segmentation* function is responsible for breaking large IP datagrams into segments that will fit within a given network's maximum frame size. The IP process in the destination host then reassembles the segments to recreate the original IP datagram. The segmentation process is sometimes called *fragmentation* in TCP/IP literature.

IP ROUTING

The routing function in a TCP/IP internet has the responsibility of determining the path over which each IP datagram travels from a source host to a destination host. A Transport layer protocol running in a host invokes the services of that host's IP process to move IP datagrams between the source host and the destination host. A Transport layer process is involved in data delivery only in the source and destination hosts. In contrast, an IP process is involved in data delivery in the source and destination hosts and in all the routers along the path between the source and destination hosts, as illustrated in Fig. 10.3.

An important point in understanding the IP routing function is that routing is concerned with delivering IP datagrams to a destination *network* and not to a partic-

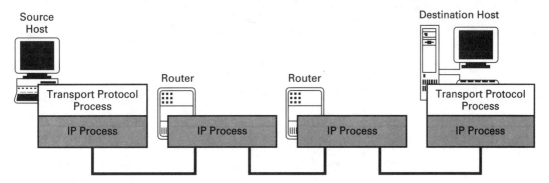

Figure 10.3   Transport protocol processes and IP processes.

ular destination *host*. Routing in a TCP/IP internet is based on the characteristic of the internet address that allows a host to quickly determine the physical network referenced by an internet address. Once the IP routing function delivers an IP datagram to a router on the destination network, another IP function directly delivers the IP datagram to a destination host on that physical network.

Each host uses the Address Resolution Protocol (ARP) to maintain an ARP cache that contains entries that describe mappings between internet addresses and physical hardware addresses for hosts on the same physical network. If the host or router running the IP process has not contacted a destination host previously, there will be no entry in the ARP cache for that destination host. ARP is then used to determine the destination host's physical hardware address. The role of ARP and the ARP cache are described further in Chapter 11.

IP may also use the services of the Internet Control Message Protocol (ICMP), described in Chapter 12, to inform hosts and routers about better routes to use.

Sample Internet

We will use the small internet shown in Fig. 10.4, which consists of three physical networks implemented using LAN technology that are interconnected using a single router. The network administrator has assigned network identifier values to each of the physical networks and also a unique internet address to each network interface card (NIC) that implements a point of physical attachment to the internet. Each host has a single NIC, and the router has three NICs, one for each of the physical networks to which it is attached.

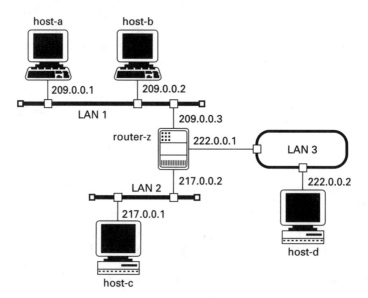

Figure 10.4   Simple internet.

IP Routing in a Host

The routing that needs to be done by an ordinary host is simple. Assume that a source host has an IP datagram to deliver. It examines the destination address contained in the IP datagram header and extracts from it the address of the physical network to which the IP datagram is destined. Two possibilities exist:

- If the source host determines that the destination network address contained in the IP datagram header is the same as its own network address, the source host delivers the IP datagram directly to the destination host.
- If the source host determines that the destination network address is different from its own network address, the source host uses the IP routing function to forward the IP datagram to a router on its own physical network that can move the IP datagram closer to its destination.

Routing Tables

Each host maintains a routing table that it uses to determine the best next destination for each IP datagram it processes that must be sent to some other physical network. The routing table must have at least one entry—an entry containing the address of a *default router*. A host's default router is assigned when the TCP/IP communication software is configured for that host.

When a host has an IP datagram to deliver in which the destination internet address refers to some other physical network, the host consults the routing table to see if it has an entry matching the address of the destination network. If the routing table has no entry corresponding to the destination network, the host sends the IP datagram to the default router. Each host directly delivers all IP datagrams destined for hosts on its own LAN and initially forwards all other IP datagrams to the default router.

In the small internet shown in Fig. 10.4, the router is directly attached to all three LANs, and each host uses the same default router. Therefore, when the router receives an IP datagram that has been forwarded to it from one of the other hosts, it extracts the network address from the destination internet address, selects the appropriate physical network, and delivers the IP datagram directly to the appropriate host.

Datagram Delivery on the Same Physical Network

Let us see how IP datagram delivery works on the same physical network by seeing how host A delivers an IP datagram to host B. When IP receives an IP datagram, it examines the destination address contained in the IP datagram header. IP uses the subnet mask to examine the destination internet address and to extract the address bits that identify the physical network to which the IP datagram is destined. IP next compares the network ID value in the IP datagram's destination address with the network ID value in host A's own internet address. If the two values are equal, as they are in our example, the IP datagram is destined for a host on host A's own physical network. Therefore, host A's IP function can deliver this IP datagram directly.

To directly deliver an IP datagram to host B, which host A has determined is on its own local area network, host A's IP process looks in its ARP cache to see if it already has an entry corresponding to the destination address contained in the IP datagram, in this case 209.0.0.2. This entry, if it exists, allows host A to find host B's physical hardware address. Host A uses this physical hardware address to directly deliver the IP datagram to host B.

Datagram Delivery on a Different Physical Network

Let us now see how IP handles the delivery of an IP datagram that is destined for a host on some other physical network by seeing how an IP datagram is delivered from host A to host D.

Again, the IP process in host A uses its subnet mask to compare the network ID value in the IP datagram to host A's own internet address. This time the network ID values are different, and IP must use its routing function to forward the IP datagram to a router on its own physical network. The IP process in host A looks for an entry in its routing table that matches the network ID value in the IP datagram's destination address. In this case, the routing table has no matching entry, so it uses the default entry to determine the address of the router to use.

The IP process in host A again uses the ARP cache to determine the physical hardware address of the default router. It then forwards the IP datagram to that router. When the router receives this IP datagram, it extracts the network ID value from the destination internet address. The IP function in the router uses the network ID value to select the physical network to which the IP datagram is destined. The router then uses its ARP cache to find the physical hardware address of the destination host. The router then delivers the IP datagram directly to host D.

Traversing Multiple Routers

Routing becomes somewhat more involved as the topology of the network increases in complexity. For example, Fig. 10.5 shows an internet consisting of three LAN data links that are interconnected using four routers and two point-to-point telecommunications data links.

With this internet, the routing function that must be performed by host A is still simple. Host A directly delivers all IP datagrams that are destined for hosts on LAN 1 and delivers all other IP datagrams to router W. Let us see what is involved in sending an IP datagram from host A to host C.

The IP function running in host A uses its ARP cache to directly deliver all IP datagrams that are destined for hosts on host A's own LAN. The IP function in host A uses its routing table to determine the next hop for all IP datagrams destined for other networks. In sending an IP datagram from host A to host C, host A uses its routing table to locate the internet address of router W, host A's default router, and forwards the IP datagram there. Router W's routing table tells the IP process in router W to forward the IP datagram to router X. Router X's routing table tells the IP process in router X to forward the

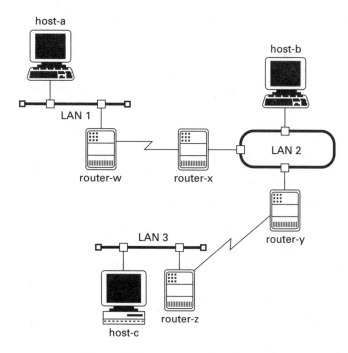

Figure 10.5   A more complex internet.

IP datagram to router Y. Router Y's routing table tells the IP process in router Y to forward the IP datagram to router Z. Router Z determines that the destination host is on router Z's own physical network, so router Z uses its ARP cache to determine host C's physical hardware address and then delivers the IP datagram to host C.

In each host and router, the routing function remains simple, but there are more intermediate steps involved as the internet increases in size and complexity. The IP functions in host A and in all the routers between host A and host C cooperate in delivering the IP datagram to its destination.

ROUTER ROUTING TABLES

The IP routing function is sufficiently powerful to allow individual hosts to maintain their own routing tables. However, a host needs to know only about the routers attached to its own physical network. Once a host delivers an IP datagram to a router, it is the responsibility of all the routers in the internet to work together in delivering the IP datagram to its destination.

The routing tables maintained by routers need to have a more global view of the network than the routing tables maintained by hosts. Therefore, routers typically run specialized routing protocols in addition to IP that allow them to keep their routing tables up-to-date. Routing protocols are discussed in Chapter 13.

SUMMARY

The Internet Protocol (IP) is an Internet layer protocol that provides a connectionless, datagram data delivery service to a process operating in the Transport layer. An IP process operates in each host and router that lies in the path over which data travels from a source host to a destination host.

TCP delivers data units called IP datagrams, sometimes called packets, from a source Transport layer process to a destination Transport layer process. The fields in the header of an IP datagram include a version number, the length of the header, the type of service, the length of the IP datagram, identification, flags, fragment offset, time to live, higher-level protocol, header checksum, source internet address, destination internet address, and options. IP employs protocol mechanisms to handle routing and segmentation functions.

The IP routing function is responsible for delivering an IP datagram to a destination network. IP then uses the host's ARP cache, running ARP if necessary, to deliver the IP datagram to the destination host. The IP function in a host or router uses a routing table to determine the next hop for each IP datagram it delivers.

Chapter 11 examines the functions provided by the Address Resolution Protocol (ARP) and the Reverse Address Resolution Protocol (RARP) in converting between internet address and physical hardware addresses.

Chapter **11**

ARP and RARP Address Resolution

Two protocols that operate in the TCP/IP Internet layer are involved in converting between internet address and physical hardware addresses. The *Address Resolution Protocol* (ARP) accepts an internet address and returns the physical hardware address of the network interface card (NIC) associated with that internet address. The Reverse Address Resolution Protocol (RARP) performs the reverse conversion. It accepts the physical hardware address of a NIC and returns the internet address by which that NIC should be known in the internet.

ADDRESS RESOLUTION PROTOCOL

ARP is a protocol that is used by IP in helping it to route IP datagrams to the correct destination host. It can be used by IP in a source host to help it deliver an IP datagram to a host or router on the same physical network as the source host.

Physical Hardware Addresses

On a typical individual physical network, such as a LAN data link, each host contains one or more NICs so that each has at least one unique physical hardware address associated with it. With local area networks, each NIC has a unique station address assigned to it in the hardware.

Local area networks that conform to the IEEE/ISO LAN architecture typically use a 48-bit *MAC address,* or *station address* that uniquely identifies each NIC. However, the IEEE/ISO LAN architecture also permits the use of 16-bit station addresses, and the vendors of proprietary LAN equipment often define their own individual station addressing schemes. Therefore, ARP must be capable of working with physical hardware addresses in any desired format. The IEEE/ISO LAN architecture and LAN and WAN physical hardware addressing are discussed further in Appendix A.

Internet Addresses

As we discussed in Chapters 4 and 10, a portion of a host's internet address uniquely identifies the physical network to which the host is attached. Therefore, the IP process running in a host can examine the destination internet address in an IP datagram and can easily determine the identity of the individual physical network to which the packet should be sent. However, a host's internet address may have no direct relationship to the host's physical hardware address. When the IP process running in one host wishes to deliver data to another host on its own network, it may know the internet address of the destination host, but it may not yet know the host's physical hardware address, which is needed by the Data Link layer for transmission over a data link.

Mapping Internet Addresses to Physical Hardware Addresses

In some cases, it is possible to provide each host on a network with a table that maps the internet addresses of all the hosts and routers on that network to their associated physical hardware addresses. However, most LANs use a 48-bit MAC address as a physical hardware address and permit a great many devices to be attached to an individual LAN. Such a LAN may be constantly changing as some users turn their machines off or remove them from the LAN and as other users attach new hosts to the LAN. For such a situation, a dynamic scheme is required that allows hosts to automatically maintain tables that are used to convert internet addresses into their associated physical hardware addresses. This is the function of ARP, as shown in Fig. 11.1.

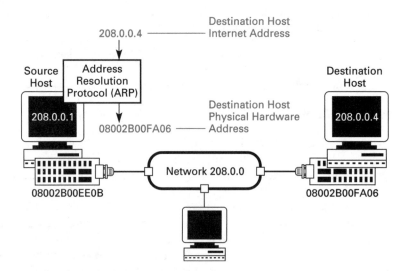

Figure 11.1   ARP conversion from an internet address to a physical hardware address.

ARP Operation

As we described in Chapter 10, when the IP process running in a source host is sending an IP datagram to a destination host, it examines the destination internet address in the IP datagram and determines whether the IP datagram is destined for a host on its own physical network or whether it is destined for a host on some other network. If the IP datagram is destined for a host on its own network, the IP process running in that host delivers the IP datagram directly; if the IP datagram is destined for a host on some other network, it sends it to a router.

To make direct delivery possible, each host maintains an *ARP cache* containing the mappings of internet addresses to physical hardware addresses for the hosts on its own physical network that it currently knows about. When the IP process running in a host needs to deliver an IP datagram to a host or router on its own LAN, it looks up the destination internet address in its ARP cache. If the cache has an entry for that internet address, IP retrieves the associated physical hardware address in that ARP cache entry and delivers the IP datagram to the NIC having that physical hardware address.

When a host or router is first powered up, its ARP cache is empty. Assume that the IP process in host A is attempting to deliver an IP datagram to host B but that host B's internet address is not yet in host A's ARP cache. In such a situation, IP runs ARP to determine host B's physical hardware address.

The following steps are performed to determine host B's physical hardware address:

1. The ARP process running in host A broadcasts on the LAN an ARP Request packet containing host B's internet address.

2. The ARP processes running in all the hosts on the LAN receive the ARP Request packet.

3. Host B recognizes its own internet address in the ARP Request packet and replies to the host that sent the ARP Request packet with an ARP Response packet containing host B's physical hardware address.

4. When host A receives the ARP Response packet from host B, host A stores host B's internet address to physical hardware address mapping in its ARP cache.

5. The IP process running in host A can now use the information in the new ARP cache entry to determine host B's physical hardware address and can directly deliver the IP datagram to host B.

Anticipating Reverse Traffic

There is a refinement to ARP that reduces the network traffic associated with running the protocol. This refinement is based on the assumption that it is likely that when host A has data to send to host B, host B may later need to send data back to host A. In anticipation of this likelihood, when the ARP process running in host A sends an ARP Request packet asking for host B's physical hardware address, host A also places into that ARP Request packet its own internet address to physical hardware address mapping. When host B receives host A's ARP Request packet, host B adds an entry for host A into its own ARP cache. This eliminates the necessity of the IP process in host B having to run ARP should it later have to send data back to host A.

ARP PACKET FORMAT

Box 11.1 shows the format of the ARP Request and Response packets and describes their fields. ARP is designed so that it can be employed with a variety of networking protocols and with any type of data link. The fields shown in Box 11.1 assume that ARP is being used on an IEEE/ISO LAN data link in a TCP/IP internet.

BOX 11.1 ARP packet format.

	← 32 bits →
Octet 0	Physical Hardware Address Type / Internet Layer Addressing Protocol
Octet 4	Physical Hardware Address Length / Internet Layer Address Length / Message Type (0001=Request; 0002=Response
Octet 8	Source Physical Hardware Address
Octet 12	Source Internet Address
Octet 16	Source Internet Address (Continued)
Octet 20	Destination Physical Hardware Address
Octet 24	Destination Internet Address

- **Physical Hardware Address Type.** Identifies the type of physical hardware address that is employed to identify network interface cards (NICs) on the network.
- **Internet Layer Addressing Protocol.** Identifies the protocol operating in the layer above the Network Interface layer or the OSI Data Link layer that is using ARP. This field allows ARP to be used by protocols other than IP.
- **Physical Hardware Address Length.** Indicates the number of octets contained in the Source and Destination Physical Hardware Address fields.
- **Internet Layer Address Length.** Indicates the number of octets contained in the Source and Destination Internet Layer Address fields.
- **Source Physical Hardware Address.** Contains the physical hardware address of the NIC in the source system.
- **Source Internet Address.** Contains the internet address assigned to the NIC in the source system.
- **Destination Physical Hardware Address.** Contains the physical hardware address of the NIC in the destination system.
- **Destination Internet Address.** Contains the internet address assigned to the NIC in the destination system.

ARP EXAMPLE

We will next use the simplified internet shown in Fig. 11.2 to show how IP uses ARP to support the requests that users make for Application layer services. We will assume that host A has just been powered up, which means that its ARP cache is empty, and that a user enters the following **telnet** command to begin a Telnet session with host D:

```
telnet host-d
```

Host A's Telnet software begins by using the name resolution function to determine the internet address associated with the host name specified in the **telnet** command.

In this simple internet, **hosts** files are used for name resolution.

The name resolution function in host A searches its **hosts** file for an entry for host D, the host referenced in the **telnet** command. This entry contains the internet address of host D. The Telnet software in host A now knows host D's internet address and next attempts to establish a TCP connection with host D. Host A's Telnet software starts this procedure by sending host D an IP datagram containing a Connect Request message asking for the establishment of a TCP connection. The destination address field in the Connect Request IP datagram contains host D's internet address.

The IP function in host A begins the process of sending the Connect Request message by using the subnet mask to extract the network ID value from the destination internet address. IP determines that this network ID value is different from host A's own network ID value. Therefore, the Connect Request IP datagram is destined for some other physical network, and host A must use its routing function to forward the Connect Request message to a router that will bring the IP datagram closer to its destination.

The IP process in host A begins the routing function by searching its routing table for a network identifier that is equal to the network identifier extracted from the destina-

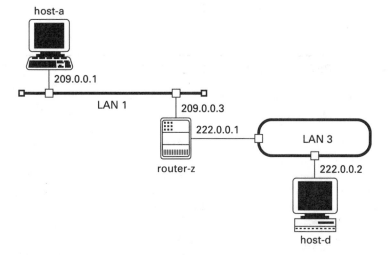

Figure 11.2   Simplified internet.

tion address contained in the Connect Request IP datagram. Since host A has just powered up, its routing table now contains only an entry for the default router. So IP forwards the Connect Request IP datagram to the default router.

Since the default router is on host A's own physical network, the IP function in host A can directly deliver the Connect Request IP datagram. To do this, host A searches its local ARP cache for an entry containing the default router's internet address. However, since host A has just powered up, its ARP cache is empty, and host A does not yet know the physical address of the default router.

In order to build the required ARP cache entry, host A now uses ARP to determine the physical hardware address of the default router. The ARP function in host A generates an ARP Request packet that contains the default router's internet address, which IP obtained from the routing table. It then broadcasts the ARP Request packet to all the devices on the LAN. The default router receives the ARP Request packet and determines that the internet address contained in the packet matches its own internet address. The default router replies to the ARP Request packet with an ARP Response packet directed to host A. This packet contains the default router's physical hardware address.

When the ARP function in host A receives the default router's ARP Response packet, it adds the address of the default router to its ARP cache. Host A now knows the physical hardware address of the default router, and it can now forward to the default router the original Connect Request message that asked for the establishment of a TCP connection. The IP function operating in the default router now finally delivers the Connect Request IP datagram to host D. Host D then sends a positive acknowledgment to the Connect Request message. When host A accepts host D's positive acknowledgment, it sends a positive acknowledgment of its own back to host D, and the TCP connection is established.

The remote host and the local host can now use the active TCP connection to conduct their Telnet dialog as if there were a simple point-to-point connection between them. IP datagrams are moved through the internet using the IP routing function running in hosts and routers.

REVERSE ADDRESS RESOLUTION PROTOCOL

A protocol related to ARP, but used for the opposite purpose, is the *Reverse Address Resolution Protocol* (RARP). RARP allows a host that knows only its physical hardware address to obtain the internet address that it should use in communicating with other hosts. RARP is typically of use only to hosts on a LAN data link that do not implement disk storage, often called *diskless workstations*. Terminals that implement the X Windows protocols—sometimes called *X Terminals*—may also use RARP to obtain their internet addresses. Such workstations or terminals typically implement file transfer code in read only memory (ROM) that allows them to download their operating system and TCP/IP communication software from some other host on the LAN.

The operating system and communication software that a particular diskless workstation downloads is generally identical to the code that other diskless workstations on the LAN download. The operating system and communication software image that diskless terminals and workstations obtain does not typically contain a separate internet address for each diskless workstation on the LAN. Diskless terminals and workstations typically implement RARP in ROM that allows them to obtain an internet address.

RARP Operation

In order for RARP to operate, at least one host on the LAN must be designated as a RARP server. A diskless workstation obtains an internet address by broadcasting on the LAN a RARP Request packet giving the workstation's physical hardware address. RARP uses a packet that is similar in format to the packet used by ARP. The RARP packet asks any RARP server on the LAN to send back the internet address that is associated with that physical hardware address.

A RARP server maintains a table that maps the physical hardware addresses of the diskless workstations it serves to the internet addresses that those diskless workstations should use. When a RARP server receives a RARP Request packet from a diskless workstation asking for an internet address, it looks up the physical hardware address in its table, obtains the internet address corresponding to that physical hardware address, and replies with a RARP Response packet containing the internet address that the diskless workstation should use.

SUMMARY

The Address Resolution Protocol (ARP) and the Reverse Address Resolution Protocol (RARP) operate in the Internet layer and convert between internet addresses and physical hardware addresses.

ARP is used by IP in a host or router to help it deliver IP datagrams to another host or router on the same physical network. ARP maintains an ARP cache that contains the results of the most recent operations that ARP performed to translate internet addresses to physical hardware addresses. To add an entry to the ARP cache for a destination system that has not been contacted for a period of time, ARP multicasts an ARP Request packet containing the destination system's internet address. The ARP Request packet also contains information about the source system's own internet address and physical hardware address in anticipation of reverse traffic. The host or router with the indicated destination internet address replies with an ARP Response packet containing its physical hardware address.

RARP services are provided by one or more hosts designated as RARP servers. A diskless workstation sends a RARP Request packet containing the workstation's physical hardware address to a RARP server. The RARP server sends the workstation a RARP Response packet containing the workstation's internet address.

Chapter 12 describes the Internet Control Message Protocol (ICMP) that allows hosts and routers to report on error conditions and to provide information about unexpected circumstances.

Chapter **12**

Internet Control Message Protocol

The *Internet Control Message Protocol* (ICMP) is another protocol that operates in the Internet layer. Its purpose is to allow hosts and routers to report on error conditions and to provide information about unexpected circumstances. Although ICMP is viewed as residing in the Internet layer, ICMP messages travel through the internet enclosed in IP datagrams. Therefore, ICMP uses the IP best-effort delivery service in a similar manner to a Transport layer protocol in moving ICMP messages through the internet, as illustrated in Fig. 12.1.

USES FOR ICMP

The following are some of the most common purposes for which ICMP is used by hosts and routers:

- A host or router can determine whether another host or router is currently reachable.
- A router can inform a source host that there is a better route that it can use in sending subsequent IP datagrams to a particular destination network.
- A host or router can tell another system that IP datagrams are arriving too fast for the host or router to process them.

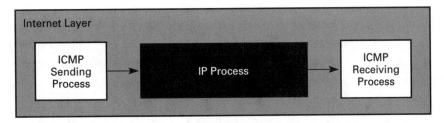

Figure 12.1   The IP connectionless, best-efforts data transfer service.

- A host or router can tell another system that it has received a bad IP datagram, such as one that has exceeded the amount of time it is allowed to exist in the internet or one that has incorrect parameter information in its header.

- Hosts can exchange messages that are used to synchronize their clocks.

- Hosts can exchange messages that inform each other of the specific formats of their internet addresses, indicating how many bits are used to identify the network and how many are used to identify individual hosts.

ICMP GENERAL MESSAGE FORMAT

As discussed earlier, ICMP messages are carried within IP datagrams and are transmitted through the internet using the services of IP. As shown in Chapter 10, a value of 1 in the Protocol field of an IP datagram header indicates that the IP datagram is carrying an ICMP message.

There are a number of different types of ICMP messages, each having a different format. However, the first three fields of all ICMP messages are the same. The common fields in all ICMP messages are shown in Box 12.1.

ICMP MESSAGE TYPES

A variety of ICMP message types are defined. They can be divided into two categories—*ICMP error messages* and *ICMP query messages*. The following sections describe some of the most commonly used messages in each of the two ICMP message categories.

ICMP ERROR MESSAGES

The most common use of ICMP is in reporting on various types of error conditions. A host or router returns an ICMP error message if it determines that an error or exceptional condition has occurred during the delivery or attempted delivery of an IP datagram. Some of the different types of conditions that result in an ICMP error message are as follows:

- **Destination Unreachable.** An IP datagram cannot be delivered to the destination host.
- **Time Exceeded.** The value contained in an IP datagram's Time-to-Live field has expired and the IP datagram has been discarded.
- **Invalid Parameters.** One or more of an IP datagram's header fields contain invalid data.
- **Source Quench.** Sent to request that the source host stop sending IP datagrams for a time.
- **Redirect.** Sent to indicate a better route to use for subsequent IP datagrams.

The volume of ICMP messages that are sent generally increases when the internet begins to experience heavy traffic volumes. In order to reduce the likelihood that ICMP messages will flood the internet with error message traffic, ICMP adheres to the following restrictions with respect to the generation of error messages:

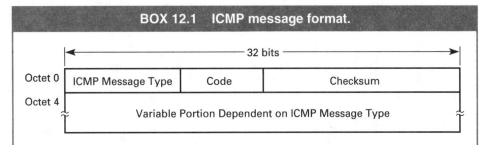

BOX 12.1   ICMP message format.

- **ICMP Message Type.** Contains a code that identifies the type of the ICMP message. The value of this field determines the format of the variable portion of the ICMP message.
- **Code.** Contains a 1-octet code in which the interpretation depends on the ICMP message type.
- **Checksum.** Contains a 16-bit checksum that is calculated based on the entire message contents and is used for detecting corrupted messages.

- No ICMP messages are generated with respect to the routing or delivery of other ICMP messages.
- No ICMP messages are generated to report on the routing or delivery of IP datagrams contained in multicast frames.
- No ICMP messages are sent to report on IP datagram segments other than the first in a set of segments.

Redirect Message Format

One of the most commonly used ICMP error messages is the Redirect message that a router uses to inform hosts about better routes to use. Box 12.2 shows the format of the ICMP Redirect message. Other ICMP error messages have a similar format in which the 4-octet Router Internet Address field is either unused or used for other purposes.

ICMP Redirect Example

Figure 12.2 shows a simple internet that allows us to illustrate how the ICMP Redirect message is used to provide hosts with information about better routes to use. In sending an IP datagram from host B to host A, host B should use router X, but in sending an IP datagram to host C, it should use router Y.

Let us see what is involved in sending an IP datagram from host B to host C. We will assume that host B starts up with a routing table that contains only a default router entry for router X. At this point, host B has no entry in its routing table for host C's network. Therefore, host B uses the default routing table entry to determine the address of the router to use and its IP process forwards the IP datagram to router X. The IP process in router X consults its routing table and determines that it should forward the IP data-

← ─────────────────── 32 bits ───────────────────→

	ICMP Message Type	Code	Checksum
Octet 0			
Octet 4	Router Internet Address		
Octet 8	Original IP Datagram Header		
	Original IP Datagram Data		

- **ICMP Message Type.** Contains a code that identifies the type of the ICMP error message.
- **Code.** Contains a 1-octet code that further describes the error message's type.
- **Checksum.** Contains a 16-bit checksum that is calculated based on the entire message contents and is used for detecting corrupted messages.
- **Router Internet Address.** Contains the internet address of the router to be used in sending subsequent IP datagrams to the destination network.
- **Original IP Datagram Header.** Contains the header of the IP datagram that caused this error message to be generated.
- **Original IP Datagram Data.** Contains the first eight octets of the data portion of the IP datagram that caused this error message to be generated.

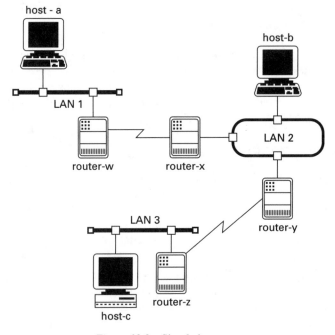

Figure 12.2 Simple internet.

gram to router Y. Router Y forwards the IP datagram to router Z. Router Z finally uses its ARP cache to deliver the IP datagram to host C.

Router X now needs to tell host B that there is a better route to use for IP datagrams that are going to host C's network. To do this, router X generates an ICMP Redirect message. The Redirect message contains the network ID value for the destination network and the internet address of the next hop router to use for IP datagrams that are destined for that physical network. Router X sends the Redirect message to host B. Host B then uses the information contained in the Redirect message to update its routing table by adding a new entry for host C's network. From this point on, when host B receives an IP datagram that is destined for the network with the network ID value contained in the new routing table entry, it sends that IP datagram to router Y. When host B receives an IP datagram destined to some other network, it uses the default entry and sends that IP datagram to router X.

ICMP QUERY MESSAGES

In addition to the ICMP messages that are generated to report on errors and exceptional conditions, there is another set of ICMP messages that can be used to request information and to reply to an ICMP request. The following sections describe some of the ICMP query messages that are commonly used.

Echo Request and Reply

The most commonly used of the ICMP query messages consists of those ICMP messages that are used to implement the Ping protocol, described in Chapter 5. These messages are used essentially to implement an "Are you alive" function. If a host or router receives an ICMP Echo Request message, it replies with an ICMP Echo Reply.

Box 12.3 shows the format of the ICMP Echo Request and Reply messages.

Timestamp Request and Reply

A host or router issues a Timestamp Request message to request that some other host or router respond with a timestamp indicating the current date and time of day. A host or router that receives a Timestamp Request message replies with a Timestamp Reply message. A timestamp contains a 32-bit value that indicates the number of seconds that have elapsed since January 1, 1900. Timestamp Request and Reply messages can be used as a simple means of synchronizing clocks or to measure elapsed time in various situations.

Box 12.4 shows the format of the ICMP Timestamp Request and Reply messages. Note that the Receive Timestamp and Transmit Timestamp fields contain zero in a Timestamp Request message; all three Timestamp fields contain data in a Timestamp Reply message.

Subnet Mask Request and Reply

Used to implement a simple client-server protocol that a host can use to obtain the subnet mask value to use. (See Chapter 4 for a discussion of subnet masks.) In an internet that

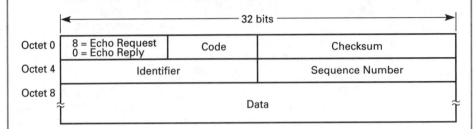

- **ICMP Message Type.** Contains the value 8 for an Echo Request message or the value 0 for an Echo Reply message.
- **Code.** Contains a 1-octet code.
- **Checksum.** Contains a 16-bit checksum that is calculated based on the entire message contents and is used for detecting corrupted messages.
- **Identifier.** Used to associate a reply message with its associated request message.
- **Sequence Number.** Used to identify each individual request or reply in a sequence of associated requests or replies with the same source and destination.
- **Data.** Generated by the sender and echoed back by the echoer. This field is variable in length, and its length and contents is set by the Echo Request sender.

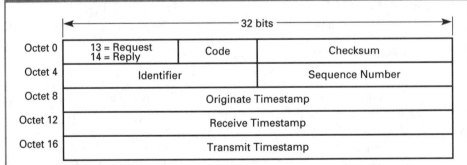

- **ICMP Message Type.** Contains the value 13 for a Timestamp Request message or the value 14 for a Timestamp Reply message.
- **Code.** Contains a 1-octet code.
- **Checksum.** Contains a 16-bit checksum that is calculated based on the entire message contents and is used for detecting corrupted messages.
- **Identifier.** Used to associate a reply message with its associated request message.

BOX 12.4   *(Continued)*

- **Sequence Number.** Used to identify each individual request or reply in a sequence of associated requests or replies having the same source and destination.
- **Originate Timestamp.** Generated by the sender and contains a time value identifying the time the original Timestamp Request message was sent.
- **Receive Timestamp.** Generated by the echoer and contains a time value identifying the time the original Timestamp Request message was received.
- **Transmit Timestamp.** Generated by the echoer and contains a time value identifying the time the Timestamp Reply message was sent.

BOX 12.5   ICMP Subnet Mask Request and Reply message format.

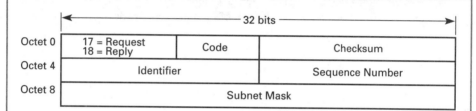

	32 bits	
Octet 0	17 = Request 18 = Reply	Code	Checksum
Octet 4	Identifier		Sequence Number
Octet 8	Subnet Mask		

- **ICMP Message Type.** Contains the value 17 for a Timestamp Request message or the value 18 for a Timestamp Reply message.
- **Code.** Contains a 1-octet code.
- **Checksum.** Contains a 16-bit checksum that is calculated based on the entire message contents and is used for detecting corrupted messages.
- **Identifier.** Used to associate a reply message with its associated request message.
- **Sequence Number.** Used to identify each individual request or reply in a sequence of associated requests or replies having the same source and destination.
- **Subnet Mask.** Generated by the echoer and contains a subnet mask value.

---

implements this protocol, one or more hosts in the internet are designated as subnet mask servers and run a process that replies to Subnet Mask Request messages. A host that needs to obtain its address mask multicasts a Subnet Mask Request message. An address mask server replies to the Subnet Mask Request message with a Subnet Mask reply message containing the subnet mask value to use.

Box 12.5 shows the format of the ICMP Subnet Mask Request and Reply messages. Note that the Subnet Mask field contains zero in a Subnet Mask Request message.

SUMMARY

The Internet Control Message Protocol (ICMP) operates in the Internet layer and allows hosts and routers to report on error conditions and to provide information about unexpected circumstances.

ICMP messages are carried within IP datagrams. There are several formats of ICMP messages, all of which have headers containing the following three fields—an ICMP message type, a message type code, and a checksum. ICMP messages can be divided into two categories: ICMP error messages and ICMP query messages.

ICMP error messages are used to report on conditions such as destination unreachable, time-to-live exceeded, and invalid parameters in an IP datagram. ICMP error messages are also sent to request that the destination system stop sending IP datagrams for a time and to inform a system of a better route to use.

ICMP query messages include the Echo Request and Reply messages used to implement the Ping protocol, the Timestamp Request and Reply messages that allow hosts to exchange date and time-of-day values, and the Subnet Mask Request and Reply messages used by hosts to exchange information about their internet address formats.

Chapter **13**

Routing Protocols

As we discussed in Chapter 10, IP includes a basic routing function that a host uses to determine the host or router to which each IP datagram that it generates should be sent. The IP function running in a host is sufficient to allow the host to maintain its own routing table. A host's routing table contains entries only for the hosts and routers on its own physical network. Once a host determines that an IP datagram is destined for a host on some other physical network, it delivers that IP datagram to a local router. It is then the responsibility of all the routers in the internet to ensure that the IP datagram is delivered to the appropriate physical network.

Each router in an internet also runs an IP process. However, the routing tables that routers maintain need to have a more global view of the internet than those maintained by individual hosts. The IP routing function alone does not provide routers with the information they need to maintain their routing tables, and routers typically run additional specialized *routing protocols* in addition to IP. Routing protocols allow routers to exchange routing information with each other for the purpose of maintaining their routing tables. The operation of these routing protocols is transparent to the hosts attached to the internet. There are many different routing protocols that routers can use, and the choice of the routing protocols that are used in any given TCP/IP internet is generally based on the size and the structure of the internet.

This chapter describes some of the routing protocols that TCP/IP routers employ. We begin by describing the general characteristics of the routing algorithms that are employed by routing protocols.

ROUTING ALGORITHMS

There are several different types of algorithms that can be used in a computer network for maintaining the routing tables employed by routers. These are summarized in Fig. 13.1 and are described in the following sections.

Routing Method	Collection	Distribution	Computation	Adaptability
Static	Through network management.	Through network management.	Routes computed offline.	None in real time.
Quasistatic	Through network management.	Through network management.	Routes computed offline.	Limited adaptability to topology changes caused by errors.
Centralized	Routers report information about the local environment to a central facility.	Central facility distributes routing information to each router.	Routes computed by central facility.	Central facility can adapt to changes, but routers have difficulty finding the central facility.
Distributed Distance-Vector	Routers report current routes to each neighbor router.	Routers accept information from neighbor routers and redistribute their view of local environment.	Routes computed by each router on receipt of information that changes their routing decisions.	Adapts to any changes that are reported by neighbor routers.
Link-State	Routers collect globally-provided information to obtain a table describing the routing domain.	Routers globally distribute information about their local environment to all other routers.	Routes computed upon receipt of information that changes a router's routing tables.	Adapts to any changes that are reported by any other router.

Figure 13.1   Characteristics of routing algorithms.

Static Routing

With *static routing,* all routing information is precomputed and is provided to each router through administrative procedures. Static routing has the advantage that sophisticated computational methods can be used for computing routes, since routes are not computed in real time. However, with static routing techniques, routing information must be recomputed and provided to the routers each time the network topology changes. Thus, static routing techniques are generally not well suited to large internets that may be constantly changing. Static routing techniques, however, may be appropriate for small internets that require few routers and have a simple, relatively unchanging topology.

Quasi-Static Routing

Quasi-static routing is similar to static routing except the routing information that is computed and provided to each router includes information about alternative paths that can be used when certain types of failures occur. Quasi-static routing techniques can handle some kinds of topological changes, such as links becoming unavailable, but major changes to the network topology still require routing information to be recomputed offline.

Centralized Routing

With *centralized routing,* hosts and routers report information about their local environments to a centralized facility. The centralized facility accumulates routing information from all the systems in the network, computes routes, and sends to each router the information it needs to make routing decisions. In effect, only the centralized facility has complete knowledge of the network topology.

Although, in theory, a centralized routing scheme can respond to topological changes, it has two major drawbacks. First, a way must be found for relaying the routing information to the centralized facility after a topological change occurs. This is difficult because the routing information maintained by the centralized facility cannot be reliably used for this purpose after the network topology changes. Second, the delays inherent in propagating routing information to and from the centralized facility can cause the calculated routes to be different from the optimal routes that should be used.

Distributed Adaptive Routing

With *distributed adaptive routing,* routers dynamically sense their local environments and exchange this information with each other in a distributed fashion. A system of routers that use distributed adaptive routing all participate in a distributed algorithm to decide on the optimal path over which each packet should travel from a source system to a destination system. Each router then periodically computes new routes for relaying packets from one router to the next. Distributed adaptive algorithms are robust, and they can quickly adapt to changing network topologies. Most routers used in TCP/IP internets employ distributed adaptive routing techniques to maintain their routing tables.

Two forms of distributed adaptive routing are in common use in TCP/IP internets—*distance-vector* routing and *link-state* routing. Each of these is briefly described next.

Distance-Vector Routing

With a *distance-vector* routing algorithm, also sometimes called a *Bellman-Ford* algorithm, each router in the internet learns about the network topology by exchanging routing information packets with its neighbor routers. A router initializes its routing table by storing information for each physical network to which it is directly attached. It stores information that identifies the physical network and the distance to that network, typically measured in hops. Periodically, each router sends out a complete copy of its routing table to all the other routers to which it is directly attached via a single data link.

When a router receives routing information from another router, it uses that information to update its own routing table. The router adds entries to its own routing table for physical networks that are not currently in its own routing table but that can be reached through the other router. If the router determines that there is a shorter route to a network already referenced in its routing table, the router updates that entry. Any other changes in distance or availability are also reflected.

By exchanging routing information with its directly attached neighbor routers, each router learns what the network topology looks like to its neighbors. Each router then constructs a new description of the network topology and communicates this new picture to its neighbor routers. The process is continually repeated and eventually stabilizes when all the routers finally have the same description of the network topology.

A distance-vector algorithm is a relatively simple algorithm and is relatively easy to design and implement. A major problem with distance-vector routing, however, is that the computational complexity of the algorithm grows rapidly as the internet grows in size. The algorithm can take many iterations to converge in a large network after a topology change occurs and can consume large amounts of network bandwidth. Also, in a network containing routers having varying levels of performance, and links having varying bandwidths, the slowest routers in the network and the slowest links tend to become convergence bottlenecks.

Link-State Routing

The other major form of distributed adaptive routing algorithm is called a *link-state* routing algorithm, sometimes called a *shortest path first* (SPF) algorithm. With link-state routing, each router periodically uses a broadcast mechanism to transmit information to all other routers in the network about the routers to which it is directly attached and the status of the data links between them. Each router then constructs a complete map of the network from the information it receives from all the other routers. Routers are then able to calculate routes from this map using the Dijkstra shortest path algorithm.

Routers continually monitor the status of their links by exchanging packets with neighboring routers. If a router does not respond after a certain number of tries, the link is assumed to be down. If the status of a router or a link changes, this information is broadcast to all the other routers in the internet. Each router then determines routes based on the new information. Since each router broadcasts information about only its own local environment to all the other routers, all the routers quickly receive a complete description of the network topology. Each router then knows where all the other routers are and what links interconnect them.

In contrast with distance-vector routing, a link-state algorithm converges in a single iteration after any topology change. Link-state routing also involves the transmission of less information than distance-vector routing. With distance-vector routing, each router broadcasts information from its entire routing table, which reflects all physical networks in the internet. With link-state routing, a router broadcasts information only about its own directly-attached links.

The main disadvantage of link-state algorithms is that they require a reliable broadcast mechanism that is difficult to design and implement.

AUTONOMOUS SYSTEMS

For the purposes of routing, a TCP/IP internet can be divided into one or more *autonomous systems.* An autonomous system consists of a set of hosts, routers, and data links, all of which make up one or more physical networks that are administered by a single authority. An authority might be, for example, a university, a corporation, or a government agency. The Internet NSFNET backbone network is an example of an autonomous system.

Routing decisions that are made within an autonomous system are completely under the control of the administering organization, and any desired routing protocol, using any type of routing algorithm, can be used within an autonomous system. Suppose Leben, Inc. maintains a relatively complex internet that is connected to the Worldwide Internet. The Leben, Inc. internet is an example of a private autonomous system. When a host in the Leben, Inc. internet sends data to another Leben, Inc. host, neither the NSFNET backbone nor any other autonomous system attached to the Internet is aware of the traffic. The NSFNET backbone network needs to get involved in routing Leben, Inc. traffic only if a Leben, Inc. host sends data to some other network in the Internet that can be reached only via NSFNET. Therefore, routing within the Leben, Inc. autonomous system is isolated from routing that occurs in any other autonomous system.

TCP/IP GATEWAY PROTOCOLS

As we mentioned earlier, routers are often called *gateways* in TCP/IP literature, and routing protocols are often referred to as *gateway protocols*. There are two general categories of TCP/IP gateway protocols:

- **Interior Gateway Protocols.** Two routers that communicate directly with one another and are both part of the same autonomous system are said to be *interior neighbors* and are called *interior gateways*. Interior neighbors communicate with one another using an *interior gateway protocol*.

- **Exterior Gateway Protocols.** Two routers that communicate directly with one another and are in different autonomous systems are said to be *exterior neighbors* and are called *exterior gateways*. Exterior gateways communicate with one another using an exterior gateway protocol.

An exterior gateway typically also functions as an interior gateway to other routers in its own autonomous system. Therefore, an exterior gateway typically runs both an exterior gateway protocol and an interior gateway protocol and functions as an exterior gateway for some traffic and an interior gateway for other traffic.

The remainder of this chapter describes commonly used interior and exterior gateway protocols.

INTERIOR GATEWAY PROTOCOLS

As described earlier, the routers in an autonomous system are free to use any desired routing protocol in communicating among themselves. In a simple autonomous system, consisting of just a few physical networks, the simple routing function provided by IP may be all the routing that is required. In larger autonomous systems, it is desirable that more sophisticated routers be used that run a distributed adaptive routing algorithm.

In an autonomous system that uses an interior gateway protocol that employs a distributed adaptive routing algorithm, it is common for hosts as well as routers to run the same routing protocol. However, hosts typically play only a passive role in routing while routers play an active role. Routers operating in an active role transmit routing information packets to the other hosts and routers; hosts operating in a passive role only listen and update their routing tables based on the routing information they receive, but they do not transmit routing information packets.

A number of interior gateway protocols are in common use in TCP/IP internets. The following sections briefly describe the more common of these.

Routing Information Protocol

The *Routing Information Protocol* (RIP) is a commonly implemented interior gateway protocol. In the UNIX environment, RIP is implemented by a daemon process typically called **routed.** The **routed** daemon is distributed as part of BSD UNIX and has become quite widely used without actually being defined in a formal specification.

RIP employs a simple distance-vector distributed adaptive routing algorithm that uses hop counts as distance measurements. With RIP, routers periodically transmit routing information, and other hosts and routers also running RIP use the received routing information to update their routing tables.

Hello

The *Hello* protocol is similar to RIP and uses a distance-vector algorithm. However, RIP makes distance measurements based on estimated propagation delays rather than on hop counts. Hello includes a mechanism for synchronizing clocks in different hosts and routers and uses timestamps on packets sent between systems to estimate routing delays.

Hello was the original routing protocol used in the NSFNET network before it became the Internet backbone. NSFNET now uses a link-state routing protocol that is similar to OSPF, described next.

Open Shortest Path First

The *Open Shortest Path First* (OSPF) Protocol uses a link-state routing algorithm that is similar to the OSI routing algorithm defined in ISO 10589. Routers use a reliable broadcast mechanism to exchange information with all other routers about their own data links and then use that information to develop a map of the network topology on which route calculations are based. OSPF allows for multiple routes to a destination based on different types of service, such as low delay or high throughput.

The OSPF specification is available in the published literature and is an open standard that many router vendors have implemented. The OSPF protocol is better suited than RIP or Hello to larger autonomous systems.

Gated Daemon

The **gated** daemon, available with many UNIX operating systems that implement TCP/IP communication software, was developed at Cornell University. It combines the RIP and Hello interior gateway protocols with EGP, a commonly used exterior gateway protocol, to provide a comprehensive routing solution for use in smaller autonomous systems.

EXTERIOR GATEWAY PROTOCOLS

As we introduced earlier in this chapter, two routers that communicate with one another and are in different autonomous systems communicate using an exterior gateway protocol. There are two exterior gateway protocols commonly used in the TCP/IP environment—the Exterior Gateway Protocol (EGP) and the Border Gateway Protocol (BGP).

Exterior Gateway Protocol

The *Exterior Gateway Protocol* (EGP) is a standardized protocol, described by a TCP/IP RFC, by which a router in one autonomous system can communicate with a router in another autonomous system. EGP is widely used and is implemented by the routers marketed by a number of different router vendors and is also implemented by **gated,** described previously.

EGP performs three major functions that are described in the following sections:

Neighbor Acquisition

The process of agreeing to exchange information with another autonomous system is called *neighbor acquisition.* When a router functioning in the role of an exterior gateway wishes to exchange information with a router in another autonomous system, it sends an EGP Acquisition Request packet to that router. The other router responds with either an Acquisition Confirm or Acquisition Refuse packet. Assuming the response is positive, the two routers are then able to exchange routing information, and the two gateways are then known as *exterior neighbors.*

As part of the acquisition packet exchange procedure, the two routers agree on how frequently each router will be tested to see if it is still responding and how frequently requests for routing information will be sent.

If, at a later time, a router no longer wishes to be available to its exterior neighbor, it sends an EGP Cease packet. The neighbor responds with an EGP Cease Confirm packet.

Neighbor Reachability

Periodically, each router that is operating in the role of an exterior gateway checks its exterior neighbors by sending them EGP Hello packets. The neighbors respond with EGP I Heard You packets. If a neighbor does not respond after a certain number of tries, it is considered to be down and is no longer available for routing.

Routing Information Updating

When a router functioning as an exterior gateway wants to receive routing information from an exterior neighbor, it sends an EGP Poll Request packet. This packet identifies a *source network* that is common to the two exterior neighbor routers. The exterior neighbor router returns routing information in an EGP Poll Response packet. Only destinations that are part of the autonomous system that is providing the information are included in the information in the Poll Response packet. The distances shown for reaching the different destination networks are based on entering the autonomous system via the specified source network.

EGP implements a distance-vector routing algorithm. However, the measurement used for distance is not defined as part of the EGP specification. Each autonomous system defines its own distance measure. This means that distance values included in a Poll Response are comparable from route to route within an autonomous system, but they may not be comparable from one autonomous system to another.

EGP Packets

Box 13.1 lists the different EGP packet types that EGP defines. Box 13.2 shows the general format of the EGP packets that routers exchange and describes their fields.

Border Gateway Protocol

The *Border Gateway Protocol* (BGP) was designed to improve on the capabilities provided by EGP. Although EGP is widely used, it does not provide a complete solution for communication between autonomous systems in a large internet. EGP defines how exterior neighbors exchange routing information but does not define the procedures that routers use in building routes. In particular, EGP does not define how hosts in two different autonomous systems can communicate through a third autonomous system.

Like EGP, BGP defines procedures that routers can use to exchange reachability information with exterior neighbor routers. However, with BGP, this reachability infor-

BOX 13.1			EGP packet types.
Packet Type	**Type**	**Code**	**Description**
Routing Update	1	–	Information on reachable networks
Poll Request	2	–	Requests a routing update
Acquisition Request	3	0	Requests a gateway to become a neighbor
Acquisition Confirm	3	1	Agrees to become a neighbor
Acquisition Refuse	3	2	Declines to become a neighbor
Cease Request	3	3	Requests termination of being a neighbor
Cease Confirm	3	4	Acknowledges termination as neighbors
Hello	5	0	Tests that a neighbor is alive
I Heard You	5	1	Response to a Hello packet

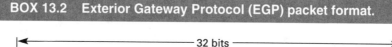

BOX 13.2   Exterior Gateway Protocol (EGP) packet format.

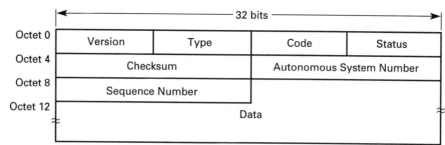

- **Version.** Identifies the version of EGP being used.
- **Type.** Identifies the type of packet.
- **Code.** Further identifies a packet type.
- **Status.** Provides type-dependent status information.
- **Checksum.** Used to verify that the packet was not damaged during transmission.
- **Autonomous system number.** Identifies the autonomous system sending the packet.
- **Sequence number.** Used to match responses to requests.
- **Data.** Contains additional information specific to a particular packet type.

mation includes the entire chain of autonomous systems that may have to be crossed in reaching a particular destination network. BGP prevents routing loops from occurring by not allowing a particular autonomous system to appear twice in a path.

SUMMARY

Each host and router in a TCP/IP internet runs an IP process that performs basic routing and relaying functions. Routers have a more global view of the internet than hosts and typically run additional routing protocols that allow them to exchange information for the purposes of maintaining their routing tables.

A number of different routing algorithms can be used to maintain the routing tables in routers, including static routing, quasi-static routing, centralized routing, and distributed adaptive routing. Most TCP/IP routers run distributed adaptive routing algorithms of which two types are commonly implemented—distance-vector algorithms and link-state algorithms.

For the purposes of routing, a TCP/IP internet can be divided into autonomous systems, each of which consists of a group of hosts, routers, and data links that are administered by a single organization. Routers in autonomous systems, often called gateways, can be divided into two types—interior gateways and exterior gateways.

Interior gateways run an interior gateway protocol for communication among the routers within an autonomous system. Some of the interior gateway protocols typically used in TCP/IP internets include the Routing Information Protocol (RIP), the Hello protocol, and the Open Shortest Path First (OSPF) protocol. The **gated** program combines the RIP and Hello protocols with EGP, a commonly used exterior gateway protocol.

Exterior gateways run an exterior gateway protocol for communicating with routers in other autonomous systems. Some of the exterior gateway protocols typically used in TCP/IP internets include the Exterior Gateway Protocol (EGP) and the Border Gateway Protocol (BGP).

Chapter 14 begins Part V that discusses internet administration functions. Chapter 15 describes network management facilities that can be used to monitor and control the operation of a TCP/IP internet.

PART **V**

INTERNET ADMINISTRATION

Chapter 14   Network Management   Chapter 16   Troubleshooting
Chapter 15   Installation and
             Administration

Chapter **14**

Network Management

TCP/IP software is being widely used to implement increasingly large and complex computer networks. The widespread use of TCP/IP in implementing large internets is generating an increasing need for standardized *network management* support in the TCP/IP environment.

Network management allows network administrators to issue commands to monitor and control the operation of various aspects of an internet. Network management also allows parameter values that have been automatically set by TCP/IP protocols to be fine-tuned as necessary. TCP/IP network management allows network administrators to start and stop internet components as needed, to monitor the operation of an internet, and to extract and analyze information relating to internet traffic and performance.

ISO CMIP APPROACH TO NETWORK MANAGEMENT

Most of today's approaches to network management, including those used in the management of TCP/IP internets, are based on the emerging international standards for network management that are being developed by ISO. ISO's approach to network management is called *Common Management Information Protocol* (CMIP). The CMIP international standards divide management functions into the following five *specific management functional areas* (SMFAs):

- Configuration management
- Fault management
- Performance management
- Security management
- Accounting management

Structure and Identification of Management Information

The ISO CMIP approach to network management defines the notion of *objects,* which are elements that need to be managed. An object might contain a value that a system administrator can inspect or set. An object might alternatively contain a value that a system administrator can only inspect.

Management information is described by the *Structure and Identification of Management Information* (SMI) developed by ISO as part of CMIP. SMI defines a set of rules for how managed objects are described and how management protocols can be used by network management applications to access the value of an object and to set an object's value.

Management Information Base

Part of the CMIP SMI is the definition of a *Management Information Base* (MIB), which is a repository, or database, that defines all the objects that can be managed in a network. Portions of the MIB are distributed among all the devices in the network—such as end systems (hosts), routers, terminal servers, and so on—that need to be managed. Managed objects are grouped according to the layering structure of the particular type of network being managed. For example, in a TCP/IP network, the objects would be organized according to the layering structure of the TCP/IP architecture. In an OSI network, the objects would be organized according to the layering structure defined by the OSI model, and so on.

Abstract Syntax Notation One

Managed objects are named and described using an international standard notation called *Abstract Syntax Notation One* (ASN.1). ASN.1 is a data description notation that allows the format and meaning of data structures to be defined without specifying how those data structures are represented in a computer or how they are encoded for transmission through a network. For example, ASN.1 allows a numeric data element to be defined as an INTEGER data type but does not specify anything about how that integer should be represented or encoded (1's complement, 2's complement, packed-decimal, etc.).

The advantage to using a notation like ASN.1 to define management information is that the management information can be described in a way that is completely independent of any particular form of information processing technology.

Object Identification and Description

With CMIP, each object that can be managed in a network is given a unique identifier and is precisely described using ASN.1 notation. These object descriptions are then stored and maintained in the MIB for access by network management applications. Communication between a network management application and a managed object takes place via a network management protocol.

APPROACHES TO TCP/IP NETWORK MANAGEMENT

There are currently two approaches that are being taken in the TCP/IP environment with respect to network management. A third approach is also being investigated as a possible long-term direction for the management of TCP/IP internets. These approaches represent an evolution toward conformance with the ISO CMIP approach to network management. The three approaches to TCP/IP network management are as follows:

- **Ad Hoc Tools.** There are a number of simple software tools that most implementations of TCP/IP communication software make available. Both users and network administrators can use these tools in performing day-to-day administration tasks and for troubleshooting. These tools take the form of commands and configuration files that most TCP/IP hosts implement.

- **Simple Network Management Protocol.** The *Simple Network Management Protocol* (SNMP) was developed at a time when the emerging international standards for network management were far from complete but when there was also a great need for improvements to the ad hoc tools that were commonly used. SNMP represents a more architectural approach to the problem of managing large internets than is provided by the ad hoc tools.

- **CMOT.** The *CMIP over TCP/IP* (CMOT) protocol specifies how the international standard *Common Management Information Protocol* (CMIP) can be used to manage TCP/IP internets. CMOT is currently being investigated as a possible long-term solution to the management of internets using the TCP/IP protocol suite.

Each of these approaches is discussed in the sections that follow.

AD HOC NETWORK MANAGEMENT TOOLS

A number of commands and configuration files are used by system and network administrators to set up and configure the TCP/IP software that runs in hosts and routers. These commands and configuration files allow the administrator to initially install an internet and to add additional hosts to it as an internet grows. Many of these tools can also be used by end users to diagnose problems that occur in an operational internet.

Network Management Commands

Most of the tools that system and network administrators have at their disposal for administering TCP/IP internets and performing troubleshooting tasks take the form of commands that most TCP/IP communication software supports. The following are the commands that are used most often to perform network management tasks:

- **The ifconfig Command.** The **ifconfig** command can be used to test the physical network interface to determine such information as whether the interface is operational and ready to receive packets, whether the network interface software is configured properly, and the internet address that is currently assigned to the physical interface.

- **The ping command.** The **ping** command can be used to determine whether a particular host is currently reachable. The host can be referenced in the **ping** command by internet address to test for internet connectivity or by name to test for proper operation of the name resolution function.

- **The traceroute Command.** The **traceroute** command can be used to diagnose internet connectivity problems by reporting on the current route that packets are taking through an internet in reaching a specified host. Like **ping, traceroute** can refer to a host by internet address or by name.
- **The netstat Command.** The **netstat** command returns a set of statistics concerning the network activity that is associated with the local host.
- **The nslookup Command.** The **nslookup** command can be used to diagnose problems in the Domain Name System by explicitly requesting name resolution operations.

Configuration Files

Most TCP/IP communication software maintains a set of configuration files that contain important information relating to TCP/IP communication options. The contents of these files can sometimes be used to pinpoint the source of problems. Three important configuration files are as follows:

- **The hosts File.** The **hosts** file is important in smaller internets when the Domain Name System is not used for name resolution. As described in Chapter 7, the **hosts** file contains a list of the name-to-address mappings that the local host has access to. It can generally be inspected and changed using an ordinary text editor to add name-to-address mappings when hosts are added to an internet.
- **The services File.** The **services** file contains information about TCP/IP application services and protocols, including the name of each service, the Transport layer protocol it employs, and its port number assignment.
- **The protocols File.** The **protocols** file contains information about the specific protocols that the local host supports and identifies the unique number assigned to each protocol.

Network Monitors

In addition to the ad hoc software tools that are available on most hosts, large internets may also implement specialized *network monitors* that keep various types of statistics during normal internet operation. Network monitors take the form of network management software that is run on one or more hosts in an internet or specialized devices that are attached to an internet in the same manner as hosts. The information that can be displayed by network monitors can often be used by network administrators in tracking down the sources of problems.

SIMPLE NETWORK MANAGEMENT PROTOCOL

The *Simple Network Management Protocol* (SNMP) was designed to provide a more comprehensive approach to network management than is provided by the simple ad hoc tools discussed previously. The SNMP approach to network management was developed at a time when work had already begun by ISO concerning the international standard CMIP approach to network management. This allowed the developers of SNMP to use the same basic concepts regarding how management information should be described and defined as those being developed as part of CMIP.

SNMP Management Information Base

As with ISO CMIP, SNMP refers to *objects,* which are elements that need to be managed. An object might contain a value that a network administrator can inspect or set. An object might alternatively contain a value that a network administrator can only inspect.

SNMP defines a *Management Information Base* (MIB) that defines all the objects that can be managed in a TCP/IP internet for each layer in the TCP/IP architecture. Portions of the MIB are distributed among all the elements in the TCP/IP internet, such as hosts, routers, and various types of servers that need to be managed.

Information about managed objects that is stored in the MIB is divided into a number of groups that reflect the fundamental organization of the TCP/IP architecture. The following are definitions of a few MIB groups that have been defined:

- **system.** Manageable objects associated with basic system information.
- **interfaces.** Manageable objects concerning network attachment.
- **at.** Manageable objects concerning address translation protocols.
- **ip.** Manageable objects concerning IP.
- **icmp.** Manageable objects concerning ICMP.
- **tcp.** Manageable objects concerning TCP.
- **udp.** Manageable objects concerning UDP.
- **egp.** Manageable objects concerning EGP routing.

Each managed host supports only the MIB groups that are appropriate given the functions that it is capable of performing.

Examples of MIB Objects

The following are a few examples of MIB objects maintained by hosts from some of the above categories:

- **sysUpTime.** This is an object from the *system* group that maintains a value giving the time since the host was last booted.
- **ifNumber.** This is an object from the *interfaces* group that indicates the number of NICs that are installed in the host.
- **ipInReceives.** This is an object from the *ip* group that contains a value indicating the number of datagrams that have been received by the IP process running in the host.
- **tcpRtoMin.** This is an object from the *tcp* group that contains a value indicating the minimum transmission time allowed by the TCP process running in the host.

As with the CMIP approach, SNMP managed objects are named and described using ASN.1. Each object that can be managed in a TCP/IP internet is given a unique identifier and is precisely described using ASN.1 notation. These object descriptions are then stored and maintained in the MIB for future access. Communication between a network management application and a managed object takes place via messages and procedures defined by SNMP.

SNMP Architecture

Figure 14.1 shows the overall architectural structure of the network management components that work with SNMP. Brief descriptions of each of the SNMP architectural components follow:

- **Network Management Station.** A *network management station* (NMS) is a host in the internet that executes a network management application. A network administrator typically uses an NMS to monitor and control the internet or a portion of it.

- **Network Management Application.** A *network management application* (NMA) is the program running in a network management station that monitors and controls one or more network elements.

- **Network Element.** A *network element* (NE) is a component in an internet that maintains a management agent and a portion of the MIB that contains manageable objects. Examples of network elements are hosts and routers.

- **Management Agent.** A *management agent* (MA) is a program running in a network element that is responsible for performing the network management functions requested by a

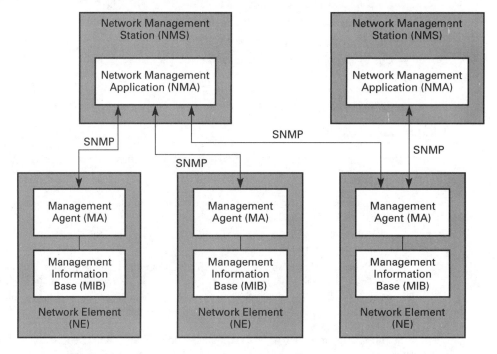

Figure 14.1 Components associated with the Simple Network Management Protocol (SNMP).

network management application. A management agent accesses the objects stored in the portion of the MIB that is maintained in that network element.

SNMP defines the formats of a set of network management messages and the rules by which those messages are exchanged when network management applications in network management stations communicate over an internet with management agents in network elements.

Network Management Application Functions

There are only two functions that a network management application can request of a management agent using SNMP:

- **Get.** A network management application can request that a management agent return the value (or values) associated with a manageable object.
- **Set.** A network management application can request that a management agent set the value (or values) associated with a manageable object.

SNMP Messages

Most of the messages that flow between a network management application and a management agent concern explicit requests that the network management application makes. SNMP also defines a limited number of unsolicited messages that a management agent can send asynchronously to a network management application regarding events that occur in the network.

Every defined SNMP message is capable of being carried in a single IP datagram and is independent of any other message. Therefore, the SNMP protocol can operate over an unreliable datagram Transport layer service, such as UDP.

CMOT (CMIP OVER TCP/IP)

As described earlier, the Common Management Information Protocol (CMIP) defines an international standard approach to management that is being developed by a subcommittee of ISO. CMOT (CMIP over TCP/IP) describes how CMIP can be used to manage a TCP/IP internet. CMOT works with the same Management Information Base (MIB) and Structure and Identification of Management Information (SMI) that has been defined for SNMP.

CMOT architectural components can be divided into two collections:

- **Agents.** An agent collects management information, executes network management commands, and performs tests on the values of managed objects.
- **Managers.** A manager receives network management information, issues network management commands, and sends instructions to agents.

Figure 14.2 shows the overall architectural structure associated with CMOT. Managers and agents contain management information that is categorized according to the

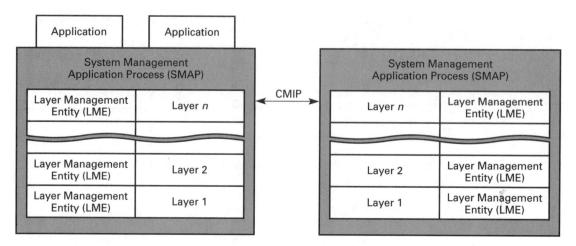

Figure 14.2   Components associated with the Common Management Information Protocol (CMIP) over TCP/IP (CMOT).

various TCP/IP architectural layers. With the management information associated with each layer is a *Layer Management Entity* (LME). A *System Management Application Process* (SMAP) in each manager and agent coordinates the information associated with all the LMEs in that component. The SMAP in a manager communicates with the SMAP in an agent over an internet using the CMOT protocol.

SUMMARY

Network management allows system and network administrators to control and monitor the operation of a TCP/IP internet. ISO is developing a comprehensive approach to network management, called Common Management Information Protocol (CMIP), with which some forms of TCP/IP network management is technically aligned. The three approaches to TCP/IP network management are represented by ad hoc tools, the Simple Network Management Protocol, and CMIP over TCP/IP.

The commands that are used most often to perform system administration tasks are **ifconfig, ping, traceroute, netstat,** and **nslookup.** The configuration files that are most useful to the network administrator are **hosts, services,** and **protocols.** Network monitors, consisting of specialized software or hardware, may also be available to aid in network management.

The Simple Network Management Protocol (SNMP) provides a more comprehensive approach to network management than is provided by the simple ad hoc tools and defines the formats of network management messages and the rules by which those messages are exchanged. SNMP refers to objects in a Management Information Base (MIB) containing values that a network administrator can inspect or set. Managed objects are named and described using Abstract Syntax Notation One (ASN.1). The architectural components making up SNMP are network management stations (NMSs), network management applications (NMAs), network elements (NEs), and management agents (MAs).

CMIP over TCP/IP (CMOT) describes how ISO CMIP can be used to manage a TCP/IP internet. CMOT architectural components can be divided into agents and managers. With the management information associated with each layer is a Layer Management Entity (LME). A System Management Application Process (SMAP) in each manager and agent coordinates the information associated with all the LMEs in that component.

Chapter 15 discusses the administration and maintenance of TCP/IP internets. It describes some of the tasks that are involved in installing a TCP/IP internet and in managing its growth.

Chapter **15**

Installation and Administration

This chapter describes some of the tasks that are involved in installing TCP/IP internets and administering them as they grow. We begin by discussing the various steps that are involved in setting up a simple, single-LAN TCP/IP internet and getting it operational. We then describe the tasks that are involved in using the Domain Name System and installing nameservers to centralize name resolution operations. Finally, we discuss how two or more separate physical networks can be interconnected using bridges or routers to create a larger internet that spans multiple physical locations and describe considerations that apply to connecting an organization's private internet to the Worldwide Internet.

CONFIGURING AN INTERNET

The evolution of a private TCP/IP internet generally begins when an individual department in an organization has a need for networking a group of workstations and server systems. The network might be necessary to support the sharing of files and peripherals and to allow users to communicate with one another using electronic mail software. TCP/IP communications software provides an attractive means of accomplishing such networking because of the broad range of computer systems on which TCP/IP communications software is implemented. TCP/IP communications is particularly appealing in the UNIX graphics workstation environment because the TCP/IP communications software often comes bundled with the operating system software.

For the purposes of introducing the tasks that are involved in the installation of a simple TCP/IP internet in the single-LAN environment, assume that a department has acquired six graphics workstations and that we wish to interconnect them with two server systems using an Ethernet LAN and TCP/IP communication software.

Installing the Physical Network

Our first task in creating a TCP/IP internet is to physically interconnect the eight hosts. It is likely that many of the systems will already have an Ethernet network interface card

(NIC) already installed in it. For those systems, the physical connectivity task consists of acquiring the appropriate cabling, connectors, transceivers, and terminators that are required to interconnect them. An Ethernet NIC must be installed in each computer system that does not already have one. Figure 15.1 shows how the eight hosts might be networked using an Ethernet LAN.

If the LAN will initially consist of more than just a few hosts, it may be beneficial to begin by creating a physical LAN containing only a small subset of the hosts in order to simplify the installation task. Other hosts can then incrementally be added to the LAN after we have made the small subset of hosts operational. In some cases, especially if we have little experience, it is best to start with a LAN containing only two hosts, perhaps one of the workstations and one of the servers.

Installing the TCP/IP Communications Software

After creating the physical network, our next task is to install the operating system software and communications software on all the systems. The individual steps involved in this task will vary depending on the particular hardware and software that is being used. The documentation that accompanies the operating system and TCP/IP communications software should be consulted to determine what is involved in performing this step.

A reasonable way to actually carry out this task is to begin with just two of the hosts that are connected to the physical LAN. The installation task is simplified by getting two hosts working and to then add hosts incrementally, making sure each new host is operational before proceeding to the next one.

During the software installation process, we will be asked to supply a number of pieces of information concerning each host. Of particular importance are the assignments of names and addresses.

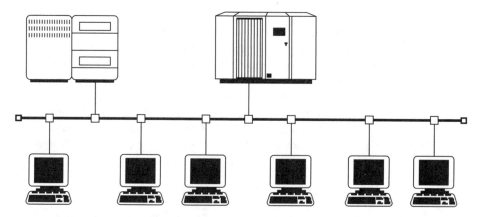

Figure 15.1   Single LAN TCP/IP internet.

Assigning Host and User Names

A unique name must be assigned to each host, and this name is typically specified during the TCP/IP software installation process. A unique name must also be assigned to each user who will be allowed to login to each host. For small internets, it is common to use a simple, flat namespace and to allow each user to choose a simple, easy-to-remember name for his or her own workstation. We can, likewise, choose a simple, descriptive host name for each of the servers. Figure 15.2 shows possible host name assignments for our sample internet.

Assigning Internet Addresses

A unique internet address must be assigned to each point of attachment to the physical network. In this simple example, each host has a single NIC and there is a one-to-one mapping between the host names assigned in the previous step and the internet addresses assigned here.

The ideal method for assigning internet addresses is to apply to the NIC for a unique internet address to use for our private internet. In this way, should we ever need to connect our internet to the Worldwide Internet, we won't have to change any of our address assignments. If our organization is large and will eventually have more than a half dozen or so individual LANs, the best approach is to apply to the NIC for a single class B address and to use subnetting to assign a different subnet ID to each LAN we create. This approach requires creating a central internet address coordination function for our organization.

If our organization is small, and it is unlikely that more than a half dozen LANs will be required, none of which will have more than a couple hundred hosts, then we can apply to the NIC for a separate class C address for each LAN and can avoid the subnetting issue.

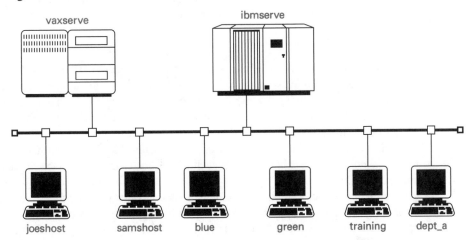

Figure 15.2   Host name assignments.

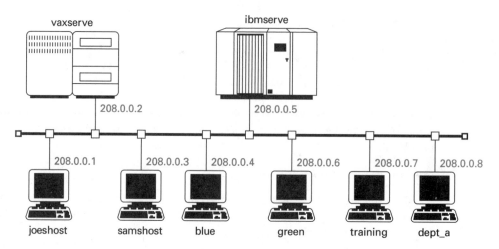

Figure 15.3 Internet address assignments.

What often happens, however, is that we will want to begin the installation process immediately without waiting for an official internet address assignment. In such a case, we will probably elect to simply choose an internet address to use. In most cases, it should be a class C address. In the absence of a central internet address coordination function, we might choose 208.0.0 for a network identification value. The first host can then be given the internet address 208.0.0.1, the second can be assigned 208.0.0.2, and so on, as shown in Fig. 15.3.

As part of the software installation process, we will typically be asked to supply the subnet mask to be used by each host. If a class C address is used without subnetting, the subnet mask will be 255.255.255.0. This value indicates that the entire first 24 bits of the address uniquely identify the physical network. The installation process might also ask for the broadcast address, which is an address of all 1s: 255.255.255.255.

Performing Name Resolution

As described in Chapter 7, the name resolution function that translates between host names and internet addresses can be performed either individually by each host using **hosts** configuration files or by the Domain Name System (DNS). To simplify matters with this small eight-host internet, we will assume that the Domain Name System will not be used and that name resolution will be performed individually by each host.

In this environment, one of our tasks is to ensure that the appropriate procedure is used to install the correct **hosts** file on each of our hosts. If we are using the incremental approach and are installing only two hosts, a workstation and a server, the **hosts** file needs only two entries containing one name to address mapping for the server and another for the workstation. This information must be placed in the **hosts** file for both hosts. In many cases, the **hosts** file is modified using a text editor, but in other cases, creating the **hosts** file is part of the software installation procedure. The system documentation must be consulted to determine the procedure to be used to create the **hosts** file on each host.

Figure 15.4 shows the contents of the **hosts** files for one of the user workstations and one of the servers in our sample internet.

Installing Server Software

As part of the software installation process, we must verify that the appropriate server software is installed on each host that will perform a server function. For example, if a particular host is going to operate as a file server, then it might be desirable to install the appropriate NFS software on that host so that other hosts can have access to the host's disk storage. If it is desirable that each workstation user be able to transfer files to and from any other workstation user or any server, then it will be necessary to ensure that FTP server software is installed on all the hosts. Similar considerations apply to other Application layer services, such as Telnet.

The installation procedures regarding server software vary from one implementation to another. The process can be simple or complex. For example, with many graphics workstations, simply selecting the networking option often causes all the appropriate server processes to be automatically installed. On other systems, each server process must

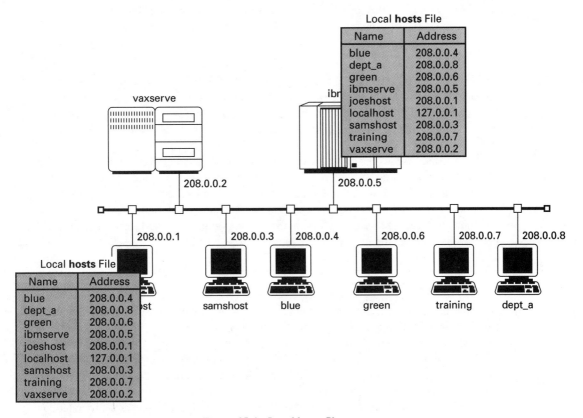

Figure 15.4   Local hosts file contents.

> ### BOX 15.1   Verifying internet installation.
>
> 1. Check to see that all the appropriate configuration files, such as **hosts, services,** and **protocols** exist, contain the appropriate entries, and are in the right directories.
> 2. Check to see that the appropriate TCP/IP communications software has been installed.
> 3. Determine that the local client and server software operate correctly. For example, if the host runs the Ping, Telnet, and FTP servers, issue **ping, telnet,** and **ftp** commands that reference the local host. Issue each command first by referencing the local host using the internet address 127.0.0.1. Then issue them again by referencing them by the host name **localhost** to verify that name resolution is operating correctly. Finally, issue them again using the actual host name.

be installed individually. The installation documentation for the particular software being used must be consulted to determine the procedures to follow with respect to installing server software.

Once the TCP/IP communications software has been installed on a particular host, we should verify that the software has been installed correctly. Box 15.1 lists some of the steps that can be performed to help verify the installation.

Testing Internet Operation

Once the physical network has been created and the TCP/IP software has been installed on each of the two hosts and verified, the first step in testing for network connectivity is to verify that a simple two-host internet is working. Assuming that each host implements a single NIC, some of the steps that are useful in testing for correct internet operation are described in Box 15.2.

After the first two hosts are operational, we can perform all the installation steps for a third host and then perform all the required testing procedures to verify that the internet now operates correctly with three hosts. The same procedures are then followed for each additional host until all of the workstations and servers are up and running and can all communicate with each other. The same procedures must then be followed each time a new host is added to the internet as the internet grows in size.

INSTALLING THE DOMAIN NAME SYSTEM

At some point in time, as more hosts and servers are added to the internet, the job of keeping **hosts** files up to date becomes unwieldy. With a half dozen hosts, the job may be manageable. With 30 or 40 hosts, with a new host possibly being added every few days, the job becomes more burdensome. The main problem with using a **hosts** file on each host to perform name resolution is that when a new host is added, the **hosts** file on every host in the internet must be updated.

With some TCP/IP communications software, this job can be semiautomated and can be coordinated from a central location. With other software, we must go from host to

---

BOX 15.2   Testing correct internet operation.

1. **Test the NIC.** The first step in testing for an operational internet is to issue the **ifconfig** command on each of the two hosts. The **ifconfig** command should name the NIC installed on that host. Consult the system documentation to determine the name to reference in the **ifconfig** command to test the NIC. Entering the **ifconfig** command allows us to determine that the NIC is operational on the host and that the correct internet address has been assigned. The **ifconfig** command tells us that the NIC is up and running and ready to receive packets. The **ifconfig** command also displays the values of the subnet mask and the broadcast address.

2. **Ping by Address.** Once **ifconfig** reports correct results, we can issue the **ping** command on each host, referencing the other host by internet address, to see if each host can reach the other. On the host with the internet address 208.0.0.1, issue a **ping** for host 208.0.0.2; on the host with the internet address 208.0.0.2, issue a **ping** for host 208.0.0.1. This tests for physical connectivity between the two hosts.

3. **Check the ARP cache contents.** If we encounter problems in pinging by address, we can issue the **arp** command, provided with most TCP/IP communications software, to verify the contents of the local ARP cache. At this point, there should be a single entry for the host being pinged, containing that host's internet address and physical hardware address.

4. **Ping by Name.** Once each host can ping the other by address, we should ping each host by name. This verifies that the name resolution function is operating correctly on each host.

5. **Testing the Server Software.** Once there is physical connectivity between the two hosts and the name resolution function is operating correctly, we should test the server software that has been installed on each of the hosts to verify that it can be accessed from the other host. For example, we might issue **telnet** and **ftp** commands on each host, referencing the other host, to verify that the Telnet and FTP servers are reachable. Any other appropriate servers, such as electronic mail servers, can be tested in the same manner.

---

host and manually update the **hosts** file on each system each time we add a new host to the internet.

In most cases, once an internet has grown to more than a dozen or so hosts, it becomes desirable to install one or more nameservers on the internet and to use the Domain Name System rather than individual **hosts** files to perform name-to-address translations.

Installing Nameservers

In installing the Domain Name System, we generally choose one or more hosts to play the role of nameservers. Any number of nameservers can be installed on the internet, but, generally, at least two hosts should be designated as nameservers. One is designated as the primary nameserver and the other as the secondary nameserver. The secondary nameserver takes over the name resolution function if the primary nameserver fails.

Configuring a host as a nameserver typically involves reconfiguring the communications software on the designated hosts to include the nameserver function. On a small internet, it is not necessary to install additional hosts to perform the nameserver function. The nameserver role can generally be played by servers that ordinarily perform other functions as well, such as hosts that operate as file servers. On large internets, it may be necessary to use dedicated nameservers to achieve the desired level of performance.

Choosing a Domain Name

As part of the nameserver configuration process, we must assign a high-level domain name to our internet. On a private internet, we can choose any high-level domain name. However, the best approach is to assign a name using the conventions established by the Internet. For example, if our private internet were operated by Leben, Inc., the high-level domain name chosen might be **lebeninc.com.** Individual users can still refer to other hosts using the simple names that were assigned earlier. For example users of hosts **blue** and **green** can still refer to each other as **blue** and **green.** However, if Leben, Inc.'s internet were connected to IBM's internet, a user on IBM's internet would refer to Leben, Inc.'s **blue** host as **blue.lebeninc.com.**

It is not possible for an organization to apply to NIC for a domain name in the same manner as applying for an internet address until the organization is actually connecting to the Internet. However, it might be desirable in choosing a high-level domain name to contact the NIC to determine if the name the organization is contemplating using has not already been appropriated by some other organization.

EXPANDING THE INTERNET

It is likely that as the LAN installed by an individual department grows, LANs installed by other departments in the organization may be growing up in parallel. It often happens during the evolution of individual LANs that it becomes necessary to interconnect them. If two LANs have grown up in parallel, both using TCP/IP communications software, it is a relatively simple task to accomplish this. This can be done either by using a bridge to interconnect the two LANs to form a single extended LAN, or it can be done by tying the two individual LANs together using a router.

Routers Versus Bridges

If the two LANs carry TCP/IP traffic exclusively, then it is almost always preferable to interconnect them using a router. A router prevents the broadcast traffic generated on one LAN from flowing across the router to the other LAN. If a bridge is used to tie together two LANs, the broadcast traffic generated on one LAN typically flows across the bridge to the other LAN. Therefore, broadcast traffic may double on each LAN as soon as they are interconnected using a bridge. In some cases, the broadcast traffic may saturate the extended LAN if the LANs being interconnected are large.

However, there are cases when a bridge should be used instead of a router to interconnect two LANs. For example, a single LAN may be carrying the traffic generated by equipment conforming to multiple protocol suites, for example TCP/IP and Digital

Equipment Corporation's DECnet. Some protocols, such as the Local Area Transport (LAT) protocol used by some Digital Equipment Corporation equipment, operate correctly only in the single-LAN environment. For such protocols to work properly across interconnected LANs, a bridge instead of a router must be used to interconnect them.

One advantage of using routers instead of bridges in the TCP/IP environment is that most TCP/IP hosts have the routing software bundled with the TCP/IP communications software. It is a simple matter to install the routing software on one or more server hosts and to use an ordinary server to perform the function of a router. Therefore, in a small internet it is possible to tie together multiple LANs without having to purchase specialized routers. In all but the smallest internets, however, it is generally desirable for performance reasons to purchase specialized routers that are dedicated to the routing function.

Addressing Considerations

In interconnecting two or more LANs that have grown up in parallel, addressing conflicts between the two LANs must be resolved before they can be effectively interconnected. When using a bridge to interconnect two LANs, the two LANs become, essentially, a single larger LAN. Therefore, all the hosts on both LANs must use the same network ID value in their internet addresses and must use the same subnet mask. Furthermore, each host on the two interconnected LANs must have a unique host ID value. Because of these restrictions, it is generally necessary to change the internet addresses of all the hosts on one of the two LANs when interconnecting them using a bridge.

When interconnecting two LANs using a router, on the other hand, it is often possible to interconnect the two LANs without having to change any internet addresses. If the LANs were installed in an organization having central coordination of internet address assignments, it is likely that the two LANs already use different network ID values in their internet addresses. In such a case, the two LANs will work correctly when they are interconnected by a router without having to modify any internet addresses. However, if both LANs grew up in an organization without central address administration and both LANs are using, say, 208.0.0 as the network ID value, then all of the hosts will have to be assigned new internet addresses on one of the two LANs before they can be interconnected using a router.

Naming Considerations

Naming considerations also play a role in what must be done before two individual LANs can be interconnected using either a bridge or a router. If both LANs use a flat namespace, with each host on each LAN having a unique simple name assigned to it, then we must get together with the network administrator for the other network to resolve any name conflicts that may exist before our two LANs can be interconnected. If a flat namespace will continue to be used, then any duplicate names must be resolved and eliminated.

It is generally recommended that the LANs being interconnected be in the same stage of evolution with respect to how name resolution is performed. If one of the two LANs is using the Domain Name System for name resolution and the other is still relying on **hosts** files, then the Domain Name System should be installed on the LAN using **hosts** files before beginning to interconnect them.

The administrators for the individual LANs should meet and decide on a strategy for name resolution for the interconnected LANs. For example, they may decide to run the primary nameserver on one LAN and the secondary nameserver on the other one. Or they may decide to decentralize the name function, assigning a different high-level domain name to each individual LAN. They may then decide to run separate nameservers for each LAN for local name resolution operations. Choosing a separate high-level domain name for each LAN avoids the problems of unique names across the two interconnected LANs. Low-level host names can be duplicated on the two individual LANs if each has a different high-level domain name to distinguish the names on one LAN from the names on the other.

Centralized Network Administration

As soon as it becomes necessary to interconnect the local area networks created by multiple departments in an organization, the need for some form of centralized network administration becomes apparent. It is simple to interconnect two LANs if their internet address assignments were centrally coordinated in the first place. By the same token, it is easy to merge two internets if the domain names they use have been centrally coordinated; it may be difficult to interconnect them if the names they use were assigned with no coordination.

As an organization's internet grows, political problems often begin to take on more importance than technical issues. It is necessary that the administrators of the various networks being interconnected be able to work together in a coordinated fashion so that the internet's growth can be controlled and coordinated.

Connecting Remote Locations

In the simplest case, two LANs being interconnected are located relatively close together and can be interconnected simply by hooking them together using a router that has a NIC connected to each of the LANs being interconnected, as shown in Fig. 15.5.

In some cases, it is necessary to interconnect two or more LANs that are located some distance away from each other. The typical way to do this is to attach a router to each of the LANs being interconnected (or use an existing router on each LAN). The two routers are then connected using a long-distance telecommunications facility, as illustrated in Fig. 15.6.

Logically, this is no more difficult to accomplish than interconnecting two LANs that are located close together. The same naming and addressing considerations apply for interconnecting two remote LANs, and the same considerations apply concerning the decision to use a bridge versus a router. Bridges can be configured in which a point-to-point telecommunications facility is used to bridge two remotely located LANs. However, if only TCP/IP traffic will flow over the interconnected LANs, routers usually offer a better solution with remotely-located LANs as well as with LANs that are located close together.

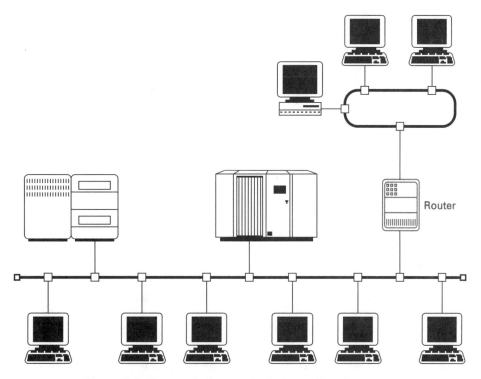

Figure 15.5   Interconnecting two physical networks using a router.

Performance must be given special emphasis when long distances separate inter-connected LANs. For example, if all the hosts on LAN 1 must access a nameserver that is attached to LAN 2, and LAN 1 and LAN 2 are connected using a low-speed telecommunications facility, the hosts on LAN 2 may experience severe performance problems in performing name resolution operations. Therefore, the location of nameservers and other server systems must be chosen with special care when low-speed telecommunications facilities are introduced into an internet.

CONNECTING TO THE WORLDWIDE INTERNET

Most private internets, especially in commercial organizations, start out with the intention of interconnecting only the organization's own equipment. Many private internets do remain private and are not connected to internets of other organizations. However, it is becoming increasingly common in government and industry for the requirement to arise for communicating with computing systems of outside organizations. If an organization applies to the NIC for its internet address assignments, it becomes a relatively simple task for an organization to interconnect one or more of its own private internets to the private internets of other organizations. It also becomes equally straightforward to connect an organization's private internet to the Worldwide Internet.

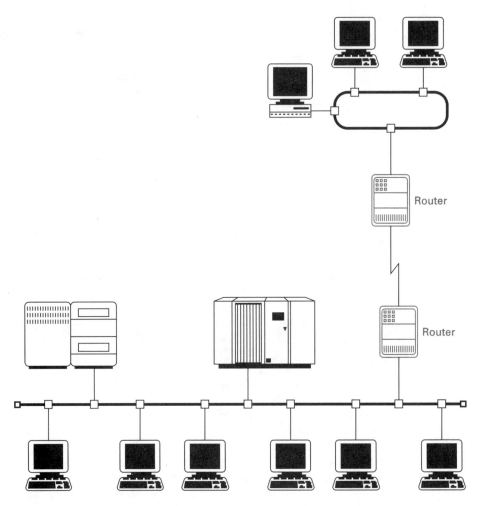

Figure 15.6   Interconnecting two physical networks using a point-to-point link.

Reasons for Connecting to the Internet

There are three reasons that a commercial organization might want to consider connecting to the Internet:

- **Accessing Internet Resources.** The Internet provides access to a wide variety of different types of information resources that may be of value to the organization.

- **Communicating with other Organizations.** The organization may need to communicate with the computers of another organization that is already on the Internet. Connecting to the Internet allows the organization to begin communicating with organizations on the Internet without having to install separate communication links to those organizations.

- **Interconnecting the Organization's Own Private Internets.** The organization may want to use the Internet as a high-speed backbone for communication within the organization's own private internet. In this case, the organization may not need to communicate with other organizations on the Internet. It simply uses the Internet as a means of interconnecting its own set of private internets.

Internet Commercial Service Providers

In the past, connection to the Internet was limited to those organizations that had the need to communicate with the government and educational institutions for which the Internet was originally created. In today's environment, however, there are a number of commercial organizations that supply Internet interconnection services to any organization that wishes to connect to the Internet. These private organizations operate their own high-speed backbone networks that connect to the NSFNET at various points.

An Internet service provider typically supplies its clients with all the hardware and software that is required to connect the organization's private internet to the Internet. A commercial provider generally provides the following services to its clients:

- Provides the client with a router that implements the required routing protocol for interconnecting with the Internet.
- Applies to the NIC for a domain name for the organization to use.
- Operates a primary and secondary nameserver on behalf of the client.

Security Considerations

The issue of security is important to consider when contemplating connecting to the Internet. While security may not have been an important issue within an organization's own private internet, it often becomes of vital importance when it becomes possible for other people to access the organization's computing systems. It must be possible to protect sensitive files and databases from unauthorized access in such an environment.

SUMMARY

Creating a simple, single-LAN TCP/IP internet involves physically interconnecting the hosts, installing the operating system and TCP/IP networking software, and assigning a unique name and internet address to each host. When **hosts** files are used for name resolution, a **hosts** file is configured on each of the hosts in the internet. As part of the software installation process, the appropriate server software is installed on each host that will perform a server function.

The steps involved in testing for network connectivity are to issue **ifconfig** to test the local NIC, issue **ping** by address and by name to test for connectivity and proper operation of the name resolution function, and issue appropriate commands to test the server software on each host.

In installing the Domain Name System, one or more hosts is chosen to play the role of a nameserver. As part of the nameserver configuration process, a high-level domain name is assigned, typically using the conventions established by the Internet.

In interconnecting two or more LANs that are running only TCP/IP networking software, it is generally preferable to interconnect them using a router. However, when a single LAN may be carrying the traffic generated by equipment conforming to multiple protocol suites, a bridge can be used to interconnect them. In interconnecting two or more LANs that have grown up in parallel, naming and addressing conflicts between the two LANs must be resolved before they can be effectively interconnected.

Many organizations eventually wish to connect their private internets to the Worldwide Internet. There are three reasons for this—to access Internet information resources, to communicate with the computers of other organizations on the Internet, and to use the Internet as a backbone to interconnect the organization's own private internets. A number of commercial organizations supply Internet interconnection services.

Chapter 16 describes procedures that may be helpful in diagnosing problems that may occur in an operational internet.

Chapter **16**

Troubleshooting

This chapter describes tools and procedures that may help you to diagnose problems that can occur in an operational internet. The chapter begins by listing typical symptoms of problems that users experience. It then lists the types of problems that can occur to cause those symptoms. Next, it describes the various tools that can be used in diagnosing problems. Finally, this chapter examines a set of procedures that can guide you in using the problem resolution tools that are available.

CATEGORIES OF PROBLEMS

The following are the six most common categories of problems that can occur in an operational internet.

- **Physical Connectivity Problems.** A physical connectivity problem is any problem that is related to the hardware that makes up the internet. It can be caused by such things as a broken cable, a failed router or network interface card (NIC), or a cable inadvertently pulled out of a connector.

- **Remote Host Hardware Problems.** The specific host that the user is trying to reach may have failed, might be in the process of booting itself, or might be temporarily overloaded or otherwise unavailable.

- **Remote Host Software Configuration Problems.** There might be a problem with the software configuration of the remote host that prevents a specific service from being made available.

- **Local Host Software Configuration Problems.** There might be a problem with the software configuration of the local host that prevents the local host from reaching the remote host.

- **Routing Configuration Problems.** The routing tables in one or more hosts or routers in the internet may contain bad information, or one or more routers may have failed.

- **Name Resolution Problems.** The host name specified in a command might have been misspelled, the **hosts** files or nameserver databases might be misconfigured, or one or more nameservers may have failed, making it impossible for name resolution to take place.

PROBLEM RESOLUTION TOOLS

The specific tools that we can use in trying to locate the source of problems may vary from one internet implementation to another. However, Box 16.1 lists some of the tools that are available in most TCP/IP internets.

The remainder of this chapter describes procedures that a user or an administrator can use in helping to decide which of the above tools can be useful in various problem situations and specifies the order in which the various tools should ordinarily be used. Since the procedures concerning the use of SNMP network management software and network monitors are implementation specific, these will not be considered further in this book.

ERROR DIAGNOSIS

When problems occur in the internet, our local host typically issues an error message at the time we attempt to access the services running on a remote host. This typically occurs when we enter a command like **telnet** or **ftp** for a remote host.

There are seven types of error messages that the TCP/IP communication software issues that account for the majority of error situations that can occur in attempting to reach a remote host:

- Service Unknown
- Protocol Unknown
- Network Unreachable
- Host Unreachable
- Connection Timed Out
- Connection Refused
- Host Unknown

The following sections discuss the above error messages and describe procedures that can be used in locating the source of the problem.

Service Unknown and Protocol Unknown

If we receive either the Service Unknown or Protocol Unknown message, the problem is almost certainly related to the software configuration of the local host. For example, a **protocols** or **services** file required by the TCP/IP communication software may not be in the appropriate directory.

The following is an example of a Service Unknown error message:

```
$ telnet ibmserve
telnet: service unknown
```

BOX 16.1   Internet problem resolution tools.

- **The ifconfig Command.** The **ifconfig** command tests the interface to the physical network and tells us if the local host's NIC is operational and if the local host software can access it.

- **The ping Command.** The **ping** command, referencing the remote host either by internet address or by name, tells us if the remote host is currently reachable.

- **The traceroute Command.** The **traceroute** command displays information about the route over which packets are traveling to the remote host. As with **ping,** we can reference the remote host either by internet address or by name.

- **Local ARP Cache Contents.** The **arp** command displays the contents of the ARP cache on the local host and tells us if there is an entry in the local host's ARP cache for a default router.

- **Local hosts File Contents.** If **hosts** files are used for name resolution, we can display the contents of the **hosts** file in the local host to see if it contains the proper entries.

- **The nslookup Command.** If the Domain Name System is used for name resolution, the **nslookup** command tells us if DNS can resolve the name of the host being contacted. The **nslookup** command has a verbose mode that directs **nslookup** to display information about each step in the name resolution process.

- **The netstat Command.** The **netstat** command displays statistics concerning network activity relating to the local host. The **netstat** command typically displays information for the local host about the state of all of its TCP/IP connections and network interfaces, the contents of its routing tables, statistics concerning routing, and statistics concerning TCP/IP protocols.

- **SNMP Network Management Software.** If the internet employs network management tools that use SNMP, these can be used to locate problems of all types in the internet. The specific procedures that are used concerning SNMP tools are implementation specific.

- **Network Monitors.** If the internet employs hardware or software network monitors, these can often be used to locate problems. The specific procedures that are used concerning network monitors are implementation specific.

When receiving a Service Unknown or Protocol Unknown error message, verify that the TCP/IP communications software has been successfully installed on the local host and that the correct configuration options have been chosen regarding the service or protocol that you are attempting to use.

Network Unreachable, Host Unreachable, and Connection Timed Out

If we receive the Network Unreachable, Host Unreachable, or Connection Timed Out message, we most likely have a connectivity problem.

The following is an example of a Host is Unreachable error message:

```
$ telnet vaxserve
  Trying 218.14.0.3 ...
  telnet: connect: Host is unreachable
```

To diagnose a connectivity problem, begin by performing the steps described in Box 16.2.

Connection Refused

If we receive the Connection Refused message when trying to request a service of a remote host, it is likely that the local host has been successful in getting through to the remote host, but the remote host is not accepting a request for the establishment of a connection between a process on the local host and a process on the remote host. In such a situation, we might first try issuing the command a few more times, possibly waiting a minute or so between tries.

When a remote server host is refusing to accept connections, it is possible that the server is simply overloaded and is temporarily unable to accept additional connections. It is also possible that the server is not configured to supply the requested service or that we

---

BOX 16.2   Diagnosing connectivity problems.

1. Issue the **ifconfig** command to ensure that the local host's NIC is operational and that the local host software can access it. This verifies that the NIC has not failed and that the software is configured properly.

2. Issue the **netstat** command to verify that the local interface to the internet is working properly.

3. If the NIC is operational, continue by issuing the **ping** command, giving the local host's own internet address or the address 127.0.0.1. If this fails, the problem, again, is a local one. Verify that the local host software is configured properly.

4. Once it has been determined that the problem is probably not with the local host, continue by trying to ping the remote host by name. If this is successful, then the remote host is reachable and the problem probably lies with the configuration of the remote host's software. Contact the administrator for the remote host for help in determining the source of the problem.

5. If the remote host cannot be pinged by name, the next step depends on whether the internet address of the remote host is known. The address of the remote host might already be known from previous contacts, or the **nslookup** can be used to determine its internet address. If the address of the remote host can be determined, ping the remote host by address. If the remote host is reachable by address but not by name, or if it is not possible to determine the address of the remote host using **nslookup,** then the problem is most probably related to name resolution. Continue by following the steps described in Box 16.3.

6. If the remote host cannot be pinged by address, the problem is probably related to faulty routing. Issue the **traceroute** command, identifying the remote host by name or address, to determine the route over which the packets are traveling to the remote host. If **traceroute** isolates the problem to a specific router, contact the administrator for that router for help in resolving the problem. If **traceroute** is not available on the local system, and the addresses of the routers are known, use the **ping** command to ping all the routers that lie in the path between the local host and the remote host in an attempt to locate the faulty router.

are not authorized to request that service on that particular server, perhaps for security reasons. If the problem persists, we should contact the administrator of the remote host for help in determining the cause of the problem.

Host Unknown

If we receive a Host Unknown message, it is likely that the local host is unable to obtain a name-to-internet-address mapping for the remote host that we are trying to contact. Use the procedures described in Box 16.3 for diagnosing name resolution problems in trying to determine the cause of the problem.

SUMMARY

When problems occur in an operational internet, the local host typically issues an error message when a user attempts to access the services of a remote host on the internet. There are seven error messages that can be received that account for the majority of problems that can occur in attempting to reach a remote host—Service Unknown, Protocol Unknown, Network Unreachable, Host Unreachable, Connection Timed Out, Connection Refused, and Host Unknown.

The six most common categories of problems that can occur are physical connectivity problems, remote host hardware problems, remote host software configuration problems, local host software configuration problems, routing configuration problems, and name resolution problems.

BOX 16.3   Diagnosing name resolution problems.

1. Begin by verifying that the name of the remote host is spelled correctly.

2. If the name is correct, the next step depends on whether **hosts** files or the Domain Name System is being used for name resolution. If a local **hosts** file is being used, the problem is probably caused by the lack of an entry in the **hosts** file for the remote host. The local **hosts** file should be updated to include an entry for that host.

3. If the Domain Name System is being used, check the local software configuration to ensure that the local host can contact a nameserver. The internet address of a nameserver is typically stored in a local configuration file.

4. If the appropriate configuration file for the local host points to a nameserver, try pinging that nameserver to ensure that it is reachable. If this fails, contact the administrator for the nameserver for help in resolving the problem.

5. If the nameserver can be reached from the local host, it is possible that the nameserver software is not running on the nameserver host. If the software is not running, the problem can be resolved by installing the nameserver software on the nameserver host.

6. If the nameserver software is running on the nameserver host, issue the **nslookup** command in verbose mode to see if the specific problem related to the name resolution problem can be located.

The specific tools that are useful in trying to locate the source of problems include the **ifconfig** command, the **ping** command, the **traceroute** command, the local ARP cache contents, local **hosts** file contents, the **nslookup** command, the **netstat** command, SNMP network management software, and network monitors.

Chapter 17 begins Part VI that discusses application programming in the TCP/IP networking environment. Chapter 17 introduces the characteristics of various forms of client-server computing.

PART VI

CLIENT-SERVER PROGRAMMING

Chapter 17   Client-Server Computing

Chapter 18   TCP/IP Programming
Fundamentals

Chapter 19   Socket Programming

Chapter 20   Remote Procedure Call
Programming

Client-Server Computing

The connectivity provided by a TCP/IP internet is often used to implement a *client-server* distributed computing environment in which networked personal computers and workstations perform tasks that were previously performed by larger, more costly mainframes and minicomputers. This chapter examines the characteristics of client-server computing.

In its most general sense, the client-server computing paradigm supports an environment in which an application component called a *client* issues requests for services. Another application component called a *server,* which may run in the same host computer as the client or in some other host, provides the requested service. When the client and server components run in different hosts, the TCP/IP internet provides a means of transporting information back and forth between them. This is illustrated in Fig. 17.1. There can be multiple clients sharing the services of a single server, and the client applications need not be aware that processing is not being performed locally.

The term *client-server computing* has many interpretations, and the term is often used in the personal computer environment to refer to client-server database systems. In a client-server database environment, desktop computers operating in the role of clients

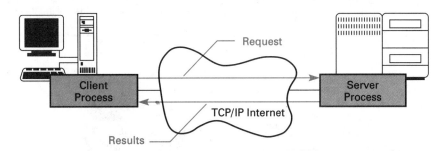

Figure 17.1   With the client-server computing paradigm, a client process issues a request to a server process, and the server passes results back to the client.

make requests for data that is maintained on other hosts operating in the role of database servers. This particular form of client-server computing is discussed further later in this chapter.

As we saw in Chapter 5, most of the TCP/IP application protocols and services operate in a client-server environment. For example, the Network File System (NFS) is a widely used TCP/IP application service in which one or more systems in the internet run NFS server software that has access to the server's file system. Other systems in the internet run NFS client software that sends file access requests to NFS servers. The NFS client software and the NFS server software employ TCP/IP communication to implement the client-server relationship between them.

The client-server computing paradigm permits many different types of server systems to be built. The following are a few types of server systems that are possible in the client-server environment:

- **File Server.** Provides file access and file management services.
- **Print Server.** Provides printing services.
- **Database Server.** Provides database access and database management services.
- **Communications Server.** Provides access to modems or other specialized communication facilities.
- **Application Server.** Provides access to application logic, allowing an application to be distributed among more than one host computer.

CLIENT-SERVER MODELS AND DISTRIBUTION TECHNOLOGIES

The distribution of application components among multiple computing systems lies at the heart of the client-server computing paradigm. In discussing the client-server computing environment, we can identify the three elements shown in Fig. 17.2 and described below:

- **Infrastructure Functions.** In constructing an application that operates in a client-server environment, it is useful for the computing environment to provide a number of general-purpose *infrastructure functions* that can be used by the various components that make up the computing application. These are functions that should be available to all systems in

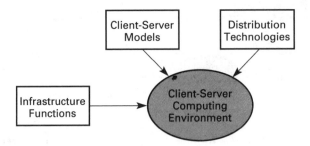

Figure 17.2   Infrastructure functions, client-server models, and distribution technologies.

the computing environment that will participate in client-server distribution. TCP/IP application services provide many of the infrastructure functions that are required to make it possible to create client-server applications.

- **Client-Server Models.** We can identify a number of different *client-server models* that can be implemented to create different types of distributed computing configurations. Each model identifies a different way in which application components can be structured and distributed.

- **Distribution Technologies.** *Distribution technologies* are the means by which the various components that make up a client-server application communicate with one another over the TCP/IP internet. A number of different technologies are available for implementing client-server communication. Any of the distribution technologies can be used to implement any of the distribution models.

Each of the above three elements of the client-server environment are described further in the sections that follow.

INFRASTRUCTURE FUNCTIONS

In building client-server applications, it is helpful if application components have available to them a number of common functions that provide useful services. We call these *infrastructure functions.* If the infrastructure functions are not ubiquitously available, then applications will have to include processing logic to implement many of them. The following are descriptions of some of the infrastructure functions that are useful in the client-server environment.

Global Naming Mechanisms

Every end user and every software component should be able to view the entire distributed environment as a single set of uniquely-named objects in which the names do not change if the objects are moved to new locations.

Unique Identifier Mechanisms

In a distributed environment, it is desirable that processes be able to create identifiers that are unique not only within their own host but unique among all the hosts in the computing environment. A mechanism for creating such globally-unique identifiers on demand is useful in the client-server environment.

Global Management Mechanisms

A single management model should govern operation throughout the distributed environment. Each component should provide a set of management services that can be used to monitor and control the operation of that component. The management model should deal with configuration, performance, error handling, security, and accounting. Components should be capable of being reconfigured dynamically and automatically to achieve high availability and good performance.

Global Time Mechanisms

All hosts in the distributed environment should have clocks that are synchronized to within a small, known degree of error. Slow or fast clocks should be resynchronized smoothly so they can be reliably used for controlling higher-level processes.

Process Activation Mechanisms

Client-server applications typically employ a large number of independent processes that run on hosts that are distributed throughout the network. In order to make the best use of computing resources, it is desirable that software components should execute only when the processing they perform is actually required. Therefore process activation mechanisms are useful in the client-server environment for loading software components and executing them on demand.

Connection Management Mechanisms

The TCP Transport layer protocol is often used to provide the underlying data transport services that are required to implement client-server distribution. As we saw in Chapter 9, TCP sets up a logical *connection* between a pair of communicating processes over which data flows. The cost of establishing a TCP connection between two processes is typically relatively high. Therefore, it is useful if mechanisms are available for reusing connections by different applications or by different components of the same application. Connection management mechanisms can reduce the number of connections that need to be established and released as client-server applications execute.

Client-Server Rendezvous Mechanisms

A fundamental task that must be performed when a client process makes a request for a service is to locate the computing system that provides the requested service. Directory services, such as the Domain Name System (DNS) provided by TCP/IP are helpful in allowing clients to locate servers in the distributed environment.

Multithreading Mechanisms

Multithreading mechanisms are useful in creating client-server applications. A *thread* consists of the execution of a piece of code that can operate concurrently with the execution of the same or different pieces of code within the same application process. Servers often allow multiple threads to execute the same code concurrently in order to be able to serve multiple clients at the same time. Client processes can also often benefit from multithreaded operation by making requests of multiple servers concurrently.

Two-Phase Commit Mechanisms

In a transaction processing environment, it is desirable to be able to define transactions that consist of a sequence of tasks that must all complete successfully before the transaction is considered complete. If any of the activities fail, the results of all previous activities must be backed out to restore the client-server application to the state in which it existed before the transaction was initiated. Such backout processing is accomplished through the use of a *two-phase commit protocol,* in which file or database updates are not considered permanent until all transaction activities have completed successfully.

Security Mechanisms

Security mechanisms are as important for client-server applications as they are for centralized applications. However, they are more difficult to implement in the distributed environment. An important aspect of security in the distributed environment is *authentication.* Authentication mechanisms make it possible for one software component to verify the identity of some other software component. Another important security feature is *data encryption,* in which enciphering and deciphering mechanisms are used to prevent unauthorized parties from eavesdropping on transmissions that take place between a client and a server component.

Data Definition Mechanisms

Mechanisms should be available that allow the data structures that are exchanged between communicating partners to be defined in a way that is independent of any particular computing or communication technology. Distribution technologies employ a wide range of methods for defining data structures, such as employing remote procedure call interface definition languages or the international standard Abstract Syntax Notation One (ASN.1) data definition notation.

CLIENT-SERVER COMPUTING MODELS

As we introduced earlier, there are a number of different models of distributed computing, all of which are based on the simple client-server paradigm. As shown in Fig. 17.3, most computing applications can be described as consisting of a collection of components that falls into one of three categories:

- User interface processing
- Function processing
- Data access processing

In a typical application that executes on a single host, components in all three categories are often intertwined in a way that makes it difficult to distinguish between the three categories. In creating distributed, client-server applications it is important that applications make clear distinctions between the three above categories of components. Understanding the distinction between these three software component categories is helpful in evaluating different models of application distribution.

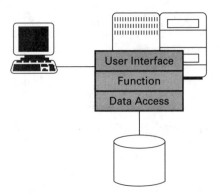

Figure 17.3 Most end user computing applications consist of *user interface* processing components, *function* processing components, and *data access* processing components.

In creating a client-server application, decisions must be made regarding how software components are distributed among a number of separate hosts in the internet. This requires identifying interfaces between components across which requests for services can be made. In the simplest forms of distribution these interfaces are defined between software components that fall into the three major software component categories.

For example, a component that implements the user interface can execute in one host, and the components that perform function processing and data access processing can run in another host, as shown in Fig. 17.4. This is a common application configuration where a personal computer is used to handle user interface tasks and a more powerful server system is used to handle all other application processing. IBM sometimes uses the term *cooperative processing* to describe this form of client-server distribution.

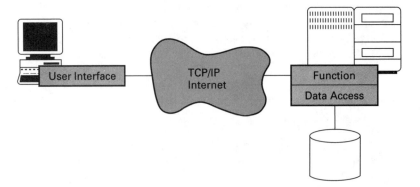

Figure 17.4 User interface processing can be performed in a different host from function processing and data access processing. IBM sometimes refers to this type of configuration as *cooperative processing.*

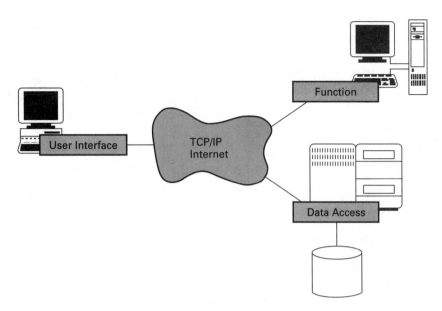

Figure 17.5 User interface processing, function processing, and data access processing can each be performed in a different host.

In a slightly more complex example, user interface processing, function processing, and data access processing can all be performed in different machines, as shown in Fig. 17.5.

The technologies that are available for creating client-server applications have grown in sophistication so that it is now desirable and feasible to distribute functions in complex ways. We next describe a number of models of client-server computing that show the wide variety of configurations that are possible in dividing the computing load among a number of networked processors.

Simple Client-Server Model

The *simple client-server* computing model is probably the most widely used form of application distribution currently in use. In the simple client-server model, the function processing components of the application are divided into two subsystems. One of the subsystems is the client process, and the other is the server process. Each of the two subsystems can run in a different host, as shown in Fig. 17.6.

In this model of client-server computing, the client process initiates a distributed activity, with the target of that activity being the server. A particular service that a server provides is made up of a set of functions that the server performs on behalf of a client.

In the simple client-server model, there can generally be multiple active client subsystems that concurrently access the server subsystem. There can also be multiple active server subsystems, giving an individual client a choice in which copy of the server process to access. In such a case, we say that the server process is *replicated* in the computing environment.

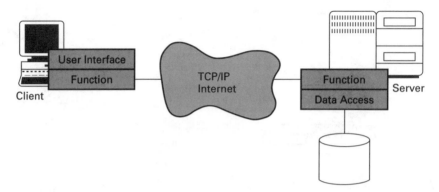

Figure 17.6   Simple client-server computing model.

Broadcast Model

The *broadcast model* is a variation of the simple client-server model. With the broadcast client-server model, a client process generates requests that are received by a number of active server processes, as shown in Fig. 17.7.

   With applications that use this model of client-server computing, it is common for the client to not expect responses from the servers. For example, in a newspaper application, a client process might be accessing wire service information and broadcasting that information to reporter desktop systems, each of which runs a server process that simply accepts the wire service information from the client.

Chained Server Model

In many client-server applications, there are multiple clients and multiple servers that are interconnected in a chain configuration or in a hierarchical tree of chains, as shown in Fig. 17.8.

   The first client makes a request of the first server. The first server then operates in the role of a client and makes a request of a second server. The fact that the first server is acting as a client and accessing a second server may be transparent to the first client. There can be any number of client-server relationships in the chain.

   A server might also have to access a number of other servers to satisfy the original client's request. For example, a client may make a request of a print server to print the contents of a file. The print server then may need to access a file server to obtain the file, a font server to obtain the required font resources, a queue server to enqueue the file while waiting for the printer to become available, and so on. Each individual application activity constitutes a separate client-server interaction, but the entire set appears to the first client process as if it is being performed by the server to which it sends the print request.

Job Contracting Model

The *job contracting model* of client-server computing is a more complex extension of the basic client-server model. In this model of client-server distribution, the client makes a

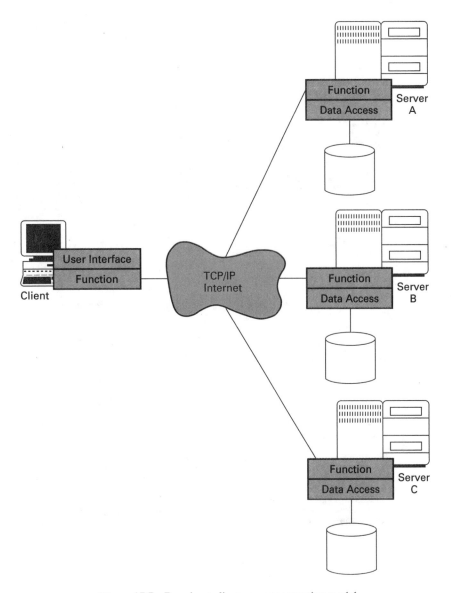

Figure 17.7   Broadcast client-server computing model.

request for a service but may not know which server will actually satisfy the request. The client sends out requests for a service that many servers may be able to satisfy. The client process may then invoke some algorithm to determine the optimum server that it should use to satisfy each request, as shown in Fig. 17.9. In very sophisticated implementations of this model, servers may actually prepare a *bid* and send it back to the client, which then selects a server based on their respective bids.

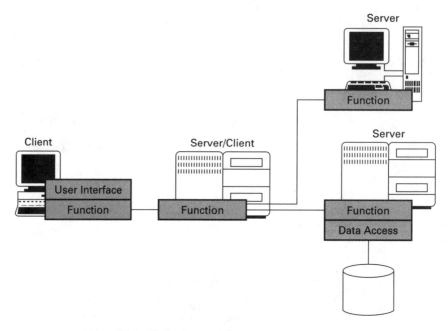

Figure 17.8 Chained server client-server computing model.

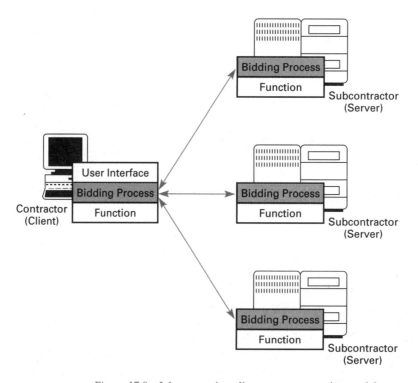

Figure 17.9 Job contracting client-server computing model.

The job contracting model can use a hierarchical structure of client and server processes to create complex and sophisticated applications. It can be used to employ small computers to do jobs that would be much too big to perform on a single system, such as performing complex, time-consuming calculations. The entire computational task could be broken into subtasks and the subtasks could be distributed to a number of computers. Each computer receiving a subtask could further subdivide that subtask and distribute those pieces to other computers. In a very large client-server application, thousands of computers might cooperate in performing the required computations. All of the computers are managed through the contractual relationships that are set up among the cooperating systems.

The job contracting model can be extended by making it possible for individual clients to employ judgment in deciding which subcontractor should perform each task. For example, the client systems can be designed to accumulate knowledge as they execute. A server might tell a client that it can perform a given task in 30 minutes. But the client might know that the last time it gave that server a 30-minute task, the job took five hours to complete. So based on that knowledge, the client might choose some other server for the task.

Object Invocation Model

The *object invocation model* of client-server computing is based on the object-oriented computing paradigm. This model, while also based on client-server relationships, is more dynamic than the previous models. With the object-oriented paradigm, any object can invoke the methods of any other object independently of where the invoked object is located.

The characteristics of object-oriented technology allow the location of invoked objects to be easily managed completely separately from other aspects of the client-server application. For example, a management component might be designed to dynamically relocate invoked objects based on various factors, such as current system load, the number of times each object is invoked, the location of the invoking objects, the cost of network access, and so on.

Flow Management Model

Flow management mechanisms can be made part of any of the distribution models discussed previously. In each of the previous models, at each point in the application, a single client makes an unconditional request of a single server. Adding flow management creates another level of control in which sequences of actions and conditional relationships can be defined apart from the client and server processes themselves. For example, an activity flow, as illustrated in Fig. 17.10, might state: Invoke server process A, then invoke server process B. If both server process A and server process B execute successfully, invoke server process C, otherwise invoke server process D.

This activity flow appears very much like something stated in a conventional programming language, and such flow management mechanisms can be directly programmed into a client-server application. However, what we are describing here is a higher-level

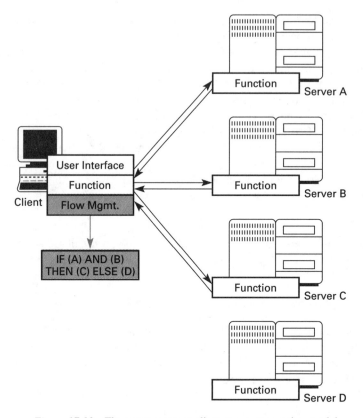

Figure 17.10   Flow management client-server computing model.

mechanism, operating above the level of the code that implements the client and server processes, for describing the behavior of the overall application. In the flow management model, the flow control operates independently of any given client or server process.

The flow management model has great potential for the future. Each of the client and server processes can be implemented in a conventional language, such as C or Visual Basic. But the meta-description that defines the flow relationships might be developed using a specialized language designed for defining the relationships among components in a client-server application and describing concurrent behavior. Unfortunately, at the time of writing, there are no languages commercially available for implementing a flow management model of client-server computing.

DISTRIBUTION TECHNOLOGIES

The technologies that are currently available for creating client-server applications are beginning to mature. There are now a great many choices facing the application developer who wishes to create applications that are based on any of the models of client-server computing we have just discussed. Each of these choices represents a particular type of distribution mechanism that has a set of specific characteristics. Each of the distribution mechanisms is typically well suited for specific types of client-server applications.

Network Transport Independence

There are a wide variety of network architectures in use today, each having its own network transport mechanism. TCP/IP is only one of the architectures currently in use. Others include DECnet, SNA, OSI, AppleTalk, Novell IPX, and so on. For the most part, all of these network transport mechanisms provide a similar range of functions. Distribution technologies are most useful if they can be used without regard to the network transport mechanism that is used to move data through the network. This makes it possible for an application developer to design a client-server application that will operate in an identical manner no matter what network architecture is used at the transport level.

TCP/IP Distribution Mechanisms

A wide range of mechanisms can be identified for creating client-server applications. In the TCP/IP environment, at the time of writing, there are three distribution technologies that are widely used and implemented on a wide range of different types of computing systems:

- Remote Database Access Mechanisms
- Message Passing Mechanisms
- Remote Procedure Call Mechanisms

The sections that follow describe the three distribution mechanisms that are generally available in the TCP/IP networking environment for building client-server applications. Box 17.1 describes two simpler mechanisms that are often also used to create a distributed computing environment but cannot be classified as true client-server mechanisms.

REMOTE DATABASE ACCESS MECHANISMS

Remote database access mechanisms are logically similar to remote file access mechanisms. The main difference between them is that the information stored in database form typically has a well-defined structure, or schema, that is stored with the data, where the information stored in files often does not.

In addition to storing databases on hosts that are remote from the hosts that process the databases, the databases themselves can be distributed among multiple hosts, as illustrated in Fig. 17.11. A number of database management systems are available that support the client-server database environment using TCP/IP networking.

Depending on the sophistication of the database management system, and the way in which functions are distributed between the client and the server systems, substantial processing might be performed by the server system on behalf of a client. At the time of writing, most examples of client-server applications that are in use or under development use a client-server

BOX 17.1 Simple distribution mechanisms.

Remote Terminal Access

The technology of remote terminal access has historically been one of the simplest and most widely used forms of distributed computing. With a remote terminal access mechanism, the end user input and output functions of the application are simply conducted using a terminal device at a location different from that of the host that performs the processing. The remote terminal access mechanisms provided in the TCP/IP environment, such as Telnet or Rlogin, are examples of this type of distribution mechanism.

The simplest applications that use remote terminal access employ inexpensive character-cell terminals to allow the end user to conduct a dialog with the application. In more sophisticated applications, personal computers or workstations are used to support a graphical user interface having windowing capabilities.

Although remote terminal access mechanism can be used to implement a rudimentary form of distributed computing, it cannot be classified as a form of client-server computing. In essence, all of the application's processing is performed on a single host using this form of distribution. Remote terminal access is, and will remain, a very useful mechanism for distributed computing. However, it does not provide any means for distributing the actual processing performed by the application. It is no more than an extension of the application's user interface across the network.

Remote File Access

An important form of distributed computing is to distribute the data files that the application accesses to hosts that are remote from the host that actually performs the processing on the data contained in those files. The remote file access facility provided in the TCP/IP environment by NFS is an example of this type of distribution tool. Again, however, with NFS all of the application's processing is performed by the client system, and an application that uses NFS to access remote files is not a true client-server application.

There are two ways in which the files that an application accesses can be distributed. The simplest way is through a network file transfer mechanism. With this method, files are distributed throughout the network to the hosts that most often access them. When a file is needed elsewhere, a copy of the entire file is transferred to the host running the application that needs it. While this is a useful method of distribution for some applications, it is not useful when a single file must be shared, and concurrently updated, by multiple users.

A more sophisticated mechanism for remote file access allows applications to transparently access the information stored in files that are maintained on remote hosts. Such distributed file access mechanisms provide a different form of information distribution and have two main advantages over file transfer mechanisms:

- A single file server can be used to maintain files that are accessed by a number of different users.

- Distributed file mechanisms can be designed so that information distribution is transparent to the application programs that use the distributed data. Applications can access files as if they were stored locally even though they may be distributed among a number of remote file servers.

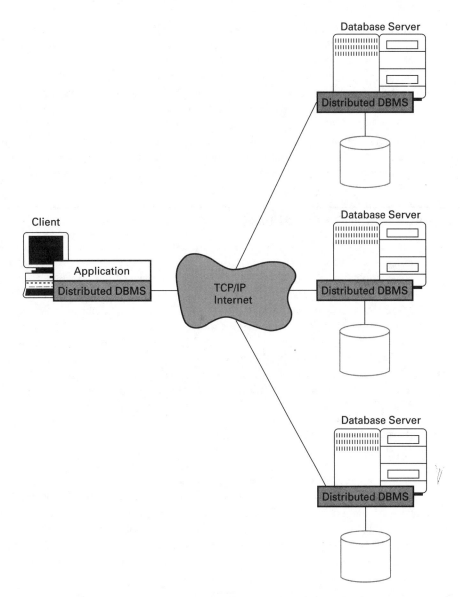

Figure 17.11   Remote database access distribution mechanism.

DBMS as a client-server application development tool. Particularly important in the client-server database environment is the *Structured Query Language* (SQL). SQL-based relational database management systems typically provide facilities that allow programs to perform database accesses in a way that is independent of the mechanisms that are used to actually store the data.

Very powerful client-server applications can be created when the DBMS allows the database itself to be distributed among multiple server systems. Database distribution is often accomplished through the mechanisms of *partitioning* and *replication*. A *partition* is a portion of the database that is administered as a unit and is maintained by a single host. A *replica* is a copy of all or a portion of the data in the database that is maintained on another host to enhance availability.

A major goal of distributed database systems is to allow any information in the database to be accessed directly from hosts anywhere in the network. It is desirable to be able to accomplish this transparently so that an application program that needs access to information stored in a remote or distributed database can access the information as if it were all stored locally. Details of distribution, such as the actual location of the data, and any partitioning or replication that is implemented, should not be seen by the applications that access the data.

MESSAGE PASSING MECHANISMS

Message passing mechanisms consist of the direct exchange of data between application processes that may be running on different hosts in the internet. With message passing, application A transmits a message across the internet to application B. Application B receives the message and may then send a reply to application A, as illustrated in Fig. 17.12. Data can be sent back and forth in the form of discrete units or in the form of a continuous stream. Distributed applications of great complexity that implement any of the client-server computing models described previously can be built using simple message passing as a distribution mechanism.

There are two forms of message passing mechanisms that can be provided for implementing client-server applications—connectionless mechanisms and connection-oriented mechanisms.

Connectionless Message Passing Mechanisms

With a *connectionless,* or *datagram,* message passing mechanism, the source application simply sends a message into the network and indicates the destination or destinations to which the message is to be sent. The message passing mechanism makes a best-efforts attempt to deliver the message to its intended destination or destinations, but the source application is not informed as to whether delivery was actually accomplished. With a connectionless message passing service, a source application can send a message to one or more destination applications in a single operation. The message passing mechanism provided in TCP/IP by the UDP Transport protocol is an example of a connectionless message passing mechanism.

Connection-Oriented Message Passing Mechanisms

With a *connection-oriented* message passing mechanism, two communicating processes exchange control messages with each other to establish an association, called a *connection,* between them. The connection is used for the purpose of ensuring that messages are exchanged reliably between the two processes. With a connection-oriented service, mech-

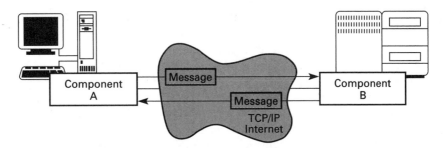

Figure 17.12   Message passing distribution mechanism.

anisms are generally provided for detecting and recovering from situations in which messages are lost, duplicated, or corrupted during transmission. With a connection-oriented message passing mechanism, a source application can send a message in a single operation to only one destination. A separate connection is required for each destination if multiple destinations are involved. Connection-oriented message passing mechanisms can provide two types of interfaces to application processes:

- **Stream Interface.** With a stream interface, the source application sends data in the form of a sequential stream of octets, and the destination application receives an identical copy of the octet stream. A stream interface operates in a similar manner to writing and reading information to and from a sequential file on a local disk storage device.

- **Message Interface.** With a message interface the application sends and receives individual units of data, much like reading and writing a record-oriented file.

The TCP Transport protocol provided by TCP/IP can be used to implement both stream and message-oriented connection-oriented message passing mechanisms. The Socket interface, implemented by most systems that support TCP/IP networking, provides an application programming interface for invoking message passing mechanisms in application programs. The Socket interface is described in Chapters 18 and 19.

Both connectionless and connection-oriented message passing mechanisms can be used to create reliable client-server applications. However, when a connectionless service is used, the application itself must implement more sophisticated reliability controls than if a connection-oriented service is available.

However, no matter what type of service is used to implement a client-server application, there can be no guarantee that a function that is invoked remotely will actually be executed. This is because even if a message is delivered to its destination reliably, the destination application process may fail before it is able to process the message. For this reason higher-level distribution technologies that employ message passing services generally implement additional mechanisms to ensure reliability.

REMOTE PROCEDURE CALL MECHANISMS

Remote procedure call (RPC) mechanisms extend the familiar procedure call programming paradigm from the local computing system environment to a distributed environment. With an RPC facility, the calling procedure and the called procedure can execute in different hosts in the internet. RPC mechanisms make it possible to hide from the application programmer the fact that distribution is taking place. A primary goal of an RPC mechanism is to make it appear to the programmer that remote procedures are invoked in exactly the same manner as local procedures.

It is not possible, however, to achieve complete transparency because the semantics of distributed operations are often substantially different from those of the same operation performed locally. For example, when the called procedure is executing on a different host from the calling procedure, a number of problems can occur that do not occur when the two procedures are running on the same host. The following are examples of some of these problems:

- Either of the two software components can independently fail in such a way that the other component is not aware of the failure.

- There can be a temporary loss of connectivity between the two components as they execute.

- Problems can occur that relate to management and security issues that do not arise in the local environment.

Most RPC mechanisms, however, provide facilities for maintaining conventional programming methods as much as possible and for handling many of the complexities that are inherent in the distributed environment.

RPC mechanisms are typically built on top of a message passing mechanism and implement a simple request-response protocol. The calling procedure makes a request for the execution of the called procedure and may pass a set of argument values to the called procedure. The called procedure then executes and may pass a set of results back to the calling procedure. An RPC mechanism handles the formatting and delivery of network messages that must flow between the calling procedure and the called procedure using a process called *marshaling*.

The main reason for using RPC mechanisms in the client-server environment is that they automatically handle much of the work involved in distributing functions, and they make it easier for application developers to design, implement, and maintain client-server applications.

The TCP/IP environment provides remote procedure mechanisms that can be used for the purposes of client-server applications. These are described in Chapter 20. The OSF Distributed Computing Environment (DCE), described in Appendix B, also includes a remote procedure call mechanism that can be used in conjunction with a variety of data transport mechanisms, including TCP/IP.

CHOOSING A DISTRIBUTION MECHANISM

Choosing a distribution technology to use in implementing a client-server application has some similarities to choosing a particular programming language for an application. An application developer may choose a particular language for a number of reasons. The chosen language may offer the best performance for a given environment, it may have language constructs that are well suited to the application, the developer may be more familiar with a particular language, and so on.

In the same way, a number of factors govern the particular distribution tool that the developer may choose to use. There are engineering tradeoffs to be made, and what may seem like an optimal solution to one developer may seem less desirable to someone else. Like the choice of a programming language, there is often no clear cut choice in selecting a distribution mechanism.

In addition to the three distribution mechanisms that we have described, additional, more sophisticated mechanisms exist in specific platform environments. Box 17.2 describes some additional distribution mechanisms that will be important in the future in creating client-server applications.

A number of different distribution technologies are available for creating client-server applications, especially if platforms can be chosen based on the technologies that are available. In addition to there being distinct differences between each of the distribution technologies we have discussed, there are also many similarities. Given any particular client-server application situation, it is likely that more than one distribution mechanism will be suitable for that application. Also, in sophisticated client-server applications, it is likely that it will be necessary or desirable to employ more than one distribution tool.

BOX 17.2   Platform-specific distribution mechanisms.

Peer-to-Peer Communication Mechanisms

Peer-to-Peer communication mechanisms provide facilities that are analogous in some ways to connection-oriented message passing mechanisms. They provide additional functions that allow communicating applications to communicate asynchronously and still retain a shared context across a dialog that may consist of multiple interactions. With this type of distribution mechanism, communication takes place between two or more software components that are organized hierarchically with the initiator of the first message exchange at the root.

The TCP/IP environment does not include a peer-to-peer communication mechanism. There are several protocol and API standards for peer-to-peer communication mechanisms. Protocol standards include those defined by ISO's TP/CCR and IBM's SNA Logical Unit 6.2 (LU 6.2). API standards for peer-to-peer communication mechanisms include IBM's CPI-C, IBM's APPC, and X/Open's DTP.

At the time of writing, it is unclear how important peer-to-peer communication mechanisms will be outside of the IBM APPC environment for creating client-server applications.

Message Queuing Mechanisms

With a message queuing mechanism, sometimes called a reliable messaging service, an application process running on one host can submit messages that are addressed to other application processes that may be running on other hosts. In many cases, the messages sub-

---

(Continued)

BOX 17.2 *(Continued)*

mitted by the source process do not require immediate responses. This makes it possible for a remote queuing mechanism to support asynchronous processing. The source process submits a message and does not wait for a response but immediately performs other required processing. The destination process may or may not be active at the time the message is submitted. If the destination process is not active, the remote queuing mechanism may wait for the destination process to become active before delivering the message, or it may take steps to activate the destination process, depending on application requirements.

A message queuing mechanism typically makes no assumptions about the structure and state of the application processes involved in the communication. For example, they do not need to implement the same mechanisms regarding recovery or consistency. As a result, queued communication can often be useful when existing applications need to exchange data with each other.

At the time of writing, the TCP/IP environment does not include a standardized mechanism for message queuing. A number of different vendor products are starting to become available for message queuing. However, at the time of writing, standardization work on message queuing mechanisms that will be useful in a heterogeneous distributed environment is just beginning. It is likely that message queuing will be an important mechanism for creating client-server applications when accepted standards begin to evolve.

Remote Object Invocation Mechanisms

A remote object invocation mechanism allows application developers to take advantage of object-oriented design and programming techniques in the client-server environment. A remote object invocation mechanism typically provides a repository for storing object methods based on a class hierarchy that allows for inheritance of attributes and behavior among related objects. It also typically allows new objects to be dynamically created and existing objects to be moved to new locations in the distributed environment. A generic object invocation mechanism may make the location of an object transparent to the invoker of that object.

Remote object invocation mechanisms are very useful for combining existing applications or creating a new application from existing software components that may or may not have been originally designed to work together. There are currently no generally accepted mechanisms for remote object invocation in the TCP/IP environment.

Transaction Processing Mechanisms

Transaction processing represents a distribution technology that has a more broad definition than those preceding. Transaction processing is often used to implement high-volume commercial applications that have strong requirements for reliability and consistency. Fundamental to all transaction processing is the two-phase commit mechanism introduced earlier. Transaction processing distribution technology often uses the two-phase commit mechanism in conjunction with other distribution technologies.

For example, a software component might start a transaction in response to a request that an end user enters using a remote terminal access mechanism. Executing the transaction

---

BOX 17.2 *(Continued)*

might require using an RPC mechanism to invoke a remote procedure. This might, in turn, require that a remote, possibly distributed, database record be updated. Finally, a software component might log a record of the database change activity by using a message queuing mechanism. The transaction is not considered to be complete, and the changes made to the database are not committed, until all processing activities have completed successfully. If one or more functions fails, the results of the entire transaction are backed out, and all resources affected by the transaction are restored to the state in which they existed before the transaction started. The transaction may then be restarted.

One of the characteristics of most transaction processing environments is that centralized control over distributed activities is required. Traditionally, this has been provided in the form of transaction processing (TP) monitor software that handles all application requests. The TP monitor can perform functions such as checking access rights to a resource, selecting a provider for that resource, determining if the resource provider is still operating and performing a given activity, recording the results of an activity for accounting purposes, and so on. As functions become more distributed, the transaction processing monitor software is itself becoming more distributed.

SUMMARY

The client-server paradigm supports an environment in which an application component called a client makes a request for a service. The service is supplied by another application component called a server. The client and server components can run in the same or in different computing systems. The client-server form of distributed computing comprises three elements—infrastructure functions, client-server models, and distribution technologies.

Infrastructure functions include generally available services that are used by a large number of application components. Some of the infrastructure functions that are useful in implementing client-server distribution include mechanisms for global naming, unique identifiers, global management, global time, process activation, connection management, client-server rendezvous, multitasking, two-phase commit, security, and data definition.

Computing applications are made up of components that can be divided into three categories—user interface processing components, function processing components, and data access components. Client-server models describe different ways in which application components can be combined to form distributed application configurations. Possible client-server models include the simple client-server model, the broadcast model, the chained server model, the job contracting model, the object invocation model, and the flow management model.

A number of different distribution technologies can be used to implement the communication functions that are necessary to implement client-server distribution. The three distribution technologies used most often in the TCP/IP networking environment include mechanisms for remote database access, message passing, and remote procedure calls.

Chapter 18 introduces a number of fundamental programming techniques that are used to implement TCP/IP communication functions in client-server application programs.

Chapter **18**

TCP/IP Programming Fundamentals

This chapter introduces the fundamentals of writing application programs that communicate over a TCP/IP internet. It is intended for programmers who are familiar with writing application programs for any computing platform that supports TCP/IP communications software.

CLIENT-SERVER RELATIONSHIP

As we introduced in Chapter 17, TCP/IP programs generally conform to a client-server form of interaction. With client-server computing, an application component running on one host issues requests for services, and those services are supplied by an application component running on another host in the internet. For example, the service requests might be for printing services or for database access that might otherwise be provided by the local operating system or by calls to a local database management system. Instead of being processed locally, the service requests are sent across the internet to another host where they are processed, and the results are returned to the application that issued the service request.

The application component issuing the service requests is called the *client*. The component running in the remote host that processes the requests and provides the results is called the *server*. There can be multiple client components sharing the services of a single server component, and the client applications need not be aware that processing is not being performed locally.

CLIENT COMPONENT

Although the specific functions performed by a client component differ depending on the application, there are certain steps that must be performed by any component functioning in the role of a client. The steps that are typically performed by a client component are described in Box 18.1.

BOX 18.1   Steps performed by a typical client component.

1. The client begins by opening a communication channel between the client component running on the local host and the server component running on a remote host. The client must know the internet address of the host running the server component, the Transport layer protocol the server is using, and the server's port number assignment. This type of open is called an *active open,* since the client expects the server to be available and waiting for communication activity.

2. The client component sends a message (or multiple messages) to the server containing details about the requested service.

3. The client accepts messages from the server containing responses to its service requests.

4. The client ends by closing the communication channel and terminating its execution.

SERVER COMPONENT

Application components that function as clients have no special design considerations associated with them. But there are two types of servers that can be employed.

Iterative Servers

An iterative server processes one client's request at a time. An iterative server is used when a client's request can be handled by the server in a known, usually short amount of time. If a second client requests a service while the server is satisfying the first client's request, the second client waits until the first client's request has been satisfied. A server that provides clients with the date and time of day is an example of a server that might be implemented as an iterative server. The client sends the server a message asking for the date and time, and the server responds with a message containing a date and time-of-day value. Such a service can be provided in a predictably short period of time using a known amount of processing.

As with clients, the detailed processing performed by a server differs from application to application, but certain steps must be performed by a server in satisfying the requests made of clients. Box 18.2 describes the steps typically performed by an iterative server.

Concurrent Servers

A concurrent server can process the requests of more than one client at the same time. It does this by issuing a function, such as the UNIX **fork** function, that creates a separate thread, task, or process to handle each client's request. A concurrent server is used when the server may not know in advance how much time and effort will be required to satisfy each request. A server that handles file transfer operations for clients is an example of a server that might be implemented as a concurrent server. The server has no idea in advance how much time it will take to satisfy each request for a file transfer operation. Therefore, in order to provide

---

BOX 18.2   Steps performed by a typical iterative server component.

1. The server begins by opening a communication channel and informing the local host of the server's willingness to accept requests from clients. It uses a Transport layer protocol port in which the number has been made known to its potential clients. This type of open is called a *passive open,* since it is possible that there may be no communication activity at the time the server opens the channel.

2. The server waits for a client's request to arrive at its port.

3. When a message arrives from a client, the server activates and performs the processing necessary to handle the request. Handling the request may require more than one message to be exchanged between the client and the server, but iterative servers are typically used only when a client's request can be handled with a single response, or a small number of responses, from the server.

4. After the server completes its processing for a given client, it waits for a request to arrive from some other client. The system typically queues requests that arrive from clients while the server is processing a previous client's request.

BOX 18.3   Steps performed by a typical concurrent server component.

1. A concurrent server begins by issuing a passive open, informing the local host of the server's willingness to accept requests from clients. It uses a Transport layer protocol port in which the number has been made known to its potential clients.

2. The server waits for a client's request to arrive at its port.

3. When a message arrives from a client, the server activates and issues a function to create an independent process to handle the client's request. The parent process then waits for a request to arrive from some other client.

4. The child process might then load and execute a program to perform the processing required to satisfy the client's request. It is typical for a concurrent server to require a number of message exchanges with the client in satisfying the client's request.

5. After the child process completes its processing for a client, it terminates its processing.

---

good service to multiple clients, it is desirable to create a separate independent process for each client so that multiple file transfer operations can be supported concurrently.

Box 18.3 describes the steps that are typically performed by a concurrent server component.

ASSOCIATIONS

In TCP/IP programming, the notion of an *association* is important. The term *association* refers to a collection of five pieces of information that are required before information can be exchanged between a component running in one host and a component running in another host.

Association Data Elements

The five pieces of information that define an association are as follows:

- **Protocol-Identifier.** An identifier that describes the Transport layer protocol (typically TCP or UDP) used to handle the transfer of data between the communicating processes.
- **Local Internet Address.** The 32-bit internet address of the local host.
- **Local Port Number.** The 16-bit port number of the Transport layer protocol port used by the local process.
- **Remote Internet Address.** The 32-bit internet address of the remote host.
- **Remote Port Number.** The 16-bit port number of the Transport layer protocol port used by the remote process.

The above five pieces of information specified in an association contain all the information that is required to unambiguously support communication between a process running on a local host and a process running on a remote host.

Half-Association Data Elements

A half-association is that part of an association that is required to define the information required by one of the hosts that participates in the association. The following pieces of information define a half-association for the local host:

- Protocol identifier
- Local internet address
- Local port number

The following pieces of information define a half-association for the remote host:

- Protocol identifier
- Remote internet address
- Remote port number

The protocol identifier must be the same in both half-associations in order for the two half-associations to form a valid association. If the client is assuming TCP and the server is designed to use UDP, communication will not be possible between that client and that server.

SUPPORT FUNCTION CALLS

TCP/IP communication software typically makes available a number of function calls that can be used to provide communication support services. Among the support services that are generally available are those for performing octet order conversions for integer information and internet address format conversions. Each of these two categories of support services are described next.

Integer Octet Order Function Calls

In writing application programs that communicate over an internet, attention must be paid to the order in which the octets that carry integer information, such as internet addresses and port numbers, are sent over the internet. Unfortunately, the computers of the world are divided into two camps with respect to the way they store data in their memories—the *big-endian* camp and the *little-endian* camp. Figure 18.1 shows the difference between how big-endian computer systems and little-endian computer systems might store a 32-bit internet address.

In a big-endian computer system, the high-order octet is stored in the lowest memory location, and the low-order octet is stored in the highest memory location. In a little-endian computer system, the high-order octet is contained in the highest memory location and the low-order octet is contained in the lowest memory location.

Examples of big-endian computers are IBM mainframes and computers using Motorola microprocessors. Examples of little-endian computers are DEC VAX processors and computers using Intel microprocessors. Networking protocols can also choose to use either a little-endian or a big-endian scheme for storing integer information in protocol headers. The scheme chosen for a particular protocol is called that protocol's *network octet order* or *network byte order*. The network octet order for all protocols in the TCP/IP protocol suite is big-endian.

A big-endian computer system need not perform any conversion in building TCP/IP protocol headers from integers stored in its memory. But little-endian computer systems need to reverse the order of the octets storing integers in building protocol headers. In order to simplify this situation and to promote portability of applications, TCP/IP communications software provides a set of functions that permit integer information, such as internet addresses and port numbers, to be reliably placed into the appropriate *network octet order*. Box 18.4 lists the octet order function calls that are useful in TCP/IP programming.

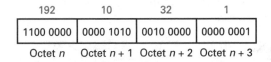

Internet Address 192.10.32.1 Stored in Big-Endian Host

Internet Address 192.10.32.1 Stored in Little-Endian Host

Figure 18.1　Difference between big-endian and little-endian integer storage.

BOX 18.4   Integer octet order function calls.

- **htons.** Host to Network Short. Converts a 16-bit integer from the octet order used by the host to network octet order. *Example:*

```
net_short = htons (host_short)
```

- **htonl.** Host to Network Long. Converts a 32-bit integer from the octet order used by the host to network octet order. *Example:*

```
net_long = htonl (host_long)
```

- **ntohs.** Network to Host Short. Converts a 16-bit integer from network octet order to the octet order used by the host. *Example:*

```
host_short = ntohs (net_short)
```

- **ntohl.** Network to Host Long. Converts a 32-bit integer from network octet order to the octet order used by the host. *Example:*

```
host_long = ntohl (net_long)
```

Since the TCP/IP network octet order is big-endian, these functions do nothing on a big-endian host. On a little-endian host, they reverse the sequence of the octets containing the integers for which they are called. It is good programming practice to always use these functions in formatting protocol header information, whether or not the program will be executed on a little-endian or a big-endian host.

Address Conversion Function Calls

Two functions are useful for performing internet address conversions when working with internet addresses in both dotted-decimal and binary form. Box 18.5 describes the address conversion function calls.

BOX 18.5   Address conversion function calls.

- **inet_addr.** Converts an internet address in ASCII dotted-decimal format to 32-bit binary format. *Example:*

```
binary_addr = inet_addr (ascii_addr)
```

- **inet_ntoa.** Converts an internet address in 32-bit binary format to ASCII dotted-decimal format. *Example:*

```
ascii_addr = inet_ntoa (binary_addr)
```

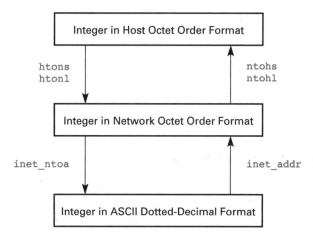

Figure 18.2   Byte order and internet address conversion function calls.

Figure 18.2 shows the relationships among the network octet order functions and the address conversion functions.

TRANSPORT LAYER PROTOCOL PORTS

As discussed earlier, a half-association identifies a Transport layer protocol, the internet address of a host, and the port number assigned to the process. Transport Layer protocol ports are important because most computing systems on which the TCP/IP communications software typically runs allow many processes to execute concurrently. Each process that uses the services of a TCP/IP Transport layer protocol on a given host is assigned a unique port number.

The port numbers for each Transport layer protocol are allocated in the following manner:

- Port 0—Not used
- Ports 1-255—Well-known port numbers
- Ports 256-1023—Reserved ports numbers
- Ports 1024-4999—Ephemeral client port numbers
- Ports 5000-65,535—User-defined server port numbers

When supporting communication in the client-server environment, the server must use a port number that is known to all of its potential clients. To support the needs of certain types of servers that are of general usefulness in most internets, a number of *well-known* port assignments have been made. For example, an application component that implements a Trivial File Transfer Protocol (TFTP) server always uses UDP port number 69 for its half-association. The port number that a user-defined server uses must be established by convention between the server and the client components it serves. These are allocated by the individual organization from the user-defined server range of port numbers.

A client component typically uses one of the ephemeral port numbers in establishing communication with the server. Most TCP/IP communications software implements a function that a client component can use to obtain the port number of an unused ephemeral port on that host. The client typically sends the server the client's own port number to which the server can then reply.

COMMUNICATION PROGRAMMING APIs

TCP/IP networking software typically supports a number of different types of application programming interfaces (APIs) for communicating over an internet. The following are descriptions of the two types of APIs that are discussed in this book.

Socket System Calls

The *socket* approach to network communication programming is generally associated with the BSD variation of UNIX, which first implemented the socket API. The socket interface provides an API for network communication that is very close to the API provided for doing ordinary I/O with local devices. The socket interface has been implemented on a wide variety of UNIX and non-UNIX operating systems, and programs that access sockets can be used for implementing network communication in a heterogeneous environment in which hosts of all types must be able to communicate. The socket API is currently the most commonly used API for network programming in the TCP/IP environment and in other networking environments as well. It is likely to remain a popular API throughout the 1990s. Socket programming is introduced in Chapter 19.

Remote Procedure Call Facilities

The *remote procedure call* (RPC) type of API provides what has the potential of being an easier to use API than is provided by the socket interface. Remote procedure calls allow a network programmer to use a simple procedure call mechanism to pass control between procedures that may be executing on different hosts in an internet. As we introduced in Chapter 5, two RPC facilities are widely used in the TCP/IP environment—the Sun RPC facility and the Hewlett-Packard RPC facility. The fundamentals of programming with the Sun RPC facility are described in Chapter 20.

Figure 18.3 shows a comparison between the location of the application programming interface when the Sun RPC facility is used and the location of the API for socket programming. With socket programming, the API interfaces directly with either the TCP or UDP Transport layer protocol. When the Sun RPC facility is used, the Sun *external data representation* (XDR) facility and the Sun RPC runtime facility sit between the application program and the Transport layer protocol. The XDR facility provides a standard method for encoding argument data and results so they can be used in a portable fashion in a heterogeneous host environment.

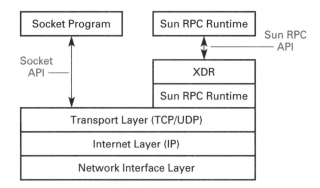

Figure 18.3   Socket and Sun RPC application programming interface relationship.

The book *UNIX Network Programming* provides detailed descriptions of the socket and RPC APIs introduced in Chapters 19 and 20 as well as a number of other APIs that are used for network programming.

SUMMARY

A form of distributed computing that is often used in the TCP/IP internet environment is *client-server computing*. With client-server computing, an application component running on one host issues requests for services (the client), and those services are supplied by an application component running on another host in the internet (the server). There are two types of server components that can be employed. An iterative server processes one client's request at a time. A concurrent server can process the requests of more than one client simultaneously.

An *association* is a collection of five pieces of information that are required before information can be exchanged between a component running in one host and a component running in another host—a value identifying the Transport layer protocol being used, the internet address of the local host, the port number of the local process, the internet address of the remote host, and the port number of the remote process.

Attention must be paid to the order in which the octets that carry integer information—such as internet addresses and port numbers—are sent over the internet. Functions are provided for converting between the network octet order and the octet ordering used by the host. Functions are also provided for converting between binary internet address values and ASCII dotted-decimal internet addresses.

Each process that uses a Transport layer protocol concurrently on a given host is assigned a unique port number. The server must use a port number that is known to all of its potential clients. A client component typically uses an ephemeral port number in establishing communication with the server and typically sends the server the client's own port number to which the server can then reply.

TCP/IP networking software supports a number of different types of application programming interfaces (APIs) for communicating over an internet. The socket approach is very close to the API provided for doing ordinary I/O with local devices. The remote procedure call (RPC) type of API provides what has the potential of being an easier to use API than sockets. Remote procedure calls allow a network programmer to use a simple procedure call mechanism to pass control between procedures that may be executing on different hosts in an internet.

Chapter 19 introduces programming techniques used in employing the socket interface for implementing client-server applications in the TCP/IP networking environment.

REFERENCE

1. W. Richard Stevens, *UNIX Network Programming,* Prentice-Hall, Inc., Englewood Cliffs, NJ, 1990.

Socket Programming

The *socket* interface was initially developed for the BSD variation of the UNIX operating system. By using the socket interface, two application programs, one running in the local system and another running in the remote system, can communicate with one another in a standardized manner. The socket interface is the most widely used TCP/IP application programming interface (API) at the time of writing.

The socket API is typically used to implement a client-server relationship between two application components running in different computing systems. The client and the server programs each invoke functions that set up an association between them. The association between the two application components is based on the use of data structures, called *sockets,* that provide access to TCP/IP communication services. The client and the server components then invoke functions to send and receive information over the internet in a similar manner to calling functions that are used to perform ordinary file I/O.

The socket API can be used to provide access to protocols other than TCP/IP. For example, sockets can be used to support process-to-process communication within the same host (UNIX domain protocols), communication using the Xerox Network System (XNS) protocols, and communication using the OSI protocols. This chapter discusses the use of sockets with only the TCP/IP protocol suite.

THREE TYPES OF SOCKETS

The socket API defines three types of sockets that can be used to support communication in the TCP/IP environment:

- **Stream Sockets.** These are sockets that can be used to communicate using the TCP Transport layer protocol. Stream sockets support a connection-oriented form of data transfer in which a stream of data can be reliably sent from one socket to another over a TCP connection.

- **Datagram Sockets.** These are sockets that can be used to communicate using the UDP Transport layer protocol. Datagram sockets support an unreliable, datagram form of data transfer in which individual user datagrams can be sent from one socket to another.

- **Raw Sockets.** These are sockets that provide access to the underlying IP and ICMP processes. Raw sockets are generally used only for specialized purposes, such as writing network troubleshooting tools. Raw sockets are not discussed further in this book.

The relationship between the three types of sockets is shown in Fig. 19.1.

Socket Addresses

Many of the socket system calls reference a pointer to a data structure containing information constituting a *socket address.* A socket address specifies one end of a communication link. A description of this data structure, and other identifiers and data structures useful in network programming, are typically contained in files that are supplied with the TCP/IP networking software.

In the typical UNIX environment, the following **include** statements make these identifiers and data structures available to the application program:

```
#include <sys/types.h>
#include <sys/sockets.h>
```

For the TCP/IP protocols, the socket address data structure contains the following information:

- **Family.** A 16-bit integer value identifying the protocol family being used. For TCP/IP communication, this value must identify the TCP/IP protocol family. The AF_INET identifier contains the appropriate integer value to identify the TCP/IP protocol family in system calls that require it.

- **Port.** A 16-bit integer value identifying the port number assigned to the process. A user-written server process uses one of the user-defined server port numbers. A client must know the port number that the server is using. A client typically asks the communications software to supply it with an ephemeral port number that it can use.

- **Address.** A 32-bit integer value containing the internet address, in binary format, of the host in which the process is running. A client process must know the internet address of the host on which the server is running.

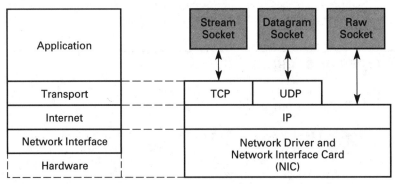

Figure 19.1   Three types of sockets.

Each of the two processes in a client-server application is identified by a separate socket address. The socket address of the server process plus the socket address of the client process make up four of the five pieces of the information necessary to create an association between the two processes. Both the client process and the server process must also identify the Transport layer protocol being used for communication, thus completing the information required for an association to exist between the two processes. Box 19.1 shows the data type definitions and data structures used to define socket addresses.

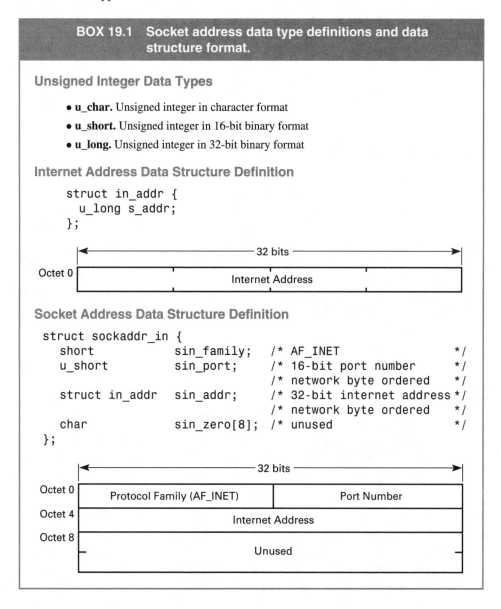

BOX 19.1   Socket address data type definitions and data structure format.

Unsigned Integer Data Types

- **u_char.** Unsigned integer in character format
- **u_short.** Unsigned integer in 16-bit binary format
- **u_long.** Unsigned integer in 32-bit binary format

Internet Address Data Structure Definition

```
struct in_addr {
  u_long s_addr;
};
```

```
                  |◄──────────────── 32 bits ────────────────►|
Octet 0 |                          Internet Address                         |
```

Socket Address Data Structure Definition

```
struct sockaddr_in {
    short           sin_family;   /* AF_INET                    */
    u_short         sin_port;     /* 16-bit port number         */
                                  /* network byte ordered       */
    struct in_addr  sin_addr;     /* 32-bit internet address    */
                                  /* network byte ordered       */
    char            sin_zero[8];  /* unused                     */
};
```

```
                  |◄──────────────── 32 bits ────────────────►|
Octet 0 |     Protocol Family (AF_INET)      |      Port Number      |
Octet 4 |                          Internet Address                         |
Octet 8 |                               Unused                              |
```

Endpoint Identifier

A socket address data structure contains data elements that constitute an *endpoint identifier* that serves as a unique identifier, or name, for a process. An endpoint address is made up of an internet address and a port number. Therefore, the following pieces of information define the endpoint address of the local host process:

- Local internet address
- Local port number

The following pieces of information define the endpoint address of the remote host process:

- Remote internet address
- Remote port number

SOCKET SYSTEM CALLS

The socket API provides a set of system calls that application programs invoke to request communication services. The system calls included in the socket interface were originally developed for use with the C programming language. API functions in other programming languages can also be used to invoke the socket system calls described here. The most commonly used socket system calls are listed in Box 19.2. Some of these system calls are described further later in this chapter.

APPLICATION PROTOCOLS

The system calls that make up the API for datagram sockets and stream sockets can be used to design client-server applications that implement either a connectionless application protocol or a connection-oriented application protocol. The following sections describe the characteristics of each.

Connectionless Application Protocols

A client-server application that implements a connectionless application protocol uses datagram sockets to communicate using UDP. Box 19.3 shows the sequence in which the socket system calls are typically issued in implementing a connectionless application protocol. No error detection and retransmission is provided by the underlying UDP data delivery service.

Note that for the server, information supplied in the **socket** and **bind** system calls and information received as a result of the **recvfrom** system call supply all five pieces of information that are required to complete the association between the client process and the server process. For a connectionless application protocol, the association need not be completed until the time that the client process actually sends data to the server process.

BOX 19.2   Socket system calls.

- **accept.** Used in a connection-oriented application protocol employing TCP by the server process to cause the server to wait for a connection request to arrive from a client.
- **bind.** Used to associate an endpoint identifier (internet address and port number) with the integer descriptor of an open socket.
- **close.** Used to close a socket descriptor in a similar manner to closing a file descriptor.
- **connect.** Used in a connection-oriented application protocol employing TCP by the client process to establish a TCP connection with the server.
- **gethostbyaddr.** Used to obtain information about a host given its internet address.
- **gethostbyname.** Used to obtain a remote host's internet address given its host name.
- **gethostid.** Used to obtain the local host's internet address.
- **gethostname.** Used to obtain the local host's name.
- **getpeername.** Used to obtain the endpoint address (internet address and port number) associated with the remote process.
- **getsockname.** Used to obtain the name associated with a given socket.
- **getprotobyname.** Used to obtain the integer value associated with a protocol given the protocol's name.
- **getservbyname.** Used to obtain the integer value associated with a well-known TCP/IP Application layer service given its name.
- **getsockopt.** Used to obtain a list of parameters associated with a socket.
- **listen.** Used in a connection-oriented application protocol employing TCP by the server process to indicate that the server is willing to accept a request from a client to establish a TCP connection.
- **read.** Used to accept incoming data from a socket.
- **readv.** Used as an alternative to **read** to accept data into noncontiguous buffers.
- **recv.** Used as an alternative to **read** to accept incoming data from a socket and uses an additional flags argument.
- **recvfrom.** Used in a connectionless application protocol employing UDP to receive a user datagram from a datagram socket and to also obtain the sender's socket address.
- **recvmsg.** Used in a connectionless application protocol employing UDP to receive a user datagram from a datagram socket. The buffer includes the user datagram's header as well as the data portion of the user datagram.
- **select.** Used to allow a process to wait for the completion of any one of multiple I/O events.
- **send.** Used as an alternative to **write** to send data over a socket and uses an additional flags argument.
- **sendmsg.** Used in a connectionless application protocol employing UDP to send a user datagram over a datagram socket. The buffer includes the user datagram's header as well as the data portion of the user datagram.

(Continued)

BOX 19.2   *(Continued)*

- **sendto.** Used in a connectionless application protocol employing UDP to send data over a datagram socket and to specify the socket address of the remote process. The **sendto** call allows an association to be established at the time data is transferred.

- **setsockopt.** Used to set values for a set of parameters associated with a socket.

- **shutdown.** Used in a connection-oriented application protocol employing TCP to close one end of an established TCP connection.

- **socket.** Used to initialize a socket data structure, to identify the Transport layer protocol to be used for communication, and to obtain an integer descriptor that subsequent socket system calls can use to refer to the socket.

- **write.** Used to send data over a socket.

- **writev.** Used as an alternative to **write** to send data from noncontiguous buffers.

BOX 19.3   Implementing a connectionless application protocol using UDP.

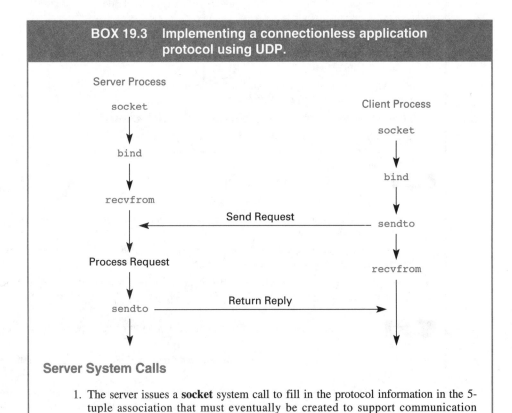

Server System Calls

1. The server issues a **socket** system call to fill in the protocol information in the 5-tuple association that must eventually be created to support communication between the client process and the server process. In a connectionless application, the **socket** system call specifies the use of UDP.

BOX 19.3 *(Continued)*

2. The server issues a **bind** system call, specifying the server's socket address, to fill in the remainder of the information making up the server's half-association. The server's half-association consists of the protocol identifier, the internet address of the host the server is running on, and the port number the server is using.

3. The server issues a **recvfrom** system call that allows the server to accept incoming data from a client. The **recvfrom** system call causes the server to wait until data arrives from any client that wishes to use the services of the server process.

4. When an incoming user datagram arrives from a client, the server performs any required processing. The header information included in the incoming user datagram includes the client host's internet address and the port number used by the client process on that host. This information provides the server with the final two pieces of information that are required to complete the 5-tuple association between the client process and the server process.

5. The server replies to the client by issuing one or more **sendto** system calls that each sends a user datagram back to the client. The **sendto** system call references the client's socket address that was determined in step 4 above.

Client System Calls

1. The client issues a **socket** system call to fill in the protocol information for its half-association. Again, in a connectionless application, the **socket** system call specifies the use of UDP.

2. The client issues a bind system call, specifying the client's socket address, to fill in the remainder of the information making up the client's half-association. The client process typically asks the networking software to supply the client's internet address and to provide it with an unused ephemeral port number to use.

3. The client then issues a **sendto** system call to transmit a user datagram to the server. The client must know the socket address of the server, and this socket address must be referenced in the **sendto** system call.

4. If the client expects to receive data from the server, it issues a **recvfrom** system call that causes the client to wait until data arrives from the server.

5. After the client finishes interacting with the server, it terminates its processing.

In the client process, the information supplied in the **socket, bind,** and **sendto** system calls supply all five pieces of information that are required to complete the association between the client process and the server process. In this example, the association is completed at the time that the client sends the first user datagram to the server.

Connection-Oriented Application Protocols

A client-server application that implements a connection-oriented application protocol uses stream sockets to communicate over a TCP connection. Box 19.4 shows the

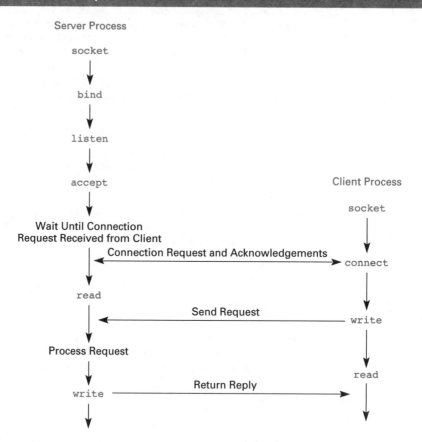

Server System Calls

1. The server issues a **socket** system call to fill in the protocol information in the 5-tuple association that must eventually be created to support communication between the client process and the server process. In a connection-oriented application, the **socket** system call specifies the use of TCP.

2. The server issues a **bind** system call, specifying the server's socket address, to fill in the remainder of the information making up the server's half-association. The server's half-association consists of the protocol identifier, the internet address of the host on which the server is running, and the port number the server is using.

3. The server issues a **listen** system call that indicates that the server is willing to accept a request from a client for the establishment of a TCP connection.

4. The server issues an **accept** system call that causes it to wait until a request for the establishment of a TCP connection is received from a client. The **accept** system

BOX 19.4   *(Continued)*

call references a socket address data structure that is filled in with the socket address of the client process when the request for the establishment of a connection is actually received.

5. The server issues either **read** or **recv** system calls that allow the server to accept incoming data from a client over the established TCP connection.

6. The server performs required processing and can issue **write** or **send** system calls that allow the server to reliably send data to the client.

Client System Calls

1. The client issues a **socket** system call to fill in the protocol information for its half-association. Again, in a connection-oriented application, the **socket** system call specifies the use of TCP.

2. The client issues a **connect** system call, referencing the client's socket address, to establish a TCP connection with the server. The client's **connect** system call causes data to flow back and forth between the client process and the server process to complete a three-way handshake procedure required to set up the connection. The data exchanged during this handshake procedure includes the information required to complete the association between the client and the server. The client must know the socket address of the server process in order to issue the **connect** system call, and it typically asks the communications software to provide the client's own internet address and an unused ephemeral port number to use for the association.

3. The client issues **write** or **send** system calls to send data to the server over the established TCP connection.

4. The client can also issue **read** or **recv** system calls to accept incoming data from the server.

5. After the client finishes interacting with the server, it terminates its processing.

sequence in which the socket system calls are typically issued in implementing a connection-oriented application protocol.

With connection-oriented data transfer operations, the server first initializes itself and then waits for a client to request a connection. The client then eventually requests a connection and transmits data to the server. The underlying TCP data delivery service provides error detection, retransmission, and flow control mechanisms.

Note that for a connection-oriented server, information supplied in the **socket** and **bind** system calls, and information received as a result of the **accept** system call, supply all five pieces of information that are required to complete the association for the server. For a connection-oriented application, the association is typically completed at the time the connection is established.

The information provided in the **socket** and **connect** system calls issued by the client process supply all five pieces of information that are required to complete the association for the client. The three-way handshake procedure that begins when the client process issues the **connect** system call allows the client and the server to exchange this information with one another. Thus, in a connection-oriented application, the association is typically completed at the time that the client issues the **connect** system call.

SOCKET SYSTEM CALL DESCRIPTIONS

The following sections describe the most commonly used socket system calls that TCP/IP communications software provides for implementing network communication.

All the socket system calls return an integer result. A result value of –1 typically means that the system call did not execute successfully. When a socket system call returns a value of –1, the global variable **errno** typically contains an integer error code that describes the problem that occurred. The documentation for the TCP/IP communication software should be consulted for error code interpretations.

socket System Call

The **socket** call is used to initialize a socket. The **socket** system call fills in only the protocol identifier of the 5-tuple that makes up an association between two communicating processes.

Arguments

The **socket** call has three integer arguments:

- **Family.** An integer describing the protocol family with which the call is associated. With TCP/IP communications, the protocol family should specify the symbolic integer value AF_INET or PF_INET.

- **Type.** An integer describing the type of socket to be initialized. The socket type should specify the symbolic identifier SOCK_STREAM for a TCP stream socket or SOCK_DGRAM for a UDP datagram socket.

- **Protocol.** An integer identifer describing the protocol associated with the call. The protocol argument is normally set to the value 0.

Result

The **socket** call returns an integer value result, similar to a file descriptor, that can be used in subsequent socket system calls to refer to the socket.

Examples

The following are examples of **socket** system calls used to establish a stream socket for a connection-oriented application protocol employing TCP and a datagram socket for a connectionless application protocol employing UDP:

```
stream_sockfd = socket(
                       AF_INET,
                       SOCK_STREAM,
                       0
                      );
```

```
dgram_sockfd = socket(
                       AF_INET,
                       SOCK_DGRAM,
                       0
                       );
```

bind System Call

The **bind** system call fills in the endpoint identifier (internet address and port number) for the local process into the association 5-tuple. A server process uses **bind** to register its own internet address and port number assignment with the TCP/IP communications software. In effect, the server uses **bind** to inform the TCP/IP communications software of the server's endpoint identifier and the transport protocol it is using.

A client process in a connectionless application protocol normally uses **bind** to register its own internet address and to assign an ephemeral port number that can be used by servers to send information back to the client process. The client can ask the TCP/IP networking software to supply the client's internet address and to assign an unused ephemeral port number to be used during the life of the association. The client process need not invoke the **bind** system call in a connection-oriented application protocol; if the client does not invoke **bind,** the **connect** system call automatically completes the binding process.

Arguments

The **bind** system call has the following three arguments:

- **Socket.** An integer descriptor identifying the socket. This argument specifies an identifier containing the integer socket descriptor that was assigned when the **socket** system call was issued.
- **Local Address.** A pointer to a socket address data structure containing the socket address of the local process.
- **Address Length.** An integer giving the length of the local address argument.

Example

The following is an example of the **bind** system call:

```
bind(
     sockfd,
     (struct sockaddr *) &own_addr,
     sizeof(own_addr)
     );
```

connect System Call

The **connect** system call is ordinarily issued by the client process in implementing a connection-oriented application protocol. It begins a three-way handshake procedure in which IP datagrams are automatically exchanged that carry all the information necessary to complete the 5-tuple making up the association between the client process and the server process.

Arguments

The **connect** system call has arguments that are similar to those for the **bind** system call:

- **Socket.** An integer descriptor identifying the socket. This argument specifies an identifier containing the integer socket descriptor that was assigned when the **socket** system call was issued.
- **Remote Address.** A pointer to a socket address data structure containing the socket address of the remote process with which the client is attempting to communicate.
- **Address Length.** An integer giving the length of the remote address argument.

Example

The following is an example of the **connect** system call:

```
connect(sockfd,
        (struct sockaddr *) &serv_addr,
        sizeof(serv_addr)
       );
```

listen System Call

The **listen** system call is issued by the server process in a connection-oriented application protocol employing TCP. The **listen** system call tells the TCP/IP communications software that the server process is willing to accept a request from a client process for the establishment of a TCP connection.

Arguments

The **listen** system call has the following two arguments:

- **Socket.** An integer descriptor identifying the socket. This argument specifies an identifier containing the integer socket descriptor that was assigned when the **socket** system call was issued.
- **Queue Length.** An integer that indicates how many connection requests the system can queue up while it waits for the server to issue an **accept** system call. This argument typically specifies a maximum value of 5.

Example

The following is an example of the **listen** system call:

```
listen(
       sockfd,
       5
      );
```

accept System Call

The **accept** system call is issued by the server process in a connection-oriented application protocol to cause the server process to wait for a connection request to arrive from a client.

Arguments

The **accept** system call has similar arguments to the **bind** system call. The **accept** system call itself fills in the values in the second and third arguments. After the **accept** system call completes, the second argument contains a pointer to a socket address data structure specifying the endpoint address of the client process that has established a connection with the server.

- **Socket.** An integer descriptor identifying the socket. This argument specifies an identifier containing the integer socket descriptor that was assigned when the **socket** system call was issued.
- **Client Address.** A pointer to a socket address data structure containing the socket address of the client process that is attempting to establish a connection with the server.
- **Address Length.** An integer giving the length of the client address argument.

Result

The **accept** system call creates a new socket data structure and returns a socket descriptor integer value that can be used to later reference this new socket data structure.

Example

The following is an example of the **accept** system call:

```
newsockfd = accept(
                    sockfd,
                    (struct sockaddr *) &cli_addr,
                    &clilen
                   );
```

write and send System Calls

The **write** and **send** system calls are used to send data to the remote process. The **write** system call can be issued referencing a socket descriptor in the same manner as issuing a **write** system call to a file descriptor. The **send** system call is similar to **write** but uses an additional argument.

Arguments

The **write** and **send** system calls use the following arguments:

- **Socket.** An integer descriptor identifying the socket. This argument specifies an identifier containing the integer socket descriptor that was assigned when the **socket** system call was issued.

- **Buffer.** A pointer to a buffer containing the data to be sent.
- **Length.** An integer specifying the number of octets to be sent.
- **Flag** (**send** system call only) An octet used to specify special options for the **send** operation.

Results

Both **write** and **send** return an integer value containing the number of octets that were actually transmitted.

Example

The following are examples of the **write** and **send** system calls:

```
nwritten = write(
                sockfd,
                buffer,
                noctets
            );
nwritten = send(
                sockfd,
                buffer,
                noctets,
                sendflag
            );
```

sendto System Call

The **sendto** system call is similar to **send** and is typically used instead of **send** or **write** by both the client process and the server process in a connectionless application protocol employing UDP. The **sendto** system call allows the 5-tuple making up the association between the client process and server process to be completed at the time that a user datagram is sent.

Arguments

In addition to the four arguments used by **send,** the **sendto** system call uses two additional arguments that identify the socket address of the remote process to which a user datagram is being sent.

- **Socket.** An integer descriptor identifying the socket. This argument specifies an identifier containing the integer socket descriptor that was assigned when the **socket** system call was issued.
- **Buffer.** A pointer to a buffer containing the data to be sent.
- **Length.** An integer specifying the number of octets to be sent.
- **Flag.** An octet used to specify special options for the **sendto** function.
- **Remote Address.** A pointer to a socket address data structure containing the socket address of the remote process.
- **Address Length.** An integer giving the length of the remote address argument.

Results

The **sendto** system call returns an integer value containing the number of octets that were actually transmitted.

Example

The following is an example of the **sendto** system call:

```
nwritten = sendto(
                sockfd,
                buffer,
                noctets,
                sendflag,
                (struct sockaddr *) &serv_addr,
                sizeof(serv_addr)
                );
```

read and recv System Calls

The **read** and **recv** system calls are used to accept incoming data from the remote process. The **read** system call can be issued referencing a socket descriptor in the same manner as issuing a **read** system call to a file descriptor. The **recv** system call is similar to **read** but uses an additional argument.

Arguments

The **read** and **recv** system calls use the following arguments:

- **Socket.** An integer descriptor identifying the socket. This argument specifies an identifier containing the integer socket descriptor that was assigned when the **socket** system call was issued.
- **Buffer.** A pointer to a buffer into which the received data can be placed.
- **Length.** An integer specifying the length of the receive buffer.
- **Flag** (**recv** system call only) An octet used to specify special options for the **recv** function.

Results

Both the **read** and **recv** system calls return integer values containing the number of octets that were actually received.

Example

The following are examples of both the **read** and **recv** system calls:

```
nread = read(
                sockfd,
                buffer,
                bufflength
                );
```

```
nread = recv(
            sockfd,
            buffer,
            bufflength,
            recvflag
         );
```

recvfrom System Call

The **recvfrom** system call is similar to **recv** and is typically used instead of **recv** or **read** by both the client process and the server process in a connectionless application protocol using UDP. The **recvfrom** system call allows the 5-tuple making up the association between the client process and the server process to be completed at the time that a user datagram is received.

Arguments

In addition to the four arguments used by **recv,** the **recvfrom** system call uses two additional arguments that identify the socket address of the remote process from which a user datagram was received:

- **Socket.** An integer descriptor identifying the socket. This argument specifies an identifier containing the integer socket descriptor that was assigned when the **socket** system call was issued.
- **Buffer.** A pointer to a buffer into which the received data can be placed.
- **Length.** An integer specifying the length of the receive buffer.
- **Flag.** An octet used to specify special options for the **recvfrom** function.
- **Remote Address.** A pointer to a socket address data structure containing the socket address of the remote process.
- **Address Length.** An integer giving the length of the remote address argument.

Result

The **readfrom** system call returns an integer value containing the number of octets that were actually read.

Example

The following is an example of the **recvfrom** system call:

```
nwritten = recvfrom(
                sockfd,
                buffer,
                bufflength,
                recvflag,
                (struct sockaddr *) &serv_addr,
                &length
            );
```

close System Call

The **close** system call can reference a socket descriptor in the same manner as for a file descriptor to close a socket after communication has been completed. It is good programming practice to always invoke the **close** system call to deallocate the socket descriptor after the program has completed its processing. With a connection-oriented application using TCP, invoking the **close** system call after communication has been completed ensures that all queued data has been sent before the connection is released.

Arguments

The **close** system call has a single argument:

- **Socket.** An integer descriptor identifying the socket. This argument specifies an identifier containing the integer socket descriptor that was assigned when the **socket** system call was issued.

Example

The following is an example of the **close** system call:

```
close(
    sockfd
);
```

SUMMARY

The socket API defines three types of sockets that can be used to support communication in the TCP/IP environment—datagram sockets that use UDP for communication, stream sockets that use TCP for communication, and raw sockets that provide access to IP and ICMP. Each of the two processes in a client-server application is identified by a separate socket address. The socket address of the server process plus the socket address of the client process make up four of the five pieces of the information necessary to create an association between the two processes. Both the client process and the server process must also identify the Transport layer protocol being used for communication.

The **socket** system call is used to initialize a socket data structure and to identify the protocol to be used for communication. The **bind** system call fills into a socket data structure the internet address and port number assignment of the local process. The **connect** system call sets up an association between communicating processes and can be issued by the client to set up a TCP connection with the server. The **listen** system call indicates that the server is willing to accept a request from a client to establish a TCP connection. The **accept** system call causes the server to wait for a connection request to arrive from a client. The **write, send, read,** and **recv** system calls are used to send and receive data over an established association by referencing socket descriptors. The **sendto** and **recvfrom** system calls are similar to **send** and **recv** but also reference the socket address of the remote process. The **close** system call closes a socket descriptor in a similar manner to closing a file descriptor.

The system calls that make up the API for datagram sockets and stream sockets can be used in client-server applications that implement either a connectionless application protocol or a connection-oriented application protocol. A client-server application that implements a connectionless application protocol uses datagram sockets to communicate using UDP. For a connectionless application, the association need not be completed until the time that the client actually sends data to the server. A client-server application that implements a connection-oriented application protocol uses stream sockets to communicate using TCP. For a connection-oriented application, the association is typically completed at the time the connection is established.

Chapter 20 introduces the remote procedure call form of network programming that can be used as an alternative to sockets for implementing client-server applications.

Remote Procedure Call Programming

A *remote procedure call* (RPC) facility can make it possible to implement client-server applications without needing to explicitly issue requests for communication services from within the application program. This chapter introduces the fundamentals of programming with an RPC facility using the Sun RPC facility as an example.

The idea behind a remote procedure call facility is that procedure calls are a well-understood mechanism for transferring control and data from one procedure to another in a computing application. It is of great utility to extend the procedure call mechanism from a set of procedures in a single-computer environment to a set of procedures in a distributed, client-server environment. Application programs that use a client-server approach can then be developed using the same procedure call techniques that are used in the single-host environment. The fact that the procedures run on different hosts connected via an internet can potentially be hidden from the application developer.

PROCEDURE CALL MECHANISM

Figure 20.1 shows the basic concept behind a procedure call mechanism. Procedure A makes a function or procedure call, possibly referencing some arguments, which passes control to procedure B. While procedure B executes, procedure A waits. When procedure B finishes its processing, it returns to the caller, which causes control to be passed to the statement immediately after the statement in procedure A that invoked procedure B. In most programming language and operating system environments, function or procedure calls can be nested to any desired level, as where procedure A in Fig. 20.1 invokes procedure C, which in turn invokes procedure D.

Procedure Calls in a Client-Server Environment

An RPC facility allows the procedure call mechanism to work in a client-server computing environment where the calling procedure (the client) and the called procedure (the

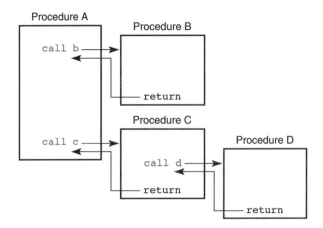

Figure 20.1　Procedure call mechanism.

server) reside in different host computers connected by an internet. Ideally, this should be done so the calling client procedure can call a remote server procedure using exactly the same technique it would use to call a procedure residing on the local host. In other words, the mechanisms that the remote procedure call facility employs should be hidden from both the client and the server procedures.

Difficulties in Achieving Transparency

None of today's RPC facilities have achieved complete transparency. The difficulties associated with making an RPC facility work in an identical manner to a local procedure call facility lie in three major areas—locating the called procedure, passing argument values and results, and binding.

Locating the Called Procedure

The RPC facility must provide a means for locating the called procedure in the network, and the calling procedure must provide the information required to do this. A directory service, such as the Domain Name System (DNS), can be used to provide the means for locating remote procedures.

Passing Arguments and Results

With the procedure call mechanism implemented in traditional programming language environments, communication between the two procedures is based on a shared address space. Argument values are sometimes passed by *reference,* which means the calling procedure passes the called procedure pointers to the argument values rather than the values themselves. When the two procedures reside on different host computers, there is no common address space. Therefore, an RPC facility must be able to handle the passing of arguments and results in both directions without the calling and called procedures having the benefit of a shared address space. There may also be differences in data formats from one type of host computer to another, including differences in integer octet ordering, number of bits used to represent binary integer values, and floating point data representation. Such differences must be resolved by the RPC facility, with data format conversions taking place when required.

Binding the Called Procedure to the Calling Procedure

With a conventional procedure call mechanism, there are many techniques that can be used for binding. With *early binding,* a linking mechanism is used to construct a single program module containing both the calling and the called procedure. Both the calling and the called procedures are then loaded into storage together. With *late binding,* the procedure call mechanism implemented by the operating system may allow the called procedure to be dynamically loaded into computer storage at the time the procedure is actually invoked. With a remote procedure call facility, binding is even more complex because it involves finding the host computer on which the desired procedure resides and loading the procedure into memory if required.

REMOTE PROCEDURE CALL FUNCTIONAL MODEL

A simplified functional model of a remote procedure call facility is shown in Fig. 20.2. In this functional model, a calling client procedure executes a procedure call in the same manner as if it were executing a procedure call to a local procedure. The called server procedure runs as if it executed in the same host as the client procedure. A module called a *stub* in the local host mimics the presence of the actual procedure to which the calling procedure is attempting to pass control. The stub, in turn, requests the services of the remote procedure call facility.

Client-Server Rendezvous

During actual operation, the RPC facility running in the client procedure's host may use a directory service, such as DNS, to determine on which remote host in the internet the called procedure resides. The server host is typically found before the calling procedure actually invokes the remote procedure.

When the RPC facility in the remote host receives the argument information generated as a result of the procedure call, it determines whether the requested server procedure already resides in computer storage there. If it does not, a facility in the remote host loads the program module containing the requested procedure and passes control to it, again using a stub unique to that procedure. The called procedure then passes results back to the calling procedure and passes control back to it using a process similar to that described for the calling procedure.

Marshaling

The RPC facility uses the services of the TCP/IP networking software to transmit argument information and results between the RPC facility in the local host and the RPC

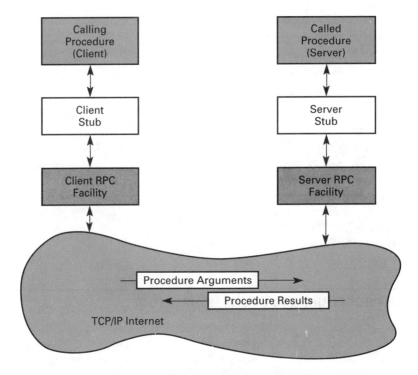

Figure 20.2 RPC facility functional model.

facility in the remote host. The process of converting the argument information in the local host into data units that can be transmitted over the internet and performing the same process in the opposite direction for results is called *marshaling*.

The marshaling process is straightforward if the two procedures represent argument values using the same form of data representation. However, to be useful in a heterogeneous environment, it is necessary for a remote procedure call facility to handle the situation where the calling procedure and the called procedure use different forms of data representation. Therefore, the marshaling routines must be capable of performing the necessary data conversions. RPC facilities use various methods for handling the marshaling process.

RPC CALL SEMANTICS

When executing procedure calls in the local environment, the question of how many times a procedure has been executed does not typically arise. If the calling procedure receives control back from the called procedure, the calling procedure knows that the called procedure was executed exactly once. But when the procedure is executing on a remote host, and the calling procedure does not regain control after some time period has passed, the calling procedure does not know if the remote procedure has executed or not.

It is possible that the remote procedure has not executed at all, it may have executed once, and it may have executed more than once.

For example, if the remote host running the server procedure fails before receiving the request for the execution of the server procedure, the called procedure will not have executed at all. If the remote host fails after the server procedure has executed but before the RPC facility in the client host has been notified of that fact, the called procedure has executed, but the calling procedure does not know about it. What is worse, if the RPC facility in the client host times out and issues a request to execute the remote procedure again, it is possible that the called procedure will be executed two or more times.

For some types of procedures, it does not matter whether a procedure is executed multiple times, as long as it can be determined that the procedure has executed at least once. Such a procedure is called *idempotent*. A procedure that simply returns an uncomplicated result, such as the time of day, or makes a complete replacement of a data value is idempotent. A procedure that adds a value to a data element, such as a bank balance, is not idempotent. The result is very different if a value is added to a bank balance once or more than once.

The differences between local procedure calling and remote procedure calling make it necessary to distinguish between three different types of remote procedure call semantics that an RPC facility may be designed to handle—at least once, at most once, and exactly once.

At Least Once

If an RPC facility provides at least once semantics, it allows the calling procedure to determine only that the procedure was executed at least one time. Such semantics are useful only for idempotent procedures. The RPC facility in the client host can keep trying the request, and once the called procedure finally responds, control can be returned to the calling procedure. The calling procedure then knows that the called procedure was executed one or more times. Many RPC facilities allow the user to specify that the called procedure is idempotent and that *at least once* semantics are all that is required for a particular call.

At Most Once Semantics

If an RPC facility provides *at most once* semantics, it allows the calling procedure to determine that if the called procedure executed at all, it executed only one time. With these semantics, if the calling procedure receives control at the statement following the statement that invoked the called procedure, it knows that the called procedure executed exactly one time. But if the called procedure does not receive control back and times out, it does not know whether the procedure executed or not. Most RPC facilities provide mechanisms that allow the user to request *at most once* semantics.

Exactly Once Semantics

If an RPC facility provides *exactly once* semantics, it allows the calling procedure to determine that the called procedure was called once and only once. Such semantics are hard for an RPC facility to achieve because of the possibility of server failures. Most RPC facilities do not provide *exactly once* semantics.

RPC IMPLEMENTATIONS

As we introduced in Chapter 5, there are two major software subsystems that are typically used to provide remote procedure call facilities in the TCP/IP environment—the RPC facility developed by Sun Microsystems and the RPC facility provided by Hewlett-Packard, Inc. Both of these provide at most once semantics and allow the use of at least once semantics for those applications that do not require at most once semantics.

Sun RPC Facility

An implementation of the *Sun RPC* facility is provided in most BSD implementations of the UNIX operating system. The Sun RPC facility is also provided on a number of other UNIX and non-UNIX operating systems and is normally available with any implementation of Sun's Network File System (NFS). Source code for the Sun RPC facility is available from Sun Microsystems for a nominal charge. The Sun RPC facility consists of the following components:

- **Rpcgen Compiler.** The Rpcgen compiler accepts remote procedure call interface definitions and generates client and server stubs that can be included with the client and server application programs.
- **External Data Representation (XDR) Facility.** The XDR facility provides a standard method for encoding argument data and results so they can be used in a portable fashion in a heterogeneous host environment.
- **Runtime Library.** The runtime library is a collection of executable routines that are required to allow client and server programs to invoke the Sun RPC facilities.
- **Portmapper Facility.** The portmapper facility provides programs with information about the location of callable services.

Hewlett-Packard RPC Facility

The *Hewlett-Packard (HP) RPC* facility (originally developed by Apollo Computer Inc., which was subsequently acquired by Hewlett-Packard) is provided as part of a software subsystem called the Network Computing System (NCS). The HP NCS is a programmer toolkit that allows programmers to access the HP RPC facilities in a similar manner to Sun RPC. Like Sun RPC, the NCS software subsystem is implemented on a wide variety of UNIX and non-UNIX operating systems. The NCS subsystem consists of the following components:

- **Network Interface Definition Language (NIDL) Compiler.** The NIDL compiler allows users to specify the interface between a client application component and a server application component. The NIDL compiler generates client and server stubs in a similar manner to the Sun Rpcgen compiler.

- **Network Data Representation (NDR) Facility.** The NDR facility allows the user to define how structured data values used in a procedure call are encoded for transmission through an internet.

- **Runtime Library.** The runtime library contains the executable code that can be included with user programs to implement remote procedure call facilities.

- **Location Broker.** The location broker maintains a database of information about the location of callable services.

SUN RPC EXAMPLES

The remainder of this chapter shows sample code used to implement remote procedure calls using the Sun RPC facility. For the examples, we will assume that the remote server process implements the following two callable procedures that provide date and the time of day services:

- **bin_time_1.** Returns the server host's internal date and time of day in binary format.
- **str_time_1.** Converts a binary date and time value into character format.

We will show the relevant code in the server procedures, the code used in the client procedures to call the remote procedures, and the code required to generate the RPC definitions needed to implement the remote procedure calls.

RPC Program Preparation

In addition to writing the code for the client and the server procedures, an RPC specification file must be prepared that describes the characteristics of the two server procedures. The RPC specification file is processed by the Sun RPC Rpcgen compiler. The Rpcgen compiler generates source code for a client stub, a server stub, and a header file. The client stub is included with the program module that contains the calling procedure code, and the server stub is included with the program module containing the server procedures. The header file contains identifier and data structure definitions that must be included in both the client and server source code modules.

Figure 20.3 summarizes the process that is used to prepare C language client and server program modules for execution.

Sun RPC Specification Statements

The following shows what the RPC specification file might look like to define our two date and time procedures:

```
/*
 * Sun RPC Specification Statements.
 */
/*
 *          bin_time_1() returns the binary date and time (no arguments).
```

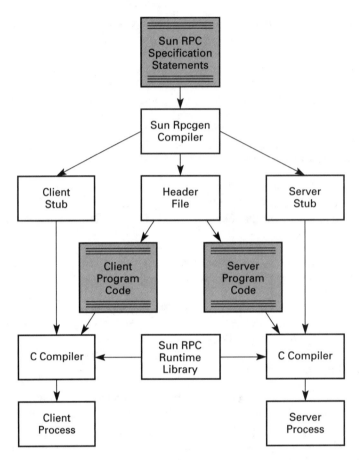

Figure 20.3   Procedure call mechanism.

```
*
*              str_time_1()  takes a binary date and time value
*                            and returns a character string.
*/
program TIME_PROG
{
    version TIME_VERS
    {
        long BIN_TIME(void) = 1;    /* procedure number = 1 */
        string STR_TIME(long) = 2;  /* procedure number = 2 */
    } = 1;                          /* version number = 1 */
} = 0x31234567;                     /* program number = 0x3000001 */
```

In the above code, the BIN_TIME procedure is defined as producing a 32-bit binary integer result, the "void" indicates that the procedure accepts no arguments, and the procedure is identified as procedure number 1 in this RPC definition. The STR_TIME procedure is defined as producing a string result, it accepts a single 32-bit binary integer, and the procedure is identified as procedure number 2.

This procedure definition is identified as version 1, and a 32-bit program number is assigned to the RPC definition using hexadecimal notation.

Sun has assigned RPC program numbers as follows:

```
00000000 - 1fffffff    • defined by Sun
20000000 - 3fffffff    • defined by the user
40000000 - 5fffffff    • transient
60000000 - ffffffff    • reserved
```

Sun Rpcgen Compiler Output

The Sun Rpcgen compiler generates the header code shown below as a result of the previous RPC specification statements:

```
#define TIME_PROG          ((u_long)0x30000001)
#define TIME_VERS          ((u_long)1)
#define BIN_TIME           ((u_long)1)
extern long        *bin_time_1();
#define STR_TIME           ((u_long)2)
extern char        **str_time_1();
```

Note that the BIN_TIME procedure is called using the name **bin_time_1,** and the STR_TIME procedure is called using the name **str_time_1.**

RPC Server Procedure Code

We next look at the code that would be used in the server program module to make the two remote procedures available to the client program module.

The bin_time_1 Remote Procedure

The code for the **bin_time_1** procedure is identical to the code that would be used if the procedure were going to be called locally. It simply obtains a binary time value using a standard UNIX function and passes control back to the calling procedure:

```
long *
bin_time_1()
{
        static long     timeval;
        long            time();

        timeval = time((long *) 0);

        return(&timeval);
}
```

The str_time_1 Remote Procedure

The code for the **str_time_1** procedure is also identical to the code that would be used if it were called locally. It accepts a long integer argument and converts the time value contained in the argument to a string time value. It then returns a pointer to the string time value to the called procedure:

```
char **
str_time_1(bintime)
long *bintime;
{
        static char        *ptr;
        char               *ctime();

        ptr = ctime(bintime);

        return(&ptr);
}
```

RPC Client Calling Code

We will next look at the relevant code in the client program module that is used to invoke the two remote procedures.

Invoking clnt_create

Before either of the procedures can be invoked, the client program module must call a procedure named **clnt_create** that is provided with the Sun RPC facility:

```
if ( (cl = clnt_create(server, TIME_PROG, TIME_VERS, "udp")) == NULL)
{
        /*
         * Couldn't establish connection with server.
         */

        clnt_pcreaterror(server);
        exit(2);
}
```

The **clnt_create** procedure is provided as part of the Sun RPC facility. The **clnt_create** procedure creates a descriptor (**cl** in the example) that can be referenced when invoking the remote procedures. Its arguments include the name of the server host, the program number, the version number, and the Transport layer protocol to use. The Sun RPC facility permits the use of either UDP or TCP to implement RPC communication.

Invoking bin_time_1

The following code invokes the **bin_time_1** remote procedure:

```
if ( (lresult = bin_time_1(NULL, cl)) == NULL)
{
      clnt_perror(cl, server);
      exit(3);
}
```

Note that the argument list indicates that the remote procedure has no arguments and references the descriptor established previously. The statement invoking the remote procedure specifies that the long integer result be placed into **lresult.**

Invoking str_tim_1

The following code invokes the **str_time_1** procedure:

```
if ( (sresult = str_time_1(lresult, cl)) == NULL)
{
         clnt_perror(cl, server);
         exit(4);
}
```

SUMMARY

A remote procedure call (RPC) facility allows a procedure call mechanism to work in a client-server environment where the calling procedure and the called procedure reside in different hosts connected by a TCP/IP internet. The difficulties associated with implementing RPC facilities lie in three major areas—locating the called procedure, passing arguments, and binding the called procedure to the calling procedure.

There are three different types of remote procedure call semantics that an RPC facility may be designed to handle—exactly once, at most once, and at least once. Most RPC facilities do not provide exactly once semantics, but most provide a choice of at most once or at least once semantics.

There are two major software subsystems that are typically used to provide remote procedure call facilities in the TCP/IP environment—the RPC facility developed by Sun Microsystems and the RPC facility provided by Hewlett-Packard, Inc. The sample code presented in this chapter showed how the Sun RPC facility can be used to implement client-server interaction.

PART **VII**

APPENDICES

Appendix A   Physical Network
             Technologies
Appendix B   OSF Distributed Computing
             Environment

Appendix C   Requests for Comments
             Glossary

Appendix **A**

Physical Network Technologies

This appendix describes the characteristics of a number of different local area network and wide area network data link technologies that are used in constructing TCP/IP internets.

LOCAL AREA NETWORK DATA LINK TECHNOLOGY

There are a great many forms of data link technology available today for implementing local area networks. An important set of standards for local area networks has been developed by the *Institute of Electrical and Electronics Engineers* (IEEE) and by the *American National Standards Institute* (ANSI). The IEEE and ANSI LAN standards have also been accepted by ISO as international standards and are published by ISO as well. These standards describe the technology that is used most often to implement LAN data links in TCP/IP internets.

Most vendors of local area network equipment market products that conform to one or more of the IEEE/ANSI/ISO LAN standards. However, many types of LAN equipment that conform to proprietary standards are in widespread use as well.

IEEE/ANSI/ISO LAN ARCHITECTURE LAYERS
AND SUBLAYERS

The IEEE/ANSI/ISO LAN standards and most proprietary LAN specifications address the Network Interface layer of the TCP/IP architecture and the underlying Hardware layer. These correspond to the Data Link and Physical layers of the OSI model. The Network Interface layer can be divided into two sublayers to accommodate different forms of LAN hardware in a standardized manner. Figure A.1 shows how the layers and sublayers of the IEEE/ANSI/ISO LAN architecture compare to the TCP/IP architectural layers.

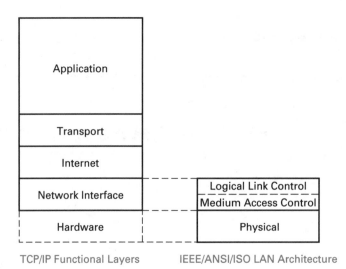

Figure A.1   TCP/IP architectural layers.

The following sections describe the layers and sublayers addressed by the IEEE/ANSI/ISO LAN standards.

Logical Link Control Sublayer

The Logical Link Control sublayer is responsible for medium-independent data link functions. It allows a LAN data link user to access the services of a local area network data link without having to be concerned with the form of medium access control or physical transmission medium that is used. A common LLC sublayer is shared by all the international standard forms of LAN data link technology.

The data unit that LLC sublayer entities exchange is called the *logical-link-control-protocol-data-unit* (LLC-PDU). The LLC sublayer adds protocol-control-information (PCI) in the form of a header to each message it receives from the LAN data link user to create an LLC-PDU. The format of the LLC-PDU is described later in this appendix.

The user of a LAN data link requests data transmission services through a *service-access-point* (SAP) into the LLC sublayer. It is possible for an implementation of Logical Link Control in a system to allow more than one user to concurrently access the services of the LAN data link. Each does so through a separate SAP having a different SAP identifier.

Medium Access Control Sublayer

A local area network typically supports multiple devices that all contend for access to a single physical transmission medium. The Medium Access Control sublayer provides services to a user of the MAC sublayer service, which is typically the LLC sublayer.

The data unit that MAC sublayer entities exchange is called the *medium-access-control-protocol-data-unit* (MAC-PDU). The MAC-PDU is often called a *MAC frame.*

The purpose of the MAC frame is to carry the LLC-PDU across a specific type of physical transmission medium from one network device to another. Each particular form of LAN data link technology employs its own unique MAC frame format.

Physical Layer

The lowest layer in the IEEE/ANSI/ISO LAN architecture corresponds directly to the Hardware layer. It provides services to a user of the Physical layer, which is typically the MAC sublayer. The PDUs that are exchanged by the Physical layer consist of signals that represent the individual bits making up a MAC frame.

IEEE/ANSI/ISO LAN STANDARDS

Early in its work on the development of local area network standards, IEEE Project 802 determined that it would not be able to develop a single local area network standard to meet the needs of all users. In recognition of this, the project developed a *family* of LAN standards. This family initially included a single standard for the LLC sublayer and three standards for the MAC sublayer and Physical layer—*CSMA/CD (Ethernet), Token Bus,* and *Token Ring.* The IEEE standards for local area networking technology were subsequently accepted by ISO as international standards and are now also described by ISO standards. ANSI then developed the *Fiber Distributed Data Interface* (FDDI) form of medium access control that has also been accepted as a MAC sublayer and Physical layer standard by ISO.

Box A.1 briefly describes each of the LAN standards defined by IEEE, ANSI, and ISO.

LOCAL AREA NETWORKING ADDRESSING

An important aspect of the IEEE/ISO/LAN architecture concerns the physical hardware addressing mechanisms that are implemented by a LAN data link. In discussing LAN addressing, we use the term *station* to mean a collection of hardware, firmware, and software that appears to other stations as a single functional and addressable unit on the LAN data link. A station implements a single physical point of connection to the transmission medium. A station is a collection of one or more hardware and/or software components that performs the functions of the LLC sublayer, the MAC sublayer, and the Physical layer.

In the TCP/IP environment, a station is implemented by a network interface card (NIC) and network driver software operating in the Network Interface layer.

The IEEE/ANSI/ISO LAN architecture provides for two levels of addressing—service-access-point (SAP) addressing and Medium Access Control (MAC) addressing:

- **SAP Addressing.** A *service-access-point (SAP) address* identifies an individual service-access-point into the LLC sublayer. SAP addressing is the concern of the Logical Link Control sublayer. A SAP address represents a particular mechanism, process, or protocol

---

BOX A.1   IEEE/ANSI/ISO LAN standards.

- **Logical Link Control.** The *Logical Link Control* standard describes the functions of the LLC sublayer of the IEEE/ISO/ANSI LAN architecture. It is defined by the IEEE 802.2 and ISO 8802-2 standards. The Logical Link Control standard describes the function of the LLC sublayer for all three forms of medium access control defined by the IEEE and can be used in conjunction with the FDDI standard as well.

- **Carrier Sense Multiple Access with Collision Detection (Ethernet).** The *Carrier Sense Multiple Access with Collision Detection* (CSMA/CD) standard describes the MAC sublayer and Physical layer functions for a bus- or tree-structured LAN using CSMA/CD as an access protocol. It is defined by the IEEE 802.3 and ISO 8802-3 CSMA/CD standards. Equipment conforming to the CSMA/CD standard is most often called *Ethernet* equipment. The CSMA/CD standard has its roots in the *Ethernet Version 2 Specification* for local area networking technology that was jointly developed by Digital Equipment Corporation, Xerox, and Intel.

- **Token Bus.** The *Token Bus* standard describes the MAC sublayer and Physical layer functions for a bus-structured LAN using token passing as an access protocol. It is defined by the IEEE 802.4 and ISO 8802-4 standards. The Token Bus form of LAN was designed to meet the needs of factory automation applications.

- **Token Ring.** The *Token Ring* standard describes the MAC sublayer and Physical layer functions for a ring-structured LAN using a token-passing access protocol. It is defined by the IEEE 802.5 and ISO 8802-5 standards. The Token Ring standard is an outgrowth of the development work that IBM did for its *Token-Ring Network* family of LAN products.

- **Fiber Distributed Data Interface.** The *Fiber Distributed Data Interface* (FDDI) standard defines a high-speed form of LAN that was standardized by a subcommittee of ANSI. It is defined by the ANSI X3T9.5 and ISO 9314 standards. FDDI uses a logical ring-structured topology using a timed token-passing access protocol that is substantially different from the token-passing protocol defined by the Token Ring standard.

---

that is requesting LLC sublayer services through the associated SAP. Each mechanism, process, or protocol that is concurrently using the services of the LLC sublayer in a given station must use a different SAP address.

- **MAC Addressing.** A *Medium Access Control (MAC) address* uniquely identifies an individual station that implements a single point of physical attachment to a LAN data link. MAC addressing is the concern of the Medium Access Control sublayer. Each station attached to a LAN data link must have a unique MAC address on that LAN data link.

The MAC addressing mechanism is used by the MAC sublayer to deliver each MAC frame to the appropriate station or stations on the LAN data link. The SAP addressing mechanism is used by the LLC sublayer to deliver LLC-PDUs to the appropriate user or users of the LLC sublayer service within a particular destination station.

MAC Addressing

The general format of the MAC frame is shown in Fig. A.2. Each type of MAC frame carries a header and a trailer that contains, among other things, destination MAC address

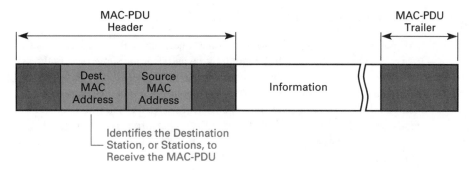

Figure A.2   MAC frame general format.

and source MAC address fields. The IEEE/ANSI/ISO LAN standards allow MAC addresses to be either 16 bits or 48 bits in length.

SAP Addressing

The LLC sublayer has the overall responsibility of controlling the exchange of messages between individual users of the LLC sublayer service. Once a MAC frame carrying an LLC-PDU arrives at an appropriate destination station, the Logical Link Control sublayer in that station uses SAP addressing to ensure that the LLC-PDU is delivered to the appropriate LAN data link user or users.

Figure A.3 shows the format of the LLC-PDU and illustrates how the LLC-PDU is carried within a MAC frame. The Information field of the LLC-PDU carries the data unit that is passed down from a user of the LAN data link. The header of the LLC-PDU contains two 1-octet SAP address values: the destination-service-access-point (DSAP) address and source-service-access-point (SSAP) address.

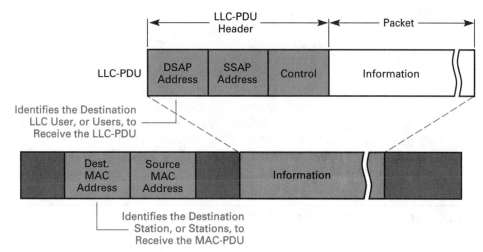

Figure A.3   Logical-link-control-protocol-data-unit (LLC-PDU) carried within a MAC frame.

LAN Data Link LLC Sublayer Users

SAP address values are used to distinguish one user of the LAN data link from another user of the same LAN data link that might be active at the same time in the same station.

The specific process that requests LLC sublayer services depends on the network architecture that is being employed in the higher layers. If the higher layer software conforms to the OSI architecture, then the user of the LAN data link is a process that implements an OSI model Network layer entity. That process will typically be running a Network layer protocol that is defined by an ISO standard. If the higher layer software conforms to some other network architecture, then the user of the LAN data link is a process running in the layer that sits above the LLC sublayer in that network architecture. In a TCP/IP internet, the layer above the LLC sublayer is the Internet layer.

It is possible for an implementation of the Logical Link Control standard to allow more than one user to concurrently request LAN data link services, each through a separate service-access-point into the LLC sublayer.

LLC Sublayer User Multiplexing

LLC sublayer SAP addresses allow stations to implement *user multiplexing* facilities that allow different types of users in the layer above the LLC sublayer to coexist on the same LAN data link. For example, an LLC sublayer user in station A might be employing the international standard ISO 8473 Internet protocol in the Network layer to communicate with a user in station B. Another LLC sublayer user in station A might be using IP to communicate with a TCP/IP user in station C. Still another LLC sublayer user in station A might be using a Network layer protocol from yet another architecture, such as Novell NetWare, to exchange information with a user in station D.

SAP Address Assigned Values

All SAP address values that have the second bit position set to 1 are reserved for definition by the IEEE, and specific meanings have been assigned to a number of these reserved SAP values. For example, the SAP address value X'FE' has been assigned by the IEEE to the ISO 8473 Internet protocol that operates in the OSI Network layer. Networking products that conform to the OSI model use LLC SAP address values of X'FE' to exchange ISO 8473 Internet protocol packets over LAN data links. With such networking products, the SAP address value X'FE' differentiates LLC-PDUs carrying ISO 8473 Internet protocol packets from LLC-PDUs carrying the traffic conforming to other Network layer protocols.

SUBNETWORK NETWORK ACCESS PROTOCOL

Very little of the traffic on today's LAN data links carries packets that conform to international standard protocols, such as the ISO 8473 Internet protocol. IEEE has defined a protocol called the *Subnetwork Access Protocol* (SNAP) that many networking products, including TCP/IP implementations, use to carry traffic that does not conform to international standards. The SNAP protocol implements another mechanism that can be used for the purpose of distinguishing LLC-PDUs that are carrying packets associated with one Network layer protocol from LLC-PDUs that are carrying packets associated with some other Network layer protocol.

Private Network Layer Protocols

The SNAP mechanism is intended for use with *private* Network layer protocols. By this we mean protocols that operate in the layer above the LLC sublayer but do not conform to international standards for the OSI model Network layer. IP is an example of such a private Network layer protocol that does not have an IEEE-defined SAP identifier. Therefore, a mechanism is needed that goes beyond SAP addressing to distinguish LLC-PDUs carrying IP datagrams from LLC-PDUs carrying packets associated with other Network layer protocols.

SNAP LLC-PDU Format

Figure A.4 shows the format of the PDUs that are defined by the SNAP mechanism. The data unit carried inside the LLC-PDU when the SNAP mechanism is used is often called a *SNAP PDU*. Notice that LLC-PDUs carrying SNAP PDUs have SSAP and DSAP address values of hex 'AA'.

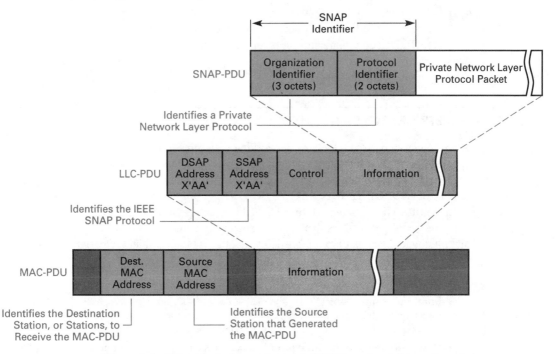

Figure A.4   Subnetwork Access Protocol (SNAP) protocol data unit carried within an LLC-PDU and a MAC frame.

The SNAP mechanism provides a level of multiplexing over and above that provided by SAP addressing to differentiate one private Network layer protocol from other private Network layer protocols. The first five octets of a SNAP PDU contain a SNAP identifier value that uniquely identifies the protocol associated with the packet the SNAP PDU is carrying.

In a SNAP PDU carrying TCP/IP traffic, the first three octets of the SNAP identifier contain a value assigned to the TCP/IP protocol suite, and the remaining two octets identify a specific TCP/IP protocol, typically a value identifying IP.

REPEATERS AND BRIDGES

Individual physical networks are interconnected in a TCP/IP internet using devices called *routers.* Other types of equipment that can be used in local area networks to interconnect local area network cable segments are *repeaters* and *bridges.*

A repeater is used in a bus- or tree-structured LAN to relay signals from one cable segment to one or more others. The main purpose of a repeater is to regenerate signals so that a LAN can be created that covers a greater distance than can be spanned by a single cable segment.

A bridge is a more intelligent device than a repeater. A bridge typically learns the addresses of the stations on each LAN segment that it bridges so that it can selectively relay only traffic that needs to flow across the bridge. Repeaters and bridges were not referenced earlier as TCP/IP internet components because repeaters and bridges are transparent to the TCP/IP communication software. A LAN constructed using repeaters and/or bridges, sometimes called an *extended LAN,* is viewed as a single physical LAN by the TCP/IP communication software.

WIDE AREA NETWORKING DATA LINKS

The most commonly used wide area networking data links in modern computer networks are point-to-point data links that interconnect a pair of devices. Point-to-point data links typically use a protocol that conforms to an international standard called *High-Level Data Link Control* (HDLC). There is a TCP/IP RFC for a *Point-to-Point Protocol* that defines a superset of the HDLC standard. In a TCP/IP internet, point-to-point data links can take the form of leased connections that are permanently established, or they can take the form of dial-up connections that are established when they are needed and released when they are not being used.

Point-to-point links are typically used for three purposes in a TCP/IP internet.

- **Router-to-Router Links.** This type of link connects a router on one physical LAN to a router on another physical LAN that is located at some distance from the first LAN. Leased lines are typically used for this type of connection.

- **Host-to-Router Links.** This type of link connects a single host to a router when the host is located at some distance from the router. Either a leased or a dial-up connection can be used for this type of connection.

- **Host-to-Host Links.** This type of link connects one host to a second host where the second host performs a routing function for the first host. Either a leased or a dial-up connection can be used for this type of connection as well.

In computer networks, wide area network (WAN) data link technology is generally used to implement point-to-point connections between devices. WAN data links can be used in an enterprise internetwork to interconnect individual computers. However, it is more common for wide area networking data links to be connected to bridges or routers that interconnect the various LAN data links that make up the enterprise internetwork. Individual computers are then typically connected to the LANs.

A number of different types of wide area networking data links can be used to interconnect LANs in an enterprise internetwork. Although the focus of this book is on the technology behind local area network data links, this appendix briefly describes the characteristics of various types of wide area networking data links that are used in enterprise internetworks. The emphasis in this appendix is on the station identification and Network layer protocol identification mechanisms that WAN data link technology implements.

CONVENTIONAL COMMON CARRIER LINKS

Conventional common carrier data links take the form of various types of analog telecommunications circuits. These range from ordinary telephone circuits that are provided via the switched telephone network to specialized high-speed telecommunications circuits that can be leased on a month-to-month basis from a common carrier.

Of particular importance, where high-speed telecommunications circuits are required, are the T1 and T3 transmission facilities that most telecommunications common carriers provide. A T1 circuit provides a 1.544 megabit per second (Mbps) digital transmission facility, and a T3 circuit provides a 45 Mbps digital transmission facility. Also available from most common carriers are fractional T1 facilities that provide a variety of transmission speeds by multiplexing a T1 facility and sharing its capacity among multiple users.

HIGH-LEVEL DATA LINK CONTROL

Point-to-point telecommunications data links typically use a data link protocol that is based on an international standard called *High-Level Data Link Control* (HDLC). The physical protocols used in conjunction with the various types of LAN technology described in this book are also based on the HDLC standard.

The HDLC protocol has its roots in the *Synchronous Data Link Control* (SDLC) protocol developed by IBM in the early 1970s for use in SNA. IBM's SDLC protocol is now considered to be a functional subset of the HDLC protocol and is in conformance with the international standard.

Frame Format

Box A.2 shows the format of the HDLC frame and describes its fields.

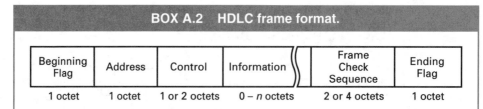

BOX A.2   HDLC frame format.

Beginning Flag	Address	Control	Information)(	Frame Check Sequence	Ending Flag
1 octet	1 octet	1 or 2 octets	0 – *n* octets	2 or 4 octets	1 octet

- **Beginning Flag.** A single octet containing the unique bit configuration 0111 1110 used to identify the beginning of the frame.
- **Address.** The Address field is used on an unbalanced data link to assign a unique station identification value to each station.
- **Control Field.** Identifies the type of frame being transmitted, conveys information necessary for the proper sequencing of frames, and carries control information.
- **Information.** Carries the user data portion of the frame. It consists of either control information or data passed down from a user. Some control frames do not include an Information field.
- **Frame Check Sequence.** Contains either a 16-bit or a 32-bit cyclic redundancy check (CRC) value used for error detection.
- **Ending Flag.** Contains the same bit configuration as the beginning flag (0111 1110) and identifies the end of the frame.

Frame Types

There are three types of HDLC frames that all share the same general format. The following are brief descriptions of each frame type:

- **Information Frames.** The primary function of Information frames (I-frames) is to carry user data.
- **Supervisory Frames.** Supervisory frames (S-frames) carry information necessary for supervisory functions that control the transmission of I-frames.
- **Unnumbered Frames.** Unnumbered frames (U-frames) are used to carry data and to perform various types of control functions.

Station Identification

On a point-to-point HDLC data link, no station identification function is necessary. While each HDLC frame has a station address field for compatibility with the standard, the value it contains is unimportant. Each frame sent has only one possible destination—the communications adapter at the other end of the data link.

Network Layer Protocol Identification

The HDLC standard makes no provision for a Network layer protocol identification function. This is a disadvantage of HDLC that makes it not well suited for use over WAN data links in an enterprise internetworking environment.

With HDLC, user data can be carried in Information frames (I-frames) by only one Network layer protocol at a time. However, some schemes have been devised for carrying information conforming to multiple protocols over an HDLC link. With these schemes, data for one Network layer protocol is carried in I-frames. Data conforming to other Network layer protocols is then carried using U-frames by including a protocol identifier in the Information field of each U-frame. Such a system of network layer protocol identification is typically suitable only for use in a situation where the amount of traffic carried in U-frames is small compared to the traffic carried in I-frames.

Because of HDLC's lack of an explicit protocol identification facility, other protocols, such as the Point-to-Point protocol and the Frame Relay protocol have been developed that are based on the HDLC standard.

SERIAL LINE INTERFACE PROTOCOL

The *Serial Line Interface Protocol* (SLIP) is a TCP/IP protocol used for transmitting IP datagrams over a point-to-point telecommunications facility. SLIP is documented in RFC 1055, *A Nonstandard for Transmission of IP Datagrams over Serial Lines.* SLIP is a very simple protocol that can be used to transmit an IP datagram, one octet at a time, between hosts, between routers, or between a host and a router.

Frame Format

SLIP uses an extremely simple framing structure. Box A.3 shows the format of the SLIP transmission frame and describes its fields.

Escape Mechanism

With SLIP, a delimiter octet having the bit configuration 11000000 (decimal 192) marks the end of each datagram. An escape mechanism is used to indicate that an octet having this bit configuration is a delimiter rather than part of an IP datagram. When SLIP encounters an octet within the IP datagram that has the delimiter bit configuration, it converts that octet to a 2-octet sequence consisting of an escape octet having the bit configu-

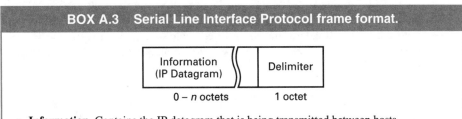

BOX A.3   Serial Line Interface Protocol frame format.

Information (IP Datagram)   Delimiter

0 – *n* octets   1 octet

- **Information.** Contains the IP datagram that is being transmitted between hosts.
- **Delimiter.** Consists of a single octet containing the unique bit configuration 11000000 and identifies the end of the IP datagram.

ration 11011011 (decimal 219) followed by an octet having the bit configuration 11011100 (decimal 220). If SLIP encounters an octet in the IP datagram having the escape character bit configuration, it converts that to a 2-octet sequence consisting of the escape character followed by an octet containing the bit configuration 11011101 (decimal 221).

SLIP Deficiencies

Although SLIP is very widely used in TCP/IP internets, it has two serious deficiencies:

- SLIP does not define any mechanisms for dynamically controlling the characteristics of the connection between the two hosts that are communicating or to identify the type of higher-level protocol to which the data traffic conforms. SLIP is typically only used when the two hosts know each others addresses and only when the two hosts are exchanging IP datagrams.
- SLIP does not provide any error detection or error correction facilities.

POINT-TO-POINT PROTOCOL

The Point-to-Point protocol is an adaptation of HDLC that grew out of work done by the Internet Engineering Task Force. The Point-to-Point protocol improves on HDLC by adding the Network layer protocol identification mechanism that is required for enterprise internetworking. The Point-to-Point protocol allows a point-to-point connection to be established between two network devices that permits frames associated with multiple Network layer protocols to flow over data links without interfering with one another.

Frame Format

The Point-to-Point protocol frame format is based on the generic HDLC transmission frame and is generally conformant with it. Box A.4 shows the format of the Point-to-Point protocol transmission frame and describes its fields.

Station Identification

On a data link that uses the Point-to-Point protocol, no station identification function is necessary. Each Point-to-Point protocol frame contains an Address field for compatibility with the HDLC standard, but the Address field's value is always hex 'FF'. Each frame sent has only one possible destination—the communications adapter at the other end of the data link.

Network Layer Protocol Identification

The Network layer protocol identification function is provided by the Protocol field that has been added to the HDLC frame between the Control field and the Information field. The documentation of the Point-to-Point protocol lists the identifier values to be used for each Network layer protocol supported by the standard. Although the Point-to-Point pro-

BOX A.4   Point-to-Point Protocol frame format.

Beginning Flag	Address (X'FF')	Control (X'03')	Protocol	Information	Frame Check Sequence	Ending Flag
1 octet	1 octet	1 octet	2 octets	0 – *n* octets	2 octets	1 octet

- **Beginning Flag.** Consists of a single octet containing the unique bit configuration 0111 1110 and identifies the beginning of the Address field.
- **Address.** Contains the value hex 'FF'.
- **Control Field.** Contains the value hex '03'.
- **Protocol Field.** Identifies the Network layer protocol with which the packet in the Information field is associated.
- **Information.** Used to carry the user data portion of the frame.
- **Frame Check Sequence.** Contains a 16-bit cyclic redundancy check (CRC) value used for error detection.
- **Ending Flag.** Contains the same bit configuration as the Beginning Flag field (0111 1110) and identifies the end of the frame.

tocol was designed primarily for use in TCP/IP internets, protocol identifiers have been assigned to other Network layer protocols as well.

X.25

One alternative to using conventional common carrier telecommunications circuits in a computer network is to use the virtual circuits provided by a public packet-switched data network (PSDN). Many of today's public data networks, especially outside of the United States, use packet-switching techniques and conform to CCITT *Recommendation X.25*. Recommendation X.25 defines a standard way for attaching a computer or other intelligent device to a PSDN.

X.25 PSDNs are generally operated by either a common carrier or a private telecommunications service provider. An organization generally contracts with a PSDN service provider to implement point-to-point connections between pairs of user computers. Each user machine has a single point of connection into the PSDN but can make logical point-to-point connections with any number of other user machines.

Virtual Circuits

A PSDN conforming to X.25 typically offers to its users two major types of point-to-point transmission facilities:

- **Permanent Virtual Circuits.** A user of a PSDN may wish to be permanently connected with another network user in much the same way as two users are connected using a leased telephone connection. A *permanent virtual circuit* (PVC) provides this facility.

- **Switched Virtual Circuits.** When an X.25 user requests the establishment of a *switched virtual circuit* (SVC), the network establishes a virtual circuit with another user, the two users exchange messages for a time over the virtual circuit, and then one of the two users requests disconnection of the virtual circuit. A switched virtual circuit is often referred to as a *virtual call* (VC).

Frame Format

The X.25 frame format conforms to the HDLC specification. Box A.5 shows the format of the X.25 frame and describes its fields.

Station Identification

Each computer that is attached to an X.25 PSDN is assigned a network address that is used to identify the computer in the network. The network addressing scheme and functions for establishing virtual circuits are defined by X.25. However, these functions operate at the level of the Network layer of the OSI model and, thus, the X.25 network addressing scheme is not equivalent to the station addressing schemes implemented for other forms of data links.

Once an X.25 virtual circuit has been established for use to connect a pair of devices in an enterprise internetwork, no station identification function is necessary at the level of the Data Link layer. The X.25 virtual circuit appears to the upper layers exactly as any other type of point-to-point communication facility. From the viewpoint of using an X.25 virtual circuit as a point-to-point data link, each packet sent has only one possible destination—the communications adapter at the other end of the virtual circuit.

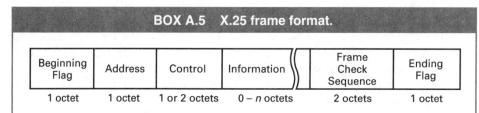

BOX A.5   X.25 frame format.

Beginning Flag	Address	Control	Information		Frame Check Sequence	Ending Flag
1 octet	1 octet	1 or 2 octets	0 – *n* octets		2 octets	1 octet

- **Beginning Flag.** Consists of a single octet containing the unique bit configuration 0111 1110 and identifies the beginning of the frame.
- **Address.** Contains hex '01' for commands flowing from the computer into the PSDN, and hex '03' for responses flowing from the PSDN to the computer.
- **Control Field.** Determines the type of frame being transmitted, conveys information necessary for the proper sequencing of frames, and carries control information.
- **Information.** Carries the user data portion of the frame.
- **Frame Check Sequence.** Contains a 16-bit cyclic redundancy check (CRC) value used for error detection.
- **Ending Flag.** Contains the same bit configuration as the Beginning Flag field (0111 1110) and identifies the end of the frame.

Network Layer Protocol Identification

A given computer attached to a given PSDN is allowed to concurrently establish up to 4095 different *logical channels* over the same virtual circuit. Each logical channel is assigned a different 12-bit *logical channel number*. Logical channels can be used to distinguish one Network layer protocol from another by using a different logical channel number in the packet header for each packet sent. Again, however, this protocol identification scheme is different from the ones used with other forms of WAN data links because it depends on information carried in the X.25 packet header rather than in the frame header. Therefore, Network layer functions are involved in handling the protocol identification mechanism when X.25 virtual circuits are used in enterprise internetworks.

X.25 facilities provide a wider range of functions for implementing multiple-protocol enterprise internetworks than do conventional telecommunication data links. However, since these facilities operate at the level of the Network layer of the OSI model, devices and software that use X.25 virtual circuits to carry data through a computer network must be aware of the protocols that they are carrying. Additional overhead is generally associated with these functions. Also, because of the complex routing decisions that must be made in moving data through an X.25 network, throughput is generally limited to relatively low levels.

Frame Relay data links, described next, provide a higher-performance alternative to X.25 virtual circuits.

FRAME RELAY

Frame Relay networks supply services that are similar to those provided by X.25 packet-switching networks. However, routing decisions in a Frame Relay network are relatively simple and are made in the Data Link layer rather than in the Network layer. Frame Relay networks support a variety of transmission speeds, but the target speed is generally in the neighborhood of the speeds supported by T1 facilities.

A major difference between Frame Relay networks and X.25 networks is that Frame Relay networks do not provide the error correction facilities that are provided by X.25 networks. If the Information field of a frame is corrupted as it moves through a Frame Relay network, the frame is discarded and does not appear at its destination. Error correction procedures must be implemented at a higher layer in the user equipment. However, this is ordinarily not a serious limitation, since error correction procedures are generally implemented in the higher layers even when X.25 virtual circuits are used.

Like X.25 networks, Frame Relay networks are generally operated by either a common carrier or by a private telecommunications service provider. An organization generally contracts with a Frame Relay service provider to implement point-to-point connections between pairs of user computers. Each user machine has a single point of connection into the Frame Relay network but can make logical point-to-point connections with any number of other user machines.

Frame Format

The Frame Relay frame is conformant with the HDLC standard. Box A.6 shows the format of the Frame Relay frame and describes its fields.

Station Identification

The *data link connection identifier* that identifies a particular virtual circuit provides the station identification mechanism that identifies the station at the other end of the virtual circuit. A computer that is connected to a Frame Relay network can communicate with any number of other computers by placing an appropriate data link connection identifier value in each frame that it transmits. Note that this station identification mechanism operates in the Data Link layer rather than in the Network layer as with X.25 virtual circuits.

Network Layer Protocol Identification

The data link connection identifier can also be used to provide the protocol identification function. One computer can establish any number of virtual circuits with another computer attached to the Frame Relay network. Each virtual circuit connecting the two computers is assigned a different data link connection identifier and can be used to carry packets associated with a different Network layer protocol.

ASYNCHRONOUS TRANSFER MODE

Asynchronous Transfer Mode (ATM) is the name of a new telecommunications technology that is currently undergoing standardization. Although the ATM standardization effort is being driven by the telephone industry, ATM has the potential for unifying many of the different forms of electronic communication that are currently in use today.

To understand the technology behind ATM, it is helpful to examine the way computer networking technology is evolving.

Circuit Switching

The earliest forms of electronic communication used *circuit switching* techniques. The telephone network is essentially a circuit switching network in which a dedicated circuit is established between two users for the duration of a telephone call. Circuit switching is ideal for ordinary telephone circuits because the required bandwidth is relatively low, the full bandwidth is ordinarily required during the entire duration of a call, and calls are relatively long (measured in minutes rather than microseconds).

Early forms of computer communication used circuit-switching techniques to interconnect computer equipment simply because the only communication facilities available that spanned long distances were ordinary telephone circuits.

BOX A.6   Frame Relay frame format.

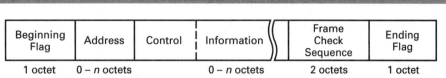

Beginning Flag	Address	Control	Information	Frame Check Sequence	Ending Flag
1 octet	0 – *n* octets		0 – *n* octets	2 octets	1 octet

- **Beginning Flag.** Containing the unique bit configuration 0111 1110.

- **Address.** The Address field is at least two octets in length and is sometimes longer. It contains a *data link connection identifier* (DLCI) that identifies the specific virtual circuit the frame is associated with. The Address field also contains bits that can be used to implement congestion control functions.

- **Control Field.** The HDLC Control Field is treated as part of the Information field by the Frame Relay protocol.

- **Information.** Carries the user data portion of the frame.

- **Frame Check Sequence.** Contains a 16-bit cyclic redundancy check (CRC) value used for error detection.

- **Ending Flag.** Contains the same bit configuration as the Beginning Flag field (0111 1110) and identifies the end of the frame.

Packet Switching

Computer communication does not lend itself well to the type of circuit switching used in the telephone system. In a typical computer application, we would like to transmit short bursts of data very rapidly between two communicating machines, but there may be relatively long periods of time between bursts. In a typical application where a person at a user-interface device communicates with a server system, we would like a communication channel having a very high transmission speed, but we typically send information over the channel for only a very small percentage of the time.

The packet-switching techniques that are used today in computer networks allow a number of users to share a high-capacity transmission channel. Packet switching works well for computer data at low to moderate transmission speeds. But packet switching is not well suited for voice or video communication. The delays introduced by the packet switches are too long and too unpredictable for voice or video applications.

It turns out that packet-switching techniques do not work well for computer data either at very high transmission speeds. On a network that supports very high transmission speeds, say billions of bits per second, the overhead introduced by conventional routers that handle the routing function in software is too high. Traditional packet switching mechanisms are especially ill-suited for a network that must handle a mix of traffic of different types, such as voice, video, and computer data.

Conventional circuit switching is also ill-suited for very-high-speed networking because no single user needs more than a small percentage of the total capacity of the transmission channel. A fundamentally different type of switching technology is needed to meet the needs of very-high-speed communication.

ATM Cell Switching Technology

ATM technology is designed to meet the needs of heterogeneous, high-speed networking. ATM implements a form of very fast packet switching in which data is carried in fixed-length units called *cells*. Each cell is 53-octets in length, with only five octets used as a header in each cell.

ATM employs mechanisms that can be used to set up virtual circuits between users, in which a pair of communicating users appear to have a dedicated circuit between them. Very fast cell-switching techniques, implemented entirely in hardware are used to implement the virtual circuits.

The result of ATM technology is to provide users with the advantages of circuit switching in that the network can guarantee a certain transmission capacity and level of service between two users. Each user can request the network bandwidth that is required for a particular application, and the ATM network provides the user with that bandwidth. The very-high-speed transmission facilities can be shared among all users, as with packet switching, with each user utilizing only the bandwidth required by that user.

ATM LANs

ATM technology can be used to create networks that have many of the characteristics of today's local area networks. With ATM, devices will be attached to interface units called *ATM switching nodes,* as shown in Fig. A.5. Switching nodes can be interconnected using dedicated cabling, as in today's LANs.

The interconnections between ATM switching nodes can be configured so that any desired amount of transmission capacity can be provided to the networked systems, giving communicating users the appearance of a very-high-speed dedicated connection between them.

ATM WANs

ATM technology can also be used to create wide area networks. When telecommunications providers make public ATM facilities available, it will be possible to interconnect ATM switching nodes using public, long-distance telecommunications facilities that use the same switching techniques as are used in a local ATM network. Such a configuration is shown in Fig. A.6.

ATM Cell Format

ATM defines two types of cells, having slightly different cell formats:

- **User-Network Interface Cells.** A *user-network interface* (UNI) cell is used to transmit data between a user device and an ATM switching node.
- **Network-Network Interface Cells.** A *network-network interface* (NNI) cell is used to transmit data between ATM switching nodes.

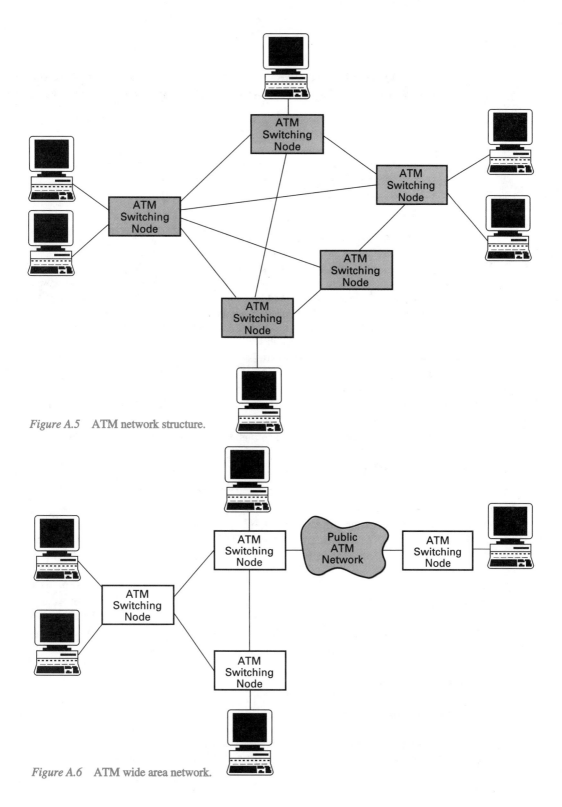

Figure A.5   ATM network structure.

Figure A.6   ATM wide area network.

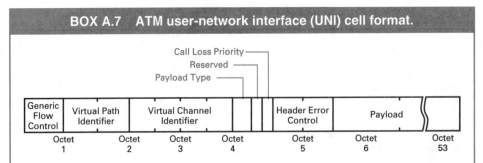

BOX A.7   ATM user-network interface (UNI) cell format.

- **Generic Flow Control.** Used to ensure that users are given fair access to the transmission facilities when a single ATM access point is serving more than one user.
- **Virtual Path Identifier.** Used, together with the Virtual Channel Identifier field, to identify a *virtual path* (VP) between two nodes. A virtual path is a collection of one or more virtual channels associated with the same user end point.
- **Virtual Channel Identifier.** Used, together with the Virtual Path Identifier field, to identify a *virtual channel* (VC) between two nodes. A virtual channel is a unidirectional virtual circuit associated with a particular user.
- **Payload Type.** Used to differentiate between cells carrying user data and cells carrying ATM control information.
- **Reserved.** Reserved for future use.
- **Call Loss Priority.** Used to determine the eligibility of a cell for being discarded during a period of network congestion.
- **Header Error Control.** Used to detect corruption of the information contained in the cell header.
- **Payload.** Contains the data portion of the cell.

Box A.7 shows the format of an ATM UNI cell and describes the fields in the cell header. An ATM NNI cell is identical to the UNI cell except that there is no Generic Flow Control field, and those bits are used as part of the Virtual Path Identifier field.

Transmission Facilities

ATM technology is designed for use over a wide range of physical transmission technologies, ranging from private cabling to various forms of long-distance telecommunications transmission. Box A.8 lists some of the transmission technologies that public ATM networks may support.

Classes of ATM Service

The ATM architecture defines four classes of service that a user connected to an ATM switching node can request, depending on the needs of the application:

BOX A.8   Representative ATM transmission technologies.

OC-1 SONET. 51 Mbps transmission over optical fiber.
OC-3 SONET. 155 Mbps transmission over optical fiber.
OC-12 SONET. 622 Mbps transmission over optical fiber.
OC-48 SONET. 2.4 Gbps transmission over optical fiber.
T1 Carrier. 1.544 Mbps using conventional telephone transmission.
T3 Carrier. 44.736 Mbps using conventional telephone transmission.

- Class A. Circuit emulation with a constant bit rate.
- Class B. Audio and/or video transmission with a variable bit rate.
- Class C. Connection-oriented service for data transmission.
- Class D. Connectionless service for data transmission.

Hybrid Networks

Although ATM technology can ultimately replace the technology used in today's LANs and WANs, it is likely that ATM switching technology will initially be used in conjunction with conventional LAN and WAN technology. For example, conventional LAN data links are likely to be connected to ATM switching nodes. This provides LAN users with another, higher-performance method of interconnecting LANs. It is also likely that conventional WAN data links will be used to connect distant ATM switching nodes in places where native ATM transmission facilities may not yet be available. A possible hybrid configuration is shown in Fig. A.7.

Future of ATM

The proponents of ATM claim that ATM technology will be the grand unifier of voice, video, and data transmission. ATM represents the closest approximation to a true bandwidth-on-demand transmission service that has yet been devised.

For the data user, ATM has the potential of removing today's distinction between local area networking and wide area networking. As we make clear in this book, the technologies used in local area networking and wide area networking are today fundamentally different. We require specialized devices, such as bridges and routers, to interconnect LAN and WAN data links. ATM technology will allow the same technology to be used over short-distance, dedicated cabling as is used over long-distance common carrier circuits.

With the high transmission speeds ATM technology is designed to support, it will be possible to make the distance between two communicating devices transparent to application programs. With such technology, it will be possible to build applications that work in an identical manner whether the two communicating systems are in the same room or across the globe.

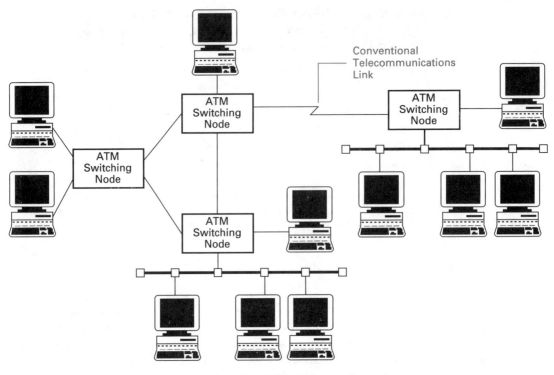

Figure A.7   ATM hybrid network.

OTHER WIDE AREA NETWORKING TECHNOLOGIES

The previous sections have introduced the most important of the wide area networking technologies that are being used today to implement wide area networking connections in enterprise internetworks. There are a number of other technologies that are in various stages of development and standardization that will become more important in the future. The following are brief descriptions of these.

ISDN

An *Integrated Services Digital Network* (ISDN) is a public telecommunications network—typically administered by a common carrier or another telecommunications provider—that supplies end-to-end digital telecommunications services that can be used for both voice and nonvoice purposes. Two levels of service have been defined for ISDN:

- **Basic Rate Interface (BRI).** This level of service defines a bit rate of 144 Kbps, which is divided into two 64-Kbps channels for the user and one 16-Kbps channel for signaling.
- **Primary Rate Interface (PRI).** The primary rate interface level of service consists of 23 64-Kbps channels and one 64-Kbps channel for signaling, providing a bit rate to the user of 1.544 Mbps.

The main data link protocol employed with ISDN circuits is called *ISDN Data Link Control* (IDLC), which is technically aligned with HDLC. Procedures for establishing ISDN connections between two computers are defined by protocols that operate at the level of the Network layer of the OSI model, and so Network layer software is typically involved in establishing an ISDN connection.

ISDN services include both packet-mode services and circuit-mode services. Packet-mode ISDN services offer services that are similar to those provided by an X.25 PSDN. Circuit-mode services can be used as replacements for conventional telecommunications circuits.

Broadband ISDN

Broadband ISDN (B-ISDN) represents a possible future direction of the telephone industry and will require that the conventional copper-wire local loops that now go into subscriber premises be replaced by optical fiber cables. B-ISDN services are built on top of a Physical layer specification called SONET. A number of bit rates have been specified for SONET signal transmission, including the following:

- SONET OC-1 — 51 Mbps
- SONET OC-3 — 155 Mbps
- SONET OC-12 — 622 Mbps
- SONET OC-48 — 2.4 Gbps

B-ISDN has the potential of providing extremely high-bandwidth wide area networking connections. For example, the OC-3 and higher levels of service provides higher bit rates than an FDDI LAN and could be used in creating enterprise internetworks that operate at higher than LAN speeds over large geographic areas.

Distributed Queue Dual Bus

The Distributed Queue Dual Bus (DQDB) protocol defines a technology that can be used to provide LAN-like services over a wider geographic area. The type of network that the DQDB protocol operates over is generally referred to as a *Metropolitan Area Network* (MAN). The DQDB protocol is relatively independent of the underlying physical transmission medium and can operate at speeds as low as 44 Mbps and as high as the SONET OC-3 speed of 155.52 Mbps. DQDB provides a service that is similar to that defined by IEEE 802.2 Logical Link Control.

Switched Multimegabit Data Service

The Switched Multimegabit Data Service (SMDS) is a wide area packet-switching service that provides packet-switching services similar to an X.25 network. However, SMDS provides services at speeds up to 44 Mbps rather than the relatively slow speeds provided by a typical X.25 PSDN.

Appendix **B**

OSF Distributed Computing Environment

An important architecture for client-server, distributed computing that is supported in many TCP/IP environments is that defined by the *Distributed Computing Environment* (DCE). The DCE is an architecture for distributed computing that has been developed by the Open Software Foundation (OSF). The OSF DCE defines a number of services that application programs can invoke in a client-server environment. These services operate above the level of the operating system and below the level of the application-oriented services that specific application programs define. Therefore, they are often referred to by the term *middleware*.

OSF took a unique approach to standardization when it defined the DCE architecture. Instead of writing specifications from scratch for each of the services that the DCE defines, OSF published requests for technology and invited all the members of OSF to submit working code that implemented each of the services the DCE was attempting to define. OSF then selected what it felt were the best technologies from among all the submissions. In this manner, each of the services that the DCE defines is based on proven, working technology rather than being abstract sets of specifications.

The DCE is not only a paper architecture; it also consists of working code that is available from OSF in source form. The source code is written in a portable fashion that is easily adapted to run on a wide variety of UNIX-type operating systems. It can also be tailored to run on other operating systems, such as Windows NT and OS/2 in the personal computer environment. It is the responsibility of a particular vendor, and not OSF, to tailor the DCE source code for a particular platform.

DCE CELL ARCHITECTURE

DCE is based on a *cell architecture* in which computing systems that must communicate frequently can be placed in a single cell. An organization can define a cell in any desired way. For example, a cell might consist of all the computing systems attached to a single organization's internet. Alternatively, an individual organization may choose to implement many cells. Provision is made for communicating between a computing system in one cell and a computing system in another cell, for example, when a computing system in a cell belonging to one organization needs to communicate with a computing system in another organization's cell.

DCE MIDDLEWARE SERVICES

The DCE defines a set of middleware services that are used to isolate application programs from the underlying computing platforms or network transport mechanisms, as shown in Fig. B.1.

The initial version of DCE is based on six distinct services:

- DCE Remote Procedure Call Service
- DCE Threads Service
- DCE Directory Service
- DCE Distributed File Service
- DCE Distributed Time Service
- DCE Security Service

Box B.1 provides brief descriptions of the six DCE services. Each service is discussed further in the sections that follow.

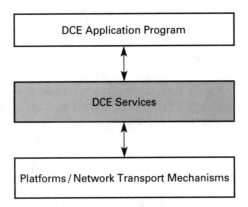

Figure B.1   DCE services operate in the role of middleware.

DCE REMOTE PROCEDURE CALL SERVICE

The DCE RPC Service is based on the RPC technology that was jointly submitted to the OSF by Digital Equipment Corporation and Hewlett-Packard and is similar to the HP RPC facility used in the TCP/IP environment.

The DCE RPC Service consists of both a development facility and a runtime service. The development facility consists of an RPC language and an associated compiler

- **DCE Remote Procedure Call Service.** The *DCE Remote Procedure Call Service* (DCE RPC) allows an application component running in one computer system to use a simple procedure call mechanism to invoke a procedure that is running in some other computing system in the network. This allows procedure calls to be used to hide many of the complexities of network communication from application developers. The DCE RPC Service is based on RPC technology that was jointly submitted to the OSF by Digital Equipment Corporation and Hewlett-Packard.

- **DCE Threads Service.** The *DCE Threads Service* provides application programmers with the ability to create independent execution threads within the same program. This gives an application the ability to carry out multiple computing tasks concurrently. The DCE Threads Service is based on the *DECthreads* implementation of the *Concert Multithread Architecture* (CMA) that was submitted to the OSF by Digital Equipment Corporation.

- **DCE Directory Service.** The *DCE Directory Service* implements a distributed repository that stores information about objects in the computing environment, including users, computing systems, and distributed services that application programs can request. The DCE Directory Service provides facilities for submitting a name to the Directory Service and getting back a list of the attributes associated with that name. The DCE Directory Service includes the following two components available from the OSF:

  — **DCE Global Directory Service.** The *DCE Global Directory Service* (DCE GDS) is designed to handle directory operations that take place between individual cells. The DCE GDS is based on the CCITT X.500 standard as implemented by the DIR-X X.500 directory service submitted to the OSF by Siemens.

  — **DCE Cell Directory Service.** The *DCE Cell Directory Service* (DCE CDS) is designed to handle name operations that take place within a single cell. The DCE CDS is based on the *DECdns* implementation of the Distributed Name Service architecture submitted to the OSF by Digital Equipment Corporation.

  In addition to the two OSF DCE directory technologies, the DCE Directory Service also integrates the TCP/IP Domain Name System (DNS) that can be used as an alternative to the DCE GDS for performing naming operations between cells. DNS is described in Chapter 7.

- **DCE Distributed File Service.** The *DCE Distributed File Service* (DCE DFS) allows users to access and share files that are maintained by computing systems operating in the role of *file servers* that can be located anywhere in the network. DCE DFS is based on the *Andrew File System* (AFS) technology submitted to the OSF by Transarc Corporation. It performs many of the same functions as the TCP/IP Network File Service, described in Chapter 6.

- **DCE Distributed Time Service.** The *DCE Distributed Time Service* allows application programs to request services that work with date and time-of-day values in a standardized manner that is the same across all computing platforms. The Distributed Time Service also implements a set of distributed algorithms that ensure that the clocks in all the computing systems in the network are synchronized and contain correct values for the date and time of day. DCE DTS is based on the *Distributed Time Service* (DTS) technology submitted to the OSF by Digital Equipment Corporation. The DCE DTS interoperates with the TCP/IP *Network Time Protocol* (NTP) introduced in Chapter 5.

(Continued)

BOX B.1   *(Continued)*

- **DCE Security Service.** The *DCE Security Service* provides facilities for implementing secure communications in a networked environment and for controlling access to resources in the computing environment. The DCE Security Service is based on the *Kerberos* security system submitted to the OSF by Project Athena. It is augmented by a number of additional security components submitted by Hewlett-Packard. Kerberos is described in Chapter 5.

---

for that language. This language and compiler are used to generate the code and data structures for the client and server stubs that allow procedure calls to be implemented using network communication. The DCE RPC Service allows programs to use procedure calls in implementing distributed applications in order to hide much of the complexity of network communication from the application.

DCE RPC Architectural Model

The architecture behind the DCE RPC facility provides support for a heterogeneous computing system environment. A somewhat simplified view of the architectural model for the DCE RPC Service is shown in Fig. B.2.

As with many TCP/IP services, the DCE RPC architecture uses a client/server model. The calling procedure operates in the role of the client, and the procedure being called operates in the role of the server. Both the client procedure and the server procedure typically execute on different computing systems but produce the same results as if they both resided in the same computing system.

DCE RPC Facility Components

The following are descriptions of the major components that make up an implementation of the DCE RPC facility:

- **Interface Definition Language (IDL) and IDL Compiler.** Application programs that make use of the DCE RPC Service specify the details of RPC interfaces by coding *interface definitions* using the *Interface Definition Language* (IDL). IDL source statements are compiled by the *IDL compiler*. The IDL compiler produces an interface header file that is used when the client and server source modules are compiled. The IDL compiler also produces two interface-specific *stub* modules, one for use by the client and the other for use by the server.

- **Application Client and Server Procedures.** An RPC application typically consists of procedures that execute on different computing systems. The server system implements the remote procedures for one or more RPC interfaces. The client system implements the corresponding calling code. The server and client procedures each contain a copy of the *RPC runtime service library,* which is part of the DCE RPC software. Each server and client procedure is linked with an associated stub procedure for each RPC interface it references.

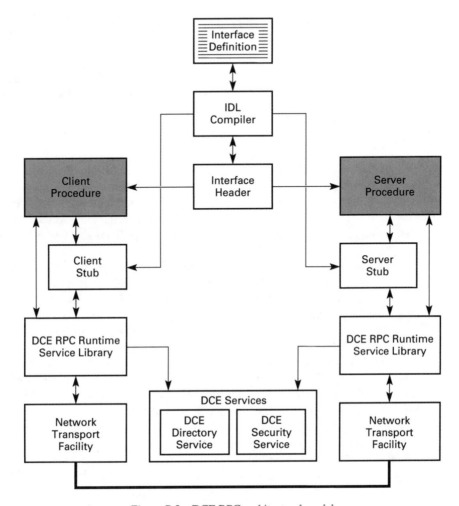

Figure B.2   DCE RPC architectural model.

- **Client and Server Stubs.** The stubs that are generated by the IDL compiler support the server remote procedures and allow the client procedures to call the remote procedures. Stubs also perform RPC support services on behalf of the application code in both the server and client procedures. The client's stub makes it *appear* to the calling procedure as if the called procedure is executing on the client's own computing system. The server's stub performs a complementary function for the server.

- **RPC Runtime Service Library.** The RPC runtime service library that is linked with each server and client procedure provides the support that is required for achieving network interoperability. Many of the runtime service library functions are invoked by the stubs, and typical RPC client and server procedures explicitly invoke only a few of the supported library functions. However, the library supports an extensive set of functions to provide RPC applications with maximum flexibility.

- **Interface to DCE Directory and Security Services.** The DCE RPC facility makes use of other DCE Services in performing its functions. For example, by coding the appropriate IDL source statements a client procedure can cause its stub to perform the function of locating an appropriate server procedure. This is done through the use of the DCE Directory Service. The DCE RPC facility can also invoke DCE Security Services to perform such functions as authentication, authorization, and data encryption on behalf of the client and server procedures.

DCE THREADS SERVICE

The DCE Threads Service is based on the *Concert Multithread Architecture* (CMA), originally implemented in the DECthreads product that was submitted to the OSF by Digital Equipment Corporation. CMA and the DECthreads product were accepted by the OSF as the technology component to form the basis of the DCE Threads Service. The application programming interface to the DCE Threads Service is based on the Pthreads API that is part of the POSIX 1003.4a standard.

A *thread* is defined as a single, sequential flow of control within a program. The DCE Threads Service provides the application programmer with the ability to create independent execution threads within the same process. This gives an application component the ability to carry out multiple computing tasks concurrently.

In some environments, a platform's underlying operating system may provide a multithreading capability of its own. If the host operating system already provides a threads facility, the DCE Threads Service can use that capability. All of the DCE technology components assume that the underlying environment supports multithreaded operations. However, not all operating systems that will participate in the DCE environment support a threads service, so the DCE Threads Service can be provided by a separate DCE component.

The DCE Threads Service is implemented by a set of portable routines that application programs can call to enable them to create multiple execution threads within the same program. Each execution thread can perform a separate computing task, and all threads within the same program can execute concurrently, sharing computing system resources. All the various threads that are started by the program operate within a shared address space and so have access to the same memory locations. The DCE Threads Service provides a set of facilities that allow the various threads to coordinate their execution and their access to shared memory to avoid unwanted conflicts.

Single Thread Process Structure

Figure B.3 shows the structure of a single-threaded process. The process has access to the computing system execution resources including processor registers and memory. The processor memory implements heap storage, static storage, stack storage, and the code the application program executes.

Multithreaded Process Structure

Figure B.4 shows the structure of a multithreaded process. In the multithreaded environment, memory is organized using a single heap storage area, static storage area, and set of

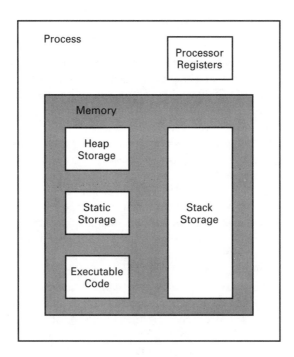

Figure B.3 Single-threaded process organization.

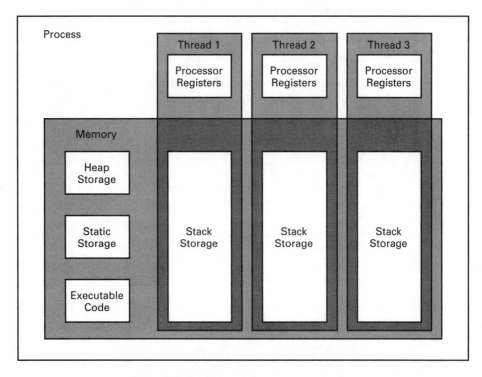

Figure B.4 Multithreaded process organization.

application code. The application code is reentrant so that it can be executed by any number of independently-executing threads, each of which may be performing different tasks at any given time. Each thread has its own stack storage allowing the DCE Threads Service to save and restore registers so that each thread executes as if it had access to its own private set of processor registers.

Multithreading facilities are especially important in the client-server environment for the implementation of server processes. Servers must often be implemented in an environment where it is difficult to predict the number of client processes that may require access to a given server. The server must be designed so that it can process any number of client processes concurrently.

Most operating systems provide facilities for starting up multiple processes that execute concurrently. But it is important to realize that a new thread is not the same as a new process. A process can contain one or more threads, but all the various threads execute within the same process context and share that context with one another. A thread has very little context associated with it, typically just a stack and a register set. A process has more context, such as a separate address space, files, devices, a user name, and privileges. So compared to a process, a thread is small: little memory is required to start one up and it is lightweight; there is low overhead associated with synchronization, and it is inexpensive; and it costs little to start one up.

Uses for Multithreading Facilities

Many classes of applications can make good use of multithreading facilities. The following are a few examples of possible uses for multithreading facilities in application programs:

- Some computing algorithms inherently define parallel processes that require the use of multiple execution threads to correctly implement the algorithm.

- Multithreading gives an application program the capability for one thread to perform useful work while another thread is waiting for I/O operations to complete.

- An application program can use multithreading to enhance the user interface it presents to a user. One execution thread might handle all interactions with the user and then pass each user request to a separate thread for execution. Such a user interface might yield faster response times and allow the user to initiate multiple actions that can all operate concurrently.

- Multithreading facilities make it possible to efficiently use the processing capabilities of powerful server systems by making it possible for a server to concurrently process the requests of multiple clients.

- Multithreading can be used to improve the response time of a server process by performing different independent units of work in separate execution threads that execute concurrently.

Thread Coordination Facilities

In some multithreaded applications, the various execution threads are completely independent of one another and need not communicate with each other as they execute. Each thread simply executes until it completes its assigned task.

In other multithreaded applications a number of independent execution threads might be working together to perform a single unit of work. In such applications, facilities are needed that allow the various execution threads to synchronize their processing.

The DCE Threads Service gives such applications the ability to create elements called *mutexes* to provide thread synchronization capabilities. The term *mutex* stands for *mut*ual *ex*clusion. A multithreaded application can create one or more mutex elements on which the various execution threads can request *holds*. Only one execution thread can hold a mutex at any given time. If one execution thread is holding a mutex, and a second thread requests a hold on that same mutex, the second thread waits until the first thread releases its hold on the mutex.

DCE DIRECTORY SERVICE

The DCE Directory Service stores information about objects in the computing environment, including users, computing systems, and distributed services that application programs can request. The information that the Directory Service maintains about objects consists of names and sets of attributes that are associated with those names. The DCE Directory Service provides facilities for submitting names to the Directory Service and getting back a list of the attributes that are associated with that name. A typical name might be the name of an end user. One of the attributes associated with that user's name might be the network address of the desktop computing system the end user is currently using.

The DCE Directory Service gives users and application programs the ability to locate and access objects in the computing environment based on their names alone without having to know where they are physically located. A primary use of the Directory service in a distributed system is to allow client processes to locate appropriate servers.

DCE Cell Architecture

One of the primary goals of the Distributed Computing Environment in general, and of the DCE Directory Service in particular, is that of scalability. Scalability is characterized by the ability to grow a distributed system to an arbitrary size without having to radically change the technology that is used to implement the distributed system.

One way in which the DCE approaches the goal of scalability is to allow computing systems to be structured into a system of *cells*. The various technologies that are integrated to make up the DCE Directory Service are closely associated with the cell structure of DCE.

Computing systems that must communicate frequently are generally placed in a single cell. The DCE architecture does not specify criteria for grouping computing systems into cells. Cells may be structured based on technological, social, political, or organizational boundaries. For example, a cell might consist of all the computing systems attached to a single local area network, those belonging to a particular department, or those residing in a particular building.

Large distributed systems are constructed by interconnecting a number of individual cells, as shown in Fig. B.5.

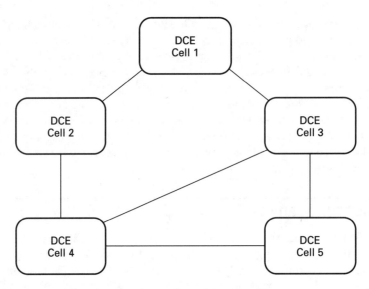

Figure B.5   DCE cell architecture.

Most communication that takes place within a single cell tends to be relatively straightforward. Communication between cells is often more complex and involves factors such as the following:

- **Longer Distances and Delays.** Individual cells may be many miles apart and interconnected by wide area networking data links that are slower than the links used in interconnecting the computing systems in a single cell.

- **Unknown, Possibly Heterogeneous Systems.** The characteristics of the systems within a cell are generally well known to the administering organization. Communication that takes place between cells may be less well known, and intercell communication cannot make assumptions about the nature of the networks and computing systems used in other cells.

- **Different Administration Policies.** Computing systems in different cells may be subject to different regulations, possibly due to security or cost considerations.

In a typical large distributed system, most communication—and therefore, most directory operations—takes place within the individual cells. The cell architecture allows the problems associated with intercell communication and name resolution to be addressed only when necessary. The DCE Directory Service can operate more efficiently when it is known that a request can be satisfied within the same cell. More general facilities needed to satisfy requests for operations involving multiple cells are employed only when they are needed.

DCE Directory Technologies

The DCE Directory Service integrates three different directory technologies in providing its services. The OSF itself distributes representative source code for the following two Directory Service technology components:

- **DCE Global Directory Service.** The *DCE Global Directory Service* (DCE GDS) is designed for performing name operations that take place between individual cells. The DCE GDS is based on the CCITT X.500 standard as implemented by the DIR-X X.500 directory service submitted to the OSF by Siemens. Compatibility with the X.500 standard is important for the eventual creation of a directory service for a worldwide computer network.

- **DCE Cell Directory Service.** The *DCE Cell Directory Service* (DCE CDS) is designed for performing name operations that take place within a single cell. The DCE CDS is based on the *DECdns* implementation of the *Distributed Name Service* architecture submitted to the OSF by Digital Equipment Corporation.

In addition to the two OSF DCE directory technologies, the DCE Directory Service also integrates the *Domain Name System* (DNS) directory technology that is used in the worldwide Internet and in many other networks that implement the TCP/IP protocol suite. DNS is widely used in the TCP/IP environment for translating host computer name references into their internet addresses. DNS is another global directory technology that can be used as an alternative to the DCE GDS for performing directory operations between cells.

Figure B.6 shows the relationship between the three directory service technologies. Each of the three directory technologies is briefly described in the following sections.

DCE Cell Directory Service

As introduced earlier, the operations used for performing name translation operations within a single cell is handled by the DCE Cell Directory Service (DCE CDS). If a user (or an application program operating on the user's behalf) requests a name translation operation for a name referring to a resource in the user's own DCE cell, the name translation operation is carried out by the DCE Cell Directory Service. The DCE Directory Service knows which directory service to use based on the format of the name that is submitted to the service. Names are made up of combinations of simple names.

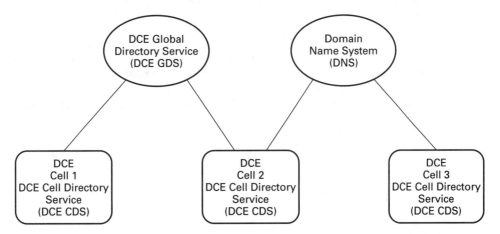

Figure B.6   Three DCE Directory Service technologies.

The following is an example of a name using the DCE CDS format:

```
/:/ENG/LEBEN/JohnFoobar
```

Slashes are used to separate individual simple names, and an initial qualifier of "/:" indicates that the name refers to a resource in the user's own cell.

DCE Global Directory Service

Directory operations that take place between cells is ordinarily handled by the DCE Global Directory Service (DCE GDS). The names that the DCE GDS works with use the X.500 name syntax to give names to individual cells. The following is an example of a cell name expressed using DCE GDS name format:

```
/.../C=US/O=LEBEN/OU=CHICAGO
```

In the above name, the "/..." indicates that the name is global and names a resource that is in a cell outside the user's own cell. The "C=US" is a *Country* entry that indicates that the cell containing the desired resource is located in the United States. The "O=LEBEN" is an *Organization* entry indicating that the cell belongs to an organization named Leben. The "OU=CHICAGO" is an *Organizational Unit* entry indicating that the cell belongs to an organizational unit, within the Leben organization, named Chicago.

Suppose the name "/:/ENG/LEBEN/JohnFoobar" refers to a resource in the above cell. A user inside that cell would then refer to that resource using a local CDS name:

```
/:/ENG/LEBEN/JohnFoobar
```

A user outside of the cell would refer to the resource using a fully-qualified global name that is a concatenation of a GDS cell name and a CDS local name:

```
/.../C=US/O=LEBEN/OU=CHICAGO/ENG/LEBEN/JohnFoobar
```

Domain Name System

The Domain Name System (DNS) technology is the third technology that is integrated with the DCE Directory Service. Although the OSF does not include the source code for a DNS implementation, DNS is implemented by a wide variety of vendors.

As described earlier, DNS can be used as an alternative to GDS to handle global name translation operations between cells. As described in Chapter 7, DNS works with names called *domain names*. Domain names can be used instead of GDS names to name individual cells. A typical domain name used to identify a cell looks like the following:

```
chicago.leben.com
```

Domain names are read from left to right with the most local domain first and the most global domain last. (Note that this is the reverse sequence from the other two Directory

Service technologies.) The above name might refer to the cell located in Chicago belonging to the organization named Leben. The **com** entry identifies the organization as a commercial organization.

Again, a user inside this cell would still refer to a resource in that cell using a local CDS name:

```
/:/ENG/LEBEN/JohnFoobar
```

A user outside of the cell would refer to a resource in this cell using a fully-qualified global name that is a combination of a DNS cell name and a CDS local name:

```
/.../chicago.leben.com/ENG/LEBEN/JohnFoobar
```

DCE Cell Directory Service Operation

This section describes how the DCE Cell Directory Service is structured and how it performs directory operations.

Even though the DCE Cell Directory Service (DCE CDS) is intended to be used within a single cell, the technology behind the DCE CDS was designed to allow very large numbers of computing systems—into the millions of systems—to be interconnected to form a single coherent network.

In operation, a DCE CDS implementation accepts the name of an object in the computing environment and passes back the set of attributes that are associated with that name. A typical attribute associated with a name is the network address of the computing system on which the named object resides. But DCE CDS can be used to store other attributes of names as well.

Namespace Structure

The full collection of directory information that DCE CDS maintains is called the *CDS namespace,* which is organized as a tree-structured system of *directories.* The directories that store names and the attributes associated with them can be distributed throughout the network and are maintained by DCE CDS software components called *CDS servers.* Figure B.7 shows a simple namespace stored in a number of directories.

A directory can contain three types of entries:

- **Child Pointer Entries.** A *child pointer entry* points to a lower-level directory. A child pointer can point to a directory maintained by the same CDS server, or it can point to a directory maintained by another CDS server. In Fig. B.7, the ENG, SITES, and EQUIPMENT directories are all pointed to by child pointer entries stored in the root directory.

- **Object Entries.** *Object entries* are the entries that are the lowermost entries in the namespace tree structure. Each object entry has a series of attributes, such as a network address, associated with it. The JohnFoobar entry in the LEBEN directory is an example of an object entry.

- **Soft Links.** *Soft links* implement pointers to other parts of the directory tree. These implement aliases that allow a single object to have multiple names. For example, we might

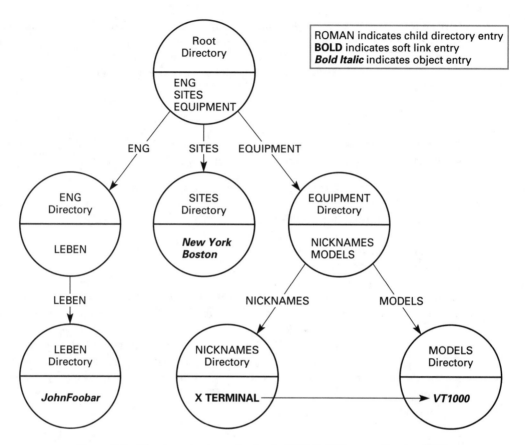

Figure B.7 Directory structure of a simple DCE Cell Directory Service (DCE CDS) namespace.

want to refer to the VT1000 product by a nickname—*X Terminal.* Soft links convert the underlying namespace tree structure into a more general directed-graph structure.

Each of the entries in the directory tree has a *simple name.* DCE CDS performs name translation operations on *full names.* A full name is formed by concatenating all of the entries from the root of the tree down to the object in question. For example, the following name is a full name:

```
:/ENG/LEBEN/JohnFoobar
```

Clearinghouses

A collection of directories stored on a particular computing system and accessible by a single CDS server is called a *clearinghouse.* Although a CDS server typically has access to a single clearinghouse, which contains all the directories the CDS server can directly access, it is possible for a CDS server to concurrently control and access multiple clearinghouses. This might be necessary when a CDS server fails and a clearinghouse has to be moved to some other CDS server.

Clerks

A *clerk* is the cell directory service component that implements the application programming interface to DCE CDS and that performs directory service operations on behalf of end users and application programs. All requests for directory operations that users make, either directly or indirectly, are made of a DCE CDS clerk. When DCE CDS is used to handle directory operations, each computing system in the network must contain an implementation of a clerk.

CDS servers

A *CDS server* is the DCE CDS component that actually accesses the clearinghouses containing the directories making up the namespace. Not all computing systems in the network implement a CDS server component. A network should include enough CDS servers to provide the performance, robustness, and availability required for a given sized network. A CDS server can be implemented in a general-purpose computing system performing other tasks as well as directory services. However, in large networks it is likely that the CDS server function will be performed by specialized processors, just as the routing function is now generally performed by specialized routers.

Partitioning and Replication

A major challenge in designing the technology behind DCE CDS was to make name translation operations work efficiently in very large networks. To meet the goal of scalability, the namespace can be *partitioned* to allow different sets of names to be maintained by different CDS servers. Directories can also be *replicated* to allow sets of names to be stored in multiple places. Partitioning and replication facilities make it possible for DCE CDS to quickly perform name translation operations in very large networks without having to refer to a single centrally-located collection of directory information. Partitioning and replication also makes DCE CDS highly available, since it can still operate if one or more CDS servers fails.

Partitioning of the namespace is accomplished by deciding which clearinghouses will contain which directories. A particular clearinghouse need not contain all the directories that make up the underlying namespace tree structure. However, it must be possible for a DCE CDS clerk to always be able to access any directory in the namespace.

Namespace replication is accomplished by storing a given directory in more than one clearinghouse. A copy of a directory stored in a particular clearinghouse is called a *replica*. There are three kinds of replicas:

- **Master Replicas.** One and only one replica of any given directory is designated the *master replica*. To simplify directory maintenance, certain types of update operations are performed only on master replicas. For example, the master replica is the only replica in which a new directory can be created by adding a child pointer to a higher-level directory.

- **Secondary Replicas.** Another type of replica is a *secondary replica.* New soft link or object entries can be added either to a master or a secondary replica, and existing directory entries can be updated in either master or secondary replicas.

- **Read-Only Replicas.** A third kind of replica is a *read-only replica.* It can handle requests for name translation operations but cannot service user requests for adding or updating directory entries. Read-only replicas are updated only at the request of DCE CDS itself.

Directory Operations

A clerk locates a CDS server by listening on the network for advertisements that are periodically broadcast by CDS servers. If the CDS server doesn't hear an advertisement, it can multicast a request for help. When a clerk finds a CDS server, it can then use that CDS server to perform directory operations on behalf of its clients.

The CDS server that receives a request from a clerk for a name translation operation may or may not have the required directories in its own clearinghouse to satisfy the request. If it does not, the CDS server queries other CDS servers to find the required directories. Special consistency guarantees make it possible for a CDS server to always navigate the directory tree and find the required directories—CDS servers are guaranteed to always be able to locate all the directories that make up the namespace, no matter what clearinghouses they are stored in.

Loose Consistency Guarantee

Since there are potentially many replicas of a given directory, it is necessary to insure that updates to a given directory are eventually applied to all replicas of that directory. The CDS architecture provides a relatively loose consistency guarantee—eventually directory replicas will be brought into synchronization, but a temporary situation may exist in which different users may get different answers when querying DCE CDS. It is up to a network administrator to decide when and how often replicas are brought into convergence for each directory in the namespace.

One of the most unusual features of the directory service is this notion of loose consistency guarantees. If two people go to the directory service and both register the name James Martin, and they happen to go to two different CDS servers, those two CDS servers will both accept the name. To handle this, CDS implements the notion of safe names and unsafe names. When you first register your name, it is unsafe. At any time you can go in and ask the directory service if your name is safe yet. Eventually either you will be told your name is safe, or you will be told someone else claimed that name before you did. The directory service takes great pains to ensure that no matter what, at some point either a name becomes safe or you are notified that someone else claimed it first.

There are two ways that the DCE CDS handles convergence of directory replicas—propagation and skulking. Certain directories may require relatively quick updates. These are handled by an efficient *propagation* function that is a one-time attempt to propagate an update to all replicas of a directory. Other directories may store names that are not as time critical, and the network administrator can choose to not perform the propagation function for these. Eventual convergence of all the replicas of a directory is always guaranteed, however, through a convergence algorithm called the *skulker*. The skulker operates periodically on each directory and insures that all replicas of a directory are eventually brought into convergence. All updates that are made to the database implementing the namespace are time stamped so that the update that entered the network most recently always wins.

Through the use of the propagation function and the skulker, the directories will all eventually come into convergence after a time, and name translation operations proceed normally after updates have been made to directory replicas.

DCE DISTRIBUTED FILE SERVICE

The DCE *Distributed File Service* (DCE DFS) is based on the *Andrew File System* (AFS), which was submitted to the OSF by Transarc Corporation. The DCE Distributed File Service allows end users and application programs to create and access files that are stored on computing systems operating in the role of *file servers* that can be located anywhere in the network. DCE DFS uses facilities provided by the DCE Directory Service so that users can access a file based on its name alone without having to know where a file is physically located.

In addition to providing users with access to remote files, DCE DFS also includes a physical file system, called the *DCE Local File System,* that is used by file servers to manipulate data in the files they maintain. The DCE Distributed File Service also provides facilities that a diskless computing system can use to download its operating system over the network, obtain configuration information, and connect to DCE DFS.

DCE DISTRIBUTED TIME SERVICE

The DCE Distributed Time Service (DCE DTS) provides facilities that programs can use to obtain correct values for the date and the time of day, as well as to request other time-related services. The DCE DTS implements algorithms that are used to synchronize the internal clocks in all the computing systems in a network. The DCE DTS is based on the DECdts distributed time service technology submitted to the OSF by Digital Equipment Corporation.

Time Value Representation

Historically, time values have been based on the rotation of the earth about its axis. A time value based on this standard is called *Universal Time* (UT) and is the basis of our international and civil time standards. Universal time corresponds with *Greenwich Mean Time* (GMT), the time of day in Greenwich, England, when Greenwich is on standard time. With Universal Time, a second is defined as 1/86400 of a mean solar day.

Coordinated Universal Time

A problem with Universal Time is that the earth's rotation is gradually slowing. To deal with this problem, in 1964, the International Congress on Weights and Measures redefined the second to be 9,192,631,770 vibrations of the characteristic frequency of an atomic clock based on the cesium atom. Unlike the earth, the cesium atom is not gradually slowing and thus provides a much more precise measure of time. This time is called *Coordinated Universal Time,* often designated by the acronym UTC. Coordinated Universal Time is maintained by an international organization called the International Time Bureau. The DCE Distributed Time Service is based on Coordinated Universal Time (UTC).

A value can be obtained for Coordinated Universal Time, via a telephone call, radio, or satellite link in many parts of the world through various organizations. For example, in the United States the radio stations WWV in Colorado and WWVH in Hawaii continuously broadcast values for Coordinated Universal Time.

Time Differential Factors

A Coordinated Universal Time value corresponds to local time in Greenwich, England. To obtain the local time and day in some other part of the world, a UTC value is often modified by a factor called the *time differential factor* (TDF). A TDF value is added to or subtracted from a UTC value to obtain a time representation corresponding to the local time in a particular time zone. For example, to obtain the standard time in the Eastern time zone of the United States, we would subtract a TDF value of 5 hours from the UTC value.

Uses for Time Values

There are three major uses for time values in computing systems:

- **Time Ordering of Events.** Given two events occurring either at the same or at different places in a distributed system, it is often useful to be able to determine which event took place first.
- **Measuring Time Intervals.** Given two events occurring either at the same or at different places in a distributed system, it is often useful to be able to determine the length of the time interval that elapsed between the times the two events occurred.
- **Scheduling of Events.** It is often useful to be able to specify that an event—or a set of distributed events—should take place either before or after some specified time.

Time Value Inaccuracy

A characteristic inherent in the measurement of time is that a time value can never be said to be completely accurate. This is because no clock can be kept perfectly in synchronization with UTC. Since a clock can never represent time completely accurately, a time-of-day value, to be useful, must include both an estimated value for UTC and an *inaccuracy value.* The inaccuracy value represents an upper bound on how inaccurate that time value is. Therefore, it is possible to determine only that the exact value for UTC at any instant falls somewhere between the estimated time value minus the inaccuracy and the estimated time value plus the inaccuracy, as shown in Fig. B.8.

When algorithms use such time values—for example to determine which of two events occurred first—the inaccuracy values must be taken into account in comparing the

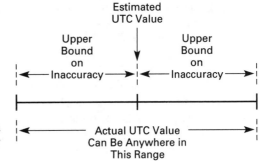

Figure B.8   A time value consists of an estimated UTC value and an inaccuracy value.

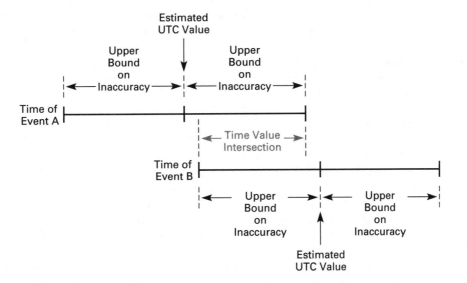

Figure B.9   Intersecting time values.

two time values. If the two events occurred relatively close together in time, it is possible for the time ranges representing the times at which the two events occurred to intersect, as shown in Fig. B.9.

When such a situation occurs, although one of the events may have occurred earlier than the other, the order in which the two events occurred cannot be determined. Since each time value must be viewed as a range of possible UTC values, the time that Event A actually occurred might be later than the estimated UTC value, and the time that Event B occurred might be earlier. Because of the time value intersection, it is possible that either Event A or Event B actually occurred first. Thus, it is not possible to say with any certainty which of the two events depicted in Fig. B.9 occurred first, and we must conclude that it is not possible to determine the order in which the two events actually occurred.

It is important in any actual implementation of the Distributed Time Service that the inaccuracy values be made as small as possible so it is possible to determine the sequence in which events occur that take place relatively close together in time.

Distributed Time Service Operation

The Distributed Time Service allows application programs to request services that work with date and time-of-day values in a standardized manner that is the same across all computing platforms. The Distributed Time Service defines a standardized format for date and time-of-day values, so applications can work with date and time-of-day values in the same format no matter what type of platform they are executing on. Application programs can use the Distributed Time Service to make requests such as obtaining current values for date and time of day, determining the order in which events have occurred, and computing the time interval between two events.

The Distributed Time Service uses a distributed algorithm, a component of which runs in every computing system in the network, that is responsible for synchronizing all the clocks in the network. Any DCE application can obtain a time value by requesting it from DTS. A major goal of DTS is to provide a time value on request with a minimum probability of the time value being incorrect. This is a difficult goal to accomplish because, unlike other services where faults or errors can be detected immediately, faulty time values are difficult to detect.

DTS Components

The two major components that implement the distributed algorithms used by DTS implementations are DTS *clerks* and DTS *servers*. Some of the servers may have access to a DTS *time provider,* a device that obtains an accurate value for UTC from a service using a telephone line, radio communication, or satellite link. Each computing system in a distributed network must contain either a DTS clerk or a DTS server. Both clerks and servers implement clocks that maintain values for the date, Coordinated Universal Time, inaccuracy, and a TDF value.

An application program can make a request of DTS for a time value. If that client's computing system implements a DTS server, the DTS server provides the time value; if the client's computing system implements a DTS clerk, the DTS clerk provides it. The application program, however, need not know whether the computing system on which it is running implements a clerk or a server; the DTS application programming interface is the same for both. Most computing systems implement DTS clerks; DTS servers are implemented in only some computing systems in the distributed environment. The complexity of synchronizing time values is handled mainly by the DTS servers.

A DTS clerk keeps its clock in synchronization by obtaining time values from some minimum number of DTS servers. The clerk then uses an algorithm to compute the intersection of all the time values it obtains to calculate a *correct* time value. The algorithm is designed so the DTS clerk obtains the correct time even if somewhat fewer than half of the DTS servers queried return incorrect time values. The function that determines how many time servers can be faulty is $int((n-1)/2)$. This means, for example, that 4 out of 9 or 4 out of 10, but not 5 out of 10, servers can be faulty, and the time service will still provide the correct time. The clerk then uses the *correct* time value it computes to adjust the time value it maintains in its own internal clock to improve its accuracy.

Typically, at least some of the DTS servers have access to a time provider that provides an accurate value for UTC. To synchronize its clock, a server that has access to a time provider periodically obtains an accurate time value from its time provider. Servers without access to a time provider periodically synchronize their clocks by obtaining the time from other DTS servers in a manner similar to that of clerks.

Local and Global Sets

DTS assumes that in most distributed systems, the majority of computing systems are connected to local area networks having relatively short communication delays and that individual LANs may be interconnected by wide area networking links that may have much longer communication delays. Each local area network implements a set of DTS servers known as the *local set*. It is possible for the local set to be empty for any given LAN. If there are enough DTS servers in a given local set, all the DTS clerks obtain time values only from servers in the local set, thus reducing communication delays and improving the accuracy of the time values maintained by the DTS clerks running on the computing systems in that LAN.

Even though there may be enough DTS servers to satisfy the needs of all the DTS clerks attached to a given LAN, it is possible that none of these DTS servers implements a DTS time provider. To handle this situation, and also the situation where there are not enough servers available in the local set, another set of DTS servers is designated as a *global set*. These DTS servers are available throughout the network. It is desirable that one or more of the DTS servers in the global set have access to a time provider that servers can use as a source of accurate Coordinated Universal Time. DTS implementations can function, however, even if no DTS server in the network has access to a time provider. In the absence of a time provider, network managers must from time to time mimic a DTS time provider on at least some of the DTS servers and must provide those servers with accurate values for Coordinated Universal Time.

Courier Servers

When a local area network does not have its own DTS server with access to a time provider, one of the servers in the local set is designated as the *courier server*. It is the responsibility of the courier server in a LAN to import an accurate UTC value from one of the global servers. The use of a courier server reduces the message traffic by requiring only a single DTS server in the local set to import a UTC value from a global DTS server.

DCE SECURITY SERVICE

The DCE Security Service is based on the *Kerberos* authentication system submitted to the OSF by Project Athena. It is augmented by a number of additional security components submitted by Hewlett-Packard. Kerberos is widely used in a number of networking environments, including the Worldwide Internet and other networks implementing the TCP/IP protocol suite.

The DCE Security Service provides facilities for implementing secure communications in a networked environment and allows access to resources in the computing environment to be controlled. The DCE Security Service defines three types of security functions that are useful in a networked computing environment.

- **Data Protection.** *Data Protection* functions are used to ensure that messages can be sent over the network privately so they cannot be read by unauthorized parties.

- **Authentication.** *Authentication* functions are used to verify the identity of an end user or an application component that is making a request for a service.

- **Authorization.** *Authorization* functions are used to provide facilities for specifying which users or application components can have access to individual resources in the computing environment.

Each of the above types of security functions is described further in the following sections.

Data Protection

Because a network must be assumed to be an inherently public medium, data that must be kept private must be protected from eavesdropping while in transit. The DCE Security Service accomplishes this with cryptographic techniques in which messages are enciphered before transmission and deciphered after receipt. A channel using a cryptography mechanism is called a *secure channel.* Cryptography also protects data integrity because an intruder cannot modify, relay, or suppress data in transit without the receiver detecting it.

Many forms of cryptography can be used to encipher data for transmission over a network to protect the data from eavesdropping. A system of cryptography is often called a *cryptosystem.* The cryptosystem used by the DCE Security System is the ANSI X3.92-1981, *American National Standard Data Encryption Algorithm* (DES). The DES form of cryptography enciphers data in 64-bit blocks using a 56-bit cryptographic key.

Authentication

The DCE Security Service discusses security in terms of *principals* that access *objects* in a distributed system. A principal can be either a human user or a program. Both principals and objects have names known throughout the distributed system. Therefore, the DCE Security Service depends on the DCE Directory Service for managing the names of principals and objects.

Authentication is the process whereby one user (either a person or an application program) verifies the identity of another user. With the DCE Security Service, an application program operating in the role of a client uses an *authentication service* to acquire the credentials that are required in order to be authenticated by a server. These credentials are called *tickets.*

A client application first acquires a *ticket-granting ticket* (TGT) from an authentication server. This is generally done at the time the user logs onto the system through the use of some direct authentication procedure, such as entering a password. The TGT is encrypted using a cryptography key that only the principal and the authentication service know. The TGT is then used to acquire the tickets that are required to authenticate each RPC call that the client application makes.

Authorization

The authorization part of the DCE Security Service is related to, but different from, authentication. Authentication verifies the identity of a user; authorization provides a means of specifying what that user is able to do after gaining access to the distributed system. For example, a human user typically performs the authentication process once, at the beginning of a session. Then authorization functions determine what operations are valid for that user during the life of the session. Authorization is accomplished through the use of *access control lists* (ACLs) that describe the resources a user is authorized to access and the type of accesses that can be made to each resource.

Appendix **C**

Requests for Comments

Requests for Comments (RFCs) are documents, available on the Internet in electronic form, that document TCP/IP protocols and contain other information of interest to the Internet community.

RFCs are stored in a number of public repositories worldwide. For example, the DDN NIC system whose host name is **nic.ddn.mil** maintains a complete set of RFCs in addition to other useful information regarding the Internet. The **/netinfo/ref-index.txt** document on **nic.ddn.mil** is a text document that contains a complete and up-to-date list of the RFCs that are available. The RFCs themselves are maintained in the **/rfc** directory on the **nic.ddn.mil** host. Any program that implements the FTP protocol can be used to download copies of the RFC list and the RFCs themselves from **nic.ddn.mil**.

The following is a partial list of the RFCs that are available from the NIC:

RFC 698	Telnet extended ASCII option.	RFC 799	Internet name domain.
RFC 726	Remote controlled transmission and echoing Telnet option.	RFC 813	Window and acknowledgment strategy in TCP.
RFC 727	Telnet logout option.	RFC 814	Names, addresses, ports, and routes.
RFC 732	Telnet data entry terminal option.	RFC 815	IP datagram reassembly algorithms.
RFC 736	Telnet SUPDUP option.		
RFC 749	Telnet SUPDUP-output option.	RFC 821	Simple Mail Transfer Protocol.
RFC 768	User Datagram Protocol.	RFC 822	Standard for the format of ARPA Internet text messages.
RFC 775	Directory-oriented FTP commands.	RFC 823	DARPA Internet gateway.
RFC 779	Telnet send-location option.	RFC 827	Exterior Gateway Protocol (EGP).
RFC 783	TFTP Protocol.		
RFC 791	Internet Protocol.	RFC 854	Telnet protocol specification.
RFC 792	Internet Control Message Protocol.	RFC 855	Telnet option specifications.
		RFC 856	Telnet binary transmission.
RFC 793	Transmission Control Protocol.	RFC 857	Telnet echo option.

RFC 858	Telnet suppress go ahead option.	RFC 932	Subnetwork addressing scheme.
RFC 859	Telnet status option.	RFC 933	Output marking Telnet option.
RFC 860	Telnet timing mark option.	RFC 941	International Organization for Standardization ISO Addendum to the network service definition covering network layer addressing.
RFC 861	Telnet extended options list option.		
RFC 863	Discard protocol.		
RFC 864	Character generator protocol.		
RFC 865	Quote of the Day protocol.	RFC 946	Telnet terminal location number option.
RFC 866	Active users.	RFC 949	FTP unique-named store command.
RFC 867	Daytime protocol.		
RFC 868	Time Protocol.	RFC 950	Internet standard subnetting procedure.
RFC 877	Standard for the transmission of IP datagrams over public data networks.	RFC 951	Bootstrap Protocol.
		RFC 954	NICKNAME/WHOIS.
RFC 879	TCP maximum segment size and related topics.	RFC 959	File Transfer Protocol.
		RFC 974	Mail routing and the domain system.
RFC 885	Telnet end of record option.		
RFC 886	Proposed standard for message header munging.	RFC 980	Protocol document order information.
RFC 888	STUB Exterior Gateway Protocol.	RFC 982	Guidelines for the specification of the structure of the Domain Specific Part (DSP) of the ISO standard NSAP address.
RFC 893	Trailer encapsulations.		
RFC 894	Standard for the transmission of IP datagrams over Ethernet networks.		
		RFC 994	ISO Final text of DIS 8473, Protocol for Providing the Connectionless-mode Network Service.
RFC 895	Standard for the transmission of IP datagrams over experimental Ethernet networks.		
		RFC 995	ISO End System to Intermediate System Routing Exchange Protocol for use in conjunction with ISO 8473.
RFC 896	Congestion control in IP/TCP internetworks.		
RFC 903	Reverse Address Resolution Protocol.		
		RFC 1001	Protocol standard for a NetBIOS service on a TCP/UDP transport: Concepts and methods.
RFC 904	Exterior Gateway Protocol formal specification.		
RFC 905	ISO Transport protocol specification ISO DP 8073.	RFC 1002	Protocol standard for a NetBIOS service on a TCP/UDP transport: Detailed specifications.
RFC 906	Bootstrap loading using TFTP IP and ICMP.		
		RFC 1006	ISO transport services on top of the TCP: Version 3.
RFC 911	EGP Gateway under Berkeley UNIX 4.2.		
RFC 919	Broadcasting Internet datagrams.	RFC 1008	Implementation guide for the ISO Transport Protocol.
RFC 920	Domain requirements.	RFC 1009	Requirements for Internet gateways.
RFC 922	Broadcasting Internet datagrams in the presence of subnets.		
		RFC 1011	Official Internet protocols.

RFC 1013   X Window System Protocol.

RFC 1014   XDR External Data Representation standard.

RFC 1027   Using ARP to implement transparent subnet gateways.

RFC 1032   Domain administrator's guide.

RFC 1033   Domain administrator's operations guide.

RFC 1034   Domain names—concepts and facilities.

RFC 1035   Domain names—implementation and specification.

RFC 1041   Telnet 3270 regime option.

RFC 1042   Standard for the transmission of IP datagrams over IEEE 802 networks.

RFC 1043   Telnet Data Entry Terminal option: DODIIS implementation.

RFC 1044   Internet Protocol on Network System's HYPERchannel Protocol specification.

RFC 1053   Telnet X3 PAD option.

RFC 1055   Nonstandard for transmission of IP datagrams over serial lines (SLIP).

RFC 1056   PCMAILA: A distributed mail system for personal computers.

RFC 1057   RPC: Remote Procedure Call Protocol specification Version 2.

RFC 1058   Routing Information Protocol.

RFC 1068   Background File Transfer Program (BFTP).

RFC 1069   Guidelines for the use of Internet-IP addresses in the ISO connectionless-mode network protocol.

RFC 1070   Use of the Internet as a subnetwork for experimentation with the OSI Network layer.

RFC 1072   TCP extensions for long-delay paths.

RFC 1073   Telnet window size option.

RFC 1074   NSFNET backbone SPF-based Interior Gateway Protocol.

RFC 1079   Telnet terminal speed option.

RFC 1080   Telnet remote flow control option.

RFC 1084   BOOTP vendor information extensions.

RFC 1085   ISO presentation services on top of TCP/IP-based internets.

RFC 1086   ISO-TP0 bridge between TCP and X25.

RFC 1088   Standard for the transmission of IP datagrams over NetBIOS networks.

RFC 1089   SNMP over Ethernet.

RFC 1090   SMTP on X25.

RFC 1091   Telnet terminal-type option.

RFC 1094   NFS: Network File System protocol specification.

RFC 1101   DNS encoding of network names and other types.

RFC 1102   Policy routing in Internet protocols.

RFC 1104   Models of policy-based routing.

RFC 1108   Security options for the Internet protocol.

RFC 1112   Host extensions for IP multicasting.

RFC 1113   Privacy enhancement for Internet electronic mail Part I—message encipherment and authentication procedures.

RFC 1114   Privacy enhancement for Internet electronic mail Part II—certificate-based key management.

RFC 1115   Privacy enhancement for Internet electronic mail.

RFC 1118   Hitchhikers guide to the Internet.

RFC 1119   Network Time Protocol (version 2) specification and implementation.

RFC 1122   Requirements for Internet hosts—Communication layers.

RFC 1123   Requirements for Internet hosts—application and support.

RFC 1124   Policy issues in interconnecting networks.

RFC 1125   Policy requirements for inter-administrative domain routing.

RFC 1127	Perspective on the Host Requirements RFCs.
RFC 1129	Internet time synchronization.
RFC 1136	Administrative domains and routing domains. A model for routing in the Internet.
RFC 1142	OSI IS-IS Intra-domain Routing Protocol.
RFC 1143	Q method of implementing Telnet option negotiation.
RFC 1147	FYI on a network management tool catalog: Tools for monitoring and debugging TCP/IP internets and interconnected devices.
RFC 1148	Mapping between X.400 (1988) / ISO 10021 and RFC 822.
RFC 1149	Standard for the transmission of IP datagrams on avian carriers.
RFC 1155	Structure and identification of management information for TCP/IP-based internets.
RFC 1156	Management Information Base for network management of TCP/IP-based internets.
RFC 1157	Simple Network Management Protocol (SNMP).
RFC 1163	Border Gateway Protocol (BGP).
RFC 1164	Application of the Border Gateway Protocol in the Internet.
RFC 1166	Internet numbers.
RFC 1169	Explaining the role of GOSIP.
RFC 1171	Point-to-Point Protocol for the transmission of multiprotocol datagrams over Point-to-Point links.
RFC 1172	Point-to-Point Protocol (PPP) initial configuration options.
RFC 1173	Responsibilities of host and network managers. A summary of the "oral tradition" of the Internet.
RFC 1175	FYI on where to start: A bibliography of internetworking information.
RFC 1178	Choosing a name for your computer.
RFC 1179	Line printer daemon protocol.
RFC 1180	TCP/IP tutorial.
RFC 1184	Telnet Linemode option.
RFC 1187	Bulk table retrieval with the SNMP.
RFC 1188	Proposed standard for the transmission of IP datagrams over FDDI networks.
RFC 1195	Use of OSI IS-IS for routing in TCP/IP and dual environments.
RFC 1196	Finger user information protocol.
RFC 1198	FYI on the X Window System.
RFC 1201	Transmitting IP traffic over ARCnet networks.
RFC 1205	Telnet 5250 interface.
RFC 1206	FYI Questions and Answers: Answers to commonly asked "new Internet user" questions.
RFC 1207	FYI on Questions and Answers: Answers to commonly asked "experienced Internet user" questions.
RFC 1208	Glossary of networking terms.
RFC 1209	Transmission of IP datagrams over the SMDS Service.
RFC 1212	Concise MIB definitions.
RFC 1213	Management Information Base for network management of TCP/IP-based internets.
RFC 1214	OSI internet management Management Information Base.
RFC 1215	Convention for defining traps for use with the SNMP.
RFC 1219	On the assignment of subnet numbers.
RFC 1220	Point-to-Point Protocol extensions for bridging.
RFC 1222	Advancing the NSFNET routing architecture.
RFC 1224	Techniques for managing asynchronously generated alerts.
RFC 1227	SNMP MUX protocol and MIB.
RFC 1228	SNMP-DPI: Simple Network Management Protocol Distributed Program Interface.

RFC 1229   Extensions to the generic-interface MIB.

RFC 1230   IEEE 802.4 Token Bus MIB.

RFC 1231   IEEE 802.5 Token Ring MIB.

RFC 1232   Definitions of managed objects for the DS1 Interface type.

RFC 1233   Definitions of managed objects for the DS3 Interface type.

RFC 1234   Tunneling IPX traffic through IP networks.

RFC 1236   IP to X.121 address mapping for DDN IP to X.121 address mapping for DDN.

RFC 1237   Guidelines for OSI NSAP allocation in the Internet.

RFC 1238   CLNS MIB for use with Connectionless Network Protocol (ISO 8473) and End System to Intermediate System (ISO 9542).

RFC 1239   Reassignment of experimental MIBs to standard MIBs.

RFC 1240   OSI connectionless transport services on top of UDP: Version 1.

RFC 1241   Scheme for an internet encapsulation protocol: Version 1.

RFC 1243   AppleTalk Management Information Base.

RFC 1244   Site security handbook.

RFC 1245   OSPF protocol analysis.

RFC 1246   Experience with the OSPF protocol.

RFC 1247   OSPF version 2.

RFC 1250   IAB official protocol standards.

RFC 1251   Who's who in the Internet. Biographies of IAB, IESG, and IRSG members.

RFC 1253   OSPF version 2 Management Information Base.

RFC 1254   Gateway congestion control survey.

RFC 1267   A Border Gateway Protocol.

RFC 1271   Remote network monitoring management information.

RFC 1340   Assigned numbers.

RFC 1341   MIME (Multipurpose Internet Mail Extensions) mechanisms for specifying and describing the format of internet message bodies.

Glossary

ABSTRACT INTERFACE. An interface describing the interactions that can occur between two layers of an architecture. An abstract interface does not specify implementation details, nor does it describe any coding syntax that must be used to implement the interface.

ABSTRACT SYNTAX NOTATION ONE (ASN.1). An international standard data description notation that allows the format and meaning of data structures to be defined without specifying how those data structures are represented in a computer or how they are encoded for transmission through a network.

ACCEPT SYSTEM CALL. Socket system call used by the server process in a connection-oriented application protocol employing TCP to cause the server to wait for a connection request to arrive from a client.

ACCESS CONTROL METHOD. In LAN technology, the mechanism by which communicating systems manage their access to a physical transmission medium.

ACCESS UNIT. See *Concentrator*.

ADDRESS CLASS. See *Internet address class*.

ADDRESS RESOLUTION PROTOCOL (ARP). An Internet layer protocol that helps a source host or router deliver data to a destination host or router on the same physical network by translating an internet address into a physical hardware address.

ADMINISTRATOR. Term used to refer to an individual or group that performs the roles of either the system administrator or the network administrator in a networking environment. See *System administrator* and *Network administrator*.

AMERICAN NATIONAL STANDARDS INSTITUTE (ANSI). The national standards organization for the United States. ANSI is a nonprofit organization that writes the rules for standards bodies to follow and publishes standards produced under its rules of consensus. ANSI accredits standards committees to write standards in areas of their expertise.

AMERICAN STANDARD CODE FOR INFORMATION INTERCHANGE (ASCII). A 7-bit code for encoding alphanumeric information and control functions that is used to achieve compatibility between data devices.

ANSI. American National Standards Institute.

API. Application programming interface.

APPLICATION LAYER. In TCP/IP, the uppermost layer of the TCP/IP architecture in which application programs and application protocols and services operate. In OSI, layer seven and the topmost layer of the OSI model. The Application layer provides a means for application programs to access the system interconnection facilities to exchange information. Communication services provided by the Application layer hide the complexity of the layers below from the communicating programs.

APPLICATION PROGRAMMING INTERFACE (API). A specification defining how an application program invokes a defined set of services.

APPLICATION SERVER. A computing system that implements software that allows other systems to request the services of application programs running on the application server.

ARCHIE SYSTEM. Facility implemented on a number of servers on the Internet, designated as *Archie servers,* that provide descriptive indexes to public information servers on the internet. Archie allows users to request keyword searches to locate hosts that have information matching the search criteria.

ARP. Address Resolution Protocol.

ARPA. Advanced Research Projects Agency. See *Defense Advanced Research Projects Agency.*

ARPANET. An early packet switching network, funded by the Defense Advanced Research Projects Agency (DARPA), that lead to the development of the Internet. See also *Internet.*

ARP CACHE. A table maintained by a system containing mappings of internet addresses to physical hardware addresses for the hosts or routers on the system's own physical network that it currently knows about.

ASC. Accredited Standards Committee.

ASCII. American Standard Code for Information Interchange.

ASN.1. Abstract Syntax Notation One.

ASSOCIATION. In socket programming, the information required in order to exchange data between a process running in the local host and a process running in a remote host. An association is made up of protocol identifier, local internet address, local port number, remote internet address, and remote port number.

ASYNCHRONOUS TRANSFER MODE (ATM). A form of very fast packet switching in which data is carried in fixed-length units called *cells.* Each cell is 53 octets in length, with 5 octets used as a header in each cell. ATM employs mechanisms that can be used to set up virtual circuits between users, in which a pair of communicating users appear to have a dedicated circuit between them.

ASYNCHRONOUS TRANSMISSION. A form of data transmission using start and stop bits to control data transfer in which a single character is transmitted in each data unit.

ATHENA. See *Project Athena.*

ATM. Asynchronous Transfer Mode.

AUTHENTICATION. A security mechanism that makes it possible for one software component to verify the identity of some other software component.

AUTONOMOUS SYSTEM. In TCP/IP, collection of hosts and routers that are administered by a single authority.

BANDWIDTH. Term, used to specify the capacity of a communication channel, that refers to the difference between the highest and the lowest frequencies that are carried over the channel. The higher the bandwidth, the more information that can be carried.

BASEBAND TRANSMISSION. A form of transmission in which data signals are carried over the physical communication medium in the form of discrete pulses of electricity or light.

BAUD. A measurement of the signaling speed of a channel that refers to the number of times in each second the condition of the transmission medium changes. Bauds are equal to bits per second when each possible line condition represents a single bit.

BELLMAN-FORD ROUTING ALGORITHM. See *Distance-vector routing algorithm.*

BEST-EFFORTS SERVICE. See *Connectionless service.*

BGP. Border Gateway Protocol.

BIG-ENDIAN COMPUTER SYSTEM. A computer system in which the high-order octet of a multiple-octet binary integer is stored in the lowest memory location, and the low-order octet is stored in the highest memory location. Examples of big-endian computers are IBM mainframes and computers using Motorola microprocessors.

BIND SYSTEM CALL. Socket system call used to associate an endpoint identifier (internet address and port number) with the integer descriptor of an open socket.

B-ISDN. Broadband ISDN.

BORDER GATEWAY PROTOCOL (BGP). A TCP/IP exterior gateway routing protocol sometimes used as an alternative to the Exterior Gateway Protocol (EGP). BGP allows routers in different autonomous systems to communicate. See also *Exterior Gateway Protocol.*

BRIDGE. A device operating at the level of the LAN Medium Access Control sublayer that is used to interconnect two or more LAN data links that use either the same or different forms of medium access control.

BROADBAND ISDN. A high-speed form of integrated services digital network, representing a probable future direction of the telephone industry, that uses fiber-optic transmission. See also *Integrated services digital network* and *SONET.*

BROUTER. A network interconnection device that combines the functions of a router and a bridge. A brouter routes the data traffic associated with certain protocols and bridges all other data traffic. See also *Bridge* and *Router.*

CABLING SYSTEM. A system of cable segments, cable connectors, and attachment units used to physically interconnect the stations to a physical network.

CARRIER SENSE MULTIPLE ACCESS WITH COLLISION DETECTION. See *CSMA/CD.*

CCITT. International Telegraph and Telephone Consultative Committee.

CCITT RECOMMENDATION X.25. See *X.25.*

CDS. Cell Directory Service. See *DCE Cell Directory Service.*

CLASS A ADDRESS. An internet address in which the first bit is set to 0. A class A address provides 7 bits to identify the physical network and 24 bits to identify hosts. In any internet there can be up to 126 networks that use class A addresses.

CLASS B ADDRESS. An internet address in which the first two bits are set to 10. A class B address provides 14 bits to identify the network and 16 bits to identify hosts. A class B address allows for up to $2^{14}-2$ different physical networks and up to $2^{16}-2$ different hosts on each network.

CLASS C ADDRESS. An internet address in which the first three bits are set to 110. A class C address provides 21 bits to identify the network and 8 bits to identify hosts. A class C address allows for up to $2^{21}-2$ different physical networks but only up to 254 different hosts on each network.

CLASS D ADDRESS. An internet address in which the first four bits are set to 1110. A class D address is used to implement a form of multicasting in which an address refers to some collection of hosts in an internet, all of which receive the IP datagrams having the specified multicast address.

CLIENT. In client-server computing, an application component that makes a request for a service of some other application component operating in the role of a server. See also *Client-server computing*.

CLIENT-SERVER COMPUTING. A form of distributed computing in which application components operating in the role of clients request the services of other application components operating in the role of servers. Client and server components can run on the same computing system or on different computing systems connected by a network.

CLOSE SYSTEM CALL. Socket system call used to close a socket descriptor in a similar manner to closing a file descriptor.

CMIP. Common Management Information Protocol.

CMIP OVER TCP/IP (CMOT). A specification that describes how the international standard Common Management Information Protocol (CMIP) can be used to manage a TCP/IP internet. See also *Common Management Information Protocol* and *Simple Network Management Protocol*.

CMOT. See *CMIP over TCP/IP*.

COLLISION. A condition on the transmission medium that occurs with the CSMA/CD (Ethernet) form of medium access control when two or more stations transmit signals concurrently.

COMMON MANAGEMENT INFORMATION PROTOCOL (CMIP). A protocol used for network management being standardized by the International Standardization Organization (ISO). The CMIP international standards divide management functions into the following five specific management functional areas (SMFAS)—configuration management, fault management, performance management, security management, and accounting management.

COMMUNICATION PROTOCOL. See *Protocol*.

CONCENTRATOR. Local area network equipment that allows multiple network devices to be connected to the LAN cabling system through a central point. Sometimes called an *Access unit* or *Hub*.

CONNECT SYSTEM CALL. Socket system call used by the client process in a connection-oriented application protocol employing TCP to establish a TCP connection with the server process.

CONNECTION. A logical association between a sender and a receiver that supports reliable communication between them.

CONNECTIONLESS SERVICE. A data transfer service provided by any layer of a network architecture in which each data unit sent is sent and processed independently of any other data units. A connectionless service is often called a *datagram* service.

CONNECTION-ORIENTED SERVICE. A data transfer service provided by any layer of a network architecture in which the delivery of data units is guaranteed as long as a logical association called a connection is maintained between communicating entities.

COOPERATIVE PROCESSING. A term, often used by IBM, to refer to a form of distributed computing in which a personal computer is used to handle user interface tasks and a more powerful server system is used to handle all other application processing.

CSMA/CD. Carrier Sense Multiple Access with Collision Detection, the Ethernet form of LAN data link technology, defined by IEEE 802.3 and ISO 8802-3. Also refers to a generic means of medium access control in which stations transmit on a bus- or tree-structured transmission medium whenever the transmission medium is available and retransmit when collisions occur.

DARPA. Defense Advanced Research Projects Agency.

DATAGRAM. An informal name for the data unit exchanged during the operation of a connectionless data delivery protocol. See also *IP datagram* and *User datagram.*

DATAGRAM SERVICE. See *Connectionless service.*

DATA LINK. A data link protocol also defines the rules that govern how those frames are exchanged. A physical circuit in conjunction with a data link protocol forms a *data link* over which data can be transmitted in an error-free fashion. Each physical network in a TCP/IP internet takes the form of a data link.

DATA LINK LAYER. Layer two of the OSI model. The Data Link layer is responsible for providing data transmission over a single link from one system to another. Control mechanisms in the Data Link layer handle the transmission of data units, often called frames, over a physical circuit.

DATA LINK PROTOCOL. A specification for controlling the transmission of data across a physical circuit that defines the formats of the data units—typically called *frames*—that are transferred across the physical circuit and procedures that govern the exchange of frames.

DCE. Distributed Computing Environment.

DCE CDS. DCE Cell Directory Service.

DCE CELL DIRECTORY SERVICE (DCE CDS). Directory service, defined by the OSF Distributed Computing Environment, designed for handling name operations that take place within a single cell. See also *DCE Directory Service.*

DCE DFS. DCE Distributed File Service.

DCE DIRECTORY SERVICE. Service, defined by the OSF Distributed Computing Environment, that implements a distributed repository that stores information about objects in the computing environment, including users, computing systems, and distributed services that application programs can request. The DCE Directory Service provides facilities for submitting a name to the Directory Service and getting back a list of the attributes associated with that name. See also *Distributed Computing Environment, DCE Cell Directory Service,* and *DCE Global Directory Service.*

DCE DISTRIBUTED FILE SERVICE. Service, defined by the OSF Distributed Computing Environment, that allows users to access and share files that are maintained by computing systems operating in the role of *file servers* that can be located anywhere in the network. See also *Distributed Computing Environment.*

DCE DISTRIBUTED TIME SERVICE. Service, defined by the OSF Distributed Computing Environment, that allows application programs to request services that work with date and time-of-day values in a standardized manner that is the same across all computing platforms. The Distributed Time Service also implements a set of distributed algorithms that ensure that the clocks in all the computing systems in the network are synchronized and contain correct values for the date and time of day. See also *Distributed Computing Environment.*

DCE DTS. DCE Distributed Time Service.

DCE GDS. DCE Global Directory Service.

DCE GLOBAL DIRECTORY SERVICE. Directory service, defined by the OSF Distributed Computing Environment, designed for handling name operations that take place between individual cells. See also *Distributed Computing Environment* and *DCE Directory Service.*

DCE REMOTE PROCEDURE CALL SERVICE. Service, defined by the OSF Distributed Computing Environment, that allows an application component running in one computer system to use a procedure call mechanism to invoke a procedure that is running in some other computing system in the network. See also *Distributed Computing Environment.*

DCE RPC. DCE Remote Procedure Call.

DCE SECURITY SERVICE. Service, defined by the OSF Distributed Computing Environment, that provides facilities for implementing secure communications in a networked environment and for controlling access to resources in the computing environment. See also *Distributed Computing Environment.*

DCE THREADS SERVICE. Service, defined by the OSF Distributed Computing Environment, that provides application programmers with the ability to create independent execution threads within the same program. Threads provide an application the ability to carry out multiple computing tasks concurrently. See also *Distributed Computing Environment.*

DEFAULT ROUTER. The router to which a host sends an IP datagram when there is no entry in the host's routing table for the physical network referenced in the destination internet address field of the IP datagram header. A host's default router is typically assigned when the TCP/IP communication software is configured for that host. See also *Routing table.*

DEFENSE ADVANCED RESEARCH PROJECTS AGENCY (DARPA). Agency of the U.S. government that funded the development of the ARPANET, the network that lead to the development of the Internet. See also *Internet.*

DESTINATION-SERVICE-ACCESS-POINT ADDRESS. See *DSAP address.*

DESTINATION UNREACHABLE MESSAGE. An ICMP error message indicating that an IP datagram could not be delivered to the destination host.

DFS. Distributed File Service. See *DCE Distributed File Service.*

DISK SERVER. A computing system that implements software that allows other network systems to share the disk server's disk units.

DISTANCE-VECTOR ROUTING ALGORITHM. A form of routing algorithm, sometimes called a *Bellman-Ford* algorithm, in which each router learns about the network topology by exchanging routing information packets with its neighbor routers. With a distance-vector routing algorithm, a router initializes its routing table by storing information for each physical network to which it is directly attached. It stores information that identifies the physical network and the distance to that network, typically measured in hops. Periodically, each router sends out a complete copy of its routing table to all the other routers to which it is directly attached via a single data link. See also *Link-state routing algorithm.*

DISTRIBUTED COMPUTING ENVIRONMENT (DCE). A specification for distributed computing, developed by the Open Software Foundation (OSF). See also *DCE Remote Procedure Call Service, DCE Threads Service, DCE Directory Service, DCE Distributed File Service, DCE Distributed Time Service,* and *DCE Security Service.*

DISTRIBUTED QUEUE DUAL BUS (DQDB). A protocol used in a form of Metropolitan Area Network (MAN) technology that can be used to provide LAN-like services over a wide geographic area. DQDB provides a service that is similar to that defined by IEEE 802.2/ISO 8802-2 Logical Link Control.

DNS. Domain Name System.

Domain. A collection of names that are administered by a single authority.

DOMAIN NAME. A name consisting of a sequence of simple names separated by periods. Each simple name, or set of simple names, identifies a *domain* under the control of some authority.

DOMAIN NAME SYSTEM (DNS). A TCP/IP directory service that can be used to maintain the mappings between names and internet addresses in a limited number of places in the internet rather than at the location of each system.

DOTTED-DECIMAL NOTATION. A form of notation used to represent 32-bit internet addresses in the form of four decimal numbers, separated by periods, with each number representing the decimal value of one octet of the address.

DQDB. Distributed Queue Dual Bus.

DSAP ADDRESS. In the IEEE/ANSI/ISO LAN architecture, an address that identifies the LLC sublayer user, or users, that are to receive the LLC-PDU. See also *SSAP address*.

DTS. Distributed Time Service. See *DCE Distributed Time Service*.

EBCDIC. Extended Binary-coded Decimal Interchange Code.

EGP. Exterior Gateway Protocol.

ENCRYPTION. A security mechanism in which enciphering and deciphering functions are used to prevent unauthorized parties from eavesdropping on transmissions that take place over a network.

ENDPOINT IDENTIFIER. In socket programming, a data structure containing an internet address and a port number that identifies either the local or the remote system.

END SYSTEM. In the OSI model, a device in a communication system that serves as the source or final destination of data. In the TCP/IP environment, an end system is typically called a host. See also *Intermediate system.*

ENTERPRISE INTERNETWORK. A computer network designed to serve the needs of an entire enterprise. TCP/IP technology can be used to construct all or part of an enterprise internetwork.

ENTITY. In the OSI model, an active element within a layer. A particular layer provides services to entities running in the layer above.

EPHEMERAL PORT. A port in which the number falls in the range from 1024–4999 that is typically used to send data from the server process back to the client process. See also *Port.*

ETHERNET. A form of LAN data link that implements the IEEE 802.3/ISO 8802-3 CSMA/CD standard. On an Ethernet LAN data link, stations are attached to a common transmission facility, such as a coaxial cable or twisted-pair cable, and a station typically attempts to transmit whenever it has data to send. See also *CSMA/CD.*

ETHERNET VERSION 2. A form of LAN data link technology, developed by Digital Equipment Corporation, Xerox, and Intel, that served as the basis for the IEEE/ISO CSMA/CD (Ethernet) standard.

EXTENDED BINARY-CODED DECIMAL INTERCHANGE CODE (EBCDIC). An 8-bit code used to encode alphanumeric information and control functions often used in the IBM environment.

EXTENDED LAN. A network that consists of two or more separate LAN data links, using either the same or different forms of medium access control, that are interconnected using bridges. See also *Bridge.*

EXTERIOR GATEWAY. A router that communicates with a router in some other autonomous system. See also *Autonomous system.*

EXTERIOR GATEWAY PROTOCOL. A routing protocol that allows routers in different autonomous systems to communicate with one another. See also *Autonomous system.*

EXTERIOR GATEWAY PROTOCOL (EGP). A standardized protocol, described by a TCP/IP RFC, by which a router in one autonomous system can communicate with a router in another autonomous system. See also *Border Gateway Protocol.*

EXTERIOR NEIGHBOR. Two routers that communicate directly with one another and are in different autonomous systems are said to be exterior neighbors. See also *Autonomous system, Exterior gateway,* and *Exterior gateway protocol.*

EXTERNAL DATA REPRESENTATION (XDR) FACILITY. In the Sun RPC facility, the facility that provides a standard method for encoding argument data and results so they can be used in a portable fashion in a heterogeneous host environment.

FAST ETHERNET. Term used to describe the standards being developed to define a 100 Mbps version of the CSMA/CD (Ethernet) standard. See also *CSMA/CD* and *Ethernet.*

FDDI. Fiber Distributed Data Interface.

FIBER DISTRIBUTED DATA INTERFACE (FDDI). A form of LAN technology, developed by members of subcommittee X3T9.5 of ANSI, in which systems are connected to one another using point-to-point fiber-optic cable segments to form a ring topology. An FDDI data link supports a data rate of 100 Mbps.

FIBER-OPTIC CABLE. A cable that contains one or more thin cylinders of glass, each of which is called a *core.* Each core is surrounded by a concentric cylinder of glass called the *cladding,* which has a different refractive index than the core. The core of a fiber-optic cable carries signals in the form of a modulated light beam.

FILE SERVER. A network system that implements software allowing other network systems to share the data files stored on the file server's disk units.

FILE TRANSFER PROTOCOL (FTP). A user-oriented TCP/IP Application layer service that allows files to be transferred in both directions between the local system and a remote system.

FILTERING BRIDGE. See *Bridge.*

FINGER FACILITY. Facility implemented by a UNIX program called **finger** that allows the user to determine a person's login name given the name of that person's host computer.

FQDN. Fully-qualified domain name.

FRAGMENTATION. See *Segmentation function.*

FRAME. An informal name for the data unit exchanged over a physical network by the TCP/IP Network Interface layer. See also *Network Interface layer* and *MAC frame.*

FRAME RELAY. A form of data link technology that provides services similar to those provided by X.25 packet-switching networks. In a Frame Relay network, routing decisions are made in the Data Link layer rather than in the Network layer. Frame Relay networks support a variety of transmission speeds, but the target speed is generally in the neighborhood of the speeds supported by T1 facilities.

FTP. File Transfer Protocol.

FULLY-QUALIFIED DOMAIN NAME (FQDN). The full domain name, consisting of simple names separated by periods, that can be used to distinguish a host from all other hosts in an internet. See also *Domain* and *Domain name.*

GATED PROGRAM. A UNIX daemon that implements the RIP and Hello interior gateway protocols and EGP to provide a comprehensive routing solution for use in relatively small autonomous systems. See also *Routing Information Protocol, Hello protocol,* and *Exterior Gateway Protocol.*

GATEWAY. In TCP/IP, the term used to refer to a device that performs the function of a router. In most other forms of networking, a network interconnection device that operates at the level of the OSI model Application layer, used to interconnect networks that may have entirely different architectures. Different protocols can be used at any of the functional layers, with the gateway converting from one set of protocols to another. See also *Router.*

GDS. Global Directory Service. See *DCE Global Directory Service.*

GET FUNCTION. In the Simple Network Management Protocol (SNMP), a function that a network management application can request of a management agent to return the value (or values) associated with a manageable object. See also *Simple Network Management Protocol, Network management application, Management agent,* and *Set function.*

GETHOSTBYADDR SYSTEM CALL. Socket system call used to obtain information about a host given its internet address.

GETHOSTBYNAME SYSTEM CALL. Socket system call used to obtain a remote host's internet address given its host name.

GETHOSTID SYSTEM CALL. Socket system call used to obtain the local host's internet address.

GETHOSTNAME SYSTEM CALL. Socket system call used to obtain the local host's name.

GETPEERNAME SYSTEM CALL. Socket system call used to obtain the endpoint address (internet address and port number) associated with the remote process.

GETPROTOBYNAME SYSTEM CALL. Socket system call used to obtain the integer value associated with a protocol given the protocol's name.

GETSERVBYNAME SYSTEM CALL. Socket system call used to obtain the integer value associated with a well-known TCP/IP Application layer service given its name.

GETSOCKNAME SYSTEM CALL. Socket system call used to obtain the name associated with a given socket.

GETSOCKOPT SYSTEM CALL. Socket system call used to obtain a list of parameters associated with a socket.

GOPHER. See *Internet Gopher.*

HALF-ASSOCIATION. In socket programming. the part of an association, consisting of protocol identifier, internet address, and port number, that is required to identify one of the processes that participates in an association. See also *Association.*

HANDSHAKE PROCEDURE. An exchange of messages that takes place between two processes implementing TCP that set up an association, called a *connection,* between them over which data can be reliably transferred. See also *Transmission Control Protocol.*

HARDWARE ADDRESS. See *Physical hardware address.*

HARDWARE LAYER. The TCP/IP functional layer, generally considered to be outside the scope of the TCP/IP architecture, that is below the Network Interface layer. The Hardware layer is concerned with physical entities, such as the NICs, transceivers, hubs, connectors, and cables that are used to physically interconnect hosts.

HDLC. High-level Data Link Control.

HELLO PROTOCOL. TCP/IP routing protocol, implementing a distance-vector routing algorithm, that makes distance measurements based on estimated propagation delays rather than on hop counts. Hello includes a mechanism for synchronizing clocks in different hosts and routers and uses timestamps on packets sent between systems to estimate routing delays.

HEWLETT-PACKARD RPC FACILITY. A remote procedure call facility that is provided by Hewlett-Packard as part of the Network Computing System (NCS). See also *Remote procedure call* and *Sun RPC facility.*

HIGH-LEVEL DATA LINK CONTROL (HDLC). An international standard, bit-oriented, wide area network protocol that operates at the level of the OSI model Data Link layer.

HOST. Term used to refer to a computing system that is attached to a TCP/IP internet, communicates using the TCP/IP protocols, and runs programs that communicate with programs running on other hosts. A host can be any type of computing system, such as a large mainframe, a mini-computer, a midrange departmental processor, a graphics workstation, or a personal computer. See also *Router.*

HOST IDENTIFIER. The portion of an internet address that identifies an individual host or router within a physical network. See also *Internet address.*

HOST NAME. A string of alphanumeric characters used to refer to a host in a TCP/IP internet.

HOSTS FILE. A TCP/IP configuration file that maintains a list of name-to-address mappings for an individual host.

HTONL FUNCTION. Host to Network Long function. Function that converts a 32-bit integer from the octet order used by the host to network octet order. See also *Network octet order.*

HTONS FUNCTION. Host to Network Short function. Function that converts a 16-bit integer from the octet order used by the host to network octet order. See also *Network octet order.*

HUB. See *Concentrator.*

IAB. Internet Activities Board.

IANA. Internet Assigned Numbers Authority.

ICMP. Internet Control Message Protocol.

ICMP ECHO REQUEST AND REPLY MESSAGES. ICMP query messages that are used to implement an echo facility. If a host or router receives an ICMP Echo Request message, it replies with an ICMP Echo Reply message. See also *Internet Control Message Protocol* and *ICMP query message.*

ICMP ERROR MESSAGE. Message used to implement the Internet Control Message Protocol (ICMP) that are used to report on errors or exceptional conditions that occur during the delivery or attempted delivery of an IP datagram. See also *Internet Control Message Protocol.*

ICMP QUERY MESSAGE. Message used to implement the Internet Control Message Protocol (ICMP) that are used to request information and to reply to an ICMP request. See also *Internet Control Message Protocol.*

ICMP SUBNET MASK REQUEST AND REPLY MESSAGES. ICMP query messages that are used by a host that needs to obtain its address mask. See also *Internet Control Message Protocol* and *ICMP query message.*

ICMP TIMESTAMP REQUEST AND REPLY MESSAGES. ICMP query messages that are used by a host to request that some other host or router respond with a timestamp indicating the current date and time of day. See also *Internet Control Message Protocol* and *ICMP query message.*

IDEMPOTENT PROCEDURE. A procedure that produces the same result whether it is executed one time or multiple times.

IEEE. Institute of Electrical and Electronics Engineers.

IETF. Internet Engineering Task Force.

IFCONFIG COMMAND. TCP/IP command that is used to test the physical network interface to determine such information as whether the interface is operational and ready to receive packets, whether the network interface software is configured properly, and the internet address that is currently assigned to the physical interface.

INET_ADDRA FUNCTION. Function that converts an internet address in ASCII dotted-decimal format to 32-bit binary format.

INET_NTOA FUNCTION. Function that converts an internet address in 32-bit binary format to ASCII dotted-decimal format.

INSTITUTE OF ELECTRICAL AND ELECTRONIC ENGINEERS (IEEE). A professional society, in which members are individual engineers, that has produced a set of standards for local area network technology that have been accepted by ISO as international standards.

INTEGRATED SERVICES DIGITAL NETWORK (ISDN). A public telecommunications network supplying end-to-end digital telecommunications services that can be used for both voice and nonvoice purposes.

INTERIOR GATEWAY. Two routers that communicate directly with one another and are both part of the same autonomous system are said to be *interior neighbors* and are called *interior gateways*. Interior neighbors communicate with one another using an *interior gateway protocol*.

INTERIOR GATEWAY PROTOCOL. A routing protocol that allows routers in the same autonomous systems to communicate with one another. See also *Autonomous system*.

INTERIOR NEIGHBOR. Two routers that communicate directly with one another and are in the same autonomous system are said to be interior neighbors. See also *Autonomous system, Interior gateway,* and *Interior gateway protocol.*

INTERMEDIATE SYSTEM. A device in a communication system that may lie between two end systems and is concerned with performing routing and relaying functions. In TCP/IP, an intermediate system is called a router. See also *Router* and *End system.*

INTERNATIONAL ORGANIZATION FOR STANDARDIZATION (ISO). The dominant information technology standardization organization in which individual members consist of individual national standards organizations. The ISO member organization from the United States is the American National Standards Institute (ANSI). See also *American National Standards Institute.*

INTERNATIONAL TELEGRAPH AND TELEPHONE CONSULTATIVE COMMITTEE (CCITT). The leading organization involved in the development of standards relating to telephone and other telecommunications services. CCITT is a part of the International Telecommunications Union (ITU), which in turn is a body of the United Nations. The delegation to the ITU from the United States is the Department of State.

INTERNET. Term used to refer to a TCP/IP network that is typically constructed using individual physical networks that are interconnected using routers and possibly wide area network data links.

INTERNET. The world's largest TCP/IP internet, which interconnects thousands of networks containing millions of computers in universities, national laboratories, and commercial organizations. Sometimes called the Worldwide Internet.

INTERNET ACTIVITIES BOARD (IAB). The organization that coordinates the development and evolution of the TCP/IP protocol suite. The IAB is staffed by volunteers, recruited from a variety of government and commercial organizations, who serve on a variety of task forces.

INTERNET ADDRESS. A 32-bit binary number that TCP/IP protocols use to uniquely identify points of attachment to the internet. Each host and router in a TCP/IP internet must have at least one unique internet address.

INTERNET ARCHITECT. The chairman of the Internet Activities Board (IAB). See also *Internet Activities Board.*

INTERNET ASSIGNED NUMBERS AUTHORITY (IANA). The organization responsible for assigning values for network parameters, special network addresses, names of services, and various types of standard identifiers. At the time of writing, the role of the IANA is performed by the University of Southern California Information Services Institute.

INTERNET CONTROL MESSAGE PROTOCOL (ICMP). In TCP/IP, an Internet layer protocol that allows end systems to report on error conditions and to provide information about unexpected circumstances. See also *ICMP error message* and *ICMP query message.*

INTERNET ENGINEERING TASK FORCE (IETF). Organization staffed by volunteers from the TCP/IP community that studies Internet technical issues and recommends Internet standards to the IAB. See also *Internet Activities Board.*

INTERNET GOPHER. A system, available on the Internet, that allows a user to browse through a set of indexed resources by selecting choices in menus.

INTERNET LAYER. TCP/IP functional layer that corresponds to the OSI model Network layer. The Internet layer provides routing and relaying functions that are used when data must be passed from a host in one network to a host in some other network in the internet. It operates in the source and destination hosts and in all the routers along the path between the hosts. See also *Network layer.*

INTERNET PROTOCOL (IP). In TCP/IP, a connectionless Internet layer protocol that provides a best-efforts datagram delivery service. See also *Internet layer.*

INTERNETWORK. See *Internet.*

INTERNETWORKING LAYER. See *Internet layer.*

INVALID PARAMETERS MESSAGE. ICMP error message that is generated by a host or router when it receives an IP datagram in which one or more of an IP datagram's header fields contain invalid data. See also *Internet Control Message Protocol, ICMP error message, IP datagram.*

IP. Internet Protocol.

IP ADDRESS. See *Internet address.*

IP DATAGRAM. The unit of data that is handled by the Internet Protocol (IP) in the TCP/IP Internet layer. See also *Internet Protocol* and *Internet layer.*

ISDN. Integrated Services Digital Network.

ISO. International Organization for Standardization.

ITERATIVE RESOLUTION. A form of name resolution performed by a Domain Name System nameserver in which the resolver client iteratively contacts nameservers until the name resolution operation has been completed. With iterative resolution, the computational complexity of name resolution is split between the resolver software and the nameservers. See also *Name resolution, Domain Name System, Resolver, Nameserver,* and *Recursive resolution.*

KERBEROS SECURITY SERVICE. An Application layer, encryption-based security system that provides mutual authentication between a client component and a server component. Kerberos also provides services that can be used to control which clients are authorized to access which servers.

LAN. Local area network.

LAN ADAPTER. IBM term for a network interface card (NIC) used to allow a device to be attached to a local area network data link. See also *Network interface card.*

LAN DATA LINK. A multiaccess communication facility that consists of two or more devices connected using local area network technology. See also *Local area network* and *Data link.*

LAN STATION. See *Station.*

LEVEL. See *Protocol status level.*

LINK-STATE ROUTING ALGORITHM. A form of distributed adaptive routing algorithm in which each router knows the complete topology of the network in terms of the existence of all other routers and the links between them. With link-state routing, each router periodically uses a broadcast mechanism to transmit information to all other routers in the network about the routers to which it is directly attached and the status of the data links between them. Each router then constructs a complete map of the network from the information it receives from all the other routers. Routers are then able to calculate routes from this map using the Dijkstra shortest path algorithm. See also *Distance-vector routing algorithm.*

LISTEN SYSTEM CALL. Socket system call used by the server process in a connection-oriented application protocol employing TCP to indicate that the server is willing to accept a request from a client to establish a TCP connection.

LITTLE-ENDIAN COMPUTER SYSTEM. A computer system in which the high-order octet of a multiple-octet binary integer is contained in the highest memory location and the low-order octet is contained in the lowest memory location. Examples of little-endian computers are DEC VAX processors and computers using Intel microprocessors.

LLC. Logical Link Control.

LLC-PDU. Logical-link-control-protocol-data-unit.

LLC-SDU. Logical-link-control-service-data-unit.

LOCAL AREA NETWORK (LAN). A term used to refer to a form of data link technology that is used to implement a high-speed, relatively short-distance form of computer communication. The term is also used to refer to a computer network constructed using LAN data link technology.

LOCATION BROKER. In the Hewlett-Packard RPC facility, the facility that maintains a database of information about the location of callable services. See also *Hewlett-Packard RPC facility.*

LOGICAL LINK CONTROL (LLC) SUBLAYER. A sublayer of the Data Link layer, defined by IEEE 802.2 and ISO 8802-2, that is responsible for medium-independent data link functions. It allows the layer entity above to access the services of a LAN data link without regard to what form of physical transmission medium is used.

LOGICAL-LINK-CONTROL-PROTOCOL-DATA-UNIT (LLC-PDU). The data unit exchanged between peer Logical Link Control sublayer entities.

LOGICAL-LINK-CONTROL-SERVICE-DATA-UNIT (LLC-SDU). The data unit that a LAN data link user passes to the Logical Link Control sublayer when requesting a data transfer service.

MA. Management agent.

MAC. Medium Access Control.

MAC Address. In the Medium Access Control sublayer of the IEEE/ISO/ANSI LAN architecture, a value that uniquely identifies an individual station that implements a single point of physical attachment to a LAN data link. Each station attached to a LAN data link must have a unique MAC address on that LAN data link. Sometimes called the *Station address.*

MAC Frame. Informal name for the medium-access-control-protocol-data-unit (MAC-PDU). See also *Frame.*

MAC-PDU. Medium-access-control-protocol-data-unit.

MAC-SDU. Medium-access-control-service-data-unit.

MAN. Metropolitan Area Network.

Management Agent (MA). In the Simple Network Management Protocol (SNMP), a program running in a network element that is responsible for performing the network management functions requested by a network management application. A management agent accesses the objects stored in the portion of the Management Information Base that is maintained in that network element. See also *Simple Network Management Protocol, Network element, Management Information Base,* and *Network management application.*

Management Information Base (MIB). In the ISO Common Management Information Protocol (CMIP) and in the Simple Network Management Protocol (SNMP), a repository, or database, that defines all the objects that can be managed in a network. Portions of the MIB are distributed among all the hosts and routers in the network. See also *Common Management Information Protocol* and *Simple Network Management Protocol.*

Marshaling. A remote procedure call mechanism that handles the formatting and delivery of network messages that must flow between the calling procedure and the called procedure. See also *Remote procedure call.*

Mbps. Megabits per second.

Medium Access Control Address. See *MAC address.*

Medium Access Control (MAC) Sublayer. A sublayer of the Data Link layer, defined by the IEEE/ISO/ANSI LAN architecture, that is concerned with how access to the physical transmission medium is managed. The MAC sublayer provides services to the Logical Link Control (LLC) sublayer.

Medium-Access-Control-Protocol-Data-Unit (MAC-PDU). The data unit exchanged between peer Medium Access Control (MAC) sublayer entities. Sometimes referred to by the informal name *MAC frame.*

Medium-Access-Control-Service-Data-Unit. The data unit that a user of the Medium Access Control (MAC) sublayer service passes to the MAC sublayer when requesting a data transfer service.

Medium Specification. The part of a local area network standard that defines for a particular type of transmission medium the physical and electrical characteristics of the transmission medium and the method by which a station is attached to the transmission medium.

Metropolitan Area Network (MAN). A form of networking technology, related to LAN technology, that spans distances up to about 20 or 30 miles. Metropolitan area networks are sometimes used to bridge the gap between wide area networks and local area networks.

MIB. Management Information Base.

MODEM. A device that implements *modulator-demodulator* functions to convert between digital data and analog signals.

MOUNT PROTOCOL. Protocol used by the Network File System to provide facilities that are required to connect directories on NFS servers to the directory structure of hosts running NFS client software. See also *Network File System* and *NFS protocol.*

MULTIHOMED HOST. A host that implements multiple network attachments, thus allowing it to send traffic directly to different physical networks.

NAME RESOLUTION. A service, typically provided by **hosts** files or the Domain Name System (DNS) that translates between host names and internet addresses. See also *hosts files* and *Domain Name System.*

NAMESERVER. Component of the Domain Name System that runs in a limited number of systems in a TCP/IP internet to provide name resolution services for other hosts. See also *Domain Name System, Name resolution,* and *Resolver.*

NAMESPACE. The collection of all the names stored in Domain Name System directory databases that are maintained by all the nameservers. The namespace contains the names of all the hosts that can be referenced anywhere in the internet. See also *Domain Name System* and *Nameserver.*

NATIONAL RESEARCH AND EDUCATION NETWORK (NREN). Very-high-speed network, which is undergoing development by the U.S. government, that may take over the role of the NSFNET as the backbone network of the Internet. See also *NSFNET* and *Internet.*

NDR. Network Data Representation.

NE. Network element.

NETSTAT COMMAND. TCP/IP command that returns a set of statistics concerning the network activity that is associated with the local host.

NETWORK. See *Physical network.*

NETWORK ADMINISTRATOR. An individual or group that assists system administrators by helping to install networking software on servers, individual workstations, and personal computers and performs networkwide tasks to ensure the proper operation of the network. See also *System administrator.*

NETWORK ARCHITECTURE. A comprehensive plan and a set of rules that governs the design and operation of the hardware and software components used to create computer networks. Network architectures define sets of communication protocols that govern how communication takes place.

NETWORK BYTE ORDER. See *Network octet order.*

NETWORK DATA REPRESENTATION (NDR) FACILITY. In the Hewlett-Packard RPC facility, the facility that allows the user to define how structured data values used in a procedure call are encoded for transmission through an internet. See also *Hewlett-Packard RPC facility.*

NETWORK ELEMENT (NE). In the Simple Network Management Protocol (SNMP), a component in an internet that maintains a management agent and a portion of the Management Information Base that contains manageable objects. Examples of network elements are hosts and routers. See also *Simple Network Management Protocol, Management agent,* and *Management Information Base.*

NETWORK FILE SYSTEM (NFS). In TCP/IP, an Application layer service that provides authorized users with access to files located on remote systems. System administrators generally designate one or more systems in the internet as NFS servers that make certain designated directories on their disk storage devices available to other systems. A user accesses an NFS-mounted directory in the same manner as accessing a directory on a local disk.

NETWORK IDENTIFIER. The portion of an internet address that identifies a physical network. See also *Internet address* and *Physical network*.

NETWORK INFORMATION CENTER (NIC). The organization responsible for collecting and distributing information about TCP/IP protocols. The NIC is also responsible for assigning unique names and addresses to the networks and systems that will be connected to the Internet by individual organizations. The NIC is operated by Government Systems, Inc. (GSI). See also *Internet*.

NETWORK INFORMATION SERVICE (NIS). Facility provided by the Network File Service (NFS) that provides some services that are similar to those provided by the Domain Name System, such as mapping between host names and internet addresses. See also *Network File System* and *Domain Name System*.

NETWORK INTERFACE CARD (NIC). A circuit board installed in a computing device used to attach the device to a network. A NIC performs the hardware functions that are required to provide a computing device with physical communication capabilities.

NETWORK INTERFACE DEFINITION LANGUAGE (NIDL). In the Hewlett-Packard RPC facility, a language that allows users to specify the interface between a client application component and a server application component. See also *Hewlett-Packard RPC facility*.

NETWORK INTERFACE LAYER. TCP/IP functional layer corresponding to the Data Link layer of the OSI model. The main function of the Network Interface layer is to handle hardware-dependent functions and to present a standardized interface to the TCP/IP Internet layer. See also *Data Link layer* and *Internet layer*.

NETWORK LAYER. Layer three of the OSI model. The Network layer is concerned with making routing decisions and relaying data from one system to another through the network. The facilities provided by the Network layer supply a service that higher layers employ for moving packets from one end system to another, where the packets may flow through any number of intermediate systems.

NETWORK MANAGEMENT APPLICATION (NMA). In the Simple Network Management Protocol (SNMP), a program running in a network management station that monitors and controls one or more network elements. See also *Simple Network Management Protocol, Network management station,* and *Network element*.

NETWORK MANAGEMENT STATION (NMS). In the Simple Network Management Protocol (SNMP), a host in the internet that executes a network management application. A network administrator typically uses an NMS to monitor and control the internet or a portion of it. See also *Simple Network Management Protocol* and *Network management application*.

NETWORK MONITOR. Network management software that is run on one or more hosts in an internet or specialized devices that are attached to an internet in the same manner as hosts to perform network management functions.

NETWORK OCTET ORDER. The octet ordering scheme, either little-endian or big-endian that a network architecture uses to order the octets in multiple-octet binary integers. Sometimes called the *network byte order*. The network octet order for all protocols in the TCP/IP protocol suite is big-endian. See also *Little-endian computer system* and *Big-endian computer system*.

NETWORK OPERATING SYSTEM. A software product, typically used in the personal computer environment, that provides high-level networking functions to users and application programs.

NETWORK OPERATIONS CENTER (NOC). Organization that manages the telecommunications links and the nodal switching systems making up the NSFNET backbone network. The NOC is operated by Merit, Inc. on behalf of the National Science Foundation. See also *NSFNET* and *Nodal switching system.*

NETWORK TIME PROTOCOL (NTP). A TCP/IP Application layer protocol that implements algorithms that permit networked computing systems to maintain common, correct values for the date and time of day.

NETWORK VIRTUAL TERMINAL (NVT). Facility defined by Telnet that provides an interface to remote hosts against which all Telnet client software is built. NVT defines an imaginary terminal device that the Telnet client software emulates. See also *Telnet.*

NFS. Network File System.

NFS PROTOCOL. Protocol used by the Network File System to handle the network transmission that is required to provide the user with local access to remote files. See also *Network File System* and *Mount protocol.*

NIC. Network interface card or, in the Internet, the Network Information Center.

NIDL. Network Interface Definition Language.

NIDL COMPILER. In the Hewlett-Packard RPC facility, a compiler that processes Network Interface Definition Language statements to generate client and server stubs. See also *Hewlett-Packard RPC facility, Network Interface Definition Language,* and *Stub.*

NIS. Network Information Service (NIS).

NMA. Network management application.

NMS. Network management station.

NOC. Network Operations Center.

NODAL SWITCHING SYSTEM. Device that plays the role of a router in the NSFNET network. See also *Router* and *NSFNET.*

NREN. National Research and Education Network.

NSFNET. A high-speed network run by the National Science Foundation (NSF) that plays the role of the Internet backbone in the United States. The NSFNET consists of a number of computers called nodal switching systems (NSSs) that are interconnected by leased T3 digital telecommunication facilities. Each of the Internet regional networks is connected to at least one of the NSFNET nodal switching systems. See also *Internet* and *T3 facility.*

NSLOOKUP COMMAND. The **nslookup** command can be used to diagnose problems in the Domain Name System by specifically requesting name resolution operations.

NSS. Nodal switching system.

NTOHL FUNCTION. Network to Host Long function. Function that converts a 32-bit integer from network octet order to the octet order used by the host. See also *Network octet order.*

NTOHS FUNCTION. Network to Host Short function. Function that converts a 16-bit integer from network octet order to the octet order used by the host. See also *Network octet order.*

NTP. Network Time Protocol.

NVT. Network virtual terminal.

OPEN SHORTEST PATH FIRST (OSPF) PROTOCOL. A TCP/IP routing protocol that operates within a single autonomous system and implements a link-state routing algorithm. See also *Routing protocol, Autonomous system,* and *Link-state routing algorithm.*

OPEN SOFTWARE FOUNDATION (OSF). A nonprofit organization established by a number of computer manufacturers to develop a common foundation for open systems computing.

OSF. Open Software Foundation.

OSF DCE. Open Software Foundation Distributed Computing Environment. See *Distributed Computing Environment.*

OSF DISTRIBUTED COMPUTING ENVIRONMENT. See *Distributed Computing Environment.*

OSI. Open systems interconnection.

OSI MODEL. The seven-layer *Reference Model for Open Systems Interconnection,* developed by members of the International Organization for Standardization (ISO) and documented in ISO 7498, that provides a common basis for the coordination of standards development for the purpose of systems interconnection.

OSPF. Open Shortest Path First.

PACKET. In TCP/IP, an informal name for the IP datagram handled by the Internet Protocol (IP). Also, informal name for the data unit handled at the level of the OSI model Network layer. See also *IP datagram* and *Internet Protocol.*

PARTITION. A portion of a distributed database that is administered as a unit and is maintained by a single system.

PCI. Protocol-control-information.

PDU. Protocol-data-unit.

PHYSICAL HARDWARE ADDRESS. Address assigned to a network interface card (NIC) installed in a host or router that uniquely identifies the NIC within an individual physical network. See also *Network interface card* and *Physical network.*

PHYSICAL LAYER. The first layer of the OSI model. The *Physical* layer is responsible for the transmission of signals, such as electrical signals, optical signals, or radio signals, between communicating machines. Physical layer mechanisms in each of the communicating machines typically control the generation and detection of signals that are interpreted as 0 bits and 1 bits.

PHYSICAL NETWORK. A collection of two or more hosts and/or routers that are interconnected using a particular form of data link technology. See also *Host, Router,* and *Data link.*

PING SERVICE. TCP/IP Application layer service, typically implemented by a program named **ping,** that is used to test for connectivity between any two hosts. Ping uses ICMP Echo Request and Reply messages in performing its functions. See also *ICMP Echo Request and Reply messages.*

POINT-TO-POINT PROTOCOL (PPP). An adaptation of High-level Data Link Control (HDLC) that grew out of work done by the Internet Engineering Task Force. PPP improves on HDLC by adding a Network layer protocol identification mechanism. The Point-to-Point protocol allows a point-to-point connection to be established between two network devices that allows frames associated with multiple Network layer protocols to flow over data links without interfering with one another. See also *High-level Data Link Control* and *Internet Engineering Task Force.*

PORT. A 16-bit number that is used to differentiate one user of a Transport layer protocol from another user of that protocol.

PORTMAPPER PROCESS. In the Sun RPC facility, the process that provides programs with information about the location of callable services. See also *Sun RPC facility.*

PPP. Point-to-Point Protocol.

PRESENTATION LAYER. Layer six of the OSI model. The Presentation layer is the lowest layer interested in the *meaning* of the streams of bits that are exchanged between communicating programs and deals with preserving the *information content* of data transmitted over the network. The Presentation layer in the two communicating systems negotiates a common syntax for transferring the messages exchanged by two communicating programs and ensures that one system does not need to care what form of internal data representation the other system is using.

PRINT SERVER. A network system that implements software allowing other network systems to share the print server's printers.

PROJECT 802. A committee of the Institute of Electrical and Electronics Engineers (IEEE) responsible for the development of an architecture and standards for local area networking. IEEE Project 802 LAN standards have been accepted as international standards by ISO. See also *Institute of Electrical and Electronics Engineers.*

PROJECT ATHENA. A cooperative effort among MIT, IBM, and Digital Equipment Corporation to develop the X Window System. See also *X Window System.*

PROTOCOL. A set of rules or conventions that define the formats of data units handled by a particular layer in a network architecture and the data flows that take place in exchanging data units between peer layer entities.

PROTOCOL-CONTROL-INFORMATION (PCI). In the OSI model, control information, taking the form of a header and sometimes also a trailer, that a layer or sublayer entity attaches to the data in a service-data-unit to create one or more protocol-data-units.

PROTOCOL-DATA-UNIT (PDU). In the OSI model, the data unit that a layer or sublayer entity transmits across the network to a peer layer or sublayer entity.

PROTOCOLS FILE. TCP/IP configuration file containing information about the specific protocols that the local host supports and identifies the unique number assigned to each protocol.

PROTOCOL STATE. Attribute of a TCP/IP protocol definition that refers to its progress in making its way through the TCP/IP standardization process. The four possible states in which a protocol can exist at any given time are: experimental, proposed, draft, or standard.

PROTOCOL STATUS LEVEL. Attribute of a TCP/IP protocol definition that refers to the way in which the protocol is used in practice. The five possible status levels are required, recommended, elective, limited use, or not recommended.

PROTOCOL SUITE. A collection of communication protocols that together define the rules governing how messages are exchanged in a computer network. The collection of TCP/IP protocols is an example of a protocol suite. See also *Protocol.*

PTT. Postal, Telegraph, and Telephone Administration.

RARP. Reverse Address Resolution Protocol.

RARP SERVER. Host implementing the Reverse Address Resolution Protocol (RARP) that converts a physical hardware address into an internet address. See also *Reverse Address Resolution Protocol.*

READ SYSTEM CALL. Socket system call used to accept incoming data from a socket.

READV SYSTEM CALL. Socket system call used as an alternative to **read** to accept data into non-contiguous buffers. See also ***read** system call.*

RECURSIVE RESOLUTION. A form of name resolution performed by a Domain Name System nameserver in which nameservers contact other nameservers, as required, to completely perform a requested name resolution operation. With recursive resolution, all the computational complexity of name resolution lies in the nameservers, and the resolver software simply makes requests for name resolution services that the nameservers satisfy. See also *Name resolution, Domain Name System, Resolver, Nameserver,* and *Iterative resolution.*

RECVFROM SYSTEM CALL. Socket system call used in a connectionless application protocol employing UDP to receive a user datagram from a datagram socket and to also obtain the sender's socket address. See also *User datagram.*

RECVMSG SYSTEM CALL. Socket system call used in a connectionless application protocol employing UDP to receive a user datagram from a datagram socket. The buffer includes the user datagram's header as well as the data portion of the user datagram.

RECV SYSTEM CALL. Socket system call used as an alternative to **read** to accept incoming data from a socket and uses an additional flags argument. See **read** *system call.*

REDIRECT MESSAGE. ICMP error message sent by a router to a host to tell the host about a better route to use for subsequent IP datagrams. See also *Internet Control Message Protocol, ICMP error message,* and *IP datagram.*

RELIABLE SERVICE. See *Connection-oriented service.*

REMOTE EXECUTION SERVICE. See *Rsh service* and *Rexec service.*

REMOTE LOGIN SERVICE. See *Telnet service* and *Rlogin service.*

REMOTE PROCEDURE CALL (RPC) FACILITY. An Application layer service for interprocess communication in which an application program issues function and procedure calls by name to program modules that may reside in other network systems. Arguments and results are automatically transmitted through the network transparently to the application program.

REPLICA. A copy of all or a portion of a distributed database that is maintained on a computing system to enhance availability.

REQUEST FOR COMMENTS (RFC). Documentation of the operation of one of the protocols making up the TCP/IP protocol suite. RFCs are available in machine-readable form on the Internet or in hard-copy form from the Internet Network Information Center (NIC). See also *Protocol, Internet,* and *Network Information Center.*

RESERVED PORT. A port in which the port number falls in the range of 256 through 1023 that are used for UNIX-related services and general-purpose services, such as certain routing functions.

RESOLVER. Component of the Domain Name System, implemented by all systems, that contacts nameservers to perform name resolution operations. See also *Domain Name System, Nameserver,* and *Name resolution.*

REVERSE ADDRESS RESOLUTION PROTOCOL (RARP). A TCP/IP Internet layer protocol that allows a host that does not yet have its internet address to obtain it. RARP is typically used to support workstations and intelligent terminals that do not have their own disk storage. See also *Internet layer* and *Internet address.*

REXEC SERVICE. A remote execution service, similar to the Rsh, that is available on some TCP/IP hosts. See also *Rsh service.*

RFC. Request for Comments.

RIP. Routing Information Protocol.

RLOGIN SERVICE. The Rlogin service is a remote login service that is related to Telnet but is typically provided only by variations of the UNIX operating systems. See also *Telnet service.*

ROUTED PROGRAM. In the UNIX environment, a daemon that implements the Routing Information Protocol (RIP). The **routed** daemon is distributed as part of BSD UNIX. See also *Routing Information Protocol.*

ROUTER. A network device that is used to interconnect physical networks and performs routing and relaying functions. Sometimes called an *intermediate system.* In TCP/IP literature, a router is sometimes called a *gateway.* See also *Host.*

ROUTING ALGORITHM. Algorithm defined by a routing protocol that describes how routers update their routing tables. See also *Routing protocol, Router, Distance-vector routing algorithm,* and *Link-state routing algorithm.*

ROUTING FUNCTION. Function of the Internet Protocol (IP) that is responsible for moving IP datagrams from the source host to the destination host, no matter how many routers the IP datagram may have to traverse in getting to the correct destination host. The routing function in a host or router must decide the next hop each received IP datagram should take in traveling to its final destination.

ROUTING INFORMATION PROTOCOL (RIP). A TCP/IP interior gateway routing protocol that allows routers within an autonomous system to communicate with one another for the purposes of maintaining their routing tables. See also *Router, Routing protocol, Routing table, Interior gateway protocol,* and *Autonomous system.*

ROUTING PROTOCOL. Protocol implemented by a system that defines how routing information is exchanged with other systems for the purpose of maintaining the system's routing table. Routing protocols are typically implemented by routers, but some functions of routing protocols can also be implemented by hosts. See also *Router, Host,* and *Routing table.*

ROUTING TABLE. Table that enables a system to determine the host or router to which the system should forward an IP datagram that is destined for a system on some other physical network. See also *IP datagram* and *Physical network.*

RPC. Remote procedure call.

RPCGEN COMPILER. In the Sun RPC facility, a compiler that accepts remote procedure call interface definitions and generates client and server stubs that can be included in the client and server application programs. See also *Sun RPC facility* and *Stub.*

RSH SERVICE. A remote execution service that allows the user to issue, at the local host, a command to request an operating system function or to request the execution of an application program on some other host in the internet. See also *Rexec.*

SAP. Service-access-point.

SAP ADDRESS. In the OSI model, a value representing a point of access into a layer. In the Logical Link Control sublayer of the IEEE/ISO/ANSI LAN architecture, a value that represents a particular mechanism, process, or protocol that is requesting LLC sublayer services. Each mechanism, process, or protocol that is concurrently using the services of the LLC sublayer in a given station must use a different SAP address.

SDU. Service-data-unit.

SEGMENT. Data units handled by the Transmission Control Protocol (TCP). Segments are transparent to TCP users and are encapsulated in IP datagrams for transmission using the services of the Internet Protocol. See also *Transmission Control Protocol, IP datagram,* and *Internet Protocol.*

SEGMENTATION FUNCTION. Function of the Internet Protocol (IP) that is responsible for breaking large IP datagrams into pieces that will fit within a given physical network's maximum frame size. The IP process in the destination host then reassembles the pieces to recreate the original IP datagram. See also *Internet Protocol, IP datagram,* and *Physical network.*

SELECT SYSTEM CALL. Socket system call used to allow a process to wait for the completion of any one of multiple I/O events.

SENDMSG SYSTEM CALL. Socket system call used in a connectionless application protocol employing UDP to send a user datagram over a datagram socket. The buffer includes the user datagram's header as well as the data portion of the user datagram.

SEND SYSTEM CALL. Socket system call used as an alternative to **write** to send data over a socket and uses an additional flags argument. See also ***write*** *system call.*

SENDTO SYSTEM CALL. Socket system call used in a connectionless application protocol employing UDP to send data over a datagram socket and to specify the socket address of the remote process. The **sendto** call allows an association to be established at the time data is transferred.

SERVER. A computing system in a network that runs software that provides services to other computing systems. In client-server computing, an application component that provides a service for one or more other application components operating in the role of clients. See also *Client* and *Client-server computing.*

SERVICE-ACCESS-POINT (SAP). In the OSI model, the point at which the services of a layer are provided. Each service-access-point has a SAP address, by which the particular entity that is employing a layer service can be differentiated from all other entities that might also be able to use that layer service. In the IEEE/ANSI/ISO LAN architecture, the Logical Link Control sublayer implements service-access-points that identify each user of the LAN data link in a particular station.

SERVICE-ACCESS-POINT ADDRESS. See *Service-access-point* and *SAP address.*

SERVICE-DATA-UNIT (SDU). In the OSI model, the data unit that a layer or sublayer entity passes down to the adjacent layer or sublayer below it in requesting a data transmission service.

SERVICES FILE. TCP/IP configuration file containing information about TCP/IP Application layer services and protocols, including the name of each service, the Transport layer protocol it employs, and its port number assignment.

SESSION LAYER. Layer five of the OSI model. The Session layer is responsible for organizing the dialog between two communicating programs and for managing the data exchanges between them. It imposes a structure on the interaction between two communicating programs and defines three types of dialogs: two-way simultaneous interaction, where both programs can send and receive concurrently; two-way alternate interaction, where the programs take turns sending and receiving; and one-way interaction, where one program sends and the other only receives. In addition to organizing the dialog, Session layer services include establishing synchronization points within the dialog, allowing a dialog to be interrupted, and resuming a dialog from a synchronization point.

SET FUNCTION. In the Simple Network Management Protocol (SNMP), a function that a network management application can request of a management agent to set the value (or values) associated with a manageable object. See also *Simple Network Management Protocol, Network management application, Management agent,* and *Get function.*

SETSOCKOPT SYSTEM CALL. Socket system call used to set values for a set of parameters associated with a socket.

SHORTEST PATH FIRST ROUTING ALGORITHM. See *Link-state routing algorithm.*

SHUTDOWN SYSTEM CALL. Socket system call used in a connection-oriented application protocol employing TCP to close one end of an established TCP connection.

SIMPLE MAIL TRANSFER PROTOCOL (SMTP). In TCP/IP, an Application layer protocol used for the transfer of electronic mail messages. SMTP is designed to be used by electronic mail software that provides the user with access to messaging facilities.

SIMPLE NETWORK MANAGEMENT PROTOCOL (SNMP). In TCP/IP, an Application layer protocol that defines the formats of network management messages and the rules by which the messages are exchanged.

SMDS. Switched Multimegabit Data Service.

SMFA. Specific management functional area.

SMI. Structure and identification of Management Information.

SMTP. Simple Mail Transfer Protocol.

SNAP. Subnetwork Access Protocol.

SNAP LLC-PDU. Data unit, sometimes called a SNAP PDU, exchanged by peer entities implementing the IEEE Subnetwork Access Protocol. SNAP LLC-PDUs carry SSAP and DSAP address values of hexadecimal 'AA'. See also *Subnetwork Access Protocol.*

SNAP PDU. See *SNAP LLC-PDU.*

SNMP. Simple Network Management Protocol.

SOCKET. A data structure that uniquely identifies a process that is communicating with some other process. A socket data structure includes a *family* consisting of a 16-bit integer value identifying the protocol family being used, a *port* consisting of a 16-bit integer identifying the port number assigned to the process, and an **address** consisting of a 32-bit integer value containing the internet address, in binary format, of the host in which the process is running.

SOCKET INTERFACE. A networking application programming interface, initially developed for BSD UNIX, that is similar to the API provided for doing ordinary I/O with local devices. By using the socket interface, two application programs, one running in the local system and another running in the remote system, can communicate with one another in a standardized manner.

SOCKET SYSTEM CALL. Socket system call is used to initialize a socket data structure, to identify the Transport layer protocol to be used for communication, and to obtain an integer descriptor that subsequent socket system calls can use to refer to the socket.

SONET. Physical layer communication facilities, using fiber optics, on which broadband ISDN services are based. OC-1 SONET provides a 51 Mbps data rate, OC-3 SONET provides a 155 Mbps data rate, OC-12 SONET provides a 622 Mbps data rate, and OC-48 SONET provides a 2.4 Gbps data rate.

SOURCE MAC ADDRESS. Address identifying the station that originated a MAC frame. See also *MAC address* and *Station.*

SOURCE QUENCH MESSAGE. ICMP message sent by a host or router to request that the source system stop sending IP datagrams for a time. See also *Internet Control Message Protocol, ICMP error message,* and *IP datagram.*

SOURCE-SERVICE-ACCESS-POINT (SSAP). A service-access-point that identifies the originator of a data unit. See also *Service-access-point.*

SPECIFIC MANAGEMENT FUNCTIONAL AREA (SMFA). See *Common Management Information Protocol.*

SPF. Shortest path first.

SQL. Structured Query Language.

SSAP Address. In the IEEE/ISO/ANSI LAN architecture, an address that identifies the service-access-point (SAP) that is responsible for originating the LLC-PDU.

State. See *Protocol state.*

Station. A collection of hardware, firmware, and software that appears to other stations as a single functional and addressable unit on a LAN data link. A station implements a single physical point of connection to the transmission medium. A station is a collection of one or more hardware and/or software components that performs the functions of the LLC sublayer, the MAC sublayer, and the Physical layer.

Station Address. See *MAC address.*

Status Level. See *Protocol status level.*

Structure and Identification of Management Information (SMI). The part of the Common Management Information Protocol (CMIP) that defines a set of rules for how managed objects are described and how management protocols can be used by network management applications to access the value of an object and to set an object's value. See also *Common Management Information Protocol.*

Structured Query Language (SQL). A language used to describe relational database queries that allows database queries to be specified in a way that is independent of the mechanisms that are used to actually store the data.

Stub. A module associated with a calling or called procedure, used in conjunction with a remote procedure call facility, that mimics the presence of the remote procedure. See also *Remote procedure call facility.*

Subnet. An individual physical network in which the same TCP/IP network identifier value can be shared with other physical networks by using some of the high-order bits in the host identifier portion of the address to identify the physical network. See also *Internet address* and *Host identifier.*

Subnet Identifier. Internet address bits, contained within the host identifier portion of the address, that is used to extend the network identifier portion of the address. See also *Internet address, Host identifier,* and *Network identifier.*

Subnet Mask. A 32-bit data structure that contains a 1 in each bit position that indicates a bit that is used to identify the network and subnet and a 0 in each bit position that is used to identify a host.

Subnetwork Access Protocol (SNAP). A protocol defined by IEEE, that implements a mechanism for distinguishing LLC-PDUs that are carrying packets associated with one Network layer protocol from LLC-PDUs that are carrying packets associated with some other Network layer protocol.

Subnetwork-Access-Protocol-Logical-Link-Control-Protocol-Data-Unit. See *SNAP LLC-PDU.*

Sun RPC Facility. A remote procedure call facility developed by Sun Microsystems that is provided in most operating systems that are based on BSD UNIX. See also *Remote procedure call.*

Switched Multimegabit Data Service (SMDS). A high-speed wide area network packet-switching service that is built on top of broadband ISDN services to provide services similar to an X.25 network.

SYSTEM. A host or router capable of running TCP/IP communication software. In the OSI model, a set of one or more computers, the associated software, peripherals, terminals, human operators, physical processes, transfer means, and so on, that forms an autonomous whole capable of performing information processing and/or information transfer.

SYSTEM ADMINISTRATOR. An individual or group responsible for installing and maintaining software on host computers that are designated as servers and for helping individual workstation or personal computer users install and maintain software on their own individual computers. See also *Network administrator.*

TCP. Transmission Control Protocol.

TCP/IP. Transmission Control Protocol/Internet Protocol.

TELNET SERVICE. A TCP/IP Application layer service that allows a user to login to some other host in the internet. The Telnet protocol establishes a client-server relationship between the local Telnet software (the client) and the remote Telnet software (the server). See also *Rlogin service.*

10BASE2. Shorthand notation for an IEEE/ISO CSMA/CD (Ethernet) LAN medium specification in which the data rate is 10 Mbps, the transmission technique is baseband, and the maximum cable segment length is 185 meters. 10BASE2 is the CSMA/CD medium specification that specifies the use of 50 Ohm, 5 mm coaxial cable, sometimes called *ThinWire* or *ThinNet* cable.

10BASE5. Shorthand notation for an IEEE/ISO CSMA/CD (Ethernet) LAN medium specification in which the data rate is 10 Mbps, the transmission technique is baseband, and the maximum cable segment length is 500 meters. 10BASE5 is the CSMA/CD medium specification that is based on the original Ethernet Version 2 specification and specifies the use of 50 Ohm, 10 mm coaxial cable often called *Ethernet cable* or *thick Ethernet cable.*

10BASE-T. Shorthand notation for an IEEE/ISO CSMA/CD (Ethernet) LAN medium specification in which the data rate is 10 Mbps, the transmission technique is baseband, and the maximum cable segment length is 100 meters. 10BASE-T is the CSMA/CD medium specification that specifies the use of twisted-pair cable.

TFTP. Trivial File Transfer Protocol.

THREAD. The execution of a piece of code that can operate concurrently with the execution of the same or different pieces of code within the same application process.

TIME EXCEEDED MESSAGE. ICMP error message sent by a host or router indicating that the value contained in a received IP datagram's Time-to-Live field has expired and the IP datagram has been discarded. See also *Internet Control Message Protocol, ICMP error message,* and *IP datagram.*

TIME SERVICE. A TCP/IP Application layer service that a host can use to contact another host to obtain a date and time-of-day value.

TLI. Transport Layer Interface.

TOKEN. A special data unit, used with Token Bus, Token Ring, and FDDI LAN data links, that is passed from station to station to control access to the transmission medium. Only a station that possesses the token is allowed to transmit MAC frames.

TOKEN BUS. A LAN data link technology, defined by IEEE 802.4 and ISO 8802-4, in which systems are connected to a common transmission medium in a similar manner to an Ethernet LAN. A system is allowed to transmit only when it has a special data unit, called the *token,* that is passed from one system to another.

TOKEN RING. A LAN data link technology, defined by IEEE 802.5 and ISO 8802-5, in which systems are connected to one another using point-to-point twisted-pair cable segments to form a ring structure. A system is allowed to transmit only when it has the token, which is passed from one system to another around the ring.

TOKEN-RING NETWORK. The name of IBM's implementation of the IEEE/ISO Token Ring standard.

T1 FACILITY. A digital telecommunication facility, available from telecommunications providers, that supports a bit rate of 1.544 Mbps.

TRACEROUTE COMMAND. A TCP/IP command used to diagnose internet connectivity problems by reporting on the current route that packets are taking through an internet in reaching a specified host.

TRANSMISSION CONTROL PROTOCOL (TCP). A connection-oriented Transport layer protocol that provides for reliable, sequenced, stream data delivery. See also *Connection-oriented service.*

TRANSMISSION CONTROL PROTOCOL/INTERNET PROTOCOL (TCP/IP). A set of communication protocols that grew out of a research project that was funded by the U.S. Department of Defense. The TCP/IP networking scheme implements a peer-to-peer client-server architecture. Any computing system in the network can run TCP/IP server software and can provide services to any other computing system that runs complementary TCP/IP client software.

TRANSPORT LAYER. TCP/IP functional layer corresponding to the Transport layer of the OSI model. The Transport layer is the lowest layer required only in two end systems that are communicating. The Transport layer forms the uppermost layer of a reliable end-to-end data transport service and hides from the higher layers all the details concerning the actual moving of streams of bits from one computer to another.

TRANSPORT LAYER INTERFACE (TLI). A networking application programming interface (API) that was originally defined for use with AT&T System V UNIX and is now implemented by a variety of networking software subsystems.

TRANSPORT LAYER PROTOCOL PORT. See *Port.*

TRIVIAL FILE TRANSFER PROTOCOL (TFTP). A TCP/IP Application layer service, providing simple file transfer facilities, that implements its own reliability controls and can run on top of any type of transport service.

T3 FACILITY. A digital telecommunication facility, available from telecommunications providers, that supports a bit rate of 45 Mbps.

TWO-PHASE COMMIT PROTOCOL. A protocol used to handle backout processing in which file or database updates are not considered permanent until all transaction activities have completed successfully.

UDP. User Datagram Protocol.

USER DATAGRAM. The data unit handled by the User Datagram Protocol (UDP). See also *User Datagram Protocol.*

USER DATAGRAM PROTOCOL (UDP). In TCP/IP, a Transport layer protocol that provides a best-efforts, connectionless datagram delivery service. See also *Connectionless service.*

USER-DEFINED PORT. Port in which the port number falls in the range from 5000-65,535 that is typically used for sending data from a client process to a user-written server process. See also *Port.*

WAIS SERVICE. A distributed text searching system that allows the user to make various types of searches based on the contents of one or more indexed text databases. A number of WAIS-structured databases are available on the Internet.

WAN. Wide area network.

WELL-KNOWN PORT. Port in which the port number falls in the range from 1 to 255 that is typically used for sending data from a client process to a server running a well-known service, such as Telnet or FTP. See also *Port.*

WHOIS SYSTEM. Facility implementing an Internet directory that is similar to a white pages telephone directory. The Whois directory is maintained by the DDN NIC and lists people who are responsible for operating the Internet and who are doing Internet research work.

Wide Area Network (WAN). Term used to refer to communication facilities that tie together computing devices or physical networks that are widely separated geographically.

WORLDWIDE INTERNET. See *Internet.*

WORLDWIDE WEB (WWW). A retrieval system in the Internet, based on hypertext technology, that attempts to organize Internet information resources as a set of hypertext documents. The user traverses the network by moving from one hypertext document to another via links that are implemented between them.

WRITE SYSTEM CALL. Socket system call used to send data over a socket.

WRITEV SYSTEM CALL. Socket system call used as an alternative to **write** to send data from non-contiguous buffers. See also **write** *System call.*

WWW. Worldwide Web.

XDR. External Data Representation.

X TERMINAL. Terminal that implements the X Window System protocols.

X.25. An international standard, documented in CCITT Recommendation X.25, that defines the interface between a computing device and a packet-switched data network (PSDN).

X Window System. An Application layer service, developed by Project Athena, consisting of a set of distributed graphical presentation services that implement a windowing system on a graphics display. The X Window System defines a protocol that is used to transmit information between a client application program and server windowing software.

Index

A

Abstract Syntax Notation One (ASN.1), 146, 181
accept system call, 217, 221
Access control lists (ACLs), 287
Access units, 10
Active open, 200
Address conversion function calls, 204–5
Addressing:
  assigning internet addresses, 157–58
  considerations related to expanding the internet, 163
  identifier conversions:
    host name to internet address conversion, 43
    internet address to physical hardware address
      conversion, 43–44
  identifiers:
    host names, 41–42
    internet addresses, 42–43
    physical hardware addresses, 43
  internet:
    address formats, 44–45
    dotted-decimal notation, 45–46
  internet addressing authority, 46
  internet routing, 48–49
  local host name and address, 49
  Medium Access Control (MAC), 243, 244–45
  routers and multihomed hosts, 48
  service-access-point (SAP), 243–44, 245
  subnetting:
    choosing subnet identifiers, 48
    subnet identifier, 46–47
    subnet mask, 47–48
Address Resolution Protocol (ARP), 39, 43, 44, 112
  anticipating reverse traffic, 119–20
  example of, 121–22
  internet addresses, 118
  mapping internet addresses to physical hardware
    addresses, 118

  operation of, 119
  packet format, 120
  physical hardware addresses, 117
Address Resolution Protocol (ARP) cache, 119
Ad hoc network management tools:
  configuration files, 148
  network management commands, 147–48
  network monitors, 148
Administration functions, 11–12
Advanced Research Projects Agency (ARPA), 3
Agents, 151
AGRICOLA, 19
Agriculture, 19
Alcoholism, 19
American National Standards Institute. *See* ANSI
Andrew File System (AFS), 281
ANSI, 241
ANSI X3.92-1981, American National Standard Data
    Encryption Algorithm (DES), 286
Anthropology, 19
Apollo Computer Inc., 71
Application layer, OSI model, 29, 31
Application layer, TCP/IP, 31–32, 53–54
  File Transfer Protocol (FTP), 18, 34
    commands and replies, 62
    data types, 60–61
    file types, 60, 61
    operation of, 61–62
    subcommands, 62–63
    transmission modes, 60, 61
  Kerberos security, 35, 69–70
  name resolution, 34–35, 43
    with Domain Name System (DNS), 65–66
    with **hosts** files, 65
  Network File System (NFS), 34, 63, 75–78
  Ping connectivity testing, 33
    examples of, 55–56
    operation of, 55

Application layer, TCP/IP *(cont.)*
  protocols and services, 32, 33–35
    end user services and protocols, 33–34, 54
    support services and protocols, 34–35, 54
  remote procedure call (RPC) facility, 35, 70–71
  Rlogin interactive login, 33–34, 59
  Rsh remote execution, 34, 59–60
  Simple Mail Transfer Protocol (SMTP), 35, 66–67
    data formats, 68
    operation, 67–68
  Simple Network Management Protocol (SNMP),
    72
  Telnet interactive login, 33
    command mode, 57
    functions of, 56
    input mode, 57–59
    operation of, 56–57
  time services:
    definition of, 71
    maintaining synchronized time values, 71–72
    Network Time Service (NTS) protocol, 35, 72
    timed daemon, 72
  Trivial File Transfer Protocol (TFTP), 34, 37, 63
  X Window System, 35, 68–69
Application programming interfaces (APIs), 32
  remote procedure call (RPC) facilities, 206–7
  socket system calls, 206, 207
Archie system, 20
ARCnet, 6
ARPANET, 3, 4, 15
arp command, 161, 171
ASCII data type, 60
Associations, 201–2
  association data elements, 202
  half-association data elements, 202
Asynchronous Transfer Mode (ATM), 8
  cell format, 258, 260
  cell switching technology, 258
  circuit switching, 256
  classes of service, 260–61
  future of, 261
  hybrid networks, 261, 262
  local area networks, 258, 259
  packet switching, 257–58
  transmission facilities, 260, 261
  wide area networks, 258, 259
At least once semantics, RPC facility, 231
At most once semantics, RPC facility, 231
Attachment units, 9
Authentication, 181, 286–87
Authorization, 286, 287
Autonomous systems, 136–37, 138, 140

B

Bellman-Ford algorithm, 135
Best-effort delivery service, 27

bind system call, 212, 215, 216, 217, 219
Block transmission mode, 61
Border Gateway Protocol (BGP), 140–41
Bridges, 162–63, 164, 248
Broadband ISDN (B-ISDN), 7, 263
Broadcast client-server model, 184, 185
Byte, 8

C

Cabling systems, 9–10
Caching, 88
Carrier Sense Multiple Access with Collision Detection
    (CSMA/CD) (Ethernet), 243, 244
CCITT Recommendation X.25, 7
Cell(s), 258
Cell switching, 8
Centralized routing, 134, 135
Cerf, Vinton G., 15
Chained server model, 184, 186
Child pointer entry, 277, 278
Chinese literature, 19
Circuit switching, 256
Class A addresses, 45, 46, 47, 48
Class B addresses, 45, 46, 47, 48
Class C addresses, 45, 46, 47, 48
Class D addresses, 45
Clearinghouses, 278–79
Clerks, 279, 284, 285
Client(s), 37, 177, 199, 200
  DCE, 268, 269
  DNS, 86–87
  FTP, 62
  NFS, 63, 75, 76
  SMTP, 67
Client-server relationship, 177–78, 199
  choosing a distribution mechanism, 194–95
    message queuing mechanisms, 195–96
    peer-to-peer communication mechanisms, 195
    remote object invocation mechanisms, 196–97
    transaction processing mechanisms, 196–97
  computing models, 181–83
    broadcast model, 184, 185
    chained server model, 184, 186
    flow management model, 187–88
    job contracting model, 184–85, 187
    object invocation model, 187
    simple client-server model, 183, 184
  distribution technologies, 188–89
    network transport independence, 189
    TCP/IP distribution mechanisms, 189
  infrastructure functions, 178–79
    client-server rendezvous mechanisms, 180
    connection management mechanisms, 180
    data definition mechanisms, 181
    global management mechanisms, 179
    global naming mechanisms, 179

global time mechanisms, 180
multithreading mechanisms, 180
process activation mechanisms, 180
security mechanisms, 181
two-phase commit mechanisms, 180–81
unique identifier mechanisms, 179
message passing mechanisms, 192, 193
connectionless message passing mechanisms, 192
connection-oriented message passing mechanisms, 192–93
models and distribution technologies, 178–79
remote database access mechanisms, 189, 191–92
remote procedure call (RPC) facility, 193–94, 227, 229
Transport layer, 37
Client-server rendezvous mechanisms, 180
close system call, 225
CMOT (CMIP over TCP/IP), 147, 151–52
Commands, File Transfer Protocol (FTP), 62
Common carrier data links, 249
Common Management Information Protocol (CMIP), 145, 146, 147, 151–52
Communication protocols, 24
connectionless protocols, 26–27
Internet Protocol (IP), 108–9
User Datagram Protocol (UDP), 95, 96
connection-oriented protocols, 25–26, 27
Transmission Control Protocol (TCP), 99–100
Compressed transmission mode, 61
Computing devices, 8
Concentrators, 10
Concert Multithread Architecture, (CMA), 270
Concurrent servers, 200–201
Configuration files, 148
Congestion control, Transmission Control Protocol (TCP), 103
Connectionless message passing mechanisms, 192
Connectionless protocols, 26–27
connection-oriented protocols versus, 27
Internet Protocol (IP), 108–9
User Datagram Protocol (UDP), 96, 96
Connection management mechanisms, 180
Connection-oriented message passing mechanisms, 192–93
Connection-oriented protocols, 25–26
connectionless protocols versus, 27
Transmission Control Protocol (TCP), 99–100
Connection Refused error message, 172–73
Connection release, Transmission Control Protocol (TCP), 104
Connection Timed Out error message, 171–72
connect system call, 217, 219–20
Control connection, File Transfer Protocol (FTP), 61
Cooking, 19
Cooperative processing, 182
Coordinated Universal Time, 281–82
Courier servers, 285
Cryptosystem, 286

D

Daemon processes, 59
Network File System, 78
Data access processing components, 181, 182, 183
Data definition mechanisms, 181
Data encryption, 181
Data formats, Simple Mail Transfer Protocol (SMTP), 68
Datagram service, 27, 192
Data link, 5
Data Link layer, OSI model, 30, 31
Data link protocol, 5
Data protection, 286
Data transfer connection:
File Transfer Protocol (FTP), 61
Transmission Control Protocol (TCP), 101–3
Data types, File Transfer Protocol (FTP), 60–61
Default router, 113
Defense Advanced Research Projects Agency (DARPA), 3
Defense Communication Agency (DCA), 15
Defense Data Network (DDN), 17
Network Information Center (NIC), 17, 46, 84, 85
Demultiplexing function, 39
Destination-service-access-point (DSAP), 245
Diskless workstations, 122
Distance-vector routing, 135–36, 140
Distributed adaptive routing, 134, 135
distance-vector routing, 135–36
link-state routing, 134, 135, 136
Distributed computing environment (DCE), 194
cell architecture, 265–66
Directory Service, 267
CDS servers, 279
cell architecture, 273–74
cell directory service, 275–76
cell directory service operation, 277
clearinghouses, 278–79
clerks, 279
directory operations, 280
directory technologies, 274–75
Domain Name System (DNS), 276–77
global directory service, 276
loose consistency guarantee, 280–81
namespace structure, 277–78
partitioning and replication, 279–80
Distributed File Service, 267, 281
Distributed Queue Dual Bus (DQDB), 8, 263
Distributed Time Service, 267
coordinated universal time, 281–82
courier servers, 285
distributed time service operation, 284
DTS components, 284–85
local and global sets, 285
time differential factors, 282
time value inaccuracy, 282–83
time value representation, 281
uses for time values, 282
middleware services, 266, 267–68

Distributed computing environment (DCE) *(cont.)*
    Remote Procedure Call Service, 266, 267, 268
        architectural model, 268, 269
        facility components, 268–70
    Security Service, 268, 285–86
        authentication, 286–87
        authorization, 287
        data protection, 286
    Threads Service, 267, 270
        multithreaded process structure, 270, 271
        single thread process structure, 270, 271
        thread coordination facilities, 272–73
        uses for multithreading facilities, 272
Distributed Queue Dual Bus (DQDB), 8, 263
Distribution technologies, 179, 188–89
    network transport independence, 189
    TCP/IP distribution mechanisms, 189
Domain name(s), 41, 84
    Internet standard, 84–86
Domain Name System (DNS), 34–35, 43, 65–66, 76, 81,
        158, 163, 164, 180, 275, 276–77
    caching, 88
    client and server software, 86–87
    installing, 160, 161
        choosing a domain name, 162
        installing nameservers, 161–62
    Internet naming scheme, 82, 84–86
    message format, 88–90
    name resolution operations, 87–88
    name resolution using, 82, 83
    query types, 90, 91
Dotted-decimal notation, 45–46, 47, 58, 81
Drosophila stocks, 19

E

EBCDIC data type, 60
Echo Reply Message, (ICMP), 33, 55, 129, 130
Echo Request Message, (ICMP), 33, 55, 129, 130
Electronic mail, 35, 66–68
End systems, 30
End user services, 33–34, 54
Error checking:
    Transmission Control Protocol (TCP), 103
    User Datagram Protocol (UDP), 97–98
Error diagnosis:
    Connection Refused, 172–73
    Host Unknown, 173
    Network Unreachable, Host Unreachable, and
        Connection Timed Out, 171–72
    Service Unknown and Protocol Unknown, 170–71
Error messages, Internet Control Message Protocol
        (ICMP), 126–27
    redirect example, 127–29
    redirect message format, 127, 128
Ethernet, 6, 243, 244

Ethernet Version 2 Specification, 244
Exactly once semantics, RPC facility, 231–32
exports configuration file, 77
Extended LAN, 248
Exterior Gateway Protocol (EGP):
    neighbor acquisition, 139
    neighbor reachability, 139
    packets, 140
    routing information updating, 140
Exterior neighbors, 139
External data representation (XDR) facility, 206

F

Fiber Distributed Data Interface (FDDI), 6, 243, 244
File structure file type, 61
File system mode, Network File System, 76–77
File Transfer Protocol (FTP), 18, 34
    commands and replies, 62
    data types, 60–61
    file types, 60, 61
    operation of, 61–62
    subcommands, 62–63
    transmission modes, 60, 61
File types, File Transfer Protocol (FTP), 61
Finger Facility, 20
Flow control, Transmission Control Protocol (TCP),
        103
Flow management client-server model, 187–88
Fragmentation, 111
Frame(s), 5, 30
Frame Relay, 7, 255
    frame format, 256, 257
    network layer protocol identification, 256
    station identification, 256
ftp command, 161
Fully-qualified domain name (FQDN), 42, 84
Functional layers:
    OSI model, 23, 24
    TCP/IP, 31
Function processing components, 181, 182, 183

G

gated daemon, 139
Gateway protocols:
    exterior, 139–41
    interior, 137–38
Genealogy, 19
Get, SNMP, 151
Global management mechanisms, 179
Global naming mechanisms, 179
Global sets, 285
Global time mechanisms, 180
Government Systems, Inc., 17
Greenwich Mean Time (GMT), 281

H

Handshake, 26, 101
Hardware addresses, 43
Hardware layer, TCP/IP, 39, 241
Hello protocol, 138
Hewlett-Packard RPC facility, 71, 206, 232
High-Level Data Link Control (HDLC), 7, 248
    frame format, 249, 250
    frame types, 250
    network layer protocol identification, 250–51
    station identification, 250
Host(s), 4, 8
    IP routing in, 113
Host identifier, 44
Host names, 41–42, 43
    assigning, 157
hosts files, 65, 82, 83, 121, 148, 158–59, 160, 161, 164,
    171, 173
Host Unknown error message, 173
Host Unreachable error message, 171–72
Hubs, 10

I

IAB Official Protocol Standards, 20, 21
Identifier(s):
    host names, 41–42
    internet addresses, 42–43
    physical hardware addresses, 43
Identifier conversions:
    host name to internet address, 43
    internet address to physical hardware address, 43–44
IEEE, 241
IEEE/ANSI/ISO LAN addressing, 243–44
IEEE/ANSI/ISO LAN architecture layers and sublayers,
    241–42
    Logical Link Control sublayer, 242, 244
    Medium Access Control sublayer, 242–43
    Physical layer, 243
IEEE/ANSI/ISO LAN standards, 243
ifconfig command, 147, 161, 171, 172
Image data type, 60, 61
Indian classical music, 19
Infrastructure functions, 178–79
    client-server rendezvous mechanisms, 180
    connection management mechanisms, 180
    data definition mechanisms, 181
    global management mechanisms, 179
    global naming mechanisms, 179
    global time mechanisms, 180
    multithreading mechanisms, 180
    process activation mechanisms, 180
    security mechanisms, 181
    two-phase commit mechanisms, 180–81
    unique identifier mechanisms, 179

Institute of Electrical and Electronics Engineers. *See* IEEE
Integer octet order function calls, 203–4
Integrated Services Digital Network (ISDN), 7, 262–63
Interface, 24
Interface Definition Language (IDL), 268
Interior gateway protocols, 137–38
    gated daemon, 139
    Hello protocol, 138
    Open Shortest Path First (OSPF), 138
    Routing Information Protocol (RIP), 138
Intermediate systems, 30
International Organization for Standardization (ISO), 27,
    145–46
International Time Bureau, 282
Internet, 3
    assigning addresses, 157–58
    configuring:
        assigning host and user names, 157
        assigning internet addresses, 157–58
        installing server software, 159–60
        installing the physical network, 155–56
        installing the TCP/IP communications software, 156
        performing name resolution, 158–59
        testing internet operation, 160, 161
    expanding:
        addressing considerations, 163
        centralized network administration, 164
        connecting remote locations, 164–65
        naming considerations, 163–64
        routers versus bridges, 162–63
    routing, 48–49
Internet (Worldwide), 4, 15
    addressing, 42–43, 118
        address formats, 44–45
        dotted-decimal notation, 45–46
    administration of:
        DDN Network Information Center (NIC), 17
        Internet Activities Board (IAB), 18
        Internet Assigned Numbers Authority (IANA), 17
        Internet Engineering Task Force (IETF), 18
        Network Operations Center (NOC), 17
    connecting to, 18, 165
        commercial service providers, 167
        reasons for, 166–67
        security considerations, 167
    hierarchical structure of:
        National Research and Education Network (NREN),
            17
        NSFNET backbone network, 16
    information resources, 18, 19–20
    naming scheme, 82
        hierarchical namespace, 84
        Internet standard domain names, 84–86
Internet Activities Board (IAB), 18
Internet addressing authority, 46
Internet Architect, 18
Internet Assigned Numbers Authority (IANA), 17, 37

Internet Control Message Protocol (ICMP), 33, 39, 112
    Echo Reply message, 33, 55, 129, 130
    Echo Request message, 33, 55, 129, 130
    error messages, 126–29
    general message format, 126, 127
    message types, 126
    query messages, 129–31
    uses for, 125–26
Internet Engineering Task Force (IETF), 18
Internet Gopher, 20
Internet layer, TCP/IP, 31, 38
    protocols, 38, 39
        Address Resolution Protocol (ARP), 39, 43, 44, 112,
            117–22
        Internet Control Message Protocol (ICMP), 125–31
        Internet Protocol (IP), 15, 27, 39, 107–15
        Reverse Address Resolution Protocol (RARP), 39, 44,
            122–23
        routing protocols, 133–41
Internet Protocol (IP), 15, 27, 39
    connectionless service, 108–9
    datagram format, 109, 110
    protocol mechanisms, 109
        routing, 111
        segmentation, 111
    router routing tables, 115
    routing, 111–112
        datagram delivery on a different physical network, 114
        datagram delivery on the same physical network,
            113–114
        as a host, 113
        sample internet, 112
        routing tables, 113
        traversing multiple routers, 114–15
    users of, 107
Internet Protocol (IP) datagram, 43, 107
    duplicate, 109
    format of, 109, 110
    lost, 108
    out-of-sequence, 108–9
Internetworking, 12–13
Internetworking layer, TCP/IP, 38
ISO 7498, 28
Iterative resolution, 88
Iterative servers, 200, 201

J, K

Job contracting client-server model, 184–85, 187
Kahn, Robert E., 15
Kerberos security, 35, 69–70, 285

L

LAN adapter, 9
Layer Management Entity (LME), 152

Library catalogs, 19
Link-state routing, 134, 135, 136
listen system call, 220
Local area network (LAN) addressing, 243–44
    LAN data link LLC sublayer users, 246
    LLC sublayer user multiplexing, 246
    MAC addressing, 244–45
    SAP address assigned values, 246
    SAP addressing, 245
Local area network (LAN) data links, 5–6, 12, 13, 241, 258
Local host name and address, 49
Local host software configuration problems, 169
Local sets, 285
LocalTalk, 6
Logical-link-control-protocol-data-unit (LLC-PDU), 242,
    245, 247
Logical Link Control sublayer, 242, 244
Logical octet size data type, 60, 61

M

MAC address, 117
MAC frame, 242–43, 245
Management agent (MA), SNMP, 150
Management Information Base (MIB), 35, 72, 146, 149–50
Managers, 151
Marshaling, 194, 229–30
Master replicas, 279
Medium-access-control-protocol-data-unit (MAC-PDU),
    242–43
Medium Access Control (MAC) addressing, 243, 244–45
Medium Access Control sublayer, 242–43
Message format, Domain Name System (DNS), 88–90
Message interface, 193
Message passing mechanisms, 192, 193
    connectionless, 192
    connection-oriented, 192–93
Message queuing mechanisms, 195–96
Metropolitan Area Network (MAN), 8
Middleware, 265, 266
MILNET, 15
Molecular graphics, 19
mount command, 77
Mount protocol, Network File System, 77
Multithreading mechanisms, 180
Mutex, 273
Multihomed hosts, 48

N

Name resolution, 34–35, 43, 81, 163, 164
    with Domain Name System (DNS), 65–66, 82, 83, 87–88
    with hosts files, 65, 82, 83
    performing, 158–59
    problems related to, 169–70, 173
Nameserver, 66, 81, 161–62

Namespace, 84, 277–78
National Aeronautics and Space Administration (NASA), 19
National Research and Education Network (NREN), 17
National Science Foundation (NSF), 16, 17
Neighbor acquisition, 139
Neighbor reachability, 139
netstat command, 148, 171, 172
Network(s), 4–5
Network adapter, 9
Network administrator, 11, 12
Network architectures, 23–25
Network byte order, 203
Network element (NE), SNMP, 150
Network File System (NFS), 34, 63, 178
    client-server architecture of, 75, 76
    file system model, 76–77
    implementation of, 78
    mount protocol, 77
    Network Information Service (NIS) and, 76
    protocol, 77, 78
    remote procedure calls (RPCs) and, 76
Network identifier, 44
Network Information Center (NIC), 17, 46, 84, 85
Network Information Service (NIS), 76
Networking software, 10–11
Network interface cards (NICs), 9, 10, 38, 43, 117, 243
Network interface layer, TCP/IP, 31, 38–39, 241
Network layer:
    OSI model, 30, 31
    TCP/IP, 38
Network management:
    approaches to, 147
        ad hoc tools, 147–148
        CMIP over TCP/IP (CMOT), 147, 151–52
        Simple Network Management Protocol (SNMP), 147, 148–49
        ISO CMIP approach to, 145
            Abstract Syntax Notation One (ASN.1), 146
            Management Information Base (MIB), 146
            object identification and description, 146
            structure and identification of management information, 146
Network management application (NMA), SNMP, 150
Network management station (NMS), SNMP, 150
Network monitors, 148, 171
Network-network interface (NNI), 258, 260
Network octet order, 203
Network operating systems, 10
Network Operations Center (NOC), 17
Network Time Service (NTS), 35, 72
Network transport independence, 189
Network Unreachable error message, 171–72
Network virtual terminal (NVT), Telnet, 56
Nodal switching systems (NSSs), 16
NSFNET, 16
NSF publications, 19
nslookup command, 148, 171, 172, 173

O

Object(s), 146, 149, 286
Object entries, 277
Object invocation client-server model, 187
Octet, 8
Open Shortest Path First (OSPF) Protocol, 138
Open Software Foundation (OSF), 265
Option negotiation, Telnet, 56
OSI reference model, 27–28
    functional layers of, 28–30
    network architecture of, 28
    purpose of, 28

P

Packet(s), 30, 107
    Address Resolution Protocol (ARP), 120
    Exterior Gateway Protocol (EGP), 140, 141
Packet InterNet Groper. *See* Ping connectivity testing
Packet-switched data network (PSDN), 7, 253
Packet switching, 257–58
Page structure file type, 61
Partitioning, 192, 279–80
Passive open, 201
Path names, 77
PC Magazine, 19
Peer-to-Peer communication mechanisms, 195
Permanent virtual circuit (PVC), 253
Physical connectivity problems, 169
Physical hardware addresses, Address Resolution Protocol (ARP), 117
    mapping Internet addresses to, 118
Physical layer:
    IEEE/ANSI/ISO LAN architecture, 243
    OSI model, 30, 31
Physical network implementation:
    access units or concentrators, 10
    cabling systems, 9–10
    computing devices, 8
    networking software, 10–11
    network interface cards (NICs), 9
Physical network technologies:
    local area network (LAN) data links, 5–6
    wide area network (WAN) data links, 6–8
ping command, 147–48, 161, 171, 172
Ping connectivity testing, 33, 129
    examples of, 55–56
    operation of, 55
Point-to-Point Protocol (PPP), 7, 248
    frame format, 252, 253
    network layer protocol identification, 252–53
    station identification, 252
Port numbers, Transport layer:
    ephemeral client ports, 38
    other reserved ports, 37
    reserved ports for well-known services, 37

Port numbers, Transport layer *(cont.)*
  user-defined server ports, 38
Presentation layer, OSI model, 29, 31
Principal, 35, 286
  Kerberos, 69
Principal identifier, Kerberos, 69
Problem resolution tools, 170, 171
Process activation mechanisms, 180
Protocol(s):
  Internet layer, 38, 39
  Internet Protocol (IP), 109
  Network File System, 77, 78
  Transmission Control Protocol (TCP), 101–4
  Transport layer, 36
  User Datagram Protocol (UDP), 96–98
Protocol-control-information (PCI), 242
Protocol ports, Transport layer, 36
protocols file, 148
Protocol states, 21
Protocol status levels, 21
Protocol suite, 3
Protocol Unknown error message, 170–71

Q

Quasi-static routing, 134
Query messages, Internet Control Message Protocol
    (ICMP):
  Echo Request and Reply, 129, 130
  Subnet Mask Request and Reply, 129, 131
  Timestamp Request and Reply, 129, 130–31
Query types, Domain Name System (DNS), 90, 91

R

rcmd, 59
Read-only replicas, 280
read system calls, 223–24
Record structure file type, 61
Recursive resolution, 88
recvfrom system call, 224
recv system call, 223–24
Reference Model for Open Systems Interconnection. *See*
    OSI reference model
Reliable messaging service, 196
Remote database access mechanisms, 189, 191–92
Remote file access, 190
Remote host hardware problems, 169
Remote host software configuration problems, 169
Remote object invocation mechanisms, 196–97
Remote procedure calls (RPCs), 35, 70–71, 76,
    193–94,206–7
  call semantics, 230–31
    exactly once, 231–32
    at least once, 231
    at most once, 231

functional model, 229, 230
  client-server rendezvous, 229
  marshaling, 229–30
implementations:
  Hewlett-Packard RPC facility, 232–33
  Sun RPC facility, 232, 233–37
procedure call mechanism, 227, 228
  in a client-server environment, 227–28
  difficulties in achieving transparency, 228–29
Remote terminal access, 190
Repeaters, 248
Replication, 192, 279–80
Replies, File Transfer Protocol (FTP), 62
Requests for comments (RFCs), 20, 289–93
Resolver, 66, 81
Retransmission, Transmission Control Protocol (TCP), 103
Reverse Address Resolution Protocol (RARP), 39, 44,
    122–23
  operation of, 123
Rexec, 34, 59
RFC 1055—A Nonstandard for Transmission of IP
    Datagrams over Serial Lines, 251
RFC 1122—Requirements for Internet Hosts—Communi-
    cation Layers, 21
RFC 1123—Requirements for Internet Hosts—Application
    and Support, 21
Rlogin remote login, 33–34, 59
routed daemon, 138
Routers, 5, 8, 48, 248
  bridges versus, 162–63, 164
Routing algorithms, 133–34
  centralized routing, 134, 135
  distributed adaptive routing, 134, 135–36
    distance-vector routing, 135–36
    link-state routing, 134, 136
  quasi-static routing, 134
  static routing, 134
Routing configuration problems, 169
Routing Information Protocol (RIP), 138
Routing protocols, 39
  autonomous systems, 136–37
  Border Gateway Protocol (BGP), 140–41
  Exterior Gateway Protocols, 139
  gateway protocols, 137
  interior gateway protocols, 137–38
    gated daemon, 139
    Hello protocol, 138
    Open Shortest Path First (OSPF), 138
    Routing Information Protocol (RIP), 138
  Internet Protocol (IP), 111–12
    datagram delivery on a different physical network, 114
    datagram delivery on the same physical network,
        113–14
    as a host, 113
    routing tables, 113
    sample Internet, 112
    traversing multiple routers, 114–15
  routing algorithms, 133–34

centralized routing, 134, 135
distributed adaptive routing, 134, 135–36
quasi-static routing, 134
static routing, 134
Routing tables, 113, 115
RPC runtime service library, 268, 269
rshd, 59
Rsh remote execution, 34, 59–60

S

San Diego Super Computer Documentation, 19
Secondary replicas, 280
Secure channel, 286
Security mechanisms, 181
Segmentation, Internet Protocol (IP), 111
Segments, 100–101, 102
send system call, 221–22
sendto system call, 215, 222–23
Serial Line Interface Protocol (SLIP):
deficiencies of, 252
escape mechanism, 251–52
frame format, 251
Servers, 5, 37, 177, 199
concurrent, 200–201
DCE, 268, 269
DNS, 86–87
DTS, 284, 285
FTP, 62
iterative, 200, 201
NFS, 63, 75, 76
SMTP, 67
Server software, 159–60
Service(s), 24
Service-access-point (SAP), 242
addressing, 243, 245, 246
services file, 148
Service Unknown error message, 170–71
Session layer, OSI model, 29–30, 31
Set, SNMP, 151
Shortest path first (SPF) algorithm, 136
Simple client-server computing, 183, 184
Simple Mail Transfer Protocol (SMTP), 35, 66–67
data formats of, 68
operation of:
connection closing, 68
connection setup, 67
mail transfer, 67
Simple Network Management Protocol (SNMP), 35, 72,
147, 148–49, 171
architecture of, 150–51
Management Information Base (MIB), 149
examples of objects, 149–50
messages, 151
network management application functions, 151
Skulker, 281
SNAP PDU, 247

Socket programming, 206, 207
application protocols:
connectionless application protocols, 212, 214–15
connection-oriented application protocols, 215–18
endpoint identifier, 212
socket addresses, 210–11
socket system calls, 212, 213–14
accept system call, 217, 221
bind system call, 212, 215, 216, 217, 219
close system call, 225
connect system call, 217, 219–20
listen system call, 220
read system call, 223–24
recvfrom system call, 224
recv system call, 223–24
send system call, 221–22
sendto system call, 215, 222–23
socket system call, 212, 213–14, 215, 216, 217,
218–19
write system call, 221–22
types of sockets, 209–10
datagram sockets, 209, 210
raw sockets, 210
stream sockets, 209, 210
socket system call, 212, 213–14, 215, 216, 217, 218–19
Soft links, 277–78
SONET, 7
Source-service-access-point (SSAP) address, 245
Space information, 19
Static routing, 134
Station address, 43, 117
Stream interface, 193
Stream transmission mode, 61
Structure and Identification of Management Information
(SMI), 146
Structured Query Language (SQL), 191
Stub, 70, 229, 269
Subcommands, File Transfer Protocol (FTP), 62–63, 64
Subnet identifiers, 46–47
choosing, 48
Subnet mask, 47–48, 129, 131
Subnetting:
choosing subnet identifiers, 48
subnet identifier, 46–47
subnet mask, 47–48
Subnetwork Access Protocol (SNAP), 246–47
LLC-PDU format, 247–48
private network layer protocols, 247
Sun Microsystems, 63
Sun RPC facility, 71, 76, 206, 232
client calling code, 236–37
program preparation, 233, 234
Rpcgen compiler output, 235
server procedure code, 235–36
specification statements, 233–35
Supercomputers, 19
Support function calls, 202–3
address conversion function calls, 204–5

Support function calls *(cont.)*
    integer octet order function calls, 203–4
Support services, 34–35, 54
Switched Multi-Megabit Data Service (SMDS), 8, 263
Switched virtual circuit (SVC), 254
Switching nodes, 258, 259
Symmetric session view, Telnet, 56
Synchronous Data Link Control (SDLC), 249
System administrator, 11, 12
System Management Application Process (SMAP),
    152

T

TCP/IP, 3
    administration functions, 11–12
    components of, 4–5
    internetworking, 12–13
    networking software, 10–11
    physical network implementation, 8–10
       access units or concentrators, 10
       cabling systems, 9–10
       computing devices, 8
       networking software, 10–11
       network interface cards (NICs), 9
    physical network technologies, 5–8
       local area network (LAN) data links, 5–6
       wide area network (WAN) data links, 6–8
Teaching, 19
telnet command, 81, 121, 161
Telnet interactive login, 33
    command mode, 57
    functions of, 56
    input mode, 57–59
    operation of, 56–57
Thai-Yunnan Project, 19
Thread, 180, 270
Ticket(s), 286
Ticket-granting ticket (TGT), 286–87
timed daemon, 72
Time differential factor (TDF), 282
Time provider, 284
Time services:
    definition of, 71
    maintaining synchronized time values, 71–72
    Network Time Service (NTS) protocol, 72
    timed daemon, 72
Timestamp Reply message, 129, 130–31
Timestamp Request message, 129, 130–31
Token, 6
Token Bus, 6, 243, 244
Token Ring, 6, 243, 244
traceroute command, 148, 171, 172
Transaction processing mechanisms, 196–97
Transmission Control Protocol/Internet Protocol. *See*
    TCP/IP
Transmission Control Protocol (TCP), 15, 27, 36

applications, 100, 101
connection-oriented service, 99–100
protocol mechanisms:
    congestion control, 103–4
    connection establishment, 101
    connection release, 104
    data transfer, 101–3
    error detection and retransmission, 103
    flow control, 103
    segment format, 100–101, 102
Transmission modes, File Transfer Protocol (FTP),
    60, 61
Transport layer:
    OSI model, 30, 31
    protocol ports, 205–6
    TCP/IP, 31, 32
       client-server relationship, 37
       port assignments, 37–38
       protocol ports, 36
       Transmission Control Protocol (TCP), 99–104
       User Datagram Protocol (UDP), 27, 36, 95–98
Trivial File Transfer Protocol (TFTP), 34, 37, 63
Troubleshooting:
    categories of problems, 169–70
    error diagnosis:
       Connection Refused, 172–73
       Host unknown, 173
       Network Unreachable, Host Unreachable, and
          Connection Timed Out, 171–72
       Service Unknown and Protocol Unknown, 170–71
    problem resolution tools, 170
Two-phase commit mechanism, 180–81

U

Unique identifier mechanisms, 179
Universal Time (UT), 281
User datagram(s), 95
    format of, 96, 97
User Datagram Protocol (UDP), 27, 36
    applications, 96, 97
    connectionless service, 95, 96
    protocol mechanisms, 96
       error checking, 97–98
       overflows, 98
    user datagram format, 96, 97
User interface processing components, 181, 182,
    183
User multiplexing, 246
User names, 157
User-network interface (UNI) cell, 258, 260

V

Virtual call (VC), 254
Virtual circuits, 253–54

W

WAIS service, 20
Whois system, 20
Whole Internet User's Guide & Catalog, The, 18
Wide area network (WAN) data links, 5, 6–8, 12, 13, 248–49, 258
Worldwide Internet. *See* Internet (Worldwide)
Worldwide Web (WWW), 20
write system call, 221–22

X

X.25 data links, 7
    frame format, 254
    network layer protocol identification, 255
    station identification, 254
    virtual circuits, 253–54
X terminals, 122
X Windows, 122
X Window System, 35, 68–69